DECISION-MAKING FOR CONSUMERS

DECISION-MAKING for CONSUMERS

An Introduction to Consumer Economics

E. SCOTT MAYNES

Cornell University

MACMILLAN PUBLISHING CO., INC.
New York
COLLIER MACMILLAN PUBLISHERS
London

Preliminary editions copyright © 1973 and 1975 by E. Scott Maynes

Macmillan Publishing Co., Inc.
866 Third Avenue, New York, New York 10022

Collier Macmillan Canada, Ltd.

Library of Congress Cataloging in Publication Data

Maynes, Edwin Scott, (date)
  Decision-making for consumers.

  Includes index.
  1. Consumers.   2. Consumer education.   3. Decision-
making. I. Title.
HC79.C6M38   640.73   75-17567
ISBN 0-02-378300-1

Printing: 1 2 3 4 5 6 7 8   Year: 6 7 8 9 0 1 2 3

To

Dr. HARTLEY W. CROSS
Professor of Economics
Springfield College, 1929–47

Dr. COLSTON E. WARNE
President, Consumers Union, 1936–

My Wife, BLANCHE

They aroused
and
she has reinforced
my interest
in the problems of consumers.

PREFACE

As you open this text for a first course in consumer economics you are already enrolled in the life-long course of consumer decisions; you are, in a sense, already an expert in this book's subject. As a consumer, however, you are also the primary component of our economic system, which, because it *is* a system, defines many of the rules of the game. It is obviously in the consumer's interest to know something of these rules, and the average person will profit, literally, from an early understanding of the broad economic rules (more accurately, principles) affecting consumer decisions. It is the purpose of this book to develop that understanding and to place some of the tools of economics, statistics, and related disciplines at the consumer's service.

In Part One of the book these tools are put to the task of helping consumers—readers like you—to make purchase decisions more effectively. In Part Two these same tools are used to undertake a critical appraisal of the United States economy from the viewpoint of consumers.

Part One starts by describing the surprisingly large payoffs in the form of lower prices or better quality that consumers can obtain through effective decision-making (Chapter 1). It goes on in Chapter 2 to explain the economic mechanisms through which payoffs arise, so that the consumer can identify them and take advantage of them. Chapter 3 answers the question of what quality is and how it may be assessed. The next chapter, Chapter 4, is a guide to how relevant purchase information may be acquired and evaluated. Probably the single most important source of information for consumers is Consumers Union, which tests consumer products and publishes its brand ratings in *Consumer Reports*. Chapter 5 describes and evaluates the activities of Consumers Union.* Possible consumer payoffs must not only be recognized; sometimes they must be bargained for. So Chapter 6 is a primer on bargaining. In making decisions in an uncertain world, all of us, know it or not, follow certain rules. Chapter 7 explains four alternative decision rules, discusses their advantages and disadvantages,

---

*Though the author has sought to be even-handed in dealing with Consumers Union and other issues, the reader is entitled to know at the outset that the author has been a member of the Board and Executive Committee of Consumers Union since 1968.

and shows how they might be applied practically—and when it is *not* practical to use them. Finally, Chapter 9 deals with "individual redress"—the actions a consumer can take when he feels he has been wronged in a purchase transaction.

The chapters in Part One take a relatively uncritical view of the economy and present, basically, what a purchaser has to know and do to purchase effectively. Part Two reverses the position and examines critically the performance of the economy in relation to the consumer.

Chapter 9, the first in Part Two, introduces the concept of *consumer sovereignty*, the familiar notion that the consumer is "king" in determining what is produced. The chapter goes on to identify the numerous and complex issues raised by the concept of consumer sovereignty. Chapter 10 summarizes and criticizes one of the major issues in contention, John Kenneth Galbraith's assertion that giant corporations flood our economy with goods consumers really do not want. But the criticisms voiced by consumerists, implicit in the consumerism movement, are different from those raised by economists, such as Galbraith. And these criticisms from the aspect of consumerism are described and assessed in Chapter 11.

Before an author can be witty or wise he must perform a task of selection. There are numerous topics in consumer economics, from the choice of occupation and the ordering of a family budget to the effect of national interest rates on home purchasing. But adequate treatment of the whole gamut is impractical. I have inclined toward presenting the relation between broad economic understanding and consumer activity rather than toward cataloguing institutions and the prescriptions for individual management of income. The bias is not intended as a slight to the immediate significance of the subjects preempted but as an acknowledgment that principles persist while facts fade.

Unless you use them rather promptly, facts either become obsolete and useless or they are forgotten. Particular solutions and specific advice fall prey to the same fates; tailored to particular situations, they lack versatility and quickly grow irrelevant. Not so principles. Principles well learned and fully understood have long lives and remarkable versatility, but they are sometimes difficult to master, sometimes difficult to recall at the appropriate time, and sometimes difficult to apply to a new situation.

The content and structure of this book and its organization reflect the primacy of principles and seek to take into account the difficulties just mentioned. Let me explain.

This book stresses a relatively small number of the most important principles. Focusing on a limited number of concepts should give you time to understand them well and help you to remember them when they are needed. Where it can, the book uses detailed examples to motivate, illuminate, test, and reinforce understanding of principles and the ability to use them. In the chapters it is the usual practice to set the problem with a short example and to employ additional short examples to illustrate the principles involved. If it is appropriate, there will appear at the end of the chapter long, detailed cases using the principles of that chapter and sometimes of the preceding chapters. If your mind works like the author's, you may find that in attempting to recall a relevant idea you succeed first in retrieving the vivid example with which it was illustrated. Memory of the example directs you to the principle. That assumption, at any rate, informs the book's organization.

I have not presented the material in this book as compactly as I might have. In truth, there is deliberate repetition. It is my hope that the recurrence of already-learned ideas in different settings will broaden understanding of them and develop the ability to apply them in situations different from those in which they were learned.

WORDS OF APPRECIATION

The long gestation period of this book—the first chapter was written in 1967—has given birth to a large number of critics and creditors. It is with great pleasure that I acknowledge my debt to the following persons:

At the University of Minnesota:
> Marjorie Brown, W. Keith Bryant (now at Cornell University), Edward M. Foster, Loren V. Geistfeld (now at Purdue University), James D. Likens (now at Pomona College), Herbert Mohring, John Neter (now at the University of Georgia), Marcel K. Richter, Irving Shapiro, Norman J. Simler, John G. Turnbull.

At the University of Michigan:
> Greg J. Duncan, John Holmes, George Katona, James N. Morgan, William G. Shepherd, Burkhard Strumpel.

At San Bernardino Valley College:
> Benjamin Torres, Jr., Roger Woods.

At Consumers Union:
> Monte Florman, Karl Nagel, George A. Pollak, Bert Strauss, E. R. Struglia, Stephen E. Taub, the late Walker Sandbach, Colston E. Warne.

At Macmillan:

   D. Anthony English.

The residual responsibility for accepting or rejecting criticisms so generously given rests, of course, with me.

Environment is important to book development. So it is with pleasure that I acknowledge three felicitous intellectual "homes" that provided me with stimulation and support during the writing of this book: first, the Department of Economics of the University of Minnesota, my "home" for 18 years; the Department of Economics of the University of California, San Diego, my host for a sabbatical leave in 1972–3; the Economic Behavior Program of the Survey Research Center of the University of Michigan where I was a Visiting Scholar during 1974–5.

Finally, a fully qualified absent-minded professor has a great need (more than most people) for competent, willing secretaries who will make good his deficiencies. It has been my fortune to be blessed with a succession of first-rate secretaries. It is with great pleasure that I acknowledge the indispensable help of Alice T. Jacobi and Lola Frederickson of the Center for Economic Research of the University of Minnesota; Marlene Moyes and Jane M. Nizyborski of the University of California, San Diego; Susan A. Hudson of the Survey Research Center of the University of Michigan; and Bonnie Huff of Cornell University.

                                                                E. S. M.

CONTENTS

PART ONE

CONSUMER PURCHASE DECISIONS

CHAPTER 1

The Case for Effective Purchase Decisions

Try the following "test." Consider an "ordinary" or "straight life" insurance policy—the type where you pay the same premium each year as long as you live. Suppose that the lowest-priced company of 88 "reliable" companies in the United States sold this policy to a particular person for $4 per $1,000 of protection. Question: What price would be charged by the *highest-priced company* to the same insured person, all "reliable" companies? Would it be $4, $4.10, $4.25, $5, $7.50, $10, $13, or $20? The correct answer is $13.00. In other words, a competent, or perhaps just "lucky," consumer, might purchase from the $4.00 company, whereas a less competent, or merely less lucky consumer, might pay three times as much.[1] The gain, or "payoff," to the competent consumer in this instance is obviously very great and is discussed in detail.

This case is just one example of the payoffs that effective consumer decision-making can bring. Part I of this book seeks to convince you of the importance of such consumer payoffs and to enable you to achieve them for yourself. Chapter 1 makes the case for effective purchase decisions.

WHY DECIDE EFFECTIVELY?

The most compelling reason for devoting time and effort to making better decisions as a consumer is to increase one's purchasing power. Such increases may be achieved by two approaches: 1) buying

---

[1] The particular facts of this and other examples in this book will quickly become obsolete. Not so—it is hoped—the principles they illustrate. The data source for this example is given in Table 1.

the same product [2] at a lower money price, or 2) for the same money price, buying a better-performing or more durable product. Table 1 gives some idea of the possible gains to competent consumers and the possible losses to incompetent consumers.

TABLE 1

**Price and Quality Variation for Typical
Consumer Products**

A. Examples of Variations in Money Prices (Quality Held Constant)

Product	Price Range (lowest to highest)
Life Insurance	
Participating straight-life policies [a]	$4 to $13 per $1,000 protection
5-year renewable term [b]	Participating: $5 to $8.50 per $1,000 or face value
	Nonparticipating: $7.50 to $10 per $1,000 of face value
Drugs [c]	
Tetracyclin, a broad-spectrum antibiotic	$0.79 to $7.45 for 30 capsules
Single-Lens Reflex Cameras [d]	
Median quality cameras	$170 to $635 in Ann Arbor, Michigan
Identical camera (Honeywell Pentax ES II)	$360 to $450 in Ann Arbor-Ypsilanti market
10-Speed Men's Racing Bicycles [e]	
Median quality bicycle	$150 in Ann Arbor-Ypsilanti (no variation at all)
Identical bicycle (Peugeot UO8 Trophée de France) [f]	$150 in Ann Arbor-Ypsilanti (no variation)
Gasoline [f]	
Regular	$0.49 to $0.62 in Ann Arbor
Automobile credit [g]	
Boston, Cleveland, Denver, St. Louis	9 per cent to 16 per cent
Detroit, New York, Pittsburgh, San Francisco	11½ per cent to 14 per cent
Home Remodeling [h]	
Remodeling specialists	$6,700 to $10,500 bids on a
General contractors	$6,500 to $10,600 standard set of
Carpenter contractors	$6,555 to $8,710 remodeling specifications

[2] Here a *product* is defined as "the set of goods or services which, for an acceptable range of outlay, will in the consumer's judgment, serve the same general purpose." The exact specification of "same purpose" is left to each individual.

TABLE 1 (Cont'd)

"Expensive" High-Fidelity Speakers [i]
(of approximately equal quality)   List Prices of $245 to $475

B. Examples of Variations in Prices and Quality

Coffee Makers [j]
The Sunbeam AP33 in the highest quality rating class listed for $16 whereas other models in the same class listed for prices from $19 to $34. By contrast, the Cory Nicro Ready Brew NRB-1 which "did not meet any of Consumer Union's criteria for standard coffee" listed for $105.

Automobile Tires [k]
A set of 4 Uniroyal Zeta 20 M tires cost $118, as compared with $121 for a set of General Poly Jet tires. After taking account of tread life, the Generals cost 2 times as much per mile as the Uniroyals.

Dehumidifiers [l]
The Ward No. 3194 dehumidifier with a price of $130 extracted roughly 50 per cent more moisture from the air than the Comfort-Aire FDHB22 with a price also in the vicinity of $130.

---

[a] Data from Joseph M. Belth, *The Retail Price Structure in American Life Insurance* (Bloomington, Ind.: Indiana University Bureau of Business Research, 1966). The "price per $1,000 of protection" is not the same as "price per $1,000 of face value." The price quoted here is calculated from a sophisticated but complex formula and is not comparable with the "price" for a 5-year renewable term policy quoted. The calculations are based on 1962 data from a sample of 88 companies. The sample includes most major companies.

The reader who wants up-to-date information on life insurance prices should consult the January, 1974 issue of *Consumer Reports* for data on term policies and the March, 1974, issue regarding straight or whole life policies. The *Consumer Reports* data on straight life policies pertain only to the *least expensive* policies. For this reason they were not cited here.

[b] Source: "Price, Options, and Reading the Fine Print," *Consumer Reports* (March 1967). The price range presented is based on prices of ten companies selected to "illustrate a wide price range." For more recent price information on term policies, see the January, 1974, issue of *Consumer Reports*.

[c] *Consumer Reports* (May 1970), pp. 278–279.

[d] Quality data taken from *Consumer Reports* (November 1974), pp. 798–801. Price data collected by the Survey Research Center of the University of Michigan for "A Pretest on Local Accessibility [to product reports in *Consumer Reports*]." The price data represent the lowest prices retailers in the Ann Arbor-Ypsilanti market were willing to quote for possible publication. They were collected in the period, November 16–26, 1974.

[e] Same source as d, except that the author simulated Consumers Union's quality index.

[f] Gasoline data were collected by the Survey Research Center of the University of Michigan in February, 1975.

[g] Allen F. Jung, "Charges for Appliance and Automobile Installment Credit in Major Cities," *Journal of Business* (October 1963), pp. 386–391. Data were collected from 123 Chevrolet and Ford dealers in 9 major cities in 1960. The price quoted assumed the purchase of a new Chevrolet or Ford with $1,500 to be financed and repaid over 36 months.

[h] Allen F. Jung, "Price Variations Among Home-Remodeling Contractors," *Journal of Business* (January 1961), pp. 52–56. Estimates were obtained from 20 firms specializing in home remodeling specialists, 10 general contractors, and 10 carpenter contractors in Chicago in 1960.

The upper part of Table 1 lists the *range* of prices for different brands of the same product. First we look in more detail at the life insurance example. If the uninformed consumer invariably purchases the "straight life" policy with a net cost of $13 per $1,000 of protection and the informed consumer invariably purchases a policy with the same provisions for $4, then the payoff for the informed consumer would be $9 per $1,000 ($13 — $4) per year. This represents an annual saving of $180 on the purchase of $20,000 of protection. But it is unrealistic to expect typical payoffs as large as this. Although it is possible that the uninformed consumer pays the highest possible price and the informed purchaser pays the lowest possible price, it is more likely that the uninformed consumer pays a "middling" price—say, $8.50—and the informed consumer pays a "low" (but not the lowest) price—say $5.50—giving a total payoff on the order of $3 or about 35 per cent of the middling price. By analogous reasoning, we might expect typical payoffs on the order of 35 per cent for all of the price ranges presented in the table.

The table is relevant for "gross" payoffs. Searching out and obtaining such payoffs is not costless, and before we fully evaluate the magnitude of such payoffs, the cost of the "search" for payoffs must be subtracted. But more about this in Chapter 2.

There is, however, another side to the payoff coin. Turning again to Table 1, we note that some products in the table are purchased in multiple units—for example, a person may buy $20,000 of protection rather than $1,000. Other goods are purchased repetitively—credit for instance. In both kinds of cases, the *dollar* quotation of the price range leads to a gross underestimate of the aggregate payoff. Supposing a family purchases $20,000 of straight life, keeps the policy for 30 years, and obtains a gross payoff of $3 per $1,000 of protection as in the previous discussion, then the total dollar payoff from this single decision is $1,800 ($20,000 × $3 payoff per $1,000 of protection per year × 30 years). To be careful about the matter, one should estimate the "present, discounted value" of this stream of payoffs. This involves asking (and then looking up in the proper tables) how much money held in a bank at typical after-tax, after-inflation interest

i *Consumer Reports* (February 1974), p. 119. In providing information in percentage terms on "the ability to reproduce sound accurately," *Consumer Reports* stated that "differences of about 8 percentage points or less in accuracy are not likely to be detected by ear." On the basis of this statement the first 10 speakers were judged to be of about the same quality.
j *Consumer Reports* (September 1974), p. 643.
k *Consumer Reports* (October 1974), p. 715.
l *Consumer Reports* (August 1974), pp. 620–622.

rates, say 3 per cent, would be sufficient to yield a payoff of $60 every year for 20 years. This would be the exact payoff. The answer is $1,176.

The possibilities evoked by Part B of Table 1 should be familiar to those who are familiar with *Consumer Reports,* the monthly magazine published by Consumers Union that reports on brand-by-brand laboratory tests of consumer products. It shows how, by choosing certain brands, the informed consumer can purchase better quality for the same money price or, better yet, superior quality at a lower money price. Thus, in Table 1 the purchasers of the Sunbeam coffee maker not only make substantial money payoffs by purchasing the cheapest model in the highest quality rating group but they obtain a better performing coffee maker than the lower quality models they might otherwise have purchased.

Finally, all of Table 1 constitutes a graphic contradiction of the long-lived, but false maxim—"Price is an indicator of quality" and its cousin—"You get what you pay for." Were either maxim even approximately correct, this book might better have been unwritten.

Open to Most. Of the two avenues to increased purchasing power —earning more or making better purchase decisions—only the latter is open to almost everyone. To "moonlight" effectively requires greater than average energy and desire. Moreover, unless you possess skills that are in unusual demand, it may require the acceptance of less than your regular earning rate. By happy contrast, most consumers can increase their capacity to make purchase decisions more effectively.

Unlike moonlighting, "earning by purchasing more effectively" need not involve more time than your present purchasing routine. Instead, it requires that your purchase activities become more effective as a result of better understanding and better planning. Needless to say, "earning by consuming better" is open to both men and women.

Consumer "Earnings" are Tax-Free. Among the least appreciated advantages of "earnings" (or "savings") from better purchase decisions is their favored tax status. Many people fail to appreciate the fact that such earnings are tax-free. They are ignorant, too, of the potential money value of this favorable tax treatment.

Consider a family of four living in New York State with a pretax income of $14,000. This was the average income for a family of four in the United States in 1973. Suppose that by means of locating lower prices or better quality our illustrative family increased the purchasing power of its income by $3,000, as compared with average families at this money level income. (In view of the spread of prices and qualities on display in Table 1, such a performance seems entirely possible.) We might well ask: how much *extra money income* would be required to enable the family to increase its spending by $3,000? The answer is about $4,400. Of this amount, $1,400 would go to federal and New York State income taxes, leaving $3,000 to be spent. Hence this family saves not only the $3,000 it might otherwise have spent for the same purpose but also the additional $1,470 it would have to have earned in order to engage in $3,000 of aftertax spending.

Table 2 shows the extra income equivalent of $1 of consumer savings for families of different sizes and income levels. Referring to Table 2, an average single person in the state with the most progressive income tax—New York—with a before-tax income of $5,000 must earn an extra $1.37 in order to increase his purchasing power by $1.00. Again, these numbers reflect the fact that federal and state income taxes siphon off $.37 leaving the taxpayer with $1.00 to spend.

The calculations in Column 3 to Table 2 refer to the state with the most progressive income tax (New York) whereas those in Column 4 assume a sales tax of 4 per cent, and no state income tax at all. If your state's tax rates are high and the structure of those rates progressive, then the value of consumer earnings will be more like those in Column 3; if your state's tax rates are low and less progressive, they will more closely resemble those of Column 4.

Table 2 expresses the value of consumer earnings in *money* terms only. In general, the money value of consumer earnings is least for those most favorably treated by the income tax and greatest for those least favorably treated by the income tax. More specifically, as income increases and family size decreases, the money value of consumer earnings increases.

To be balanced against this is the *subjective worth* of consumer earnings to families in different situations. Although no one can prove it, almost everyone would accept the proposition that an additional dollar of income is worth more *subjectively* to a low-income or large-sized household on the one hand, as compared with a high-income or small-sized household on the other.

The Divergence of the Seller's and Consumer's Interest. A fourth reason for considering alternatives in consumer purchases is defensive in nature: to avoid being bilked. Too many consumers fail to understand that the seller's interest may not be the consumer's interest, and that neither an implied fiducial relationship (a relationship based on trust) between buyer and seller nor the discipline of markets, as they exist, is sufficient to ensure optimal outcomes from the consumer's viewpoint. This point is spelled out in several examples.

TABLE 2

The Extra Income Equivalent of One Dollar of Consumer "Savings" [a]

$1 saved = this amount of extra income in: [b]

(1) Before-Tax Family Income	(2) Number of Persons in Family	(3) Highest Income Tax State (New York)	(4) State with No Income Tax
$ 5,000	1	$1.37	$1.30
$10,000	1	1.49	1.41
$15,000	1	1.61	1.45
$20,000	1	1.82	1.54
$25,000	1	2.13	1.67
$30,000	1	2.38	1.79
$ 5,000	2	1.30	1.25
$10,000	2	1.39	1.30
$15,000	2	1.49	1.35
$20,000	2	1.64	1.41
$25,000	2	1.75	1.47
$30,000	2	2.00	1.56
$35,000	2	2.22	1.67
$40,000	2	2.38	1.75
$ 5,000	4	1.27	1.22
$10,000	4	1.39	1.30
$15,000	4	1.47	1.35
$20,000	4	1.61	1.41
$25,000	4	1.75	1.47
$30,000	4	1.96	1.56
$35,000	4	2.22	1.67
$40,000	4	2.44	1.75

[a] Interpretation: an average single person with a $5,000 pretax income in the state with the highest income tax rates—New York—can achieve a $1.00 increase in purchasing power by either 1) earning an additional $1.37 of money income on which he will pay a total of $.37 in federal and New York State income taxes as well as New York sales taxes; or 2) "saving" $1.00 through a more effective purchase decision ("Saved" income is not taxed.)

The estimates in Columns 3 and 4 probably bracket the range of values to be found in various states. Rates for the New York income tax are among the most progressive in the country. Furthermore, they are *not* attenuated through the device of allowing the deduction of federal income tax in calculating New York taxable income. This procedure is permitted among a number of other states whose rates *appear* as progressive as those in New York.

At the other extreme lies a state such as Nevada, which assesses a sales tax, but no income tax. The value of a dollar "saved" by more effective consumer purchases in such a state is estimated in Column 4.

The calculations are based on a 4 per cent sales tax and on 1974 tax rates for both federal and New York State income taxes. The taxpaying unit itemized deductions and had average deductions for its income class size.

[b] The estimates of "average deductions" closely approximate those in Joseph A. Pech-

A chairman of the board of trustees of a church had occasion to review the fire insurance coverage of his church. The policy was purchased, and had been for many years, from a member of the congregation at an annual cost of $500. Other agents, the chairman discovered, were prepared to provide identical coverage from reputable companies for about $400. When confronted with these lower bids, the church member-insurance agent affirmed that he could and would match these lower prices. But why so late?

This episode was related to a conference of clergymen. The knowing smiles after the telling of the story suggested that the situation described is by no means unique. Some of you may be in a position to cite instances where sellers have dealt faithfully with churches or have even given their client church "a break." The point of this story is that neither the presumably strong fiducial relationship between seller and purchaser nor competition in the local insurance market will *guarantee* the desired outcome.

A second illustration comes from the securities market. By many of the usual canons of financial investment and especially from a growth viewpoint, IBM in the spring of 1967 represented an excellent investment. Its price per share, however, was in the vicinity of $500. At this price the commission charged for a purchase of 100 shares (a $50,000 purchase) would be $75, of which the customer's representative would receive only a portion. On the other hand, a purchase of $50,000 worth of a stock selling for $5 per share would involve a brokerage fee of $1,200. The question, put to an audience of frequent purchasers of securities, was "Have any of your brokers recommended IBM lately?" The nature of the responses made the question rhetorical. (It is readily acknowledged that there may have been other valid reasons why a broker would not have advised the purchase of IBM at that time.)

Both of these examples underline the possibility that the seller's and the consumer's interest may not overlap. Even where a church was the "consumer," and where fiducial relationships between seller and purchaser would be presumed to be very strong, the income-maximizing motivations of the seller apparently outweighed altruistic considerations.

---

man, *Federal Tax Policy,* rev. ed. (New York: W. W. Norton & Company, Inc., 1966, 1971), Table C–12, p. 300.

The extra income equivalent was calculated from the formula:

$$S = \$1/(1 - t)$$

where S = the extra income equivalent of $1 saved, and

t = the net effective marginal tax rates on the last dollar earned, taking account of all income taxes and, in both cases, a 4 per cent sales tax.

The fact that considerable price disparities exist for identical products suggests that churches—and other consumers, too—are less active in obtaining price information than they might be.

One final lesson from these two examples is that the sellers receive their compensation for *selling* and not for providing the services that consumers really desire. In the church example, the seller obtains his income by selling insurance policies. The higher the premiums paid, the greater is his compensation. The basic interest of the church, on the other hand, is in obtaining fire protection at the lowest possible price.

In the securities market example, a broker's compensation depends upon the number and character of the securities transfers that he executes. He is not compensated directly for the investment advice that his clients sometimes want and that he often gives. Because of the structure of commissions, his advice may be biased in the direction of too frequent transfers, and purchases of lower-priced rather than higher-priced securities.

Pride in Deciding Effectively. You need not be much of a perfectionist to garner considerable satisfaction from doing anything well. Consumer purchase decisions commend themselves as a potential source of such satisfaction, especially since your purchase decisions are so numerous and affect your pocketbook so tellingly.

Shopping As a "Game." Paul Rosenblatt, a social psychologist at the University of Minnesota, has suggested to the author that it is fruitful to view shopping as a mass participation "game." Specifically, it is a mental game with a quantified scoring system, yielding both material rewards and a feeling of competence to the winners.

A central feature of the shopping game is the battle of wits and information between sellers and you, and between you and other consumers. The object, of course, is to obtain "bargains." The greater the bargain, the greater is your score. From the viewpoint of some of you, the "game" and the motivations of participants can be summed up succinctly: nothing is sweeter than winning!

For some, the *process* of shopping has entertainment value, regardless of whether purchase decisions are made effectively or bargains achieved. Such people—perhaps you are one of them—enjoy the chance to get out, the opportunities for contacts with other people whether friends or merely chance acquaintances, the access to pleasant surroundings, and other pleasurable experiences that shopping makes possible.

The Social Payoff. Consumers, no less than sellers, are strongly propelled by self-interest. What induces many of them to invest more time and effort in making purchases effectively is the expectation that *their own* purchasing power will be substantially increased.

Nonetheless, it is comforting to reflect that this is one of those too rare instances in which individual and social interest overlap completely. Individual consumers serve themselves when they search out and obtain lower prices and better quality. But the same actions serve other consumers by reinforcing the reward-punishment mechanism that is at the heart of the market economy. When this mechanism works, less enterprising and less competent consumers benefit from purchases under more favorable terms.

Ordinarily the impact of the individual consumer's actions on terms offered is imperceptible, much like the single vote in an election involving large numbers of voters. But occasionally, the means by which the individual consumer influences terms become visible as in the following example. A large department store in our area proclaims that "——— is never undersold!" To implement this policy, this store will meet the lower price of its competitors in selling to any *individual* who shows that he can buy a comparable good at a lower price in a competitive store. But if enough customers cite lower prices in other outlets, the never-to-be-undersold store may post a lower matching price that thereafter becomes available to all buyers. By this means the enterprising consumer, in the aggregate, serves not only himself but also others who are less energetic and less competent.

CHAPTER 2

Achieving Consumer Purchase Payoffs

How is it possible that the drug tetracyclin can sell for as low as $.75 and as high as $7.50 in the same city?[1] What makes a car dealer willing to sell to some customers for only $75 over genuine dealer costs? What accounts for the fact that one vacuum cleaner is not only priced 30 per cent less than most of its competitors, but outperforms them as well?[2] What actions must I take to be fairly certain that I will be able to make purchases at the lower price and the higher quality? These are the questions that this chapter seeks to answer.

More formally, this chapter faces the question of how consumer purchase payoffs may be achieved. It deals with the nature, origin, and accessibility of such payoffs, establishes some tentative operating rules for consumer purchases, and winds up by presenting detailed examples of how particular payoffs were achieved.

But before proceeding with the analysis of purchase payoffs, it will be useful to pause and familiarize ourselves with the entire range of economic activity and choice-making in the household.

ECONOMIC ACTIVITY OF THE HOUSEHOLD: AN OVERVIEW

"Consumption," Adam Smith wrote 200 years ago, "is the end purpose of economic activity . . ."[3] By *consumption*, Smith meant the enjoyment of goods and services. It was consumption that gave

---

[1] *Consumer Reports* (May 1970), pp. 278–279.
[2] *Consumer Reports* (June 1974), p. 480, canister vacuum cleaner with powered nozzle.
[3] Adam Smith, *The Wealth of Nations*, 3rd ed. (London: J. Dove, 1826), Book IV, chap. VIII, p. 620.

rise to "satisfaction" or *utility,* to use the name economists have given to satisfaction. Complementary to consumption, in Smith's view, was *production,* meaning the creation of goods and services. Household members sell their labor services in order to earn income. This income is then used to purchase goods and services (consumption). Thus, "working" yields satisfaction not directly but rather indirectly through the consumption it makes possible.[4]

In this view, which has been embodied in most economic analysis until recently, the central task of the *household as a consuming unit* is to choose consumer goods, given a certain income, in such a way as to maximize utility. In other words, the household so spends its income that it "gets the most" from its income.

Time enters the picture in that the household can choose between current consumption or consumption in some future period. It can increase *current* consumption in three ways: 1) by using money or goods carried over from earlier periods; 2) by allotting a larger fraction of its current income to consumption, rather than saving it; 3) by borrowing and using the money thus obtained for purposes of current consumption. The household can increase *future* consumption by "saving" and carrying over to the next period a greater fraction of its income or of the durable goods that it possesses.

Time also enters the picture as household members choose between working and not working. If they work more, they will earn more, making possible greater consumption and greater utility. But work is thought to be "hard" or distasteful, yielding negative utility. And it is the increasing disutility (distaste) of work which sets a limit on the number of hours an individual is willing to work.

Although traditional analysis does assign importance to the choice between present and future consumption, as well as the choice between working and not working, the fact that the current use of consumption goods and services requires time does not influence current purchases of consumer goods.

This book is imbued with a newer and broader view of the functioning of households. This view, based in part on the model of household behavior in Staffan B. Linder's *The Harried Leisure Class,* contrasts greatly with the traditional analysis of household consumption activity.[5]

[4] Classical economists, such as Smith, recognized the existence of "psychic income,"—that is, the satisfactions from work above and beyond that conferred by money income. But "psychic income" played a subsidiary role in their analysis.

[5] See Staffan B. Linder, *The Harried Leisure Class* (New York: Columbia University Press, 1970). The formal model in Linder is identical with that in Gary S. Becker, "A Theory of the Allocation of Time," *Economic Journal* (September 1965), pp. 493–517. Linder's book is less formal and hence more accessible to a larger audience.

In this revised view it is activities that give rise to utility. The household is a "firm" that combines such inputs as the time of household members, their skills (human "capital"), their durable goods, their money (from current income, accumulated savings, or borrowings) to produce activities that in turn yield utility. For example, to produce an hour of tennis requires the participants' tennis skills, their time, their racquets, and possibly some money for the rental of a court.

In this newer view, time is very important. For instance, no formal demonstration is required to show that individuals with ample incomes and little spare time will have a greater preference for time-saving equipment than will individuals with small incomes and abundant "idle" time.

Part I of this book does not analyze the influence of time directly, but peoples' preferences for particular goods and their procedures in purchasing goods reflect indirectly the fact that time is scarce.

The Kinds of Decisions That Consumers Make. Although this book focuses on purchase decisions, the intelligent consumer will want to be familiar with the entire range of decisions that consumers undertake.

Purchase decisions, as most of us know from experience, involve the acquisition of goods and services in exchange for a payment.

Sometimes purchases also represent *investment.* This occurs when the purchase results in the acquisition of *capital*—something that will yield a return in the future. Capital may take many forms, some familiar, some unfamiliar. For instance, capital may be *tangible* as in the cases of houses, cars, washing machines, and clothes. Each of these will yield a portion of their services during some future period. Equally familiar will be *financial capital,* as illustrated by savings accounts or mutual fund shares. These yield future income in the form of interest, dividends, and, sometimes, capital gains or losses.

Still reasonably familiar, especially to college students, is *human capital*—the skills and knowledge that enable a person to earn more and (it is to be hoped!) to "enjoy" more in the future. Less familiar examples might be one's *state of health* and his *stock of memories.* One's health enables the human body to function effectively and one's memories make possible reminiscence, a mental exercise permitting the same experience to be enjoyed more than once. When a person goes on a vacation, it is proper to interpret this as an investment in both health and in a stock of future memories.

The concept of *saving,* defined as "nonconsumption," emphasizes the negative: the current consumption that is given up. *Consumption,* as we use the term, refers to the utility derived currently from either the use or possession of goods and services, or from both use and possession.

Sometimes the same action will at once represent several types of decisions. For example, adding to one's saving account will represent a decision both to invest and to save, in equal amounts. Similarly, the purchase of a washing machine—to the extent that it will wash clothes in future periods—will again represent both investment and saving. The current use of the washing machine will, of course, represent consumption.

Finally, consumers make decisions regarding the *use of time.* For example, a particular afternoon can be devoted to "working," loafing, shopping, or studying.

The principles governing the making of *purchase decisions* occupy us throughout Part I of this book. Nonetheless, it is helpful for students to be aware that consumers make many other types of decisions, and that purchase decisions often involve saving and investment, as well as the use of time.

Whose Preferences? Whose Values? De gustibus non disputandum est—or, in English, "There is no disputing tastes" [6]—is the viewpoint that infuses this book. In different words, we assume, generally, that the individual knows what he likes, given the information in his possession. We do not try to tell the person what he *should* like or what is "good for him." Our goal is to aid the consumer in obtaining what he believes he wants. One way of achieving the goal involves showing the consumer how to search out information more effectively. It is possible that the new information may, in turn, alter his preferences. But we generally respect the individual's preferences and take no actions aimed directly at changing them.

As an example, some consumers may wish to purchase a "hot" sports car because of the status value they believe it confers. This view is not the author's to dispute.

This neutrality applies not only to preferences for a particular product but even more strongly to "values." *Values* may be defined as "criteria of desirability." [7] As such, they represent higher-order

[6] The terms *tastes, likes,* and *preferences* are used interchangeably.

[7] For a fuller discussion of values, see Robin M. Williams, Jr., "The Concept of Values" in David M. Sills, ed., *International Encyclopedia of the Social Sciences* (New York: Macmillan Publishing Co. Inc., and the Free Press, 1968).

In an unpublished paper, "Values and the Family: Consensus, Conflict, and preferences that help us determine our preferences for lesser objects or lesser actions. For example, an individual for whom the "simple life" is an important value will quickly conclude that gold-handled faucets are not for him, even as a gift. More generally, the person who prizes the simple life will have weak or negative preferences for material goods and services above some relatively low minimum level. We do not try to judge the rightness or the wrongness of the simple life or of any other value.

The viewpoint just expressed is, of course, the traditional position taken by the economics profession.

This Book and Economic Theory. Economic theory consists of systems of interrelated hypotheses representing simplified models of the economy or its parts. The objective of economic theory is to explain, predict, and evaluate the workings of the economy or its parts.

This book seeks to make economic theory the servant of consumers. It asks, and seeks to answer the question: in what ways can economic theory help me to function better as a consumer?

In order to serve consumers effectively, economic theory has to be modified in several ways. First, it must be made more realistic. This usually involves the inclusion of details that are important to consumers, but can be neglected by economic theorists. For example, in our discussion of shopping ("searching"), we explain the concept of *subjective* costs of the search. Ordinarily, economic theory does not, and need not, deal separately with such subjective costs. However, if consumers do not take account of subjective costs, they may make incorrect decisions. For this reason the book deals at length with subjective costs.

Second, for our purposes, economic theory must be rendered understandable to consumers. This implies that economic principles must be explained in words rather than symbols, and at some length rather than in their most compact form.

Later in this chapter we present examples of this approach at

---

Change" (Minneapolis, Minn.: Arny Symposium on Family Values, March 15, 1970), Williams commented usefully on the meaning of values: "They [values] serve as selective standards in conduct: in choosing a course of action, in justifying such selections to oneself and others, in appraising policies, in judging the conduct of others, in evaluating events and objects (physical, social, cultural)."

Those who would like to know more regarding the economic values held by Americans should consult Burkhard Strümpel, "Economic Life Styles, Values and Subjective Welfare—An Empirical Approach," in Eleanor B. Sheldon, ed., *Family Economic Behavior: Problems and Prospects* (Philadelphia: J. B. Lippincott Co., 1973), pp. 69–125.

work. As one example, consider "price discrimination."[8] In economics texts, this concept is helpful in explaining how prices are set by sellers. In this book, an understanding of this phenomenon is used to help the consumer achieve consumer payoffs. In an economics text, price discrimination is presented in diagrammatic or mathematical form; here it is explained in words, abetted by detailed examples.

THE QUEST FOR CONSUMER PAYOFFS

Relevant Concepts

Consumer payoffs have already been identified as the "gains obtained through effective purchasing via lower prices, better quality, or both." To obtain such payoffs you must "search" directly or indirectly for information regarding the prices and qualities of goods in which you are interested, and then you must act on the basis of the information you have accumulated. We define search as follows:

> *Search* is "each attempt to secure and to act on information regarding the price and quality of a product."

Thus, the concept of a search includes all of the following: "shopping," consulting publications giving product information, telephoning retailers to ask if they carry a given brand, getting information from the Yellow Pages of the telephone directory, consulting a mail-order catalog, and—very important—bargaining.

What kinds of payoff result from a search? It is useful to distinguish:

> A *gross payoff* is the "total gain *before* the costs of obtaining it have been subtracted"; and
> A *net payoff* is the "aftercost gain."

We should also differentiate between *objective* and *subjective* payoffs. An example makes the difference clear. Consider a person who by searching has succeeded in reducing the price of a television set he wishes to buy by $50. This $50 constitutes the "objective" payoff. But he may be so pleased with this outcome that the subjective value of this $50 will exceed the amount of utility, or subjective satisfaction,

---

[8] The discussion of price discrimination starts on page 23.

that he usually associates with $50. To reckon the gross payoff correctly, one should add to the objective payoff the dollar amount of the "subjective" payoff—that is, the money equivalent of the extra satisfaction afforded by the result. How do you assign a money equivalent? Simply ask yourself how much money—given your financial position and family situation—you would be willing to pay to achieve this result. No actual payment will be involved. What you are doing is assessing, in money terms, the subjective satisfaction you expect this outcome to yield.

The achievement of a better quality specimen as a result of a search is another example of a subjective payoff.[9] Here the problem is to assess the worth to you of the improvement in quality you have achieved. Again, the appropriate procedure is to ask yourself—and to answer on the basis of whatever information you possess—what is the dollar equivalent to you of the better quality embodied in the better specimen.

The *gross payoff* includes both the objective payoff and either of the two types of subjective payoff just described.

We turn now to the *cost of the search*. In general,

a *cost* is "anything that is undergone or foregone (or given up) in order to attain a given end."

When this definition is applied to a search, some kinds of search costs are obvious and readily understood. Many searches, for instance, involve *direct money costs,* such as payments for telephone calls and automobile operating expenses. *Direct, but subjective costs* raise problems not of recognition but of valuation. Anyone with a family recognizes that shopping (searching) with young children is difficult, in essence a cost to be borne. How do we assign a money value to such costs? As in the case of subjective payoffs, ask yourself how much money you would be willing to pay to shop without your children. Again, no actual payments will be involved. But you will be accounting for a real life, although difficult-to-value cost.

The *indirect* costs of a search consist of that which is foregone in order to undertake the search. These costs may be "objective" and readily valued. Such is the case when the head of a household gives up a day's pay in order to search for new housing in a different city. Or these costs may be "subjective." This would be the case when someone gives up an afternoon's sailing in order to visit used car lots.

[9] The concept and measurement of quality is discussed in Chapter 3.

In this case, the indirect subjective cost of the search is the dollar equivalent of the satisfaction that the sailing would have yielded. The crucial idea in identifying indirect search costs is that you consider *only* the second-best activity: what you would have done had you not engaged in the search whose costs you are evaluating.

Someone may object: "But I enjoy shopping." The objection is pertinent and introduces two additional observations. First, for those who like shopping, the subjective costs of the search may indeed be negative; that is, they are not costs at all in the usual sense. Second, it may be difficult in mentally calculating net payoffs to separate gross payoffs from subjective costs of the search. In general, such a separation is unnecessary. But for correct mental calculations it is important not to count the same source of subjective satisfaction twice.

RATIONALITY AND CALCULATION

To some, rationality in decision-making erroneously implies constant, detailed calculation of payoffs and costs as well as an exclusive preoccupation with material well-being. This caricature has paraded under the label of the "economic man." The concepts developed previously should help dislodge the mistaken notion of the economic man.

The identification of rationality with constant, detailed calculation fails by definition. Recall that a search was defined as an attempt to secure and act upon information. Most assuredly, the calculation of payoffs and costs are themselves part of the cost of the search. And, just as assuredly, it is unreasonable and irrational to incur large costs of calculation when the expected payoff is small. By the same token, it is highly reasonable to undertake extensive calculations when the payoff is expected to be large. A house purchase comes readily to mind as an example of a purchase that is likely to yield a large payoff and hence justifying extensive search costs. The corrected version of rationality, as far as calculation is concerned, calls for only the quickest, rudest calculations for "small" decisions, whereas "important" matters call for careful as well as extensive calculations.

Failure to consider subjective payoffs or costs often results in frustrating, erroneous decisions. For example, how many of us have made a wrong decision to engage in a do-it-yourself home improvement project because we failed to take into account the indirect subjective cost of the project—the satisfaction of a Saturday's recreation that might have been? Numerous homemakers complain that they lack the time to read books. How many of this group fail to recognize that an important cost of reading a book might be a dirty house? And how many are unwilling to own up to the fact that *for them* having a clean house is really more important than the subjective satisfactions derived from reading a book?

Or, to change scenes, how many students incorrectly accept part-time jobs, failing to recognize that the "free" time they've replaced with work was not really free? One cost of the part-time job may be the anguish generated by lower grades.

This parade of examples could be lengthened without end. But these should convey the point: subjective elements of payoffs and costs must be considered if correct decisions are to be made.

WHERE ARE THE PAYOFFS?

The central question for any consumer contemplating a purchase is: How many searches should I make? The general answer is:

> *Keep making searches as long as the expected net payoff from that search is positive,* that is, as long as the expected gross payoff from a search exceeds the expected total cost of that search.[10]

Like most general rules, it is less an answer than a prelude to a number of questions. And so let us press on to progressively more specific analysis and recommendation.

On a somewhat more particular level, consumers will find it profitable to search widely under the following conditions, other factors held constant:

1. When an item looms *relatively large in the long-run* household *budget;*
2. When the consumer is *less affluent* rather than more affluent;
3. When the cost of the search is low;
4. When the *expected variation in money price,* or *quality,* or *both is large.*

An item may qualify as "relatively large in the long-run household budget" in two ways: 1) by virtue of a large unit price, for example,

---

[10] Economists have called this the marginal rule, which is worded as follows: "Keep searching as long as expected marginal (incremental) payoffs exceed expected marginal costs."

an automobile or a house; or 2) through repetitive purchases. For example, a gallon of gasoline is scarcely a "big ticket" item, but the $500 or so required to buy the 850 gallons of gasoline the typical family uses in a year could be clearly considered as looming relatively large in the long-run budget.

Turning to the second item in the list, some affluent persons feel guilty when they fail to "shop" for a major purchase, in most cases wrongly so. Commented one such person, "I just call up _____ (a prominent department store) and ask them to send their best. I know you wouldn't approve." Not at all. Affluent people are ordinarily possessed of abundant money and, frequently, have little time. Thus, it is rational for them to utilize tested sources on all but the very largest transactions and save the scarce commodity of time at the expense of somewhat higher prices and possibly lesser quality.

The third and fourth items in the list deserve fuller discussion.

Reducing the Cost of the Search. Any source of product information that is available in your own home greatly economizes on search costs. Three sources in particular commend themselves: *Consumer Reports* or *Consumers' Research Magazine,* a Sears or Montgomery Ward catalog, and the classified telephone directory.[11]

Consumer Reports and *Consumers' Research Magazine* facilitate the making of informed brand choices and also provide preliminary price information for a limited range of products and brands. The catalog of a large mail-order firm is, in the author's judgment, indispensable for obtaining information regarding reasonable prices for a vast array of products. Although Sears and Montgomery Ward prices are not always the lowest, they are usually in the bottom quarter of the price range. (Remember, however, that mail-order prices are usually final and may not include additional transportation costs, whereas other list prices may be lowered through discounts.) Finally, the Yellow Pages of the telephone book provide the most readily accessible list of sellers of any product, and the telephone is the cheapest means of obtaining either preliminary or final price information.

The use of the telephone for obtaining price information raises the problem of accuracy of information. You can secure partial protection against false or incomplete information by asking for the name of your informant and declaring that you will not purchase if the

---

[11] This discussion of procedures for obtaining consumer information is preliminary. Chapter 4 discusses the subject at length.

information given you turns out to be seriously incomplete or false.

A final means of economizing on search costs is to conduct a number of different searches on the same shopping expedition.

Determinants of Price and Quality Variation. As suggested earlier, the existence of substantial price and quality variation raises the possibility of large consumer payoffs. What, then, determines the extent of price/quality variation? The preliminary answer—to be developed —is that price and/or quality variations are greatest where:

1. Sellers practice *price discrimination;*
2. *Product differentiation* is substantial;
3. *Consumers fail to obtain and use price-quality information;*
4. The number of *sellers is large;*
5. *Price-fixing* by sellers or by law *is minimal;*
6. *Sellers conduct* genuine *sales.*

Price Discrimination. The practice of price discrimination results in substantial *within-brand* and *within-dealer* variation in prices. By definition, price discrimination is practiced when a single seller charges different customers different prices for the same good. To be a valid example of price discrimination, the differences in prices charged should not be attributable to differences in selling costs.

For a seller to engage in price discrimination two conditions must be met: 1) different customers (or the same customer at different times) must have differing urgencies of demand for his products—that is, be willing to pay different prices: 2) barriers must exist that prevent resale of his product from the customers charged the lower price to those charged the higher price. A classic example shows why price discrimination is profitable and lays bare the importance of the two conditions.

In the era prior to modern packaging a grocer purchased tea by the barrel. Upon receiving a new shipment, the competent grocer would first divide its content between one display case labeled "good" and a second proclaiming the tea to be "better." "Good" tea was priced at $.30 a pound and "better" tea at $.45 a pound. What made the purchasers of the higher-priced $.45 tea willing to pay more was their naïve belief that either the *better* label really meant "better" or that price is a reliable guide to quality. For these purchasers the same invincible innocence killed any appetite for the cheaper tea, and thus prevented resale from the $.30 purchasers to the $.45 purchasers.

Since the cost of posting the "better" sign was near-zero, the added $.15 per pound represented pure profit to the seller.

Differential transportation prices (lower fares for children, students, servicemen, round trippers), physicians charging lower fees to those they identify as "poor," and lower prices charged in sales are all relevant examples of price discrimination.

In the examples given, price discrimination was undertaken at the initiative of the seller (except for perhaps physicians' fees). It need not be. An enterprising consumer can induce a seller to practice price discrimination. When such a consumer asks, "What discount do you offer?" and actually succeeds in purchasing a good at a price that is genuinely lower than the usual price, he has induced the seller to practice price discrimination.

It will be profitable for the seller to accept the consumer's initiative as long as his receipts exceed the costs directly attributable to this sale *and* as long as he does not have to generalize the lower price to all of his customers. The latter requirement invariably will be met in the case of a new car purchase where the vast variety of engines, accessories, and lines makes it almost impossible to say what *the* price of *the* car is. It will also be met wherever there is a trade-in since the value of the trade-in is so subjective that it is difficult to say whether a particular used item has been over- or undervalued. These factors make it very difficult for a less favorably treated buyer to know whether the "deal" he is being offered is really more favorable or less favorable than that offered to other purchasers.

Price discrimination, then, is a major source of price variation. Knowledge of its practice and of the opportunity to induce sellers to engage in individual price discrimination favorable to them open up attractive possibilities for consumer profit.[12]

Product Differentiation. To abuse Gertrude Stein: A toothpaste is not a toothpaste is not a toothpaste. For a variety of reasons, some real, some imagined, some perhaps induced by "successful" advertising, consumers may develop a strong preference for a particular brand (or seller) and be willing to pay more for it (him).

In the case of toothpaste, a successful advertising campaign may persuade some consumers that Colgate (substitute any other name) performs better than its competitors, and hence they may be willing to pay a higher price for it. Alternatively, recognizing the value of a

---

[12] For a formal, yet clear discussion of price discrimination, see Richard H. Leftwich, *The Price System and Resource Allocation.* 5th ed. (Hinsdale, Ill.: Dryden Press, 1973), chap. 11.

convenient location, they may be willing to pay more for Colgate when they buy it at their neighborhood drugstore. Indeed, there are other reasons why consumers may be willing to pay more for any product at the local drugstore: they may like the druggist and the salespeople and enjoy dealing with them; they may feel, rightly or wrongly, that they can count on the druggist's honesty and his knowledge of their household medical needs.

All of these factors come under the heading of product differentiation.[13] Successful product differentiation enables a particular brand (particular seller) to command a higher price than its (his) competitors. Product differentiation gives rise to *within-brand, interbrand,* and *interdealer* variation in prices.

Some ideas of economist Kelvin Lancaster further illuminate the nature of product differentiation.[14] According to Lancaster, a specimen of a "product" consists of a "collection of characteristics or attributes."[15] Thus, a pair of ice skates on sale in a particular store may be viewed as a composite of basic characteristics—the "intrinsic" qualities of ice skates, durability, appearance, locational convenience of the store, as well as pleasantness and other attributes of the store or its salespeople. Prices of the "combined" product will vary, of course, depending upon how much of each characteristic the particular item possesses and how much consumers want each characteristic embodied in the item. To achieve profits, the seller seeks to put together a set of characteristics that appeals to a large number of consumers and at the same time differentiates his offering from that of his competitors.

For the intelligent consumer there are two sources of consumer payoffs in product differentiation. Gains are to be had from information revealing the real, as opposed to the advertised or imaginary, characteristics of a particular item. Moreover, gains are to be had by searching out the most satisfying set of characteristics. After all, the consumer does not willingly pay for characteristics that he does not want. For many consumers, this desire for certain product characteristics suggests

[13] The concept of *product differentiation* was developed by Edward H. Chamberlin in *The Theory of Monopolistic Competition* (Cambridge, Mass.: Harvard University Press, 1933; 6th ed., 1951).

[14] The basic reference is Kelvin J. Lancaster, "A New Approach to Consumer Demand," *Journal of Political Economy* (April 1966), pp. 132–57. A more readable version is Kelvin J. Lancaster, "Changes and Innovation in the Technology of Consumption," *American Economic Review* (May 1966), pp. 14–37. The latest version is Lancaster's book, *Consumer Demand: A New Approach* (New York: Columbia University Press, 1971).

[15] A *characteristic* is "a basic factor giving rise to utility," for example comfort, durability, safety. The concepts of *specimen* and *product* are defined in Chapter 3.

a search for discount outlets where the product mix offers less in terms of service, decor, and the like.

Consumers Fail to Obtain and Use Relevant Information.[16] The consumer's role in a well-functioning market is to identify and reward good performance on the part of sellers. To perform his role effectively, the consumer, in turn, needs to know the following:

1. What products, brands, and sellers exist and where they may be found;
2. What characteristics of a product are desirable ("general" product information);
3. The extent to which particular specimens in a product class possess the desired characteristics ("specific" product information);
4. Money prices and other terms ("free" delivery).

It goes without saying that consumers must not only possess the required information. They must also be willing and able to act on it, all at low cost.

The importance of complete and accurate consumer information —or its lack—in explaining variations in prices and quality can hardly be overemphasized.

If consumers possessed complete and accurate information regarding prices and qualities, the importance of price discrimination and product differentiation as sources of variations in price and quality would be reduced considerably. Gone would be price discrimination based on the inability of consumers to compare prices and qualities. In the tea example cited earlier, the grocer would not be able to induce innocent snobs to pay a higher price for the "better" tea that was better in name only. Gone also would be the high prices resulting from "successful" advertising not grounded in reproducible fact. Clorox, for instance, would no longer command $.58 a gallon while chemically identical bleaches were priced at $.37; Bayer's brand of aspirin would no longer command $.78 per 100 tablets while medically equivalent unbranded aspirin sells for $.18;[17] Kasar's brand of the sedative chloral hydrate would no longer command $14.00 per

---

[16] Chapter 4 is devoted to "The Acquisition and Evaluation of Consumer Information."

[17] Source: author's observations, Safeway Stores, San Diego, February 1972. These figures correspond closely to those obtained in Minneapolis in June, 1969.

100 capsules at wholesale while an alternative brand by Columbia Medical Company sells at $1.20.[18]

Some sources of price and quality variation would survive in a world of perfect information. One example would be price discrimination based on the different treatment of objectively defined classes, as in the case of discounts offered to elderly people. Also surviving would be product differentiation and associated price-quality variation arising from individuals' differing preferences for services, decor, durability, and "frills."

In real life, consumers never possess complete and accurate price-quality information. As we saw earlier, this ignorance of prices and qualities increases the opportunities for the profitable application of price discrimination by both sellers and buyers and of product differentiation by sellers. But even if—by a turn of magic—price discrimination and product differentiation were eliminated, the fact that consumers fail to obtain and use relevant information would, by itself, give rise to substantial variations in prices and quality. What accounts for the failure of consumers to obtain and use information? The answer comes in three parts.

1. Consumers Do Not Seek Relevant Information. That consumers search relatively little for information is attested by numerous consumer surveys.[19]

A first reason for this is that many consumers believe that markets work better than they really do. If markets did work well, the payoffs to information seeking would be small, and little searching would be justified.

Recall the question on the price of life insurance with which Chapter 1 opened: "If the price of the *cheapest* ordinary life policy was $4 per $1,000 of protection, what is the price charged by the highest-priced company (same policy, same insured person, all "good" companies)?" The correct answer was $13. But the answer most frequently given in the dozens of groups to whom this question was addressed is $5. Clearly, people in these groups believe that the market for life insurance works better than it really does.

[18] Richard F. Burack, *The New Handbook of Prescription Drugs* (New York: Pantheon Books, Inc., 1970), pp. 288–289.

[19] See George Katona and Eva Mueller, "A Study of Consumer Purchase Decisions," in Lincoln H. Clark, ed., *Consumer Behavior—The Dynamics of Consumer Reactions* (New York: New York University Press, 1958), pp. 30–87; H. Behrend, "Price Images, Inflation, and National Income Policy," *Scottish Journal of Political Economy* (November 1966); Reuben Hill, et al., *Family Development in Three Generations* (Cambridge, Mass.: Schenkman Publishing Co., Inc., 1970), especially chap. 9, "Correlates of Family Consumership."

Why should consumers hold such a favorable view of the workings of consumer markets? First, a belief in the effectiveness of "free enterprise" has been disseminated in thousands of speeches, magazine articles, advertisements, tracts, and books over a very long period. An additional explanation, applicable to a select few among the larger body of consumers, is that they may misremember and misapply what they learned a long time ago in courses in economics. These former students may remember correctly that "perfect competition" yields a single, lowest price for any product. But they may forget that perfect competition does not describe the real world in which most consumers make most of their purchases.[20]

Another, though more prosaic, reason for the failure of many consumers to seek information is that the "facts" of how badly markets work have been little researched, little recognized, and even less publicized.[21]

Another major reason for nonsearching or (more accurately) little searching on the part of consumers is affluence. As Staffan Linder has so cogently pointed out in *The Harried Leisure Class*,[22] affluence has brought us more goods, but we are still stuck with the 168-hour week. Interpreted: time is scarcer and worth more now; hence the cost of information-seeking has increased. A rational reaction to such an increased cost, other things being equal, is to reduce the amount

---

[20] Perfect competition assumes 1) homogeneous (undifferentiated) products, 2) "many" sellers, 3) "many" buyers, 4) perfect knowledge of prices and quality on the part of the buyers, 5) perfect mobility of resources. For a detailed discussion of perfect competition, see Richard H. Leftwich, *The Price System and Resource Allocation*, 5th ed. (Hinsdale, Ill.: (Dryden) 1973), pp. 27–29.

[21] We refer here to facts of variations in prices and quality. The consumer's chief source of information on quality variation is *Consumer Reports*. The extent of its influence is probably well represented by the extent of its circulation since World War II:

	Average Circulation	As Per Cent of Households
1947	175,000	0.47
1957	780,000	1.12
1967	1,100,000	1.82
1975	2,000,000	2.83

In explaining the lack of knowledge regarding price and quality variation, it is noteworthy that the author had to search with some diligence to locate those examples of price and quality variation in Table 1 of Chapter 1 that did not come from *Consumer Reports*. Consumer awareness of other market defects—the effects of monopoly, for example—is much more widespread.

[22] Linder, op. cit.

of information seeking in which we engage. It would appear that consumers have reacted rationally to the increase in affluence.

A final reason for nonsearching on the part of some consumers is supplied by sociologists. People, they assert, obtain satisfaction not merely from the goods they consume but also from the *roles* they perform or appear to perform in society. Some roles rule out careful shopping. Such is the case with the "liberal woman," a role identified in some recent research.[23] Besides searching less, the "liberal woman" has an unfavorable attitude toward trading stamps, is not familiar with top store personnel, is not active in social (as distinct from political or intellectual) organizations, gets her shopping done quickly, believes that working for fun is important, and makes infrequent trips away from home. The research does not tell us how many consumers follow this pattern.

Many other roles certainly exist—some requiring less careful searching as the example just cited, others requiring more careful searching, and still others that have no effect.

2. Consumers Are Unable to Obtain Relevant Information. Even when willing to seek out information on price and quality, consumers are often unable to obtain the relevant information. It is convenient to divide the discussion here into two parts; 1) what the consumer can achieve *through his own personal efforts;* 2) what the consumer can achieve *through services provided by others.* We address each in turn.

The basic obstacle to obtaining accurate price and quality information is the technical complexity of contemporary products. To solve the previously cited life insurance problem, one must be an insurance scholar, or be able to hire such a person, or to locate and digest his results. None of these tasks is easy.

Unfortunately, similar obstacles exist for most products. And, unfortunately, too, they apply to three of the four major categories of information—what characteristics are desirable, the extent to which particular specimens possess the desired characteristics, and the ascertaining of price.

As an example, consider transportation. Two hundred years ago, no one had any difficulty in understanding how a horse "worked." And, despite a classic literature on horse trading and the people taken in thereby, most people could identify good-performing and poor-

[23] Louis P. Bucklin, "Consumer Search, Role Enactment, and Market Efficiency," *Journal of Business* (October 1969), pp. 416–438.

performing horses. Not so with the modern automobile. One may ask: what consumer before Ralph Nader had any idea whatsoever regarding the characteristics of a safe car? And the matter of brand-specific information is no easier. For an individual to assess successfuly the quality of various makes of automobiles, he would have to possess the skills of a trained engineer, have access to a test track, and possess enough capital to finance controlled tests for several months!

Even for such apparently "simple" products as aspirin, one would need to undertake laboratory tests before he could assert with confidence that an unbranded aspirin was therapeutically equivalent to the widely advertised Bayer's brand of aspirin.[24]

The difficulties of the unaided consumer extend also to money prices as a consequence of multicomponent products and "packages" of sales terms. For example, in order to know and compare the prices of different automobiles, the consumer has to be sure that each car includes the same (or highly similar) components: body type, "line," transmission, motor size, type of brakes, trim, and numerous accessories. As to packages of sales terms, the consumer frequently purchases a "package" of goods-plus-ancillary arrangements (delivery, credit, service contract) for a single price. To make valid price comparisons, the package has either to be held constant or adjusted in terms of its components.

If the consumer's personal efforts to obtain price information and to judge quality are likely to be relatively ineffective, what possibilities exist for purchasing price-quality information from organizations specializing in this function? The answer is that relatively little exists for reasons we investigate presently. But first a few words regarding what assistance is now available to the consumer.[25]

The most conspicuous source of systematic consumer information regarding quality and, to a lesser extent, prices, is Consumers Union, which publishes the results of laboratory tests relating to about 110 widely distributed products per year in its monthly magazine, *Consumer Reports*. With a 1974 circulation of 2 million [26] *Consumer Reports* reaches up to 11 million families, or about one-sixth of all American homes. Other consumer information periodicals include

[24] Burack, op. cit., p. 69 states: "All aspirin tablets sold in the United States must by law meet U.S.P. [United States Pharmacopeia] standards. Therefore, patients should buy the least expensive aspirin tablets. . . ."

[25] The reader is again reminded that Chapter 4 contains a full discussion of sources of consumer information.

[26] *The 1974 Buying Guide Issue of Consumer Reports* (December 1974), p. 447. By mid-1975, as a result of the 1974–5 recession, the circulation of *Consumer Reports* had fallen to 1,800,000.

Changing Times (general information, circulation of 1.5 million),[27] *Consumers' Research Magazine* (product tests, circulation of 111,000),[28] *Moneysworth* (general and brand information, circulation of 996,000),[29] and *Money* (general information, circulation of 500,000).[30] As to systematic sources of price information, almost none exist.[31]

Given the wide range of price and quality variation displayed in Table 1, why is there so little systematic information? We have already encountered the first part of the answer: consumers are not widely aware of the potential payoffs to price-quality information. Hence, there has not been a great demand for information.

A second part of the explanation is the credibility problem. Product tests by consumer-controlled organizations by government or by universities are more believable to most than are tests performed by private businesses. It is noteworthy that the two *commercial* publications cited previously specialize in general product information (no brand comparisons) or in the dissemination of brand information already in the public domain or produced by other organizations.[32]

Although consumer controlled-cooperatives such as Consumers Union possess credibility, cooperatives are difficult to organize, perhaps because of the lack of large financial rewards to their organizers.

Another problem shared by many publishing activities is the "public good" nature of consumer information: published test results are not "used up" by the person purchasing them. Borrowers can make use of the information without paying for it. Although the "dog-eared" condition of library copies of *Consumer Reports* attests to their social usefulness, it does nothing to help finance a larger supply of information.

Still another problem is that much consumer information is local and subjective—what doctors to choose or how to locate a reliable roofer. The per-unit cost of obtaining such information may exceed

[27] 1975 Ayer Directory of Publications (Philadelphia: Ayer Press, 1975), p. 223. By mid-1975, according to industry scuttlebutt, the circulation of *Changing Times* had fallen to 1,200,000.

[28] *Consumers' Research Magazine* (November 1974), p. 35.

[29] Source: industry scuttlebutt.

[30] *1975 Ayer Directory of Publications, op. cit.,* p. 634.

[31] A major exception: information on dealers' prices for new cars and both whole sale and retail prices of used cars. See *Edmund's 1975 Car Prices* (Edmund Publications Corp., 295 Northern Boulevard, Great Neck, N. Y. 11021).

[32] Before jumping to any overly hasty conclusion regarding the noncredibility of profit-making organizations, consider the success of the *Mobil Travel Guide* whose regional editions have rated restaurants, hotels, and motels in the United States since 1958. The Mobil Guide is published by Rand McNally & Co. in collaboration with the Mobil Oil Corporation.

its worth to individual consumers, unless a large demand for this information materializes from the outset.[33]

As to the production and distribution of price-quality information by government, universities, or research organizations, political-ideological considerations have thus far kept these organizations from acting very positively on behalf of consumers. With the advent of "consumerism" as a political factor in the late 1960s and the 1970s, this could change.

A final factor reducing the supply of price-quality information from what it might otherwise be is technological. Consumer information has thus far been disseminated by the printed word. This form of distribution, as research has repeatedly shown, restricts the audience to high-education, high-income families.[34] The other technological limitation comes from the time required to test products. Too often the information is obsolete by the time it is published.[35] Thus, even those who would welcome and use it, are unable to do so.

3. Consumers Are Unwilling/Unable to Act on Information They Possess. Seeking and obtaining price-quality information are by themselves insufficient to ensure the application of market discipline to sellers. Consumers must be willing to *act* on the basis of the information they possess. Everyone "knows" that new automobile prices are bargainable, but some may find bargaining distasteful or uncomfortable, and be *unwilling* to engage in it. Some may have a distaste for the conflict that bargaining often engenders. Others may find that bargaining runs against early engrained beliefs that sellers are to be trusted, rather than questioned. Others may feel uncomfortable, because of a felt lack of skill or of supporting information. Finally, bargaining takes time and some may feel that the payoff to bargaining does not justify the time required. Still others are *unable* to bargain effectively, lacking the skills, the supporting information, or the personality.

Whether it stems from unwillingness or an inability, the failure to bargain has the effect of reducing market discipline and permits price and quality variations that would otherwise be eliminated.

Summing up, if consumers fail to obtain and act on the relevant

[33] The Survey Research Center of the University of Michigan is seeking financial support so it can test the feasibility of a local consumer information system.

[34] Colston E. Warne, "The Impact of Consumerism on the Market," *The San Diego Law Review* (February 1971), p. 31; also Ruby Turner Morris, *Consumers Unions— Methods, Implications, Weaknesses, and Strengths* (New London, Conn.: Litfield Publications, 1971), pp. 52–53.

[35] See Morris, op. cit., p. 50.

price/quality information, then sellers will not be disciplined, and consumer markets will be characterized by large variations in prices and quality. This opens up delicious opportunities for those consumers who successfully search out and act on the relevant information.

Where the Number of Sellers Is Larger. It will be an unusual consumer who for a particular product has access to more than 20 sellers at search costs he finds acceptable. For a market of this size it is our expectation that the greater the number of sellers, other things being equal, the greater will be the variation in price and quality confronting the purchaser of this particular product. The reasons for this expectation are several.

Prices *initially* set are likely to be tailored to fit the objectives of the seller, and a number of objectives are possible. One student of the subject, Alfred Oxenfeldt, lists 20: [36]

1. Maximize long-run profits;
2. Maximize short-run profits;
3. Maximize growth in sales;
4. Stabilize markets;
5. Desensitize customers to price;
6. Maintain a price leadership arrangement;
7. Discourage new entrants into this product line;
8. Speed the exit(s) of existing firms;
9. Avoid government investment and/or control;
10. Maintain loyalty of middlemen and obtain their sales support;
11. Avoid demands for "more" from suppliers, particularly labor;
12. Enhance image of the firm and its offerings;
13. Be regarded as "fair" by customers;
14. Be considered trustworthy and reliable by rivals;
15. Help sale of weak items in product line;
16. Create interest and excitement about an item;
17. Discourage others from cutting prices;
18. Make a product "visible";
19. "Spoil market" to obtain a high price from the sale of the business;
20. Build traffic.

The larger the number of firms, the more likely it is that their decision-makers will give precedence to *different objectives*. And to the extent

[36] Alfred R. Oxenfeldt, "A Decision-Making Structure for Price Decisions," *Journal of Marketing* (January 1973), pp. 48–53.

that the pursuit of different objectives implies different prices for variants of the same product, then we may expect greater variation in prices for the product category as a whole.

But, given the uncertainties of the market, different sellers may feel that the *same objective* is served by *different pricing strategies.* For example, think of two retailers both hoping to maximize their profits in the long run. But one follows a high markup policy (over cost) and the other a low markup policy. From such ambiguities regarding cause and effect comes greater variation in prices (and, by parallel argument, in quality).

At a somewhat lower level of abstraction, sellers can utilize a variety of price-setting practices: they can accept the manufacturer's "suggested price" (if there is one); they may apply markups to the wholesale prices they pay that are "customary" for that product and area; they can accept the "conventional" prices that exist for certain products ($9.95; not $10, not $9.67); finally, they can follow their "hunches" or intuition. This list is not exhaustive.[37] The point of the list is to show that the number of price-setting principles is fairly large, and to suggest that the larger the number of sellers, the greater is the number of price-setting principles likely to be used. Since different principles typically result in different prices, the effect will be to increase the variation in prices as the number of sellers increases.

Even if the same principle is followed by different firms in the setting of initial prices, its application in different firms can give rise to different prices. Consider the practice of setting the retail prices as a certain percentage markup over wholesale. The possibility that different firms pay different wholesale prices would yield different retail prices. Or, alternatively, different firms may use different markups,[38] thus yielding different retail prices. So, from this factor, too, follows the conclusion that the greater the number of sellers, the greater is the variation in prices.

Also related to price-setting practices are the costs experienced by different sellers. Regardless of the principle employed in setting initial prices, each firm that remains in the industry indefinitely must set prices that, on the average, will cover total costs, including a level

[37] For more on alternative pricing principles, see Delbert J. Duncan and Charles F. Phillips, *Retailing, Principles and Methods* (Homewood, Ill.: Richard D. Irwin, Inc., 1963), chap. 16, "Pricing Merchandise"; or M. A. G. van Meerhaerghe, *Price Theory and Price Policy* (London: Longmans, Green, 1969), chap. 2.

[38] The author queried an executive of the "number two" department store in a large metropolitan area regarding the fact that his store charged a lower price on an identical appliance than did the dominant number one store. "We would like to use the same markup as _____ (the dominant store), but we can't get away with it."

of profits enough to induce the owner(s) to continue that line of production. If different sellers experience different costs and if these costs must be covered in the long run then high-cost firms will tend to set higher prices (on the average) than low-cost sellers. The greater the number of sellers, the greater is the variation we would expect in costs, and hence the greater the variation in prices.

A final major factor accounting for variations in prices initially set is the inability of sellers either to gauge in advance, or to control consumer reactions, after the introduction of either new prices or products. As most people know, the Ford Motor Company invested millions of dollars in the design and marketing of the Edsel automobile in 1958. Still the Edsel failed and was withdrawn in 1961. This large-scale failure to anticipate consumer reactions is probably matched by countless smaller-scale failures.[39]

Earlier, we discussed *initial* prices. If consumers were able and willing to obtain and act on relevant price-quality information at negligible cost, then the initial price variations for which we have just argued would vanish. Consumers would patronize the low price-per-unit-of-quality sellers, and other sellers would be forced to accept the lowest prices offered.[40] The rub is—as we argued earlier—consumers are unable or unwilling to do so. Hence, the larger the number of sellers, other things being equal, the greater is the variation in price.

Price-Fixing. Successful price-fixing at the retail level reduces price variations and hence opportunities for consumer profit. When instigated by sellers, the impetus for price-fixing usually comes from the least efficient and hence most vulnerable retail sellers with the likely result that higher prices are established than would otherwise prevail. When sought by consumers, price-fixing may or may not succeed in establishing lower prices.

Successful price-fixing at the retail level may be instituted by manufacturers, retailers, or the government. It may take the form of laws, contractual agreements among the concerned parties, or of collusive or quasicollusive behavior on the part of retailers. An example of collusive price-fixing would be a meeting of owners of local gas stations in which all owners agreed (orally or in writing) to adopt the pattern of prices set by Brand X. *Quasicollusive* price fixing might occur if the same persons, without consultation, developed a practice of following the same pattern of prices as Brand X.

---

[39] See Chapter 10 for evidence regarding failure rates for new products.

[40] The final, single price would be reached, not immediately, but after a series of adjustments.

Surprising though it may seem, it is, under certain circumstances, legal for manufacturers to set and enforce minimum retail prices of their products.[41] There are two methods of setting and enforcing retail prices. The first is to sell only to retail dealers who are willing to sign a manufacturer-retailer contract calling for the retailer to follow the manufacturer's suggested price. Where a manufacturer has few products, susceptible to wide distribution by a "small' dealer network, this is feasible. Thus, Volkswagen, which follows this practice, has been quite successful in maintaining its suggested retail prices.

The second method relies on the "nonsigner" clauses that were part of the resale price maintenance [42] laws passed in many states during the 1930s. If a manufacturer enters into a contract setting the retail price for a single retailer, the nonsigner clause makes this price binding for all other retailers—*whether they signed a contract with the manufacturer or not*. The effect of the nonsigner clause, when enacted, was to reduce greatly the cost to the manufacturer of setting and enforcing his preferred retail price. Resale price maintenance legislation (misleadingly labeled "Fair Trade" legislation) was enacted in many states with the strong support of small retailers, particularly druggists, who feared the competition of chain stores. In December 1975, Congress finally repealed "Fair Trade." [43]

Since World War II both forms of price-setting by manufacturers have become less effective. The causes are several: the high cost of enforcement to manufacturers even when aided by the nonsigner clause, successful legal challenges to the nonsigner clause in several states, the manufacturer's interest in selling to high-volume, price-cutting retailers, and the introduction of "house" brands. In general, price-fixing by manufacturers has been ineffective where the number of products marketed is high (for example, General Electric with its thousands of products) and where the number of retail outlets to be policed is large.

Local retailers can agree, explicitly or implicitly, to set a single

[41] The Miller-Tydings Resale Price Maintenance Act in 1937 amended Section 1 of the Sherman Anti-Trust Act to exempt from antitrust prohibition contracts prescribing minimum prices for the resale of trade-marketed or branded commodities "in free and open competition." Cf. F. M. Scherer, *Industrial Market Structure and Economic Performance* (Chicago: Rand McNally & Company, 1970), pp. 512–16.

[42] For a brief discussion of resale price maintenance, see F. M. Scherer, *Industrial Market Structure and Economic Performance* (Chicago: Rand-McNally & Co., 1970), pp. 512–516. For an authoritative review, see Stanley C. Hollander's chapter in B. S. Yamey, ed., *Resale Price Maintenance* (Chicago: Aldine Publishing Company, 1966).

[43] It achieved this by repealing the McGuire Act of 1952 that exempted nonsigner clauses from the Sherman Act prohibition.

price. But, as noted previously, such price agreements become increasingly difficult to enforce as the number of sellers increases. As this occurs, it becomes increasingly likely that some seller will feel that *his* interest is best served by a different price, usually lower, and *not* by common price. As numbers of sellers increase, it also becomes increasingly difficult and costly for nonprice-cutters to police the price agreement.

A final observation: such collusive price-setting is easier to initiate and to continue when the product in question is relatively "standard," for example, a car wash at an automated installation. As the product becomes more complex, it becomes easier for the price-cutting retailer to offer a disguised price cut in the form of an additional service or a "break" on some other term. (For example, a price-cutting dealer in high-fidelity equipment charges the full "Fair Trade" price on a speaker, but makes no charge at all for a cartridge and needle with a list price of $50!)

"Sales." Thus far, we have focused on factors giving rise to price variations at a given point in time. Sales give rise to price variations over time. A genuine *sale* occurs "when a retailer's usual line of merchandise is sold at reduced prices."

A number of factors account for the conduct of sales by sellers:

1. *Price Discrimination.* Once the retailer has sold to his "regular" customers at "regular" prices, he can achieve additional sales by reducing prices. (Of course, the same individual may be a "regular" customer for some product and a sales customer for other products.)

2. *Seller's Planning Error.* The seller may have overestimated the demand for a certain product. Or—and it comes to the same thing —the seller's judgment as to what his customers wanted in terms of style may have been deficient.

3. *Loss Leaders.* The seller may set sales prices—even below cost —on certain products in order to attract "new" customers to his store. He expects to sell other products to these new customers at the usual or even higher-than-usual prices. In terms of cost, any loss incurred by this device may be viewed as a promotional expenditure.

4. *Seasonal Factors.* Many products, for example, bathing suits or ice skates, are time-specific. When the appropriate season has passed, they can be sold only at reduced prices.

5. *Tradition.* Many stores establish a pattern of sales that becomes "traditional." Often traditional sales may be continued even when economic conditions would indicate otherwise.

6. *Concessions for Shopworn Merchandise.* Money prices are

often reduced on merchandise whose condition has suffered by virtue of customer handling.

TENTATIVE OPERATING RULES FOR CONSUMER PURCHASES

In this chapter we have sought to be progressively more specific in both analysis and recommendations.

In the last section we dealt at length with factors accounting for variations in price and quality. We believe that a deeper understanding of the causes of price and quality variation *in general* would help the consumer to estimate better the expected variation in price/quality for the product whose purchase he contemplates. And the expected variation in price and quality for *his* product is important since it is in turn an important determinant of how much he should search.

This chapter ends with the spelling out of tentative operating rules for consumer purchases.

1. *Before Purchasing*

a. Ask yourself whether the product of interest is subject to substantial variations in price and quality.

(1) For relatively objective information on this point, consult *Consumer Reports, Consumers' Research Magazine,* or specialized publications such as *Popular Photography.*

(2) If objective information is *not* available, ask yourself:

(a) Whether the *prices* of the product (or brand) *are fixed* by law, manufacturers, or retailers, and how effective any price-fixing arrangements are. If they are effectively fixed (and the fixed price cannot be avoided by buying elsewhere), buy promptly and waste no further effort.

(b) Whether the product is *subject to product differentiation* as a result of characteristics of the individual seller (friendliness, reliability, background information he possesses) or characteristics of the outlet (reliability, decor, extent of service, location). If yes, ask yourself what characteristics you want and how much you are willing to pay to obtain these characteristics.

(c) Whether *the seller practices price discrimination.* The relevant question is whether there are classes of consumers who will buy the product only at reduced prices. Price discrimination will be practiced only when the seller does not have to generalize the lower price. This condition is met when the favored groups are kept separate through classification, ignorance, or some other device. If you expect sellers to initiate or to accept price discrimination, ask yourself whether you belong to a group likely to be favored, how you might join such a group, or in what capacity a seller could be induced to practice price discrimination in your favor.

(d) Whether this is a *product for which consumers cannot or do not obtain and act on accurate price-quality information.* A subjective question such as this can only have a subjective answer. We suggest that you consider whether you personally believe that you can make valid comparisons of the prices and qualities of different brands with little effort. If not, expect substantial payoffs from any information, which you obtain, even though it may be imperfect.

Also ask if you yourself would normally act to take advantage of the price-quality information you possess. If not, expect substantial payoffs from efforts to act on information.

(e) Whether a *sale* involving this product or brand is *likely* —perhaps as a result of the practice of price discrimination over time, a planning error by the seller, seasonal considerations, loss leader sales, or the timing of traditional sales.

2. *While Purchasing:*

a. Deal in markets with the *largest possible number of sellers.* Be sure to consider mail-order sellers, where relevant.

b. *Whenever* there is a *trade-in* or *the price of the good is $100 or more* (set your own minimum), always seek a particularly favorable price—that is, *try to persuade the seller to practice individual price discrimination.*

c. *Whenever the price of a good is $100 or more*—again set your own minimum—*always contact at least three sellers.* Search more if:

(1) You have reason to expect more than average price-quality variation, or

(2) The expected outlay is very high, or

(3) The costs of the search, including time and effort, are relatively low.

These rules are neither final nor complete. They could not be. Consumer decisions are too complex. In addition, the discussion from which they were constructed did not deal in detail with such important matters as sources of product information, negotiating the purchase, or the possibilities for consumer redress. These are discussed in later chapters.

EXAMPLES OF THE RULES AT WORK [44]

Air Transportation. Mr. A flies rather frequently from San Diego to New York and back again in connection with his work. Occasionally, some of Mr. A's family—his wife, daughter age seven, or son age five, accompany him to visit the family's relatives who live in the East. What is more, neither Mr. A nor his family is averse to taking a vacation en route if the price is right. The problem of the A family is to ascertain the cheapest means of getting to New York and back for different combinations of family members.

From past experience, the A's know that American Airlines is the dominant airline to New York, offering both nonstop and frequent direct flights. United offers a number of direct flights, and Delta can get you to New York at the cost of possible plane changes and considerably longer trip time. In terms of the analysis of this chapter, Delta suffers a kind of "negative" product differentiation.

Thus, the A's were not surprised when an advertisement alerted them to the No. 7 offering in Table 1. In essence, if you accept the inconvenience of flying to New York via Atlanta, then Delta/Eastern/Western together will "make it up to you" by letting you return to San Diego via Mexico City—a 1,800 mile "diversion." In terms of what you would pay to fly the regular round trip from San Diego to Mexico City, the Mexico City stopover is "worth" $162. Subtract this from the price of the total package—$308—and your "inconvenient" New York trip costs only $146, less than half the regular round-trip fare of $326.

Why do the airlines do it? The answer is straightforward: it is profitable. If there are empty seats on these flights—and note that you cannot depart during a peak period—then the cost of carrying one more passenger is very low, perhaps the wholesale cost of a single meal. But in order to induce people to put up with a much less attractive San Diego-to-New York segment, the three airlines have to

---

[44] To repeat an earlier observation: the facts of these examples will quickly become obsolete. Not so—it is hoped—the principles that they illustrate.

TABLE 1

Alternative Air Fares—San Diego to New York and Return (January, 1972):

A Sampler of Legal Price Discrimination Arrangements

Fare Designation	Eligibility Criteria	Fare	Restrictions
1. Regular Coach	Anyone	$326	None
2. Summer Excursion	Anyone	$284	1. Away from 7 to 29 days. 2. No departures during peak hours.[a] 3. Payment for ticket within 3 days of reservation.
3. Winter Excursion	Anyone	$245	Same as Summer Excursion
4. Tour-Based Fare	Anyone booking through 1) airline "tour department" or 2) travel agent.	$228 [b]	1. Requires at least $65 of expenditures for hotels, car rentals, entertainment. 2. No departures during peak hours. 3. Departure for return trip no earlier than the next Sunday.
5. Youth Standby	Age 12–21	$216	1. Seats not guaranteed.
6. Children	Age 4–11	$163	None.
7. Mexico-for-Atlanta Exchange [d]	Anyone	$146 + 162—Mexico [c] / $308 [c]	1. Travel one way via Atlanta. 2. Travel the other way via Mexico City with stopover. 3. Away less than 30 days.
8. Additional Family Member	Family member accompanying person paying full coach fare.	$107	1. Return trip must be mde within 4 days 2. No departures during peak hours.[a]

[a] Peak hours: 2 P.M. to Midnight, Fridays and Sundays.

[b] A minimum expenditure of $65 on ground services would bring the total outlay to $291, but the additional $65 does purchase services that may be of use to you. You are not required to *use* all services, but you must *pay* for them.

[c] The total fare is $308. However, if one subtracts the San Diego-to-Mexico City round-trip fare of $162, then the cost of the New York round trip becomes $146, as noted previously.

[d] Except for one through flight, this will require a change of planes.

sweeten the rest of the package. Hence, the $146 fare and the jaunt to Mexico.

This is not the only price discrimination arrangement available out of San Diego. The creativity of airline planners in concocting alternative fares is formidable, as Table 1 shows.[45] Indeed, the number of price discrimination fares established by various airlines has been sufficient to create a serious problem of information retrieval on the part of airline clerks and travel agents. The lesson to travelers is to check and check and check—to make sure that you are paying the lowest fare available and that you are aware of the restrictions on each.

Table 1 sets forth a large, though incomplete menu of price discrimination arrangements available from San Diego. The payoffs to the A's may be considerable indeed. Take a dependent for less than four days, avoiding the peak departure hours, and you save $219 from the regular fare—See No. 8. Book your trip through the "tour" department of an airline and return on the following Sunday or later and you have "earned" a payoff of $98. (Again, you must avoid a peak-hour departure.)

The airline's objective in all this is to entice you to travel as often as possible, paying the highest fare you will accept each time. Family A, of course, aims at the lowest fare. Mr. A encountered a delicious conflict of objectives between one airline's management and its tour department. The tour representative, evidently paid on a commission basis, worked overtime to show Mr. A how he could get to New York on the tour-based fare of $228 instead of the regular $326 fare.

Some footnotes are applicable to this and other air ticket situations. First, some airline or travel agents will only provide the information about cheaper fares if you ask directly: "Is that the cheapest way to get to New York and back?" Second, small travel agencies will sometimes be ignorant of advantageous lower fares, because of their inexperience combined with the number and complexity of airline tariffs.

If the total price of a trip is very large as in the case of a European or Asiatic trip, it might be worth the search cost to find a "natural" group (members of an art institute, a fraternal organization) who have arranged for group fares or who have chartered an entire plane or block of seats on certain dates. Alternatively, travel agents sometimes organize artificial groups of people—nonaffinity groups—who want

[45] The Civil Aeronautics Board has authority to approve or disapprove fares proposed by individual airlines. Prior to 1973, and resuming in 1976, the CAB usually approved fares embodying price discrimination since they were consistent with the board's general policy of encouraging lower air fares.

Type of Fare	Fare
First Class	$1,262
Standard "Economy"	668
14–21 Day Excursion	598
14–21 Day Group Inclusive Tour	429
22–45 Day Excursion	387
7–8 Day Winter Group Inclusive Tour	351
Affinity/Incentive Group	338

	Cost if:	
All Expense Group Tours by Air	Purchased As "Package"	Purchased Separately
New York to London: Saturday to Saturday	$599	$999
New York to Paris: Saturday to Saturday	699	1,235

to make the same flight(s) at the same time. Neither of these approaches is "pure" price discrimination since some of the reduction in price may arise from a reduction in airline costs. Yet the question put by the inquiring consumer is the same: Is this a group of people who are likely to make this trip only when accorded an attractively low price? Can I qualify as a member of the group? [46]

The Purchase of a New Car. Mr. B wished to purchase a new car. A reading of *Consumer Reports* led him to settle on a particular Plymouth with a particular set of accessories.

The problem was how to obtain the lowest price. Mr. B was aware, of course, that automobile manufacturers cannot set retail prices and that, therefore, the competent consumer can negotiate advantageous terms for himself. He was also aware that dealers have established different reputations with respect to reliability and willingness to quote lower prices. Through casual conversations with friends and acquaintances Mr. B became convinced that a certain Plymouth dealer in his large city had a reputation for both reliability and favorable prices. It might be noted parenthetically that the subjective, indirect costs of such information are usually low: for the most part the conversations foregone were not "pearls of great value!" Finally, Mr. B was aware that car dealers are more willing to discount heavily in the winter when the demand for cars usually falls short of the supply of cars.

The gambit Mr. B employed in talking with the car salesman is arresting in its simplicity and effectiveness and reflects Mr. B's great

[46] Footnote 1 in Chapter 1 was right: facts do become obsolete. The facts of this example—correct in January, 1972—are totally outdated. Some of the arrangements are no longer available. And for those that remain, most of the numbers have changed.

But the principles live on, triumphantly. Note the following "menu" of New York to Switzerland fares offered by the airlines in February, 1975:

distaste for shopping and bargaining, that is, high subjective search costs. His conversation with the salesman went something like this: "I am going to buy a new Plymouth. I've written down on this piece of paper the exact model and accessories I want. I'll be trading in my present car, a '63 Chevy II, which is outside. I'll pay cash for what I owe beyond the trade-in."

"I don't want to waste time in bargaining. What I want you to do is to give me *your best price*. On the basis of this I'll make up my mind as to whether I'll buy from you. . . . I know figuring prices is complicated. So take your time and come up with a price that you and your sales manager will stick to."

This gambit is effective only if the seller accepts the notion that this is *his single chance* to sell to *this* customer. The no-nonsense manner, serious mien, and general aura of knowledgeability of Mr. B —he is a real person and this is a real incident—probably reinforced the salesman's conviction in this instance that he had to offer quite a low price or lose this customer to another dealer. (In fact, Mr. B intended to contact only one dealer, but the seller had no way of knowing this.)

The result was an on-the-spot offer by the seller of $2,313 plus the old car. Mr. B retired saying that he would think it over. Time is usually on the side of the patient consumer. The next day Mr. B received by mail a second, lower offer of $2,263 ($50 less) plus the old car. This he accepted.

Subsequent analysis disclosed that this was a favorable price. But how was the car buyer to know? Two pieces of information were critical in appraising this offer: 1) the wholesale prices the dealer had to pay Plymouth for the new car and accessories, 2) the wholesale value of the used car Mr. B was trading in. Mr. B's credit union provides such information to its members.

Their analysis of this offer in November, 1967 was as follows:

Dealer Receives:		Dealer Pays (Wholesale):	
Cash: Down payment	$ 100	Basic car (1967 Plymouth	
at delivery	2,163	Belvedere II, 4-dr. sedan,	
Old Car: Wholesale value	465	V-8 engine)	$2,121
	———	Tinted windshield	16
	$2,728	Power steering	69
		Air conditioning	274
		Deluxe wheel discs	30
			———
			$2,510

The dealer's gross profit comes to $218 ($2,728 — $2,510). This $218 is by no means clear profits. Out of it must come the salesman's commission, contributions to rent, office salaries, interest, and depreciation as well as other such items. Although this price is not excessive, it is certainly high enough for the buyer to insist that he has not traded away his right to, or expectation of, a satisfactory level of after-purchase service.

Individuals may obtain information on wholesale prices for all makes and accessories from the current issue of *Edmund's 1975 Car Prices* (published at 295 Northern Boulevard, Great Neck, N. Y. 11021) and available on newsstands. Current used car quotations are published monthly in the *N.A.D.A. Official Used Car Guide* (Washington: National Automobile Dealers Used Car Guide Co., published weekly), also available at newsstands.

The purchaser's invoice in this transaction bears almost no resemblance to the figures given. In fact, only two numbers were the same: the down payment of $100 and the additional cash required of the purchaser, $2,163. The invoice was as follows:

Item	List or "Sticker" Price
Basic car (1967 Plymouth Belvedere II 4-dr. sedan, V-8 engine)	$2,569
Power steering	89
Tinted windshield	21
Air conditioning	338
Deluxe wheel discs	39
Total	$3,056
Less: Trade-in (1963 Chevy II 100 2-dr. sedan $793) Down payment $100	$ 893
Equals: Cash to be paid by buyer at delivery	$2,163

There are—car dealers tell us—naïve persons who accept list prices as final. From this data we can calculate the gross profit a dealer would make if he sold the car at list without a trade-in. From the $3,056 he would charge the customer, we subtract the $2,510 he pays Plymouth, leaving him a gross profit of $546, $328 more than he would get from selling to the knowledgeable Mr. B. This is $328 that most consumers can ill afford to give up.

Analytically, the reader will at once recognize this as an instance when the buyer's ploy led the seller to practice price discrimination.

Mr. C Buys a Camera. An expensive camera is a complex product, and its purchase is a complex process. Here we follow such a purchase in most of its details.

Mr. C knows what he wants in a new camera. He travels abroad frequently. What he prizes most from his past travels is close-up photographs of people. But like many tourists, he finds it embarrassing to attempt close-ups of people he doesn't know. This dilemma pushes him inexorably in the direction of telephoto lenses and a camera that will accommodate them. (His present camera does not.) Unlike many camera enthusiasts, he abhors baggage. And this dislike leads him to prefer a camera with a built-in exposure meter. (His present camera requires a separate exposure meter.) Thus, he was in a state of psychological readiness when *Consumer Reports* tested single-lens reflex cameras.

On the basis of its tests, *Consumer Reports* picked the Miranda Sensorex as the best of the "Very Good," followed by the comparable models of Canon, Pentax, Nikkormat, and Minolta. A Miranda for Mr. C? Before accepting *Consumer Reports'* preference as his own, he "tested" this choice on camera enthusiast-friends and camera sellers. Most accepted Miranda's right to membership in the select group, but not all accepted its right to *leadership*. One disconcerting note was the question raised by several as to whether Mirandas experienced mechanical breakdowns more frequently than other makes. The question arose most dramatically when one dealer (authorized to sell Miranda and other makes as well) said he would accept an order for Miranda, but would urge Mr. C to consider a $100-more-expensive Nikon, citing its "solid" body. Mr. C set against these comments the three-year-guarantee that Miranda offers and decided to go ahead with the Miranda.

Mr. C is sufficiently knowledgeable about statistics to realize that on matters of camera quality no one can be certain. All of us—consumers, dealers, the Consumers Union tests—are dependent upon the unknown quality-control procedures of Miranda and other manufacturers. If these procedures are technically sound and executed frequently and carefully, their results are significant. If the testing is inadequate, the results lose their meaning as guides. But can knowledgeable users of expensive cameras effectively "monitor" camera quality? I think not. Most such users have neither the time nor the inclination to make the large-sample tests necessary for effective monitoring over long production runs.

Hence, with every camera purchase the nagging uncertainty lingers, unanswerable: Is this the best camera in its class? Is the camera in my hand representative of Miranda quality (substitute any other name)?

Mr. C at any rate decided on a Miranda. But which Miranda? He wanted the least automatic (fewer things to go wrong) Miranda that would give him a built-in exposure meter. The Miranda FVT model met this specification. As for the choice of lens, Mr. C, after discussions of focal lengths, maximum lens openings, and within-brand list prices, settled on a 135 mm. automatic Miranda f/3.5 telescopic lens (image magnified 2½ times). This, then, would be the package to price.

In buying a camera, the camera will be the same, but the service may differ from dealer to dealer. One dealer, for example, may be willing to make an .on-the-spot exchange of a new camera that the customer finds unsatisfactory. Some offer free trial periods, others do not. Some are prepared to make on-the-premise repairs, whereas others perform no repair work at all.

Mr. C's preliminary visit to camera shops and his perusal of photography magazines enabled him to make a preliminary analysis of price as well as service variation. Price-fixing is impossible for most camera manufacturers: too many retail sellers. As in the case of automobiles, the quotation of different prices to different buyers (that is, individual price discrimination) is frequent. Given the multitude of lenses, camera body options, and accessories, each "deal" is different, and hence the dealer need not offer his lowest price to all purchasers. At the same time these factors make it possible for sellers to practice product differentiation galore. On the basis of his "searches," Mr. C distinguished the following types of camera dealers in his Midwest city.

(This list is necessarily incomplete. Our purchaser could not and **did not wish to** contact every seller in his locale. Nonetheless, the cost of this information is relatively low, since Mr. C—like many camera enthusiasts—enjoys visiting with the knowledgeable young sellers who populate most camera shops. The more experienced camera "bugs" may possess most of this information initially as a matter of common knowledge.)

Mr. C's impression is that price decreases and service increases as one goes down the list. This is true with one exception: the time and mistakes of communicating by mail keep mail-order houses from rendering as good a service as local establishments. At any rate, this

Reference Number	Location	Photographic Products Only?	Emphasis on Film Processing versus Camera Sales	On-Premise Camera Repair
1	Downtown (high-cost)	No, also sells records	Equal	No
2	Downtown	Yes	Film processing	No
3	Downtown	Yes	Camera specialists	No
4	Downtown	Yes	Camera specialists	No
5	Suburban (low-cost?)	Yes	Both, but emphasis on cameras	No
6	Mail order No. 1 N.Y.	Yes	Equal	Yes
7	Mail order No. 2 N.Y.	Yes	Equal	Yes
8	Mail order No. 3 Chicago	Yes	Equal	Yes

analysis leads Mr. C to his final purchase objective: to buy the camera from the suburban camera specialist at the mail-order price.

He then proceeded to obtain price quotations for his package from different dealers. With each, after appropriate discussion of cameras in general, he asked, "What is the best price you can give me?" This yielded the following list of offers:

Seller Number	"Best Price" [a]
1. Downtown	About $273 (includes sales tax) [b]
2. Downtown	No quote sought
3. Downtown	About $247 (includes sales tax)
4. Downtown	No price quoted, urged Nikon
5. Suburban	$229 (includes sales tax)
6. Mail order-NYC	$221 (no sales tax)
7. Mail order-NYC	$205 (no sales tax) [c]
8. Mail order-Chicago	$215 (no sales tax)

[a] In several cases the manager was not present. Hence, these are estimates of what the purchaser believes the best price would be—another source of uncertainty.

[b] A camera purchaser in Mr. C's state is legally liable for the sales tax, regardless of the location of the seller. In practice, mail-order sellers in other states do not collect it, and purchasers do not volunteer to pay it.

[c] But this dealer gave his quotation on the basis of a Soligor lens. Thus, a new uncertainty enters. Mr. C decided to ignore this bid.

The final act came when our purchaser visited the suburban shop listed as No. 5, "armed" with the Chicago offer. Upon seeking the best price, he received the $229 offer recorded. He then showed the dealer the $215 quotation from the Chicago mail-order house. "Can you match that?" was Mr. C's query.

"No," was the reply. "I've got to pay the sales tax and he doesn't."

Our purchaser then asked, "Is there any reason I should buy from you rather than from him?"

The suburban dealer replied, "I stand behind my sales. If you buy that Miranda from me and it isn't right, I'll give you a new one on the spot. With ——— you'll have to send it to Chicago and wait a month or more for the Miranda people to act. The same thing with repairs. We do small repairs ourselves."

This had a convincing ring for Mr. C who then suggested: "Why don't we split the difference between $215 and $229? Then I'd pay $222, sales tax included." This arrangement was accepted, and Mr. C had almost what he had set his sights on—suburban store service at a near-mail-house-price.

Five-Year Footnote to Example C. A well-known line of the Scottish poet, Bobbie Burns, reads: "The best laid schemes o' mice and men gang aft a-gley. An' lea'e us nought but grief and pain, for promis'd joy." Translated: Despite their best efforts, individuals err, yielding untoward results. See the example at the end of Chapter 4 for a post mortem on Mr. C under the heading, "Epitaph for a Sound Decision," p. 110.

CHAPTER 3

Product Quality: Meaning, Measurement, and Implications

Almost every purchase decision that consumers make involves the assessment of quality. Indeed, it is the judgment as to which specimen is better or which is worse (and by how much) that converts many easy decisions into hard ones. Yet, strangely enough, most consumers do not know what "quality" *is*. And even stranger, the professionals on whom they might expect to rely—economists, home economists, engineers, and statisticians—have little help to offer.

Section 1 of this chapter seeks to remedy this situation by proposing and explaining a concept of quality and showing how it might be measured.[1] An understanding of product quality should help you make more effective purchase decisions.

Section 2 characterizes local consumer markets by the nature of the price-quality relationships they embody. It then goes on to point out the possibilities and problems each type of market poses for consumers and specifies procedures by which consumers can make more effective purchases in such markets.

THE CONCEPT AND MEASUREMENT OF PRODUCT QUALITY

We start with the definition:

The *quality* of a specimen (a product/brand/seller/combination)

[1] For a detailed and rigorous exposition of the concept of quality proposed here, see E. Scott Maynes, "The Concept and Measurement of Product Quality," in Nestor E. Terleckyj, ed., *Household Production and Consumption*, Studies in Income and Wealth, Volume 40 (New York: National Bureau of Economic Research, 1976). The same volume contains critical comments by F. Thomas Juster and Jack E. Triplett as well as a reply by the author.

consists of "the extent to which the specimen provides the service characteristics that the individual consumer desires."

Before this proposed definition can become fully meaningful, a number of subsidiary concepts must be introduced and explained. For convenience, some concepts that were partially introduced earlier are discussed more fully here.

Characteristic

A *service characteristic,* or more simply, a *characteristic,* is defined as "the basic factor giving rise to utility."

Examples are durability, beauty, and safety—things that consumers desire.

In our usage a characteristic is defined in terms of services provided, not in terms of the input(s) "producing" the service. Thus, we might speak of the durability of a hot water heater as a characteristic. The glass lining or copper pipe that contributes to its durability would *not* be considered as characteristics of the heater. There are two reasons for defining characteristics in terms of services rendered. First, it simplifies the problem of thinking about quality since there are usually fewer services than means of producing them. Second, it is our hypothesis that the utility arising from *service* characteristics can be more easily measured than the utility associated with the objective features of goods, for example, the glass lining on the heater.

Characteristics may pertain to the good itself, the hot water heater; or to the retail seller of that particular water heater, his reliability; or to the manufacturer of the good, the prestige of the brand name.

In our usage the extent to which a specimen provides a characteristic is considered subjective and nonuniversal. That is, the individual consumer will form his own judgment regarding the extent to which a specimen yields a given characteristic. For some goods and for some characteristics this proposed property of characteristics seems not only readily defensible but natural. It would be rash indeed to assert that there exists an "objective" means of assessing the "beauty" of a soprano's rendering of a particular piece of music. It would be equally rash to assert that everyone in a large audience would judge the soprano's performance equally beautiful.

For some other characteristics, the sensitivity of a radio receiver, for example, it may be possible to develop valid objective (reproducible) tests. But this does not lead necessarily to an objective and universally acceptable determination of how much of a given characteristic a given specimen provides. It will be up to the individual consumer to accept wholly, partially, or not at all the evidence from objective tests in determining for himself the amount of the characteristics that the specimen possesses.[2]

A vexatious problem in the identification of characteristics is the determination of the optimal level of abstraction. An example should help clarify the nature of the problem. Consider the performance of the soprano mentioned previously. Should we consider "beauty" as a characteristic? Or, assuming that beauty in a vocal performance has as its components such things as "color" and "range," should we consider *each of these components* of beauty as a separate characteristic? Our recommendation is that each individual use that level of abstraction or aggregation at which he feels he can make the most accurate overall judgment of quality. Some may feel that they will gain greater accuracy by judging each component and then combining judgments on the separate components. Others will feel that greater accuracy will be obtained by forming an overall judgment at the outset. The level of abstraction each chooses is likely to be affected by his level of knowledge of the product.

Of course, goods sometimes possess negative or undesirable characteristics. An example is "ugliness." A moment's reflection will confirm that "ugliness" is not the mere absence of beauty.

Product. In our subsequent discussion we need the notion of "product" to delineate the set of items within which it is appropriate to compare quality. With that introductory statement we are ready to define *product* as:

> the set of goods which, for some maximum outlay, will serve the same general purpose in the judgment of the purchasing consumer.

[2] Kelvin Lancaster, an originator of the characteristics approach to the analysis of consumer demand, assumes that characteristics are both objective and universal. These assumptions serve two ends: 1) they enable him to deduce certain propositions regarding consumer demand, and 2) they permit a clear division of labor between engineers whose responsibility it is to determine how much of a characteristic(s) a good(s) possesses, and economists who deal with the demand for characteristics.

See Kelvin Lancaster, *Consumer Demand* (New York: Columbia University Press, 1971), 113–115.

Our objection to Lancaster's approach is that the objective-universal assumptions do not correspond to real-life behavior.

In other words, this is the set of items among which the consumer will choose. Examples are single-lens reflex cameras, ten-speed racing bicycles under $225, and compact sedans under $5,000. Additional comments should illuminate these examples.

The "maximum outlay" specification in the definition is necessary since most consumers, in trying to allocate their scarce income to yield maximum satisfaction, will have in mind some upper limit on outlay, based on their own or others' prior experience with this product. Should they go beyond this limit they will reduce satisfaction. Turning back to the examples, a Mercedes-Benz sedan would qualify as a "compact sedan" in terms of size and a number of other characteristics. But many consumers who would consider paying $4,000 for a Dodge Dart would be unwilling to consider the purchase of a Mercedes at $9,000. For this reason, the Mercedes would not be included in *their* "compact sedan" product class.

The concept of *product* is subjective and personal. Each consumer decides for himself what specimens will "serve the same general purpose." Even though product classes as defined by different consumers differ from one another, it is expected that there will be enough uniformity from the opinion of one individual to that of another so that discussions of "average" products will be meaningful. Different specimens within a product class will have rather similar characteristics.

In practice, it would appear that the delineation of product classes has posed few problems. None of the 30 or more student investigators who made quality assessments under the direction of the author in 1970 reported any difficulty in determining which specimens were appropriately included and which were appropriately excluded from the relevant product classes.

Market. Just as the concept of *product* is needed to delineate the *items* whose quality and price it is appropriate to compare, the concept of "market" is also needed to delineate the set of *sellers* whose price and quality offerings it is appropriate to compare. This brings us to the definition of a *market.*

A *market,* from the consumer's viewpoint, consists of "the set of sellers the consumer might consider if he possessed accurate information regarding the existence of sellers and brands as well as the range of prices and qualities available."

In identifying sellers whose offerings he "might consider," the consumer is assumed to shop according to the marginal rule: keep making searches as long as the expected gross payoff from the search exceeds the expected cost of that search. Hence, the extent of the market, in terms of the sellers it will include, is limited by two factors: 1) search costs (both objective and subjective), and 2) *accurate* information regarding the range of prices and quality.

Thus, once again, a subjective concept is proposed. Two consumers, living in adjacent homes, might conceive of markets of different sizes because one found shopping more distasteful than the other.

It is worth remarking that a market need not be limited spatially. It might include mail-order or out-of-town sellers, depending upon the consumer's evaluation of the cost of the search in such cases.

What should be underlined is that the consumer is assumed, contrary to fact, to possess accurate information regarding the existence of sellers and of brands as well as variations in prices and quality. Our anticipated use of the concept, however, justifies this assumption. We wish to measure *possible* payoffs for consumers. Were sellers omitted because it was assumed, more realistically, that the consumer may be unaware of their existence or of their wares, then the *possible* payoff to the search would be underestimated.

From our earlier discussion of searches, it should be repeated that the subjective cost of the search includes not only the process of obtaining information but also the cost of acting upon the information obtained.

In fact, of course, a consumer may search over a narrower set of sellers and brands because he underestimates the "true" variations in price and quality.

As in the case of the concept of *product*, the problem of delineating a market has proved to be easier in practice than in principle. The same student investigators who reported no difficulty in delineating "product" classes also reported no problems in deciding what sellers to include or exclude from particular "markets."

Markets consist of both sellers and buyers. Our *market* also includes any consumers who might purchase from the sellers included under the original definition.

Quality.[3] We return now to the definition of quality stated earlier:

---

[3] See Maynes, op. cit., for a rigorous development of two alternative models for conceptualizing quality.

The *quality* of a specimen consists of "the extent to which the specimen provides the service characteristics that the individual consumer desires."

This definition may be expressed arithmetically as follows:

$$G \text{ (for "goodness") } = \text{Quality Score of a Specimen}$$
$$= \frac{\text{Sum of (Weights} \times \text{Characteristics Scores)}}{\text{Sum of Weights}}$$

where:

Weight = a number of 0.00 to 1.00 representing the relative importance assigned to a particular characteristic by the individual consumer. For convenience, the weights should be assigned so that they sum to 1.00.

Characteristic
Score = a score with values from 0.00 to 1.00 denoting the extent to which a particular specimen yields satisfaction, in the consumer's judgment, as compared with the best conceivable specimen. A score of 0.00 denotes that the specimen provides no satisfaction whatsoever on this characteristic. 1.00 denotes that the specimen yields the maximal satisfaction conceivable, given the consumer's level of knowledge.

A hypothetical example should clarify the use of this formula. Suppose a consumer wishes to assess the quality of two alternative television models, A and B. For this consumer, only two characteristics are important: 1) sensitivity, meaning the extent to which weak signals are picked up, and 2) resolution, meaning the sharpness of the picture. The judgments of this consumer are set forth as follows:

Characteristic Scores for:

Characteristic	Weights	Specimen A	Specimen B
I. Sensitivity	0.3	0.5	0.8
II. Resolution	0.7	1.0	0.8
Total	1.0		

The quality score for Specimen A is calculated as follows:

$$G_A = \frac{(0.3 \times 0.5) + 0.7 \times 1.0)}{(0.3 + 0.7)}$$

$$= \frac{(0.15 + 0.70)}{1.0}$$

$$= 0.85$$

The quality score for Specimen B is similarly calculated:

$$G_B = \frac{(0.3 \times 0.8) + (0.7 \times 0.8)}{1.0}$$

$$= \frac{(0.24 + 0.56)}{1.0}$$

$$= 0.80$$

Note that the weights are the same for both specimens. This will always be the case, since these weights express the consumer's preference for these characteristics regardless of the extent to which a particular model provides them. The *relative* weights, 0.3 for sensitivity and 0.7 for resolution, express this consumer's belief that sensitivity is 43 per cent as important as resolution (0.3 ÷ 0.7).

When compared with one another, the characteristic scores have a similar interpretation. In the judgment of this consumer the sensitivity of Specimen A yields 63 per cent as much satisfaction as that provided by Specimen B (0.5 ÷ 0.8).

Finally, the overall quality scores for model A and B indicate that A is expected to yield 85 per cent as much satisfaction as the best conceivable whereas B is expected to yield 80 per cent as much satisfaction as the "best."

Although our example contained no negative characteristics, some products and some specimens might yield negative characteristics, such as "ugliness." These would be assigned negative weights. Hence, if they were predominant, the result would be a negative overall quality score. The meaning is that this specimen is positively disliked!

Quality, as proposed here, is subjective and personal. Each individual will identify certain relevant characteristics. Each individual will also decide for himself what weight to assign to each characteristic. Finally, each individual will assign a characteristic score. The individual consumer may seek information from any sources—friends and acquaintances, advertising, sellers, and consumer publications. But the decision as to which information received is accepted, and to what extent, will be made by the individual himself.

Quality judgments are anticipatory in nature. The quality assessor expresses the satisfaction he expects to receive from the specimen in the future.

The identification of a complete set of relevant characteristics poses a problem. Unless prompted, consumers will omit relevant characteristics that they would otherwise accept as "their own." [4] Ruby Morris reports an episode where a group of middle-class housewives, after much consideration, came up with an average of three or four relevant characteristics for electric frying pans. By contrast, Consumers Union's test engineers identified and evaluated 12 characteristics in arriving at their quality scores. [5] When the housewives were told of the additional characteristics utilized by Consumers Union's engineers, they were pleased to accept them as their own.

The accuracy of any overall quality score will thus depend upon the knowledgeability of the assessor and the care he or she invests in evaluating quality. If he omits an "important" characteristic or if he makes a serious error in assigning a characteristic score for an "important" characteristic, this may lead him to a wrong purchase decision.

Quality scores are, of course, time-specific. As the consumer receives more information, he may modify his weights (general product information) or the characteristic scores for particular models. Presumably the more knowledgeable and the more careful the consumer is at the time of his initial quality assessment, the more stable successive quality assessments of the same specimen will be over time.

Knowledgeability also affects the specification of the "ideal" amount of a characteristic that the best specimen might provide ($= 1.0$). When and as the consumer's perception of the ideal changes, then the characteristic scores of all specimens have to be revised since they are expressed in numbers *relative* to the ideal.

Safety Thresholds and Other Nonadditivities. The concept of quality proposed here is "additive." By that we mean that the overall quality of a specimen is simply a subjectively weighted *sum* of the satisfaction that its performance yields on various characteristics. For each specimen you assign a characteristic score, weight this score, and

[4] Morris Kaplan, late, longtime technical director of Consumers Union, asserted this proposition on the basis of many episodes in which consumers identified fewer characteristics than test engineers. Personal conversation with Morris Kaplan on August 12, 1971.

[5] Ruby Turner Morris, *Consumers Union: Methods, Implications, Weaknesses, and Strengths* (New London, Conn.: Litfield Publications, 1971), p. 51.

then add up the weighted characteristic scores to obtain an overall measure of quality, or of the same thing, satisfaction.

There are two types of departures from the additivity approach that we wish to explain and commend. The first consists of safety and other thresholds, and the second involves quality homogeneity (uniformity) *within* a single specimen.

The threshold notion embodies the idea that minimum amounts of desirable characteristics are required if the quality of a specimen is to be recognized as minimally acceptable. An example may help. Unless the brakes of an automobile conform to a certain minimum standard—a "critical value"—the quality of that automobile will be designated as "unacceptable." This idea can be implemented arithmetically by providing that a characteristic score less than the critical value on the critical characteristic will automatically lead the assessor to assign a quality score of 0.

In all countries, the consumer product-testing organizations utilize thresholds in determining which specimens are "unacceptable." In so doing, they are acting on the view that an additive formula does not assign sufficient importance to what they would term to be a "crucial" factor.

Is quality uniformity or homogeneity across characteristics a desirable characteristic of a specimen? If you answer "yes," you will have announced your support for a second type of departure from additivity. Consider two cars with identical overall quality scores on an additive basis. One car has characteristic scores of 0.8 on *all* the characteristics we assume relevant for illustrative purposes: comfort, safety, aesthetic qualities, performance, and convenience. The second car is outstanding (characteristic scores of 0.9 or more) on comfort, safety, and aesthetic aspects, but mediocre (scores less than 0.7) with respect to performance and convenience. Some individuals—and many of the product-testing organizations would downgrade the overall quality rating of the second car on the subjective grounds that the second car does not embody a characteristic that they prize: quality uniformity. In implementing this view, the German product-testing organization, Stiftung Warentest, adjusts the extent of downgrading to the extent of nonuniformity in characteristic scores: the greater the nonuniformity, the more extensive is the downgrading of the overall quality score.[6]

Specimen versus Variety. Here our discussion has centered on the

---

[6] Roland Hüttenrauch, "Probleme um Qualität und Preis beim Warentest," *Markenartikel* (September 1973), pp. 434–444.

assessment of quality for a *specimen* of a product. Thus, the quality score reflects the characteristics of *both* the "thing" itself and the seller.

Quality may also be assessed for *varieties* of products. Such a quality assessment omits consideration of the characteristics of the retail seller. The quality information distributed by the product-testing organizations pertains to *varieties* of products, not to specimens.

PURCHASE DECISIONS WITH QUALITY EXPLICIT

Now, armed with an understanding of the meaning of quality and knowing—at least in principle—how to measure it, we are ready to use this knowledge in the making of purchase decisions. The great virtue of the quality concept proposed here is that it permits us to compare quality among alternative specimens in the same way we compare prices. We can say that the quality of Specimen A, a single-lens reflex camera, is roughly three-eighths better than Specimen B, another single-lens reflex camera. And then we can ask ourselves: is this 38 per cent increase in quality obtained by buying Specimen A rather than Specimen B "worth" the 60 per cent increase in price?

In this section we deal with the possibilities and the problems that quality poses for purchase decisions.

To facilitate the discussion here, we sidestep two important problems by making two assumptions.

1. We assume that fully informed consumers would make approximately *uniform quality assessments* of the same specimen. That is, different individuals would agree that Specimen A is approximately 20 per cent better in quality than Specimen B and that Specimen B in turn is about 10 per cent better than Specimen C. We assume further that everyone agrees as to which varieties are included in the product class and which sellers are included in the market class.

2. We assume that everyone has access to *complete and accurate information concerning price and qualities offered* for sale in the local market. This would be the case if an effective local consumer information system was operating in the market under discussion.

With these assumptions in place, we can identify four types of local markets that confront consumers with distinctly different problems and possibilities. These four types of markets are the products of two factors, considered jointly:

1. Whether quality varies for this product class;
2. The extent of the correlation between quality and price.

The following table shows the four markets and lists examples of each that are discussed for illustrative purposes.

A Taxonomy of Local Consumer Markets

The Correlation Between Price and Quality:

Quality Varies?	Low	High
Yes	Single-lens reflex cameras	10-speed racing bicycles
No	Life insurance, "regular" gasoline	Shares of General Motors stock

In the following examples, Ann Arbor, Michigan, is the local market to which price and quality pertain. Its 1973 population was probably 150,000. For those with local knowledge or interest, this market is assumed to include all of Ann Arbor plus the readily accessible Western outskirts of the closest adjacent city, Ypsilanti. Depending upon the nature of the area in which you live and your search costs, the market in which you deal may contain fewer or more specimens for these products than Ann Arbor.

The quality scores for single-lens reflex cameras are those of Consumers Union whereas the quality scores for ten-speed bicycles represent the author's quantifications of the verbal judgments expressed in the ratings tables of *Consumer Reports*. Conceptually, both measures conform to these proposed earlier in this chapter. Both of these quality measurements are partial, however. They do not reflect such intrinsically subjective characteristics as the "appearance" of a camera or a bicycle. Nor do they take account of the characteristics of the retail dealers. Thus, the quality assessments are for *varieties* of products whereas the prices necessarily relate to *specimens* of cameras or of bicycles.

We turn first to single-lens reflex cameras for two reasons. First, in the author's judgment, the market they typify is that most commonly encountered by consumers. Second, this example has more to teach us than the others.

Single-lens Reflex Cameras. A complete understanding of Chart 1 will turn away unnecessary questions. Chart 1 depicts the prices and quality of each single-lens camera for which a quality rating was published in the November, 1974, issue of *Consumer Reports.* Each variety of camera is designated by a letter or double letter (A, B, C, . . . AA, BB, and so on). Some of the cameras tested by *Consumer Reports* could not be purchased in the Ann Arbor market, for example, Specimen E. These are designated by o, and the price shown is the "list price." In November, 1974, eleven retail establishments were selling single-lens reflex cameras in the Ann Arbor market.[7] Each point (not o) represents a price quoted by one of these retailers. Each price is the lowest price the seller was willing to quote when told that the information he provided would be widely distributed. Hence, these prices do not include the possibly lower prices accessible to a knowledgeable consumer who was well endowed with bargaining skills.

Consumers Union's quality scores are "based primarily on judgments and measurements of convenience, overall optical quality of normal lenses, and freedom from blur in hand-held use at 1/30 and 1/60 second. . . . Versatility achievable with accessories was not a Ratings factor."[8] Regarding the accuracy of its numerical quality scores, *Consumer Reports* states: "Differences of less than about 10 points in the Overall Ratings Score (the quality score) were judged not very significant."[9]

Turning now to the data in Chart 1, it can be seen that cameras of approximately the same quality sell for as little as $170 or as much as $635 in the same market. (Compare Specimens I and O in Chart 1).[10]

---

[7] Mail-order sellers in Ann Arbor or elsewhere are excluded from this compilation even though some consumers would include such mail-order sellers in "their" markets.

To clarify terms, each retail location where sales are consummated is considered an "establishment." Thus, branch stores are counted as separate establishments. In this sample, different establishments with common ownership exhibited considerable independence in setting prices.

[8] *Consumer Reports* (November 1974), pp. 798–799.

[9] Ibid.

[10] By the time you see these data, they are likely to be obsolete. Some models will have been withdrawn from the market, others superseded. For this reason they are identified here as Specimens A, B, and so on rather than by name. For those whose urge to know is very strong, Specimen A is the Olympus OM-1, Specimen B is the Minolta SRT 100, and so on down *Consumer Reports'* rating list, ibid., pp. 798–802.

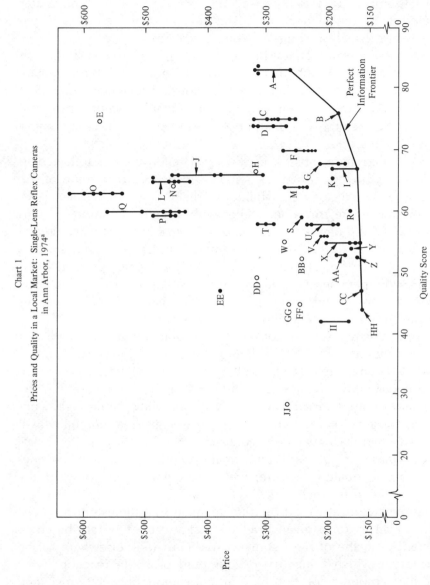

Chart 1

Prices and Quality in a Local Market: Single-Lens Reflex Cameras
in Ann Arbor, 1974[a]

[a]Source: Quality Scores—*Consumer Reports*, November, 1974.

Prices—Collected by Blanche R. Maynes, November 18–26, 1974

The symbol o denotes the list prices of specimens which could not be purchased in Ann Arbor.
The others points plotted represent actual prices.

If your first reaction to this price spread was one of astonishment, your second is likely to be that there must be "something wrong" with the measurement of prices or quality. And, of course, there might be. As to prices, a check by a second investigator two months later revealed much the same picture. The possibility of blemishes in the assessment of quality requires further discussion.

As noted previously, intrinsically subjective characteristics, such as the reputation of the manufacturer, do not enter these quality scores. Further, these quality scores appear designed to reflect the needs of the individual who might use as many as three lenses, not those of the semiprofessional or professional who uses an entire family of accessories.

Since the characteristics of the retail seller are not reflected in the quality scores, you may be tempted to believe that some of the higher prices reflect the reliability and helpfulness of particular retailers. If this were true, the retailer with a high reputation for reliability and helpfulness could (and presumably would) command consistently high prices across specimens. The facts do not support this hypothesis. The establishment exacting the highest price in Chart 1—$635 for Specimen O—charged the lowest price for Specimen G ($190) and the second lowest price for Specimen F ($252). Thus, this possible blemish in the quality estimates is eliminated.

Alternatively, you may observe that durability is not listed as a characteristic in the quality ratings published in *Consumer Reports*. In fact, CU's engineers examined all of the tested cameras for evidence of poor durability. None was found, so it appears unlikely that the varieties examined varied significantly in durability. Nonetheless, uncertainty lingers on. Conclusive evidence regarding durability will come after months, or even years of use.[11]

For those of you who still remain skeptical regarding the adequacy of the quality measure, we recommend a rereading of the *Consumer Reports* article.

Summing up, it would be our judgment that the astonishing disparity of prices for a given level of quality cannot be attributed to deficiencies in the quality estimates. We must look elsewhere for an explanation, which brings us to your third probable reaction: what *is* it that accounts for this lack of correlation between price and quality? Chapter 2 provides the framework for a detailed analysis, but the simple answer is consumer ignorance. And this in turn is traceable to the technical complexity of the product, successful product differ-

[11] Correspondence with Monte Florman, technical director of Consumers Union, September 8, 1975.

entiation, and high search costs for consumers. Had consumers been able themselves to undertake exhaustive product testing, Specimen O would certainly not have successfully commanded prices in the vicinity of $600. Or, had most camera purchasers seen and acted on the data of Chart 1, most of the higher prices in Chart 1 would have disappeared.

A second factor worthy of mention is the extent of retailer competition. At most, six retailers in Ann Arbor sell a given variety of camera and Chart 1 demonstrates the effect of multiple sellers on the range of prices (the difference between the highest and lowest price for a specimen). At lower price levels—under $300—the prices display a range of about $50 to $80 when sellers of those specimens number four or more. For models with average prices of $400 or more, the range is much greater, running from $70 for Specimen L to an astounding range of $160 for Specimen J.

What choice should the camera purchaser make? The answer seems obvious: he should purchase a specimen on or near to the *perfect information frontier.*[12]

> The *perfect information frontier* consists of the positively sloped line segments connecting those points, representing price and quality, for which a given quality may be purchased for the lowest price.[12]

The buyer might purchase a specimen *near* rather than on the frontier because he expects to obtain characteristics that are not reflected in the quality measure, for example, the services of a highly reliable retailer.

The meaning of the *perfect information frontier* is revealed by its name. It is the set of specimens, and their prices, among which consumers would choose, had they perfect information regarding prices and quality in the market. To depart from the frontier, you would have to pay more for equivalent quality.

To say *which specimen on the frontier* the consumer should buy requires the application of the *marginal rule.* Start with Specimen HH, the lowest quality specimen on the frontier. (The rational consumer would pay no attention to Specimen II, for example, because Specimen

---

[12] Edward M. Foster suggested the concept of perfect information frontier to the author. In earlier publications it was labeled as the *efficiency frontier.* The restriction of the perfect information frontier to positively sloped line segments is dictated by the interests of consumers. Points on negatively or zero sloped line segments would be "dominated" by other points lying to the right: the points to the right would offer higher quality at either the same or lower prices. Sharyn Beth Adelstein called the author's attention to this point.

HH offers more quality at a lower price.) He can then ask, moving to the right on the frontier, whether the improvement in quality offered by successive specimens is "worth" the increase in cost. Specifically, the consumer might ask about Specimens HH and I whether the increase in quality from 44 to 67 is worth an increase in price of $10 ($160 for Specimen HH to $170 for Specimen I).[13] Or, comparing Specimens I and B, he might ask whether the improvement of quality from 67 to 76 is worth the increase in price of $30 ($170 to $200). In answering, the consumer will seek to apply the general utility-maximizing rule: spend your income so that, at the margin, each penny spent on purchases yields the same increment of utility (or quality).

The lessons for consumers regarding this type of market are two. First, the low correlation between price and quality, as indicated by the existence of many prices far above the perfect information frontier, signals very large positive payoffs for the consumer. By purchasing the on-frontier variety from an on-frontier retailer a consumer can greatly extend the purchasing power of his income from what it might otherwise be. Second, for persons who insist on purchasing a particular specimen regardless of whether it lies on the frontier, substantial payoffs may accrue from identifying and purchasing from the retailer with the lowest price.

It is natural to speculate as to whether there exist certain retailers, particularly those identified as "discounters," whose prices tend to be low across all varieties of cameras. As stated earlier, the answer for single-lens reflex cameras in Ann Arbor is emphatically "no."

Do the models offered and prices remain stable over periods of two or three months? We do not know. A general answer across many products would require statistical investigations that have not yet been carried out. For single-lens reflex cameras we do know. The data in Chart 1 pertain to November 18–26, 1974; the same market was resurveyed two and one-half months later during February 3–14, 1975. If any period was susceptible to dynamic changes in the market, this was it. The February period was post-Christmas rather than pre-Christmas. Further, during these two and one-half months, the 1974–75 recession accelerated at an alarming and highly visible rate, especially in Michigan, which is so heavily affected by the automobile industry.

What happened to our market for single-lens reflex cameras over this period? First, the extent of choice was reduced with the removal of two establishments from the market, which accounted for the re-

---

[13] In this particular example, the increased cost of shifting from Specimen HH to either Z or X is so small that we have ignored these possibilities. The near-zero slope on this particular frontier is probably peculiar to single-lens reflex cameras and is not typical of other products.

moval of 28 specimens from Chart 1. Second, our object of prime concern—the perfect information frontier—was truncated by the disappearance from the frontier of Specimens B, CC, and HH, and on the high quality side it shifted upward because of the disappearance of the lowest price quotation for Specimen A. Third, among the remaining specimens, upward shifts in prices were roughly offset by downward shifts.

Nonetheless, as a guide to the individual purchaser, the data of November—including the frontier—remained useful, though less accurate, even in February.

We now turn to Chart 2 for a discussion of men's 10-speed racing bicycles.

Ten-Speed Racing Bicycles. If the data on single-lens reflex cameras came as a surprise, the data on ten-speed bicycles under $225 will come as a further jolt—to you and to the author and others as well. This is especially true since we may have been "preconditioned" by our exposure to the case of single-lens reflex cameras.

Chart 2 constitutes a graphic display of a near-perfect price-quality correlation.[14] Why are there so few off-frontier prices? [15] The answer comes in two parts. First, buyers in this market can assess quality with some accuracy, or, at least, manufacturers believe that they can and price accordingly. Second, the market is structurally deficient, with two retailers *at most* selling the same variety of bicycle. Both points require elaboration.

If you read a hobby book on cycling, you may become confused by talk of reinforced butts and Reynolds 521 metal. And you may conclude that the assessment of bicycle quality is an esoteric business. In reality, a bicycle is a relatively simple instrument whose purpose is to get you from one place to another quickly (requiring lightweight and proper gearing), easily (again requiring lightweight, proper gears, good machining), safely, and reliably. The crude "testing" of a bicycle's

[14] The quality scores plotted in Chart 2 represent the author's quantification of the verbal judgments expressed in the ratings tables published in *Consumer Reports.* Characteristics with the weights assigned them by the author were as follows: weight of the bicycle (20), ease of shifting (9), handling and stability at low speeds (13), pedal response (5), saddle comfort (10), seal in crank bearing, as a proxy for care in design and manufacturing (10), shifting range (6), rolling resistance of tires (9), equipped with chain guard/kickstand (3), reflectors (2), fenders (3), wet brake effectiveness (10). The weights summed to 100. The additive quality model employed by the author reproduced Consumer Union's ordering perfectly for the first eight varieties and less than perfectly for the last six varieties.

[15] Note that the perfect information frontier is drawn on the basis of *actual* prices of specimens that can be purchased in the local market. Hence, varieties available elsewhere, but not in Ann Arbor, may be located *below* the frontier.

performance is not so difficult: ride it. And, if you do not have time to do that (or the experience to do it well), "borrow" the experience of knowledgeable enthusiasts by asking them. Thus, reasonably good information on the quality of bicycles is fairly easy to obtain, and once secured by some buyers, it will tend to push prices toward the frontier.[16]

As to the structural deficiencies of the market, it is a fact that a given variety of bicycle can be purchased in Ann Arbor from, at most, two retailers. As Chart 2 reveals, this fact has given rise to different price quotations for only two varieties, B and E. For varieties A, C, and F, both retailers quoted the same list price. No one knows how many retail sellers would have to enter the Ann Arbor market in order to produce a range of prices for a given variety comparable to that which we found in the camera case. At present, nine retail outlets sell this set of ten-speed bicycles.[17]

What are the lessons of this information and this type of market for consumers? Further information-seeking does not pay. In selecting a variety to purchase, simply follow the marginal rule. Then go to the most convenient retailer offering that variety. Remember, however, that consumer-induced price discrimination is still possible. The purchaser with bargaining skill may be able to negotiate a price lower than the frontier price for a particular specimen shown on Chart 2.

Products of Roughly Uniform Quality: Life Insurance, "Regular" Gasoline. If variations in product quality are eliminated, the problem of choice is vastly simplified. With variations in quality out of the way, you can concentrate on locating the lowest price. Such is the case with life insurance and regular gasoline. But before we proceed further, we should make the case that life insurance and regular gasoline are indeed products of roughly uniform quality.

Essentially, life insurance is a product with a single characteristic: protection. Die, and the payment of the policy's face value provides income replacement, or "protection," for your beneficiary.[18] There is

[16] We simply do not know how many knowledgeable purchasers are required in a given market to force all prices down to the perfect information frontier.

[17] The investigation of prices reported here was confined to those reported in *Consumer Reports* (January 1974).

[18] The attentive student may argue that the quality of life insurance should also include such characteristics of the local agent as his capacity to provide insurance counseling, his friendliness, and so on. On a more sophisticated level, some have argued that by possibly overpaying an agent on a policy, you are enhancing the chances for favorable settlements when these settlements are of a discretionary nature. Stated concretely, your agent may be decisive in seeing whether a borderline claim under your homeowners' policy is paid.

The attentive student is, of course, correct. But here we argue that such factors

Chart 2

Price and Quality in a Local Market: 10-Speed Bicycles
in Ann Arbor, January, 1975[a]

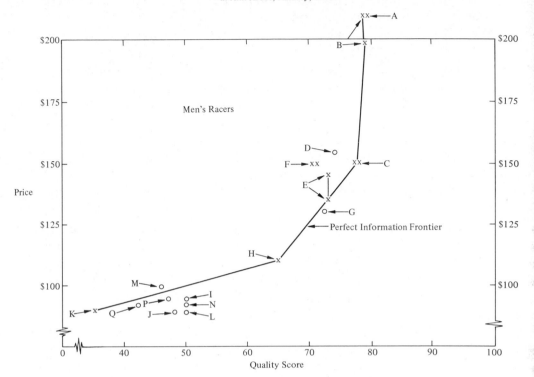

[a]Symbols: x denotes *actual* price quotations; o denotes list prices published 12 months earlier in *Consumer Reports*. Hence, they are probably lower than current actual prices. Models so designated could not be purchased in Ann Arbor in January, 1975. Sources: (1) Price quotations obtained by Jane Zale; (2) Quality scores represent E. Scott Maynes' quantification of ratings and descriptive materials appearing in *Consumer Reports* for January, 1974.

the additional issue of whether your life insurance company is likely to be around and able to pay off when you die. If you confine your choice to companies with highly favorable financial ratings, this problem is largely answered.[19]

Gasoline, too, is essentially a single-characteristic product. Its major characteristic: X miles of transportation, the value of X depending upon the size of your car, the average speed and character of

---

are minor and may be ignored. We consider protection to be the sole charactristic of life insurance.

However, a life insurance buyer, confronted with a small difference in price between two policies, might be justified in paying the larger price to obtain additional benefits of the type mentioned.

[19] *Best's Insurance Reports, Life-Health, 1974* (Morristown, N.J.: A. M. Best Company, 1974) provides financial ratings of life insurance companies.

your driving, and so on. It is possible to count the characteristics of the seller—friendliness, ancillary services (checking tires, oil, and so on)—as components of the quality of the product, gasoline. But these extras are minor and we ignore them in our analysis.

Turning now to Chart 3, we can see that the highest price of gasoline charged in Ann Arbor in February 1975 was 24 per cent higher than the lowest, 60.9¢ versus 48.9¢. What accounts for this difference? Probably site monopolies (stations adjacent to the expressways charge more), product differentiation (the reputation of the station and the ancillary services it offers and the belief that Brand X gas is better), and consumer ignorance (many probably do not know about the lowest 20 per cent of prices, and others, rationally or irrationally, would not purchase at the lower prices).

The lesson for the purchaser of gasoline is to remember the marginal rule. The most you can save on a 20-gallon purchase is the difference between what you have been paying and the lowest, 48.9¢. On a 20-gallon purchase, for example, a savings of 5¢ per gallon comes to a total saving of $1.00. That gain should be taken only if it exceeds the marginal cost of getting it, for example, driving out of your way, the extra time involved, and frayed nerves.

Chart 3

Regular Gasoline: Prices in Ann Arbor, February, 1975[a]

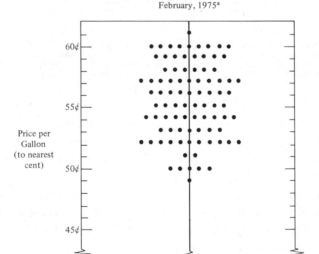

Regular Gasoline

[a]Data obtained by Jane Zale, February 5-9, 1975. Each point represents the price charged by a different establishment.

The life insurance data are much more interesting because the numbers are bigger. First, let us be sure that we understand these numbers. The data pertain to five-year renewable term policies, under which you pay a fixed premium per year for five years. If you die, your beneficiary receives the face amount of the policy. At the end of five years, you are guaranteed the right to purchase a new policy, but at a higher price for the next five years, and so on. The sophisticated price graphed here—the 20-year interest-adjusted index—is for a 25-year-old male purchasing a face amount of $25,000. The concept is explained in the basic reference.[20]

Data are provided for both nonparticipating and participating policies. As the name suggests, purchasers of participating policies "participate" or share in the company's financial fortunes. This participation takes the form of a year-end dividend, reflecting the experience of the last year. If the company's costs were lower than expected—because of fewer-than-expected deaths in the insured group or more efficient operations—then the year-end dividend will be larger and the policyholder's net premiums (gross premium less dividend) will be lower. Contrariwise, if deaths or expenses were higher than expected, then dividends will be smaller and net premiums higher. Thus, in a participating policy, the policyholder "participates" in the risks; in a nonparticipating policy there are no dividends and the risks are born entirely by the company. For this reason, the 20-year interest-adjusted index for nonparticipating policies (Column 1 in Chart 4) is higher on the average than that for participating policies (Column 2).

We are now ready to assess the market for *nonparticipating policies*—Column 1 in Chart 4. The informational imperfections of this market operate through two channels. For one thing, the sophisticated price, the "20-year interest-adjusted index," is difficult to understand. The sources from which it can be obtained—consumer periodicals [21] and helpful, sophisticated insurance agents—are likely to be utilized only by sophisticated purchasers. The second channel is the difficulty of contacting companies selling low-priced policies. Of the companies offering the 25 cheapest policies, only two were "easily accessible" from Ann Arbor. (By this we mean that these were the only two companies of the 25 that were listed in the Yellow Pages of the local telephone directory.) The remaining companies with low-priced policies could only be contacted by mail (after you located their

20 *Consumer Reports* (January 1974), pp. 35–66.
21 *Consumer Reports,* op. cit.; *Changing Times* (June 1973), pp. 38–44; Pennsylvania Insurance Department, *A Shopper's Guide to Term Life Insurance* (Harrisburg: 1972).

address) or via a general insurance agent (an agent authorized to sell the policies of a number of companies).

Thus, in this market, informational deficiencies reinforced the structural deficiencies. The combined effect of these informational and structural deficiencies is visible for all to see in Chart 4: a range of prices from $1,680 to $3,100 for 20 years of coverage.[22] The differ-

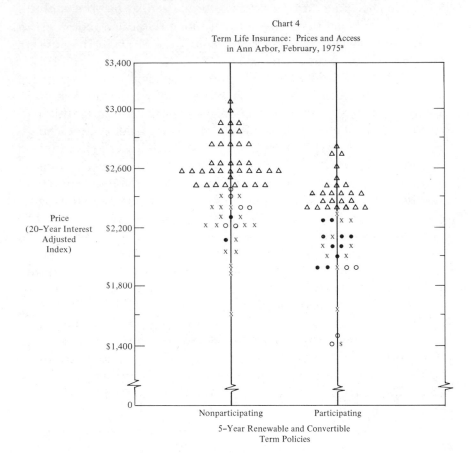

Chart 4

Term Life Insurance: Prices and Access
in Ann Arbor, February, 1975[a]

Symbols: • Readily accessible (company listed in Yellow Pages)
x Accessible with difficulty (sales by mail, or company
has agent in Michigan; *not* listed in Yellow Pages)
s Special clientele: available only to special class of buyers,
e.g., teachers
○ No access from Ann Arbor (not licensed in Michigan, no
agents in Michigan)
△ Accessibility not investigated.

[a]Source: Price data from *Consumer Reports,* January, 1974, pp. 43–45, accessibility
data from Survey Research Center, University of Michigan.

[b]Price estimates pertain to 25-year-old male in good health assumed to have purchased
face amount of $25,000. The price charted represents the 20-year cumulative cost.

[22] The possible savings over 20 years was discounted at a rate of 0 per cent, it being hoped—in March, 1975—that the rate of return on savings would match the rate of inflation.

ence of approximately $1,400 between the highest and lowest cost is an amount that most consumers cannot afford to sacrifice.

The lesson for consumers is again that there is a payoff for knowledge. The enterprising consumer who identifies and buys from the company with the lowest price earns a very substantial return on his efforts. One qualification is in order. Companies sometimes reduce their prices by selling only to the very healthy. This means that you have to qualify, by virtue of good health, in order to be eligible to purchase some of the lowest priced policies.

The local market for participating five-year term policies—see Column 2 of Chart 4—is both better and worse. It is better because 11 of the cheapest 25 policies are "readily accessible." It is worse because access to the three "very cheap" policies is practically zero. Two of these three policies—those sold by savings banks in Massachusetts and New York—are, by law, unavailable to residents of other states. And the third, policies sold by Teachers Insurance and Annuity Association of America, are sold only to persons employed by educational institutions.

So, once again, we encounter a market characterized by informational and structural imperfections. But in this case, the most conspicuous structural deficiency—the exclusion of savings bank life insurance policies from the national market—is traceable to successful political efforts on the part of life insurance agents to have restrictive laws passed.[23]

The lesson in the case of participating policies is the same: information pays, and handsomely!

Perfect Competition—A Share Is a Share Is a Share. The topic is perfect competition, the example is a share of General Motors common stock, and the paraphrase represents a further abuse of Gertrude Stein. If you combine a homogeneous product (where every share of General Motors is indistinguishable from every other share of General Motors, regardless of who owns it), many sellers, and many buyers, *and* perfect information on the part of all participants, you will get the result depicted in Chart 5, a single price. Stated differently, it makes no difference which of the eight brokers you contact in the Ann Arbor market, they will all quote exactly the same price for a share of

[23] Belth, a leading insurance scholar, comments: "The fourth reason for the predominance of agents in the sale of life insurance is their political prowess. They have been successful in persuading state legislatures to enact and retain restrictions that make it difficult to market life insurance other than through agents." He goes on to cite successful actions by insurance agents in Connecticut to prevent that state from relaxing the restrictions on sales of savings bank life insurance. See Joseph M. Belth, *Life Insurance, A Consumer's Handbook* (Bloomington, Ind.: Indiana University Press, 1973), pp. 108–109.

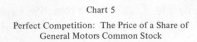

Chart 5

Perfect Competition: The Price of a Share of
General Motors Common Stock

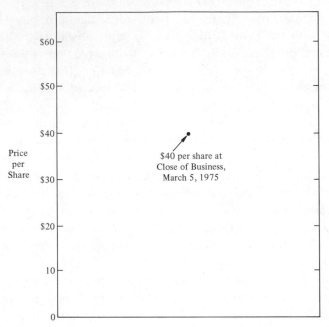

$40 per share at
Close of Business,
March 5, 1975

General Motors—provided that you contact them at exactly the same moment! [24]

It is little wonder that this type of market is so beloved by economists. It gives a lovely result, automatically. But note that it is really a special case of the perfect information frontier—where that frontier has been collapsed into a single point.

Once you have decided to purchase this product, there are no further problems: simply buy from the nearest seller. In this market you always get the same quality (there is no other!) for the same lowest price.

But perfect competition is not perfection. It applies only to a tiny portion of the spectrum of products—products having a single characteristic, or complex products where only a single variant is offered. For more complex products, the analogue to perfect competition is a market where all prices are located on the perfect information frontier and where this frontier is established in a market with many sellers. The ten-speed bicycle market would be an example, if it were populated by a large number of wholesale and retail sellers.

Alternative Classifications of Markets and Their Uses. We thus have the following four types of markets:

[24] However, the commissions they charge may differ.

Description of Market	Example
1. Quality variable, informationally imperfect	Single-lens reflex cameras
2. Quality variable, informationally near-perfect	Ten-speed racing bicycle
3. Quality uniform, informationally imperfect	Life insurance, regular gasoline
4. Quality uniform, informationally perfect [25]	Shares of General Motors stock

The alert readers will note that in *this* summary table we have sub-stituted "informationally imperfect" or "informationally near-perfect" (or "perfect") in place of the "low" or "high" correlation between price and quality that we used previously. The reason is straightforward: the two are linked causally. Imperfect information gives rise to a low correlation between price and quality whereas near-perfect information produces a high correlation between price and quality. These phrases seem easier to use and are in fact used later in this book.

If you have mastered, perhaps with some pain, the traditional classification of markets in economics—perfect competition, monopolistic competition, oligopoly, and pure monopoly—you may wonder why we have gone through the trouble of establishing a new classification. The answer is that the traditional market classification is designed to explain the differential behavior of firms, and this is how we have used it, both in Chapter 2 and in this chapter. The four types of markets presented are designed to aid consumers in making purchases. Once you correctly identify the type of market, you know how to proceed in order to choose effectively.

The Assumption of Uniform Quality Assessments. You may have bridled when we assumed, provisionally, at the outset of this section that fully informed consumers "would make approximately uniform assessments of the same specimen." An appraisal of this assumption is now in order.

At the beginning of this chapter we defined a *product* as consisting of "the set of goods that, for some maximum outlay, will serve the same general purpose in the judgment of the purchasing consumer." For illustrative purposes, think of automobiles. It seems likely that teen-agers' product grouping would *include* "high performance" varieties (with the ability to accelerate very rapidly) whereas the

---

[25] In this case potential buyers possessed accurate information on the prices at which shares are offered. They also know that each particular share is as good as any other. But they are likely to be imperfectly informed regarding factors making shares of General Motors stock more or less valuable at a particular time.

product grouping of middle-aged consumers would not. Unless you forced the teen-agers to assess the quality of varieties in the middle-aged consumers' product grouping, they would never consider those varieties. ("Underpowered!" would be the teen-agers' complaint.) *Valid comparisons are made only within the same product grouping.* And this means that assessments of quality are confined to consumers with approximately the same product set. This line of reasoning removes a major source of potential nonuniformity in quality assessments.

The same line of reasoning applies to the concept of a *market,* which, as we have noted, consists, from the consumer's viewpoint, of "the set of sellers the consumer might consider if he possessed accurate information regarding the existence of sellers and brands as well as the range of prices and qualities available." The number of sellers in an individual's market will depend upon how much he searches. This is critical. A high-income individual, whose time in terms of foregone income is highly valuable, may search less for a given product than a person of smaller income. Hence, the market of the high-income person is likely to include fewer sellers—and the specimens they sell—than the market of the less affluent persons. Again, valid comparisons can be made only within the same product *and* market grouping.

This restriction removes another potential source of nonuniformity in quality assessments. Even though a high income person is likely to assign greater weight than a low income buyer to a characteristic such as "convenience/timesaving capacity" the different weights assigned will not produce nonuniform quality assessments because they apply to quality comparisons that are unlikely to be made.

But there exists some real-life evidence based on a sampling of *Consumer Reports* subscribers that supports the uniformity assumption. For a set of products including hair shampoo, color television sets, coffee makers, sewing machines, record changers, TV antennas, and AM/FM radios, anywhere from 48 per cent (AM/FM radios) to 81 per cent (hair shampoo) of the subscribers who purchased these goods reported that they purchased "top-rated models." [26] Although we have no information as to how many subscribers purchased top-rated automobiles, we do know that 74 per cent of shoppers consulted *Consumer Reports* before purchasing.[27] Thus, after sifting the information in *Consumer Reports* before purchasing, most subscribers made their purchases in a way that suggests they had accepted *Consumer Reports'* quality ratings.

[26] See Table 3 in Chapter 5 for details.
[27] Ibid.

Nonetheless, the possibility remains that, even within identical product/market groups, different individuals will make nonuniform assessments of quality. If your quality assessments differ from those of others, this means that you must mentally "correct" the price-quality chart to reflect your preferences, which is no mean task. And, if the differences are great, you may have to conceive a new price-quality chart for yourself.

Quality and the Acquisition and Evaluation of Information. Contrary to the assumption made at the beginning of this section, consumers do not ordinarily have price-quality charts of local markets at hand. It is our hope that the discussion in this section will help you to organize your information-decision problem so that you will in fact be able to make more effective purchases in these four types of markets.

The problem of acquiring and evaluating the relevant information is the next topic on our agenda and is dealt with in Chapter 4.

CHAPTER 4

The Acquisition and Evaluation of Consumer Information

It is one thing to say, in principle, how much effort the consumer should invest in obtaining price-quality information. This was our concern in Chapter 2. It is another thing to understand what quality is, to be able to classify markets by the nature of their price-quality relationships, and—again, in principle—to know how to proceed in making effective purchases in each of these markets. This was our focus in Chapter 3. It is yet another thing to say how and where the relevant information may be acquired and evaluated. This chapter is concerned with the "how and where."

The chapter turns first to a specification of the information the consumer needs and then to the enumeration and the critical review of sources of consumer information. It also includes a discussion of the special problems of obtaining information regarding services, choosing a house painter or a lawyer, for example. We start by specifying what the consumer needs to know.

THE INFORMATION THE CONSUMER NEEDS

The information the purchasing consumer requires may be organized in terms of four major problems confronting him: the "problems" of product, market, quality, and price. Each problem is elaborated in question form. Amplifying comments are added where they seem appropriate.

1. *The Product Problem*
    a. *What alternative product sets exist that might fit my needs?*
    Comment: the car purchaser, for example, must "discover" and possibly redefine for his particular needs the product group-

ings that are most relevant to him. In this example, he may wish to consider groupings such as "compact sedans," "compact station wagons," and "intermediate sedans."

The consumer product-testing publications—*Consumer Reports* and *Consumers' Research Magazine*—may be helpful in this connection. In publishing quality ratings of varieties of products that they consider "comparable," these publications have had to answer this question on behalf of their readers.

Manufacturers, too, may be helpful since they tailor certain of their product "lines" for particular types of consumers, and often identify the group to which particular models belong.

For some lines recognized "standards" or "grades" may be helpful, for example, "fancy" apples, or "prime" steak.

In setting the boundaries for his product group, the consumer must decide on the maximum amount he is willing to spend to meet this need. Thus, he may specify: compact sedans under $5,000.

b. *From what product set should I choose?*

c. *What varieties of products belong to the product group from which I expect to choose?*

Comment: Again, the product-testing organizations may be helpful because they had to answer this same question. Specifically, in testing "compact sedans" they had to form judgments as to what brand/models belonged to the "compact sedan" category.

2. *The Market Problem*

a. *What are the boundaries of my market for this product?*

Comment: These "boundaries" may be geographic, representing the distance the consumer is willing to travel to search for this product. But they need not be: one's "market" can include telephone and mail-order sellers.

To answer this question of boundary, the intelligent consumer must form a judgment—perhaps by obtaining more information—on the extent of variation in quality and price. He will also want to estimate the extent to which quality is *not* correlated with price. Other things being equal, the greater the variation in quality not correlated with price the larger one's market should be.

Note that search costs, of both money and time, will affect the size of one's market: the lower the search costs, the larger will be the market (other things being equal).

b. *How do I "discover" the sellers in my market?*

Comment: The Yellow Pages of the telephone book are a

good starting point. And, of course, one of the main points of local newspaper, radio, and television advertising is to make consumers aware of the existence of sellers and of the types of products they sell.

3. *The Quality Problem*

Comment: We purchase specimens, not varieties of products. Therefore, we must obtain information regarding the characteristics of both the "core product"—the automobile or the television set itself—and of the seller. Hence, the questions here apply both to 1) the core product, and 2) the seller.

a. *What characteristics are desirable?*

Comment: For the core product, the answer may include such service characteristics as durability, comfort, and safety. For the seller it might include such characteristics as technical competence, friendliness, honesty, promptness, and locational convenience.

Here we seek to identify *all* the relevant characteristics. Both the consumer product-testing magazines and the nontesting consumer publications may be helpful in suggesting characteristics, which, upon consideration, we may adopt as "our own."

This type of information is often called "general" product information.

b. *What weights shall we assign to characteristics?*

Comment: Remember that weights remain constant for all specimens in the product class.

c. *To what extent do particular specimens possess the characteristics we desire?*

This type of information is sometimes called "specific" product information.

d. *Are direct measures of quality available? Do I wish to use them?*

For a limited set of products, mostly appliances and durable goods, the consumer product-testing organizations do publish direct quality ratings.

An important question for the consumer is whether the testing organization's weights need to be modified to fit his own preferences. If they do not fit, he must "adjust" the quality ratings to his preferences.

4. *The Price Problem*

a. *What is the money price of the specimen?*

Comment: For some products the "thing" purchased may represent an assemblage of components, each with its own quality and its own price. An automobile, for example, combines a particular engine, transmission, body type, and a particular set of accessories. In analogous situations, different sellers may "include" different services in their price, for example, credit with no charge, a better or poorer guarantee, trading stamps. Both the quality index and the money price must be adjusted to take account of these component "services" if valid comparisons are to be made.

Some of the seller-provided services that must be taken into account are:
1. Service contract
2. Guarantee of parts
3. Credit with no charge (90-day cash)
4. Delivery at no extra charge
5. Extras and accessories
6. Installation at no extra charge
7. Trading stamps or "bonuses"
8. Trade-in allowance
9. Possibility of returns
  b. *How do I discover the prices in my product-market set?*
  c. *Is a particular price bargainable?*

MODERN DEVELOPMENTS AND THE NATURE OF THE INFORMATION PROBLEM

The nature of the information problem that consumers face is strongly influenced by several modern developments—affluence, the automobile, and modern technology. It will perhaps be helpful to the reader to discuss the effect of these developments in a single section, although they enter our analysis elsewhere.

Most obviously, affluence, by which we mean high and rising levels of real income, confers potentially greater satisfaction on consumers through the greater array of goods and services its possessors command. But, unless the means of delivering consumer information improves or unless consumers work harder to obtain information, affluence condemns consumers to less informed purchase decisions and to greater residual uncertainty. And to the extent that this uncertainty makes them uncomfortable, consumers may become increasingly disgruntled with the fruits of their affluence.

The reason for less informed purchase decisions is straightforward. With greater income the consumer can purchase more goods.

But the total time available for making these more numerous purchases remains unchanged. Small wonder that today's consumer may be more "harried" than happy.[1] This effect also applies to each person as he passes through the typical family life cycle. As his income rises, he can expect to have less time for the making of each purchase decision.

The automobile both eases and worsens the consumer's information problem. It reduces the money-time-effort costs of reaching a particular seller. On the other hand, it increases the number of sellers who can be reached for a given expenditure of money-time-effort. And obtaining information about these additional now-reachable sellers and brands becomes part of the consumer's information "problem."

The greater carrying capacity of the automobile as compared with the arms-carrying capacity of the pedestrian or transit-using shopper has radically changed shopping from what it was one or two generations ago. It leads many of us to undertake more purchases per shopping trip and to make different kinds of purchases in the same expedition, thus reducing the shopping costs per purchase. Over time, retailers have responded to the purchaser's new capacity by first organizing food supermarkets, and then, more recently, shopping plazas or super supermarkets in which the consumer may purchase many different types of merchandise at one location. These larger units compound the consumer's information problem by offering more stores, more products, and more brands. Thus the preplanning consumer has a greater need to organize his efforts carefully.

To date, technology has done more to create than to solve the conusmer's information problem. As products become technically more complex, the assessment of quality becomes more difficult, and hence more costly. As products become increasingly multicomponent, even the determination of money price becomes difficult and costly.

In response to the problem just posed, there is coming into existence a consumer information "industry," some elements of which are readily identified. Most conspicuous of these are the consumer product-testing organizations: Consumers Union with its *Consumer Reports* and Consumers' Research with its *Consumers' Research Magazine*. Then there are the publications that purvey

---

[1] This line of analysis is attributable to Staffan Linder. Small wonder that he titled his book embodying this analysis, *The Harried Leisure Class* (New York: Columbia University Press, 1970). Partially offsetting harriedness for the individual consumer is his ability, which increases with affluence, to purchase more by way of information services.

general consumer information: *Changing Times, Money,* and *Moneysworth.* Next come compilations of "inside" price information under titles such as "1975 Car prices." Finally—and clearly it is only the beginning of a long stream—there are the "how to" manuals such as Richard Burack's *New Handbook of Prescription Drugs,*[2] revealing the possible payoffs that may be obtained by buying generic drugs or the cheapest proprietary brand drugs, *How It Works and How to Fix It.*[3]

As yet, however, the infant consumer-information industry has relied on the technology of the printed page for the dissemination of quality and price information. Still in the future is the development of telephonic access to a computer "bank" of accurate, price-quality information. When this comes, some of the deleterious effects of affluence on the quality of consumer purchase decisions may be offset.[4]

In the meantime, many consumers find themselves frustrated by very real difficulties in obtaining and evaluating information regarding product prices and qualities. In seeking to avoid the information problem, some ask whether simple rules exist that might substitute for tiresome business of securing and using price/quality information. Still others adopt simple rules without stopping to consider their validity, which brings us to a discussion of "rules" as a substitute for consumer information per se.

RULES RATHER THAN INFORMATION [5]

Four simple rules were considered. Unfortunately all but one were found wanting. We examine each in turn.

Price As an Indicator of Quality. A natural first candidate was that old saw, "Price is an indicator of quality," and its cousin, "You get what you pay for." Were either approximately correct, the shopping process would be greatly simplified. The consumer could choose a higher or lower quality by selecting a higher or lower price.

It is thus worth asking under what conditions price *is* a valid

[2] (New York: Ballantine Books, Inc., 1970.)

[3] (New York: The New American Library, Inc., 1974.)

[4] In spring, 1975, the Survey Research Center of The University of Michigan was seeking financing for a large-scale research project designed to test the feasibility of a local consumer information system.

[5] This section is heavily dependent upon the research of Ruby Turner Morris as summarized in her book, *Consumers Union—Methods, Implications, Weaknesses, and Strengths* (New London, Conn.: Litfield Publications, 1971).

indicator of quality? The answer that economic theory gives is that markets will yield a *single price* for goods *of the same quality* in the same product group under conditions of "perfect information." [6] Perfect information means that consumers can obtain and act on price-quality-seller existence information at zero cost. The rationale for this outcome is straightforward. If consumers can discern quality differences with perfect accuracy and at zero cost, why should they pay more for equivalent quality?

In real life, of course, the cost of obtaining and acting on information is never zero. But a typical farmers' market with numerous farm families selling fruits and vegetables in adjacent stands to large numbers of food shoppers serves as a satisfactory first-approximation model. In such a setting, most consumers are fairly capable of judging the quality of produce offered and can make a rapid survey of the offerings at various stands. The result will be relatively little price variation for the same quality and a high correlation between price and quality. Price in this situation is likely to be a valid indicator of quality. In this situation, the consumer ironically does not need the rule since he can easily judge quality without it.

Consider another apparently "simple" product, aspirin. Although competent authorities agree that "aspirin is aspirin" (since by law it must meet standards set by the United States Government),[7] the Bayer brand of aspirin at one time sold for $.78 per 100 while an equivalent amount of a less well-known brand of aspirin on the same shelf was priced at $.18.[8] Apparently many consumers could not "see through" Bayer's advertising claim that it *is* different. In this instance, price is emphatically not an indicator of quality.

The aspirin illustration makes the point, but the questioning student will ask for more solid evidence, based on many products over a period of time. Morris and Bronson,[9] who correlated prices and quality ratings by Consumers Union for 48 sets of products, mostly major household appliances, over the 1957–68 period, concluded "that price and quality do correlate, but at a level so low as to lack practical significance." [10]

[6] So that the student will not be misled, perfect *competition* implies a single, *lowest* price. Perfect competition makes stronger assumptions, however, one of which is perfect information.

[7] See Richard Burack, *The New Handbook of Prescription Drugs, rev. ed.* (New York: Ballantine Books, Inc., 1970), p. 69.

[8] Source: author's observations in San Diego, California, February, 1972.

[9] Ruby Turner Morris and Claire Sekulski Bronson, "The Chaos of Competition Indicated by Consumer Reports," *Journal of Marketing* (July 1969), pp. 26–34.

[10] Ibid., p. 33. During the period to which the Morris-Sekulski data pertain, the quality ratings of Consumers Union did not take account of durability.

Some of their lesser findings illuminate both the conclusions and the problems they pose. Of the 48 correlations estimated, 12 were statistically significant at the 5 per cent level. (In other words the positive relationship between price and quality was highly unlikely to have occurred by chance.) Unfortunately for the practicing consumer, there was no obvious method by which he could identify the set of products for which the price-as-an-indicator-of-quality rule apparently "worked."

And, even if there were a method, a further result of the Morris-Bronson study would have proved discouraging. For ten products, the investigators were able to calculate price-quality correlations for different points in time. In the case of air conditioners, for example, they correlated price-quality data for five different times (1960, 1961, 1963, 1965, and 1967). The results showed that a statistically significant price-quality relationship in one period did not guarantee a statistically significant price-quality relationship in a second (or third or fourth) period. Thus, even if the consumer discovered that the price-as-an-indicator-of-quality "worked" at one time for a particular product, he could not rely on this relationship's obtaining at any other time.

Once Excellent, Always Excellent? Another Morris-Bronson result makes the same point in an even stronger way. It would be enormously convenient if the consumer could confidently operate on a "once excellent, always excellent" rule or assumption. Unfortunately, he cannot. Bronson-Morris correlated the quality ratings of given models and their "successor" models (same brand, same position in the distributor's "line") for 10 product classes (16 sets of correlations). In only two product classes (washing machines and freezers) and three tests did a statistically significant relationship hold between a model's quality rating on a first occasion and the quality rating of its successor.[11] Again, this result is based mainly on data for major household appliances. We have no evidence on the validity or invalidity of this relationship for other product categories.

The negative conclusions on the price-as-an-indicator-of-quality family of rules perhaps understates how badly markets for appliances

---

For a critical discussion of Consumers Union product testing procedures and data, see Chapter 5 of this book.

For four examples of near-zero price-quality correlations based on a more comprehensive quality index, see E. Scott Maynes, "Consumerism: Origin and Research Implications," in Eleanor B. Sheldon, ed., *Family Economic Behavior, Problems and Prospects* (Philadelphia: J. B. Lippincott, Inc., 1973), pp. 281–283.

[11] Ibid., Table 3, p. 31.

operate in terms of price-quality relationship. Another result underlines this point: in 87 per cent of 637 product tests over 10 years the
brands placed in the "worst" quality ranking by Consumers Union
actually carried list prices that were higher than the best-quality
brands in the same product category.[12] Thus, the inept consumer
might not only purchase a lower quality brand but pay more for it!

Data on quality are hard to find, and careful analyses of the price-
quality relationship are even rarer. There is every reason to believe
that the Morris-Bronson results, despite certain statistical limitations [13]
and their concentration on major appliances, would hold for most of
the products that consumers purchase.

The Morris-Bronson study did not try to evaluate what we might
dub "the rich man's rule," namely—"Buy the highest-priced item in a
product category." The crucial question, which remains unresolved by
the Morris-Bronson investigations, is whether the application of such
a rule would "usually" yield "high" quality. If it did, it would seem to
be a plausible rule for the wealthy to follow since, for such persons,
time and inconvenience are presumably more important than the
expenditure of money.

Buy the Products of the Same Excellent Firm? For this rule to
work, two related questions require positive answers: 1) Are there
firms in most product categories whose models rank consistently
high in quality? 2) Is there a reliable way of identifying such firms?
For our answer to the first question, we again rely on a study by
Morris,[14] this one involving 500 tests of 2,341 models of 18 makers of
appliances over the 1960–69 period.[15] Again, the quality data come
from *Consumer Reports*. Several different statistics give congruent
results and the author concludes emphatically:

> Can one rely upon the names of Zenith, and other top-rated
> firms, and omit a detailed model-by-model, year-by-year com-

---

[12] Ruby Turner Morris and Claire Sekulski Bronson, "The Potential Loss in Money
Income to the American People by Haphazard Purchasing," *Journal of Consumer Affairs*
(Winter 1970), Table 1.

[13] The statistical limitations were two: 1) the use of quality rating groups rather
than numerical quality scores for each sample, and 2) the restriction of Consumer
Unions quality scores to 1) objective characteristics, and 2) varieties of products.
Neither limitation is attributable to the authors.

[14] Ruby Turner Morris, "Major Firms Comparatively Evaluated?", *Journal of Consumer Affairs* (Winter 1971), pp. 119–139.

[15] The firms, ranked by the average quality of their products, from top to bottom,
included: Zenith, Whirlpool, Sunbeam, RCA, General Electric, Magnavox, Frigidaire,
Sears, Westinghouse, Motorola, Penney's, Wards, Hotpoint, Philco, Kelvinator, Emerson,
Wizard, Admiral.

parison? . . . the answer is no. The immense instability of annual ratings . . . and we do live by the year . . . absolutely requires taking constant advice on a current basis. There is not a firm . . . which did not put out one or more models receiving a rock-bottom rating. Nor was there any firm which did not market [in a decade] one or more top-rated items.[16]

We might note, however, that for the three best firms—Zenith, Whirlpool, and Sunbeam—the fractions of their models in the upper quartile with respect to quality were 47 per cent, 32 per cent, and 40 per cent, respectively.

Since there appear to be at best very few consistently excellent firms, the question of identifying such firms becomes academic.[17]

Buy "Top of the Line?" For most appliances and for many other product categories firms market a "line" of product variants. Ordinarily, the bottom-of-the-line model is utilitarian and free of frills. As you proceed up the line, there is ordinarily an escalation in the number of "features," in the packaging and appearance, in the advertising rhetoric (custom, deluxe, superdeluxe), as well as in the price associated with successive product variants.

Although the "price-is-an-indicator-of-quality" rule is invalid for *interbrand* comparisons, one might legitimately ask whether it works *within* brand lines. Can the consumer expect—*within brand lines,* to obtain better quality if he pays more?

The evidence, again from an analysis by Morris of Consumers Union data, seems to warrant a qualified "yes" answer—at least for "big" jumps up the brand line.[18] More specifically, if you move from

[16] Ibid., p. 131.

[17] A possible exception would be manufacturers of electronic products.

[18] Morris, op. cit., pp. 135–139.

Neither the data nor the analysis are fully adequate. The problem with the data is that Consumers Union hardly ever tests a manufacturer's full line. Instead, Consumers Union selects for tests those models that are expected to sell best. Further, Consumers Union does not evaluate *all* the characteristics of a product, especially those that are likely to differentiate adjacent models in a product line, for example, differences in "packaging" or appearance and in "small" convenience features.

The analysis, too, was somewhat crude. Morris classified as "orderly" (or consistent with the hypothesis) cases where, as one moves up the product line, both price and placement in a quality rating group increase. A "disorderly" case would be one in which price and quality are inversely related, where price increased with no improvement in quality, or where quality improved with no price change. Bear in mind that prices cited are list prices and quality is measured by placement in a rating *group*, not by a numerical quality score. (These deficiencies are inherent in the data, and not the fault of Morris.)

the bottommost model up (say) two steps, you are likely to attain a gain in quality; at a higher price, of course. And it is impossible to say on the available evidence whether the higher price justifies the presumably higher quality.

OBTAINING AND EVALUATING CONSUMER INFORMATION

None of us is going to possess—nor should we want to possess—complete and accurate information regarding *all* sellers, *all* product and brand characteristics, and *all* prices. The application of the marginal rule—seek further information as long as it "pays"—combined with the fact that additional information is costly and decreases in usefulness as we obtain more of it, implies that we will make our consumer purchase decisions on the basis of *partial* information. A knowledge of the best techniques for collecting and testing information will help us to make the best use of our limited information-seeking efforts.

It is instructive to borrow from the thinking of professional data collectors—those who conduct our best sample surveys. To ensure the collection of accurate responses to questions on a sample survey, the following requirements must be met: [19]

1. *Your informant must have access to the required information.*
2. *Your informant must be favorably motivated* to give accurate information, and not to distort or conceal information.
3. *The information must be communicated accurately* from supplier to user.

We now apply these ideas to the situation faced by the consumer as information-seeker.

Where Consumers Union tested two models in the same line, 66 per cent of 218 cases were orderly, or consistent with the hypothesis. Where Consumers Union tested three models, only 32 per cent of 85 cases were consistent.

In view of this discussion, it is my belief that these results provide partial support for the hypothesis. Morris believes otherwise. She states (p. 139): "it is the bold—and quite possibly foolish—buyer who selects the 'top of the line' with confidence that he is getting the best."

[19] This framework for the study of response errors in sample surveys was suggested by John B. Lansing. See John B. Lansing, Gerald Ginsberg, and Kaisa Braaten, *An Investigation of Response Error* (Urbana, Ill.: Bureau of Business and Economic Research, University of Illinois, 1961), pp. 188–189.

Access to the Required Information. Some sources of information merit priority attention because they concentrate great quantities of relevant information in contrast to other sources that provide only small amounts of information. Thus, for a particular product, *Consumer Reports*—which is subjected to a critical review later in the next chapter—concentrates in a single article a large amount of information regarding what characteristics are desirable, what varieties are available, to what extent they possess the desired characteristics, and, finally, some price information. By contrast, personal contact with a particular seller may disclose only fragmentary information in each of these categories. A rough ordering of sources of information by the extent to which they concentrate information might go as follows, from most to least: reports of product-testing organizations, nontest consumer periodicals and books, mail-order catalogs and telephone directories, the "expert consumer," friends and acquaintances, sellers contacted in person, and advertising.

In the case of seller-informants, other factors affecting the amount of information possessed will be their experience and position. In general, we would expect the more experienced salesman to have accumulated more information of all sorts.[20] As to position, sometimes only a decision-maker can possess and transmit the required information. Often, for example, only the owner or department manager can say how far an organization will go in the granting of price discounts. The lesson is clear: try to deal with persons of experience and authority.

The consumer information-seeker will inevitably be concerned with how accurately his informant retrieves information—whether from records or from his own memory. The failings of memory are too commonly known to require documentation. Be careful! Be skeptical!

Many record sources are often themselves inaccurate or complex. Consider the unsettling experience of the author, who made air travel plans on the basis of a fare quotation that was $200 too low, on a correct total of $840. This is an instance where the airline clerk wrestled with and lost to a fat and complex book of air tariffs. (After much disputation, the airline later agreed to split the difference between its initial erroneous fare quotation and the correct fare.) Again the lesson is clear. Where possible, obtain an *independent* check of any information based on memory or complicated records. (An *independent* check of the airline fare cited could have been obtained

---

[20] A caveat, however: the more experienced salesman may be more selective in dispensing information!

from a clerk who started "from scratch," neither knowing the original fare quoted nor relying on the original informant.)

As mentioned earlier, information transmitted in printed or written form with its source clearly indicated is to be preferred to that conveyed from someone's memory and transmitted orally.

A Favorably Motivated Informant. Can anyone seriously doubt that most sellers are motivated, by the source of their income, to suppress and distort information in favor of the products and brands they sell? This does not mean that useful information cannot be obtained from seller sources (sellers contacted in person or heard through advertising), but rather that information so obtained should be accepted conditionally and tested carefully for accuracy.

What about the motivation of consumer periodicals? Since their future prosperity depends upon their perceived usefulness to consumers and since their reliance on advertising is zero (for some) and relatively small (for others), they lack any reason to suppress or distort. This does not, however, imply that the information they provide is necessarily accurate. It merely says that there appears to exist no reason for them to conceal or distort information.

What about the motivations of friends and acquaintances? To some of us, the moment when we take possession of a new car (or a new anything) signals a drastic transformation in our attitude toward the object. Now it is "ours." Formerly skeptical, we are now at once prideful and forgiving. And, to the extent that this caricature is correct, we are motivated to communicate an excessively favorable picture of our recent purchase. Against this will be an opposing motivation of uncertain strength—our desire to help our friends and acquaintances. If this admittedly superficial analysis is correct, we should be aware that the dominant motivation of friends and acquaintances in reporting consumer information may be to buttress their own image rather to serve their friends and acquaintances by providing accurate information.

Finally, we come to the "expert consumer" who derives major satisfaction from his role as consumer consultant to his friends and acquaintances. To the extent that this role is important, he should be motivated to provide accurate information.

Accurate Communication. In obtaining information via personal or telephone conversation, the careful consumer can increase the likelihood of accurate communication in several ways. First, *before* the conversation takes place, he can list the items of information he wants.

Next, he can take the trouble to formulate questions carefully so that they ask what he wants to ask. Third, recognizing that his memory too is fallible, he can record answers to his questions in writing.

Perhaps the consumer's most useful tool in attaining accurate communication is the clarifying or follow-up question. This question can come when the original conversation takes place, or it can be asked later. Since failures in communication are a fruitful source of subsequent disputes between buyers and sellers, it seems prudent to verify your understanding of the information offered. It is better to be redundant than to be wrong.

The Sampling Problem. Some items of consumer information— the existence (and sometimes the location) of a seller, brand, or model, the price of a good in a "single-price" store, the published technical specifications—are invariant. If you solve the problem of accurate communication, a single source of information will meet your needs.

Other properties of goods about which we may wish to know— the overall length of a car, for example—may exhibit specimen-to-specimen variations of such small magnitude as to be of no practical importance. For this class, too, we can rely on a single source of information once the problem of accurate communication is solved. Here, there is a "sampling problem," but it is of negligible proportions. In most cases our common sense and background information will enable us to identify the items of information belonging to this class.

Many properties of goods, however, exhibit considerable item-to-item variation. The quality of a wine, the quality of frozen food, gas consumption for a given automobile model, the quality of a house painting job, and the price paid for a given model of used car come to mind as examples. Here a single accurate report may mislead rather than inform.

Some needed items of information—the probability of breakdown of a machine, for example—make sense only when reported on the basis of a large number of observations.

For many types of goods, item-to-item variation spells difficulties and frustration for the information-seeking consumer, problems that we have placed under the "sampling problem" heading. Our further discussion shows why. In the discussion that follows we assume (unrealistically) that all informants provide accurate reports of their experience.

Consider for illustrative purposes the auto-purchasing consumer who wishes to ascertain the likelihood (probability) of a "front-suspension" repair and the size of the typical repair bill that will result.

The information the consumer would ideally like is summarized in Column 1 of Table 1. It consists of accurate reports from all owners possessing the car in question—"the relevant population." The probability of trouble, as shown in Table 1, is 21 per cent and the average repair bill is $50. If "our" consumer purchased an "average" specimen and enjoyed "average" experience, then his chances of trouble are 21 per cent and the best estimate of his likely repair bill is $50.

Of course, almost no one obtains information from reports of an entire population. The time and money costs of information collection for a complete enumeration are prohibitive. Besides, a complete enumeration is unnecessary; a well-conducted sample survey is almost as good.

The sample for the survey is drawn in such a way that every element in the parent population—in our example, all the cars of a spe-

TABLE 1

Hypothetical Data on Repair Bills Resulting from Front Suspension Trouble: Different Information Sources

Information obtained from:

	(1) Entire Population (all owners)	(2) Unbiased Sample	(3) Biased Sample	(4) Consumers' Acquaintances
Per Cent of Owners with No Trouble	79%	81%	75%	100%
Per Cent Experiencing Trouble	21%	19%	25%	0%
Size of Repair Bill				
Less than $20	41%	43%	37%	0%
$20–$39	15	16	13	0
$40–$59	14	13	17	0
$50–$89	20	18	19	0
$90–139	5	7	6	0
$140–$239	3	2	4	0
$240 or more	2	1	4	0
Total	100%	100%	100%	100%
Average Repair Bill (for those with repairs)	$50	$45	$70	0
Number Reporting	879,754	1,000	1,000	4

cified make-model-year—have an equal probability of selection. This assures us that our sample will be "representative" of the parent population and that statistics estimated from the sample will correspond closely to those obtained from the entire population. Notice that in Column 2 of Table 1, the probability of breakdown as estimated from the unbiased sample is .19, only .02 away from the probability in Column 1; similarly, the average repair bill is $45, only $5 lower than the Column 1 figure. In general, as the sample size increases, the discrepancy between the sample estimate and the population estimate will tend to become smaller. Samples of 1,000 as in Column 2 are precise enough to serve most purposes,[21] and even sample sizes of 75 or 100 will serve many purposes. But the number of reports (= "sample size") that the typical consumer is likely to obtain—say 2, 3, 4, or even 10—will usually be too small, subject to too much error to give information representative of the population.

Very occasionally, the consumer may encounter useful information collected from sample surveys. For example, *Consumer Reports* publishes data on the "frequency of repair" for automobiles and other household durables collected from its subscribers.

Column 3 illustrates the problem of bias in sample surveys. This occurs when the sample is *not* representative because some elements in the population had a greater or lesser probability of selection in the sample. Suppose, in our probability of breakdown survey, that people with favorable breakdown experiences tended not to return a questionnaire and that people with *un*favorable experiences returned questionnaires more frequently than the average. This would give results such as those in Column 3. They indicate, misleadingly, an erroneously higher probability of breakdown as compared to the correct figure (Column 1) and an erroneously high average repair figure.

Most of the time the information-collecting consumer will have to do without sample survey information, whether biased or unbiased. The information he gains from his own efforts are likely to resemble that in Column 4, based on 4 reports.

Several lessons can be drawn from Table 1. First, all sample information is subject to sampling errors. In forming judgments, the consumer should ask how large the sampling errors are likely to be for the data in which he is interested. (Sampling errors can be calculated.) This will help in forming a judgment as to the likely probability

---

[21] This is not true when either ownership/use or the event being estimated is "rare." A harp would be an example of a *product* whose ownership/use is rare whereas an explosion (for most products) is an example of an *event* that is rare.

of need for repairs and the average repair bill (or whatever statistic he is interested in). Second, he should be alert to the possibility of bias in the sample selection. If the suspected bias is too great or too complicated, he may probably decide to reject data from this source. Third, he will be aware that for the small number of reports he may be able to collect via his own efforts, sampling variability will dominate. What can he do? The next section seeks to help the consumer in evaluating the inferior information on which he must usually rely in making decisions.

Evaluating the Information Received. A "Missouri," or skeptical, viewpoint is appropriate to the evaluation of much of the consumer information we receive. In implementing this viewpoint, however, a number of specific "tests" may be helpful.

Building on this discussion, a first step in evaluating an item of consumer information might be to review the process by which the information was obtained. To what extent did the informant have access to the information desired? To what extent was the informant favorably motivated to communicate accurately and fully? To what extent was communication both to and from the informant accurate?

A second step is to ask whether the item of information is subject to non-negligible sample variation? If sampling variation is not a problem, then a single source of information will suffice. If sampling variation is likely to be a problem, we will want, if possible, to know the sample size on which our information was based. And, preferably, we would like to know about the sampling process to judge if, and how, the sample selection process was biased. As soon as these questions are answered, we will want to engage in the impossible-to-specify process of "adjusting" the information or deciding to reject it.

In this process of assessment our most important aid is that marvelous instrument—the human mind. For it constitutes a storehouse of useful information: our past experience, favorable or unfavorable, with particular information sources; our memory of our personal past experience as well as that of our friends with particular kinds of products and particular brands or models; and our understanding of how particular products or mechanisms work. Each person's "store" of pertinent knowledge will be larger or smaller depending upon such factors as intelligence, memory, type and extent of both formal and informal education, and range of experience and contacts.

We can use this accumulated experience to help evaluate new consumer information. A first question to be asked relates to our previous experience with a particular information source. If it was favorable and involved many episodes, then we should give heavy weight to it. Obviously, if it was unfavorable or based on a small number of incidents, we should view it more skeptically. Indeed, cumulative experience may lead us to discard some sources as completely useless.

A second test is conformity to expectations. No matter how ill-informed we are, most of us will probably have formed some expectations regarding desirable characteristics, the extent to which particular brands or models possess them, and prices. In general, it is advisable to accept information conforming to our expectations more readily than information that differs from what we expect. When differences arise, this is a signal to search for more information especially when the information is important, for example, safety aspects of a particular product.

Several additional tests may be helpful when we are confronted with unexpected information. First, we can be aware of the "sampling problem" discussed previously. Could it be that the unexpected information is unrepresentative of the "typical" specimen of that brand or model? In the parlance of the car market, does the information we have received describe a "lemon" instead of the typical car? We can never be sure, but by obtaining more information, we will be in a better position to make this judgment. Second, regarding the unexpected information, we can ask whether there is a good explanation that "fits" the unexpected information better than it fits our prior expectations? Most of us have probably heard favorable reports of automobile disc brakes. If someone tells us that a particular car, so equipped, braked faultily, we would probably be quite skeptical. But, suppose they told us further that oil tended to get into the brakes (thus reducing the coefficient of friction). This explanation would tend to make the initial information more credible, though we might still seek corroboration of both judgment and explanation from a different, independent source.

The word *independent* raises another relevant point—the extent to which information received actually comes from *different* sources unaffected by each other. Consider the consumer who is contemplating a particular purchase, carefully reads *Consumer Reports,* and then happily finds that the judgment of a friend-expert consumer on the purchase agrees with that of *Consumer Reports*. This is fine until he discovers that his friend was relying almost wholly on *Consumer Reports*. What is needed is genuinely new information or judgments and not a recirculation of information from a source already tapped.

Finally, in evaluating consumer information it is useful to undertake a critical review of the sources of consumer information in general.

Our next selection undertakes this task.

SOURCES OF INFORMATION: A CRITICAL REVIEW

Advertising. Informationally, advertising is indispensable to the operating consumer in the American economy. Advertising has the virtue of informing consumers recurrently of the existence of:

1. New or alternative *products;*
2. New or alternative *brands* or *models;*
3. New or alternative *characteristics;*
4. New or alternative *price possibilities;*
5. New or alternative *retail establishments;* [22]
6. "Sales."

To judge whether advertising has informational content in addition to that specified, we must first analyze the purposes of the advertisers. The objective of advertisers is to encourage initial and repeated sales to the point at which the seller's profits are maximized. Let there be no mistake about it: our market economy is based on the strongest and most selfish motives, not on altruistic impulses.

Informationally, these motivations may badly bias sellers and the advertisers they employ. If it is profitable, you may rely on some advertisers to try to persuade you that demonstrably undesirable characteristics are desirable. Thus, the increasingly strong evidence linking cancer to cigarette smoking does not deter the tobacco companies from spending millions of dollars to try to persuade us to smoke.

Consider the case of STP, an oil additive for use in cars. In 1971, its advertising claimed that STP "makes your ailing motor healthy and powerful again." *Consumer Reports* concluded that this was not the case and the use of STP was unnecessary since it did nothing more than a thicker (than you are now using), multiviscosity motor oil would do.[23] What is more, according to representatives of General Motors and Ford, the use of STP on new automobiles could, under

---

[22] But sometimes advertising seeks to blur the distinction between old and new, trying to pass off as "new" a product, brand, model, characteristic, price, or even establishment that is not really new.

[23] *Consumer Reports* (July 1971), p. 422.

certain circumstances affect the terms of their warranties.[24] All this for a product that retailed in 1971 for three to six times as much (per quart) as ordinary motor oil.

Roughly coincident with the *Consumer Reports* article, the price of STP stock plummeted. Did the STP Corporation withdraw its product or its advertising from the market? Not at all. A year later the *Wall Street Journal* reported: "What STP did . . . was spend money like crazy on advertising and promotion to maintain its key oil-additive market. . . ."[25] The motivations of the seller were revealed in a comment by one of its directors, Leslie T. Welsh: "Andy (the president of STP) could have laid low after the *Consumer Reports* article, but he went all out, and I think he did right."

It is thus the effective working of the *system,* not the goodness or badness of the participant's motivations, that makes a market system deliver a high performance in terms of high quality and low prices. When the system works well, it rewards good performance and punishes poor performance.

Informationally, the system yields accurate and complete advertising regarding the characteristics of brands *only when the failure to provide such information places heavy costs on the seller.* When is this likely to occur?

First, it tends to happen in the case of *mail-order houses.* Here, misrepresentation would result in returns that are costly to the seller. In the short run, a return may make the particular sale unprofitable. But the long-run effect of misrepresentation may be the loss of a customer "for good." This is why mail-order catalogs are so refreshingly informative. Relatively untouched pictures are combined with careful text so that potentially "weasel" phrases, such as "better" and "best," are less likely to be used.

A second case is *newspaper classified advertisements.* The seller of a house who fails to tell the reader that the house has but two bedrooms will spend valuable time and effort turning away would-be buyers who want more than two bedrooms.

A further case is *simple,* as opposed to complex products, such as newspaper advertising of canned vegetables or fruits. When the advertisement states that a store is offering "California" oranges or "locally grown" corn, these specifications are likely to be correct.

Finally, advertising directed to *professional buyers* tends to be somewhat more accurate and complete. No doubt this is the consequence of the fact that such buyers possess the qualifications to judge

[24] Ibid.
[25] *Wall Street Journal,* June 13, 1972, p. 40.

for themselves which characteristics of a product are desirable and the extent to which a given brand possesses these characteristics. But there are degrees of expertness. One is impressed, for example, that judging from the exaggerated character of drug advertising in some medical journals, doctors may not be "expert" buyers when it comes to the purchase or recommendations regarding drugs.

It is worth noting that for all of these four classes, little effort tends to be devoted to persuading the consumer as to what characteristics are desirable. Instead, the consumers' desires tend to be taken as given, and the advertising inclines toward providing reproducible information regarding the degree to which the brands advertised possess various characteristics.

That advertisements outside these four classes possess *some* accurate information for the consumer can scarcely be denied. It may be possible for some ingenious person to devise a reliable means of separating "truth" from "untruth," and of identifying significant omissions from advertisements. But, as of now, no such system exists. And so we arrive at the conclusion that the informational value of advertising—the four classes cited excepted—generally reduces to the lowest common denominator mentioned at the outset: the identification of new or alternative products, brand/models, characteristics, retail establishments, and prices.[26]

Sellers Contacted in Person. All of us have approached a seller with the request: "I need something to—." And here we specify some need that is sufficiently urgent to put us on the seller's doorstep or telephone. Informationally, perhaps the most valuable service that sellers perform is to identify products and varieties that will meet our specifications. If the particular seller has such a product, he will recommend "his own" brand. But if he does not, he will often serve as well by recommending another seller who can meet our needs.

Aside from identifying needed products, brands, models, characteristics, and sellers, what can be said in general about the *character* of information that sellers provide? First, it is usually biased. This applies both to information regarding what characteristics are desirable for a particular need as well as information regarding the extent to which a particular brand (or model) provides the desired characteristics. There are a number of reasons for this.

As noted earlier, sellers are compensated for selling, not for pro-

[26] For a closely reasoned article more supportive of advertising's information-giving role, see Phillip Nelson, "Advertising as Information," *Journal of Political Economy* (July–August 1974), pp. 729–754.

viding consumer information. Furthermore, sellers are compensated for selling "their own" brands. It brings a Ford salesman neither comfort nor compensation if a would-be customer subsequently buys a Chevrolet, or even a Ford, if it is purchased from another dealer. And this fact significantly biases sellers as sources of information. It would be fatuous to expect the Ford salesman to suggest a Chevrolet, rather than a Ford, has the particular desired characteristics. And, of course, the same would be true for the Chevrolet salesman with the automobiles interchanged.

By the same token, compensation arrangements influence judgments regarding what characteristics of a product are desirable. Imagine a Buick salesman (substitute almost any other make)—whose product has a conventional gasoline engine—extolling the virtues of a diesel. It is unlikely to happen, at least until Buick has such an engine to sell!

One might be tempted to argue that multibrand sellers—for example, department stores or "general" insurance agents—can make interbrand judgments without bias. They may in some cases, be able to do so, but there remains the possibility that interbrand differences in commissions are large enough to bias the information given.[27] To put the point in the form of a rhetorical question: Which will more affect the recommendations of a department store seller of electric shavers—a low rating for Brand X in *Consumer Reports* (if he's aware of it) or a higher commission for Brand X?

A final source of bias is the so-called "ethical" codes of many industries by which sellers agree not to criticize their competitors (even when they deserve it). Doctors, for example, are constrained by their code of "ethics" not to comment negatively on either the competence of another physician or on the quality of service rendered in a particular case. In some cases such codes prohibit the quotation of competitors' prices, even from the competitors' own literature. Companies selling major medical insurance follow this practice. In essence, such codes represent perversions of what the term *ethics* usually conveys: they protect "insiders" from competitive forces by withholding information. In so doing, they increase the probability that "outsiders" —consumers in this case—will purchase inferior goods or services and pay higher prices.

But there are some offsetting factors to the sources of bias cited previously. Some salespersons, acting on a broader social view of their

---

[27] Surreptitious commissions—"push money" or "spiff" in the trade—have been a part of American retailing for a long time. See "Push Money = Spiff = Bribe," *Consumer Reports* (January 1971), p. 24.

responsibilities, invest a considerable effort in obtaining and disseminating fuller and more accurate product information, sometimes at the expense of their own income. And, in some lines where repeated contacts between salesman and client are possible—men's suits, for example—it is probable that greater, rather than less, candor pays off in the long run in the form of larger sales to a particular customer.

In general, the payoff for providing relatively less biased consumer information is greater for the larger multiproduct, multibrand sellers than for sellers whose range of products and brands is more limited. The former gain more than the latter when particular customers return for repeat purchases of other goods.

What lessons are there in this for the consumer? First, he should be aware that compensation arrangements seriously bias information provided by sellers. Second, wherever possible, he should obtain information from sources other than sellers. Third, if you do need seller advice, obtain it from the multiproduct, multibrand seller. Finally, you may have discovered from past experience particular sellers who have served you well. In seeking their advice, it is probably best to expect them to be less biased in giving general information on which characteristics are desirable than in selecting a particular brand.

Friends and Acquaintances. Consumer surveys tell us that friends and acquaintances are the most common source of consumer knowledge. This should not come as a surprise to you, and it probably bears out your personal experience. And for good reason. It is a reticent person indeed who does not wish to relate for your benefit his experience with his purchases, especially his recent ones. Furthermore, as we remarked earlier, the cost of this information is low—the conversation you might have had with your informant on another unrelated topic.

But, aside from the evaluation of certain simple products or characteristics, the low quality of information provided by most friends and acquaintances may match its low cost. As noted earlier, pride of ownership can produce a powerful bias to forget and forgive the weaknesses of what one owns—even when giving information to a friend. Furthermore, most friends and acquaintances lack an understanding of sampling and an in-depth knowledge of the competing brands as well as "their own" brand. Both are necessary to make a valid comparison.

Can a layman, on the basis of incomplete information, evaluate the performance of a physician whose treatment presumably saved a life (or failed to save a life)? It seems doubtful. Is it surprising that a person who has just replaced his 6-year-old, 100,000-mile-old clunker with the newest model car is well pleased with his new car? Scarcely. Is it useful information? Hardly. What we want is the informed, preferably reproducible judgment of someone who has intimate knowledge of Brands A, B, C . . . Z, and not just Brand A. Even if our friend reports persistent trouble with rain leaks in his own examplar of Brand A, how can we be sure that this defect would be characteristic of the particular Brand A we might buy?

These criticisms notwithstanding, we will continue to form brand judgments on the basis of our friends' experiences and judgments. But we should—and we can—weigh experiences, pro and con, and weight different person's evaluations in the light of their track record.

These observations bring us to the subject of the "expert consumer."

The Expert Consumer. All of us know individuals whose enthusiasms have led them into expertness in particular areas, for example, high-fidelity equipment, photography, cars, housing, or even consumer information itself. Many such persons derive satisfaction not only from using their expertness for their own gain but also from sharing their expertness with others in the form of advice.

Locating an expert consumer is a simple matter. In groups to which you already belong, you will know them automatically. In groups to which you are a newcomer, a simple question as to who knows about high-fidelity equipment (or cameras or cars or any other subject you mention) will usually yield several names. So there is no problem here.

The effective use of your expert consumer is something else and there are several caveats. In the first place, not all enthusiasts are equally "expert." So, as in the case of other information sources, it is prudent to learn what you can, both firsthand and from the experiences of others, regarding the past performance of your prospective consultant. Have others who have followed his advice found it to be efficacious?

The expertise of some individuals is strictly "temporary." With an eye toward making an effective purchase for themselves, they carefully investigate desirable characteristics, alternative varieties and sellers, prices, and discounts. Their purchase completed, they "retire" from this particular area. The obvious doubt for someone wishing to "borrow" their knowledge is its relevance at a later point in time.

Another question to ask is whether your expert consumer (consultant) is capable of providing information and advice that is appropriate to *your* problem and *your* tastes rather than his. To put the point more concretely, can he and will he advise you to purchase high-fidelity equipment in the low-price range appropriate to *your* budget and *your* tastes, rather than the middle-price range that he would prefer given *his* budget and *his* tastes?

A final proposition is that expert consumers may be specialized. The high-fidelity "consultant" just mentioned may be extremely knowledgeable regarding middle- or high-priced high-fidelity equipment and relatively ignorant of low-priced equipment. Obviously, you must check to see that the expertness of your consultant fits your needs.

Better Business Bureaus. In any big purchase consumers are understandably desirous of dealing with reliable firms who treat their consumers fairly. But how do you find such firms? Many of our most sophisticated consumers believe that a phone call to the local Better Business Bureau (BBB) will give accurate information on a firm's reputability and fairness.

Unfortunately, the facts do not always support the expectation. The BBB's reports are only partly credible. If the BBB reports that a firm is unreliable, then the consumer is well advised to believe it. A "clean" report by the BBB, unhappily, is not necessarily to be believed. The firm may or may not be one with which you would like to deal.

The basis for this harsh appraisal of the BBB's reports lies in the manner that the BBB counts and reports consumer complaints. See Chapter 8 for a detailed discussion of the BBB complaint system and its deficiencies.

Obtaining Information on Services: The Two-Stage Sift. Tacitly the discussion until now has focused on *tangible* consumer products. Suppose, however, that the consumer must make a choice regarding services, for example, those rendered by doctors, bankers, lawyers, painters (house or otherwise), plumbers, and other craftsmen. What procedures and what information sources are available to the consumer interested in obtaining these services?

To a certain extent both search procedures and information sources must be tailored to the service in question. But the two-stage sift described as follows should have wide applicability.

In essence, the two-stage sift consists of a *nomination stage* in which a locally knowledgeable person(s) suggests a list of potential service providers and an *elimination stage* in which a different locally knowledgeable person(s) chooses those service-providers who would serve you best.

Operationally, a two-stage sift might be carried out in steps as follows:

1. Consider the service in question and ask what person or types of persons, *accessible to you,* are most competent to judge the quality of service provided.

2. Approach one or more such "judges" and ask them to nominate a number (perhaps four to eight) of "very good" persons, firms, or institutions in that line.

3. Ask a second judge whose basis for judgment is different— perhaps from a different occupation—to select the "best" two or three from the list obtained in the first sift.

Ideally, this process should yield the names of two or three service providers who will serve you well.

A couple of examples may illuminate the working of the two-stage sift approach. Suppose you want to select a house painter. A possible nomination stage source of information is the paint store where you purchase supplies and that may also cater to professional painters. You might ask the store manager to give you the name of several painters who would do a good job for you. In so doing, you are assuming that the paint store people will be able to form worthwhile judgments of painter quality on the basis of such factors as the supplementary materials they buy, the care they exhibit in the purchase, informal chats that reveal their attitude toward their work, and their reputation based on the "scuttlebutt" of the trade. The paint store's recommendation may or may not be based on a firsthand scrutiny of various painters' work. You are aware, of course, that the paint store's recommendation might be contaminated by such considerations as long-standing friendships, or the extent to which a painter is "their" faithful customer. Offsetting this, presumably, is the paint store's own reputation for reliability and helpfulness, and in particular its hoped-for continuing relationship with you.

Most of us would view the paint store's recommendation as imperfect. And it is this that justifies the second sift.

In this example, the elimination stage sift is performed by former customers of the painters whose names were obtained from the paint store's nominations. The information-seeking consumer asked each painter to supply him with the names and addresses of people for whom he has performed major paint jobs, both recent and some time ago (since the length of time a paint job lasts is crucial). Any painter who is unwilling or is slow in supplying such a list is automatically disqualified. It is inferred that he has unsatisfactory jobs to conceal, or that he is likely to be as dilatory in doing the job as he is in supplying the list.

The consumer can make a quick "drive-by" survey. Conversations with purchasers of the painting jobs will be confined to those painters whose work "passed" the drive-by "test." In these chats, the consumer checks to see how well satisfied those people were with their painter, their experience regarding such matters as promptness, the care taken in doing the job (cleaning up, for example), the business aspects of the job, and finally their judgment regarding the price paid.

The choice of a personal physician—perhaps an internist—involves similar principles, but different information sources. Here, more than in the case of the painter, the quality of the information received will depend upon the extent and quality of your personal contacts.

It is probably easier to obtain a larger list of doctors from impersonal sources and then ask your personal contacts to narrow it down to a few names. For the nomination stage one might start with a university medical school or hospital if there is one, with a large, accredited, nonprofit hospital, or with the county medical society and ask them to recommend four to six "very good" internists. Conforming to accepted norms regarding appraisals of doctors, these sources would be unwilling to nominate a single physician (or to give negative information), but they probably would be willing to recommend a list from which a choice might be made. It is assumed that institutions such as these—and the secretaries and minor officials who actually give the required information—will feel a sufficient sense of pride and social responsibility to nominate only the "better" physicians.

In the second stage one must first ask whether he has access to someone who is both familiar with and competent to judge the quality of the doctors on the initial list. A specialist, for example, an eye doctor, might be such a judge since internists often function as first-stage diagnosticians and thus have frequent interactions with other specialists. It is not unreasonable that the specialist will have some knowledge of, and ability to evaluate, the training, the quality of diagnosis, the carefulness, and the judgment of internists with whom they deal. If you have access to a specialist, he would be an ideal judge.

If you do not have such access, less satisfactory information sources are available. You might consider nurses associated with hospitals or pharmacists in large drugstores. There is, moreover, nothing in the two-stage sift approach that prevents you from obtaining and using sources of objective information. In selecting a physician, it is certainly appropriate to telephone a "candidate" physician and ask him (or his secretary) about the date and source of his medical degree, with what hospital(s) he is affiliated, what specialist "Boards" he has passed. An internist should have passed an examination conducted by the Board of Internal Medicine and should therefore be designated as a Fellow of the American College of Physicians (FACP). Other things being equal, a higher quality medical school and more recent training (a physician five to ten years out of school) are likely to assure a more competent physician. Alternatively, you can telephone the reference room of your local library and collect much of the same information. The best source is the *Directory of Medical Specialists* (Chicago: *Marquis Who's Who*, revised periodically).

From the foregoing discussion it is obvious that the two-stage sift may give variable results. Its efficacy will depend upon the contacts of the consumer, his ability to determine what sorts of people can judge different areas of competence, the size of the community, and his own ability to judge other persons' capacity to judge.

Because the consumer product-testing organizations concentrate information so prodigiously and serve consumers in other ways, they have been allotted a chapter of "their own," Chapter 5.

But first we turn to some examples of the principles of this chapter "at work."

THE PRINCIPLES AT WORK: DETAILED EXAMPLES

What You Can and Cannot See: The Purchase of a New Car. It was spring, 1971, and the G's wanted to buy a new car. With three children ages 11, 8, and 6 and a penchant for camping, it did not take the G's long to determine that they wanted an intermediate station wagon. A full-sized wagon was too big to park and too expensive to buy and operate, and the compacts were too small.

Their first step was to consult *Consumer Reports,* but it had no clear-cut recommendations. *Consumer Reports* liked some features of the Ford Torino; but it liked the Chevrolet Chevelle for quite different reasons. The result was that the G's—for reasons they would hate to defend—decided to look first at a Chevelle. They did note that the

Oldsmobile Cutlass and the Buick Sport Wagon were "twins" to the Chevelle—the same design, but produced in different plants under different names.

With three Chevrolet dealers in their city, the G's went first to a dealer, Midwest Motors, who gave discounts to members of the credit union to which they belonged. The Midwest salesman with whom they dealt was neither particularly helpful nor particularly knowledgeable. But what struck the G's with full force was their own ignorance about cars; they knew absolutely nothing about engines. But, as they looked at the Chevelles that the salesmen showed them, one thing attracted their attention. The paint finish on every Chevelle they looked at appeared rough, as though it had not received the final buffing it needed. And, on many of the cars, the trim was loose, ready to rattle (they thought) and perhaps fall off. They were struck with doubts. If the finish was badly turned out, what of the more important parts they could neither see nor understand?

Since the Oldsmobile Cutlass was the "twin" of the Chevelle, they decided to see whether the Oldsmobile label made any difference. So they made their way to an Oldsmobile dealer in a near-by suburb.

In a single glance the G's could see that this Oldsmobile dealership was indeed different. Its new showroom and younger salesmen contrasted vividly with the Chevrolet dealer back in the central city. But, they thought, you don't buy decor, you buy a car and, it is hoped, service. On the important matter of the car they discovered a difference, too. The paint jobs on *all* the Cutlass wagons they saw were finished, satisfactorily. And, although they could still find some loose trim, there was much less of this than in the Chevelles. They were also pleasantly surprised about the price. Without investigating they had assumed that the "step-up" from a Chevy to an Olds would cost a lot, but, upon inquiry, they learned that the initial quote from the Olds salesman was only about $75 more than the Chevy price.

What they had learned at the Oldsmobile dealer whetted their appetite for what they might learn about the third "twin," the Buick. So off they went to the Buick dealer.

And here their revelation regarding paint and trim became complete: not one of the Buick Sport Wagons they saw suffered from either a poor paint finish or loose trim. The G's were at once surprised and delighted. And their delight was compounded when they discovered that the Buick salesman's price quotation (which they regarded as preliminary) was only $100 higher than that for the Chevelle. But now they began to have their doubts. Was the difference in paint and trim between the Buick, the Olds, and the Chevelle real? Or was it merely a figment of their imagination? It was now 8:30 and toward the end of the car-selling evening. But, as a last gambit, they decided to visit a second Chevrolet dealer, happily located no more than two blocks from the Buick dealer.

The visit was short. This time the G's knew what they wanted to see. And, with closing time approaching, the salesman was less expansive than he might have been earlier in the evening. But this last visit was worthwhile nonetheless. Although the shapes were the same, the Chevelles at this second Chevrolet outlet suffered the same defect as the first Chevelles they had seen: poor finish and much loose trim. The G's thanked the salesman and retired to digest their viewing.

Once they were home, their first step was to get out *Consumer Reports* to see if it provided any clues to the differences they had observed between Chevelle, Olds Cutlass, and Buick Sport Wagon. (*Consumer Reports* had tested only the Chevelle, and not the similar Olds and Buick.) It did not take long. Although *Consumer Reports* did not publish separate frequency-of-repair data for station wagons, it did publish such data for all cars of the same "line" (Chevelle, Buick Special, Skylark, and so on). The correspondence between what the G's thought they had seen and the frequency-of-repair data was uncanny: the Chevelles with their loose trim and poor finishes were "worse-than-average" on frequency-of-repairs; the Cutlasses were "average"; and the Buicks were "better-than-average."

Frequency of repairs was very important to the G's. Mr. G had a strong distaste for breakdowns and unplanned trips to automobile repair departments distressed him. Both the G's believed that auto repair costs were likely to rise in the future.

The "discovery" of a relationship between what they could see (and judge) and the all-important frequency-of-repair record was decisive for the G's. It would make more sense to buy the Buick even if it cost $100 more. They agreed that this had been a profitable evening.

The only thing left was the buying. There were two Buick dealers —City Buick nearer to them in the central city (and, in fact, the one they had visited) and Suburban Buick. Inquiries to friends and acquaintances yielded consistent reports—City Buick had a favorable and well-deserved reputation for delivering new cars in good shape and for correcting faults that appeared. And the reputation of Suburban Buick was not far behind. Since City was closer, the G's decided to try them first.

Some preliminary bargaining, which we do not review here,

indicated that neither City nor Suburban would "give" much on price. If the G's wanted to buy a Buick, they would have to pay about $200 over dealer cost and at least $100 more than the best price they could get on a Chevelle. This gave them pause, but not for long. The recollection of the paint-trim differences and its correlation with the frequency-of-repair records reinforced their original decision in favor of a Buick.

They were also impressed by what the City salesman had said when they tried to beat his price down (even if it *did* sound like a "line"): "If I gave you a lower price, we wouldn't be able to prep your car and still make a profit." And despite pressure, he refused to budge further on price.

For their part the G's were not passive. They told the salesman: "Our car had better be right. We are aggressive consumers. And we'll camp on your doorstep until it *is* right. What's more, all our friends will hear about it!" The salesman assured them that he would contact the delivery manager personally to make sure that the dealer preparation on their car was performed with care. Was this a "snow job" or a commitment with some substance? Neither you nor I nor the G's will ever know.

What we do know is that on a lovely June evening seven weeks later the G's checked over their new Buick, decided it was "as promised," and drove off very pleased. Their first crisis with the car was not long in coming. The next morning the tailgate window was derailed (jarred out of its track) when their son closed the tailgate (too hard?). Was this a serious malfunction or an easy correction (by applying pressure with your thumbs)? With a brand new car caution was in order. The next day, after having driven it only 100 miles, the G's returned their car to the Buick dealer for a warranty repair. That night, when they picked up their car, they discovered that it was indeed a serious problem. According to the service manager: "We had to dismantle the entire tailgate and then reassemble it right. But I'll tell you now. You might have trouble with something else, but you won't have trouble with this!"

As it turned out, that was the only significant failure the G's experienced with their car over the two years it took them to drive 20,000 miles.

We will never know whether this was luck or a singularly savvy assessment of uncertainties. When some of Consumers Union's automobile testers were told of the G's belief that their paint-trim observations were causally related to the care the manufacturer exercised in production, they scoffed. Nonetheless, the G's remained unrepentant in their belief that the paint-trim clue was real evidence of care in construction. What can be stated with certainty is that the frequency-of-repair record for the 1971 Buick Special with a V-8 motor (the "family" to which their car belonged) remained "better-than-average" through to at least 1975.

And, whether the G's declaration of aggressiveness to the salesman had any effect whatsoever, we will never know. What can be said is that this step and their investigation of alternative makes and dealers represented a highly defensible approach to these decisions.

Epitaph for a Sound Decision

Remember Mr. C back at the end of Chapter 2 who purchased a Miranda Sensorex single-lens reflex camera? And he did it so well that we held him up as a "model."

Now shed a tear for Mr. C. His model purchase procedures, unhappily, did not yield model results.

Before he had purchased his single-lens reflex, Mr. C had owned a nonreflex 35 mm. camera that had served him well. It was convenient, and most of his color slides were sharp and appropriately exposed.

What pushed him toward a single-lens reflex were the possibilities opened up by interchangeable lenses, in particular a telephoto lens. With a telephoto lens, he felt, he could take "natural," unposed pictures from so far away that his subjects would be unaware that they were being photographed. This was important to Mr. C because the oldest of his children was now eight years old and becoming self-conscious about being photographed. The same advantage would pertain to taking pictures of people, close-up, when traveling. Finally, Mr. C thought that the telephoto lens would enable him to "get close" (in pictures at least) to mountains and other scenery. So, when he purchased his Miranda, he also bought a 135 mm. telephoto lens.

A few weeks after the purchase of his single-lens reflex, Mr. C and his family went off on a two-week vacation to a Maine beach. There, he expected, his conception of "natural" pictures would become a reality. And on their Maine vacation Mr. C took a boyish pleasure in trying out the features of his new camera.

But his experience was instructive. Usage impressed upon him the fact that a second lens was not altogether convenient. The shift from one lens to another took time, and if he didn't adjust the exposure meter (to take account of the fact that his regular lens was f. 1.9 and his telephoto was f. 3.5) he would get the wrong reading, and hence the wrong exposure. What's more, he had to carry the extra lens.

The revelation that his single-lens camera was not the complete answer to Mr. C's photographic aspirations came when his vacation slides were developed. To his chagrin he found that he had harvested a far greater than usual number of overexposed slides, especially with the telephoto lens. (He could identify the objects all right, but color and detail were lacking.) At the same time his vacation batch included some genuine "gems," which fully realized his best hopes. Mr. C chalked up these partial failures to photographic error and resolved to improve his mastery of his camera. (In this he may have been wrong. A survey by *Consumer Reports* in 1972 of 8,600 owners of single-lens cameras showed that the major malfunction of such cameras involved the metering or shutter system.) [28]

The experience with his vacation photographs put a damper on Mr. C's enthusiasm for his new single-lens camera and for photography, in general. Over the next year or two his average of taking good pictures fell as did the total number of pictures he took. His fading enthusiasm for photography was further dampened when the film advance lever broke and required four weeks and $48 (on a camera for which he had paid $222) to fix.

Mr. C's feelings about his Miranda and about *Consumer Reports* were not improved when in 1972 *Consumer Reports* published frequency-of-repair records for single-lens cameras. Unfortunately, Miranda "led" all the rest with the worst frequency-of-repair record: 60 per cent of *Consumer Reports* sample of Miranda purchasers in 1968 had taken them for repairs at some time during the four-year period, as compared with only 18 per cent of Canon owners.[29]

Three lessons may be learned from Mr. C's experience. First, even well-conceived search-shopping procedures can yield disappointing results. Second, the product tests of *Consumer Reports,* even though they probably represent the consumer's best single source of information, are not infallible. (In the tests upon which Mr. C relied, *Consumer Reports* provided no information on durability. On this point, one of Mr. C's friends, a statistician, emerged "one up." The statistician-friend also bought a single-lens reflex at about the same time and also relied on *Consumer Reports*. But he dug out two earlier tests of single-lens reflexes and discovered that, although there was considerable shifting among makes over three successive tests, the

---

28 *Consumer Reports* (August 1972), pp. 514–515.
29 Ibid.

Canon consistently ranked high. He bought a Canon, and his results were most favorable: well-exposed, sharp slides and no repairs.)

A third lesson pertains to the value of individuals' experience with a product. When purchasers of the camera with the worst frequency-of-repair record (the Miranda) were questioned about their "satisfaction with their camera," 95 per cent (!) expressed "high satisfaction." [30] Our interpretation would be that camera users can discriminate very well on matters of sharpness and exposures of their pictures. But they are likely to be ignorant regarding what constitutes a "normal" frequency-of-repair rate.

What finally happened to Mr. C and his Miranda? Two years after the film advance lever was fixed, it failed again. This time Mr. C balked at doing any new repair. He quietly put away his single-lens reflex in a drawer and forgot about it. Since then he has purchased a Minolta nonreflex 35 mm. camera (again relying on *Consumer Reports)* and this time he is well pleased.

Perhaps Mr. C erred at the beginning when he attributed his failure rate on slides to himself and not the camera. Or, perhaps, he really is not a single-lens reflex person. Perhaps the simpler camera with some reduction in performance possibilities fits him better.

Deceptive Advertising: An Exercise in Inoculation. "Know thine adversary," an old saying advises. Better yet, know your adversary's weapons so that you can counter them or use them to your own advantage.

Here the subject is advertising and the weapon is the psychology of advertising. Your "guide" to the psychology of advertising is David M. Gardner, professor of marketing at the University of Illinois and a specialist on the topic. The vehicle for your introduction to the subject is a paper of Gardner's presented at a seminar on "Consumer Action Research" conducted by the International Institute of Management in Berlin in April, 1975. The paper has been edited by the author so that its terminology fits the concepts and framework of this book.

Part I of Gardner's paper explains many of the psychological principles embodied in successful advertising, whether it be deceptive or nondeceptive. In Part II, Gardner describes deceptive and nondeceptive advertising and discusses the means by which deception in advertising might be assessed.

Gardner's paper aids the reader in two important ways: 1) it pro-

[30] Ibid.

vides him with a knowledge of the psychology of advertising (and thereby perhaps aids him in not becoming its victim), and 2) acquaints him with a sophisticated concept of deception in advertising.

"DECEPTION IN ADVERTISING: A RECEIVER ORIENTED APPROACH TO UNDERSTANDING" [31]

David M. Gardner

Deception in advertising interests governments, business firms, and academics for at least two reasons. First, lying in advertising—communicating untruths—is to some degree illegal in all countries. However, in general, there is no objective standard by which a "lie" is defined. In some countries certain specific practices are spelled out as being illegal, whereas in other countries broad principles guide both the regulator and the business firm. A second reason for interest is the persistent ambiguity in the conception of "deception." Some advertisements, containing no explicit untruths whatever, may have an effect on both competition and consumers that is indistinguishable from advertisements containing explicit lies.

This paper examines deception in advertising from a behavioral perspective, seeking a definition of "deceptive advertising" that can guide both research and government regulation.

A Behavioral Perspective

The basic premise underlying the outlawing of deceptive advertising is the assumption that such advertising affects some buyers' behavior. When this occurs, free competition is hindered. The winners are the firms that deceive; the losers are the consumers who are misled and the honest firms who would otherwise have the misled as *their* customers.

Because of the difficulty of assessing the effects of advertising (whether truthful or otherwise), governments have traditionally focused on the content of the message itself: are certain words, pictures, or statements not truthful and hence deceptive? The emphasis given to the content of advertising has led quite naturally to such issues as to whether intent to deceive must be shown, and how many

[31] Reprinted with permission of the author from Folke Ölander (ed.), *Proceedings of the Conference on Consumer Action Research—II* (Berlin: International Institute of Management, 1975).

people need to be deceived for deception to exist. In those countries that have rigorously policed deception in advertising, the volume of explicit lies has been greatly reduced. But serious doubts remain. Has the rigorous policing of explicit lies solved the problem of deception in advertising? My answer is emphatically no! The excessive attention paid to the contents of advertising ignores the receiver of the communication (the advertisement). It will turn out that some advertisements containing explicit lies may *not* be deceptive to consumers whereas other advertisements that are literally true may in fact be deceptive.

It is the thesis of this paper that deception in advertising will only be properly understood when attention is focused on the receiver of the communication. Only when we assess the behavioral impact of a message on the receiver will we be able to determine in a meaningful way that a given advertisement is "deceptive." We can call certain statements "lies" without reference to the receiver of the communication, but we cannot determine if the advertisement is deceptive without knowing its behavioral impact on the receiver.

Therefore, it appears necessary to study deception in advertising within the framework of a communication theory such as that of Weaver.[32] According to Weaver, communication is a system and this fact makes the treatment of the isolated parts of the system potentially misleading. The lesson for us is that the receiver is of vital importance in understanding the message.

If we are to include the receiver of the communication in our understanding of deception in advertising, it is both necessary and appropriate to review briefly several aspects of perception. Everything we call perception is the end product of a categorization process. But in order to engage in the categorization process, receivers must first learn. They must learn the relations between properties of products, social objects, and events that are encountered or likely to be encountered. The product of learning is a series of category systems that are used to predict what properties go with what products, social objects, and events. But also, these category systems are used to check on what goes with what.[33]

These category systems are largely learned by exposure to stimuli, for example, advertisements. Krech, Crutchfield, and Ballachey suggest that these category systems are a product of each individual's

[32] Warren Weaver, "The Mathematics of Communication," *Scientific American*, Vol. 181 (1949), pp. 11–15.

[33] Jerome S. Bruner, "On Perceptual Readiness," *Psychological Review* (March 1957), p. 126.

physical and social environment, physiological structure, wants and goals, and past experiences.[34] Clearly, however, not all stimuli enter into the individual's view of the world. There are two reasons for this. First, there are factors associated with the stimuli such as figure-ground (how much the figure differs from its background), frequency of presentation, stimulus intensity (the brightness of color, the size of type used), movement and change, and the number of objects in the stimulus. Advertisers are keenly aware that it is necessary to get the attention of the receiver before the message can be categorized. For this reason they invest heavily to obtain high levels of exposure and try to build attention-getting devices into their advertisements along with factors that improve the chances that the receiver will note the aspects of the message they wish to emphasize.[35]

Personal factors constitute the second major reason why not all stimuli enter into the individual's view of the world. Factors such as the span of apprehension (that is, how much we can take into account at one time), mental set (that is, a momentary disposition to react in some preferential way), emotions, and wants operate in such a way that the number of objects that can be perceived varies from moment to moment and from individual to individual. Sometimes these personal factors cause the receiver to become selectively sensitized to stimulus objects. Sometimes, too, they distort the perception of the stimuli so that they "fit" the personal factors of a particular receiver.

These personal factors are very important to advertisers. For, as Maloney has stated,[36] "Each person's predisposition to note, understand, and accept or reject certain messages is learned. Different people have different expectations about the trustworthiness of various kinds of advertising. They have developed different kinds of knowledge and different types of feelings about the products or brands being advertised." Therefore, the advertiser is concerned that the receiver of his advertisement should respond correctly to an object to which he is sensitive or, alternatively, that any distortion of the stimuli should work to the advertiser's advantage.

In addition to the categorization process, another aspect of perception of interest to students of deception in advertising is the predictive process. Bruner refers to *predictive veridicality*.[37] This means

---

[34] David Krech, Richard Crutchfield, and Egerton Ballachey, *Individual in Society* (New York: McGraw-Hill, Inc., 1962).

[35] *Cognition Selectivity,* is the technical phrase.

[36] John C. Maloney, "Is Advertising Believability Really Important?", *Journal of Marketing* (January 1975), pp. 40–46.

[37] Bruner, op. cit., p. 126.

"simply that perceptional organization of an object or event permits one to 'go beyond' the properties of the object not yet tested. The more adequate the category systems constructed for coding environmental events in this way, the greater the predictive veridicality that results." This implies that the receiver learns a set of probabilities expressing what goes with what. As a result, the receiver of advertisement almost automatically adds to an advertised object attributes that are neither depicted nor dealt with in the advertisement. When he sees an advertisement for flour, he need not examine the flour to know its texture and basic baking properties because past experience or learning has taught him the general characteristics of all flour.[38]

In the case of advertising, we are concerned, not so much with the question of how category systems are developed but more with how these categories are *used* in the perceptive process.

A review of the literature suggests that the receiver reacts to an advertisement by engaging in the categorization process at two levels. The first consists of an evaluation of specific product information and recommendations and the second consists of some type of total impression, or "gestalt."

But in both cases the receiver is engaging in predictive veridicality. He goes beyond the information presented in the advertisement to anticipate (or predict) properties neither depicted not dealt with directly in the advertisement. This process of predictive veridicality serves as a basis for understanding, detecting, and correcting much of the deception in advertising.

So far predictive veridicality has been applied to the advertised good itself and we see that the receiver adds unadvertised properties to those properties that are advertised. But the situation is more complex, and predictive veridicality applies to other facets of advertisements. To be specific, the receiver also has expectations regarding the *set of words* used to describe the object, the *setting* in which the object is presented, the *communicator,* and/or the *sponsor* of the advertisement.

The receiver may use the literal meaning of a word or collection

---

[38] Bruner states it more formally: "Veridical perception, consists of the coding of stimulus inputs in appropriate categories such that one may go from cue to categorical identification, and thence to the correct inference or prediction of other properties of the object so categorized. Thus, veridical perception requires the learning of categories and category systems appropriate to the events and objects with which the person has commerce in the physical world. When we speak of the representative function of perception, we speak of the adequacy of the categorizing system of the individual in permitting him to infer the nature of events and to go beyond them to the correct prediction of other events." Ibid., p. 133.

of words. But he may also go beyond the literal meaning and add different meanings and expectations.

For this reason it is not the literal meaning of a word or collection of words that renders it deceptive. To determine whether a word, or collection of words, is deceptive it is necessary to understand how the receiver is categorizing them and what is being added by process of predictive veridicality. Since the categorization and predictive veridicality processes are affected by the setting in which the object is presented, the communicator, and/or the sponsor of the advertisement (the gestalt), it is necessary to take these into account in assessing deception.

Without the analysis of the categorization process at both the word and the gestalt level, and without an analysis of the resultant predictive veridicality, it is impossible to judge if, in fact, deception in advertising is taking place. Failure to undertake these analyses will result in erroneous conclusions: some advertisements that are judged "deceptive" will, in fact, be innocent of deception in a behavioral sense, whereas others that in terms of their behavior impact are deceptive will be found innocent of deception.

A Behavioral Definition of Deceptive Advertising

This background leads us to a behaviorally valid definition of deceptive advertising. The definition offered has two merits. First, it is based on the interaction of the advertisement with the categorization process of the receiver. Second, it is operational; that is, it can be used in practice for the detection and avoidance of deception in advertising.

The definition, first offered by Gardner: [39]

An advertisement (or advertising campaign) is *deceptive* when both:

1. the advertisement leaves the consumer with an impression(s) and/or belief(s) different from what normally would be expected if the consumer had reasonable knowledge; and
2. the advertisement leaves the consumer with impressions and/or beliefs that are factually untrue or potentially misleading.

This definition assumes that the end product of the perception

[39] David M. Gardner, "Deception in Advertising: A Conceptual Approach," *Journal of Marketing* (January 1975), pp. 40–46.

process is the chief matter of interest. What the receiver perceives rather than what the advertisement either intended or states literally is most important. It should be clear that untrue statements are of only limited relevance to this definition.

This definition leads us at once to two major classes of deception:

1. *The Claim-Fact Discrepancy* in which the processes of categorization and predictive veridicality lead to a deceptive impression of the advertised object, as compared with the facts.
2. *The Unconscionable Lie,* in which there exists no way for receivers to achieve the claimed results, attributes, or benefits.

The following discussion and examples should clarify the meaning of these two categories.

The Claim-Fact Discrepancy. In one type of claim-fact discrepancy *the central issue is whether or not the receiver has enough accurate information* to add to that contained in the advertisement *to yield a nondeceptive impression* of whatever is advertised. Consider an advertisement of the format: "Three out of five doctors recommend . . ." For most receivers the word, *doctors,* is associated with someone who holds an M.D. degree, takes care of you when you are sick, prescribes medicine, and so on. In general, doctors are held in rather high esteem and are thought to be honest. Therefore, the advertisement that asserts that "three out of five doctors recommend" is, through the process of veridical perception, likely to add the positive view of doctors to these words and hence increase the acceptance of the recommendation. The potential for deception exists because there is no way to tell what quality of doctor made this recommendation, the circumstances under which the recommendation was made, the representativeness of the sample, or why the other 40 per cent of the doctors questioned did not join in this recommendation.

Under a second type of claim-fact discrepancy, *a correct claim* for a product *is made, but it is not clear under what circumstances the claim is correct.* For instance, the use of a certain type of oil in automobiles may increase the useful life of the vehicle, but only if used in conjunction with certain other practices and in certain types of automobiles. Deception in this instance could result if receivers tended to overlook the restriction of benefits to certain types of automobiles on which certain complementary practices were followed.

A third type of claim-fact discrepancy occurs *when a uniqueness claim is made for a particular brand that is said to contain attribute X, and X is in fact contained in all other comparable brands.* It is easy to see how veridical perception could result in the conclusion, contrary to fact, that only the advertised brand contains attribute X. Only "outside" information could prevent the receiver from falling victim to this type of deception.

The second major type of deception is The Unconscionable Lie. For this class *there exists no way by which receivers could achieve the claimed results, attributes, or benefits.* Deception of this type could occur when a communicator whom the receiver has come to trust transmits a claim that is completely false. For instance, suppose the communicator makes the factually untrue claim that a watch has 21 jewels and that the receiver accepts the claim as valid. This would be an "unconscionable lie." To fit this category, an advertisement must make a claim that is completely false.

A Research Orientation

The processes of cognitive (perceptual) categorization and veridical perception are complex. Thus, it is unlikely that answers will come easily regarding what is deception and how it is to be detected and measured. Nonetheless, enough is known about information processing by humans that tentative efforts in this direction are appropriate.

It should be clear that, in referring to deception in advertising, we are dealing primarily with attitudes. [From the discussion that follows, it becomes clear that Gardner's *attitude toward a product* is identical to the definition of the *quality of a specimen* that you encountered at the beginning of Chapter 3.] Hansen presents an excellent development of the formation of cognitive categories and the relationship of these categories to attitudes.[40] From the work of Hansen and others, it can be argued that an attitude toward a product is a function of (1) beliefs about the product, and (2) the evaluations of each such belief.

Let us assume that the perception process discussed in the previous section is appropriate. Then we can say that advertising influences the addition of attributes [Gardner's words for the "characteristics" referred to earlier in this book] making up an attitude, and their importance or weighting. Therefore, the generalized, multi-attribute model presented by Pessemier and Wilkie [41] seems appropriate as the

[40] Flemming Hansen, *Consumer Choice Behavior* (New York: The Free Press, 1972).
[41] Edgar A. Pessemier and William L. Wilkie, "Multi-Attribute Choice Theory—A Review and Analysis," Working Paper No. 372, Herman C. Krannert Graduate School of Industrial Administration, Purdue University, 1972.

basis of a detailed discussion of deception in advertising leading to a measure of deception. This model may be expressed as follows: [42]

> (1) Attitudes toward = Sum of (Importance Weights X Characteristic Scores) Product A

This type of model is widely used in studies of consumer behavior and reflects the work of Rosenberg and Fishbein.[43] The foundations of these theories suggest that attitudes are learned as part of the concept formation, or labeling process. Fishbein places his theory within the framework of behavior theory. This, in turn, allows him to hypothesize that once a concept has been learned, many new things are subsequently learned about it. This means that a consumer associates many different objects, concepts, values, or goals with the product or service (the attitude object or stimulus concept). These different objects, concepts, values, or goals associated with the concept of a particular product make up a belief system that is organized into a hierarchy of responses.[44]

Therefore, an individual's attitude toward any product or service can be seen as a function of (1) the strength or importance of his

---

[42] Maynes: The Pessemier-Wilkie "multi-attribute model" is identical to the concept of "quality" introduced in Chapter 3. The correspondences are as follows: Maynes' *quality* = Pessemier-Wilkie's *attitude* (or attitude score); Maynes' *weights* = Pessemier-Wilkie's *importance weights;* Maynes' *characteristic scores* = Pessemier-Wilkie's *attribute* or *product characteristic* (defined by them as the "consumer's belief regarding the extent to which attribute i is offered by brand j").

For those interested in the problems posed to the development of science by disciplinary boundaries, it is worth noting that Maynes' quality paper was presented in 1974–75 to three audiences (among others), heavily populated by marketers. No one recognized the identity of the Pessemier-Wilkie and Maynes models.

On the other hand, none of the economists to whom the same materials had been presented over a three- to four-year period were familiar with Pessemier-Wilkie and related papers.

[43] Milton J. Rosenberg, "Cognitive Structure and Attitudinal Affect," *Journal of Abnormal and Social Psychology,* Vol. 53, pp. 367–372; Martin Fishbein, "A Behavior Theory Approach to the Relations Between Beliefs About an Object and the Attitude Toward the Object," in M. Fishbein, ed., *Readings in Attitude Theory and Measurement* (New York: John Wiley, 1967), pp. 389–399.

[44] Fishbein elaborates on this point: "The higher the response in the hierarchy, the greater the probability that the response is associated with the stimulus concept, that is, the stronger the belief. Each of these associated responses may also be viewed as stimuli, which themselves elicit a learned mediating evaluative response. These mediating evaluative responses are viewed as summative; through the processes of mediated generalization and conditioning, this summated evaluative response becomes associated with the stimulus concept. Thus, when the concept is presented, it will elicit this summated evaluated response, that is, it will elicit this learned attitude." Op. cit., p. 394.

beliefs about the product, that is, those beliefs in his response hierarchy, and (b) the evaluation of those beliefs, that is, the evaluation of associated responses.

Applying this logic to consumers, we find that consumers learn to associate certain product attributes with a given product class and with certain brands within that class. Furthermore, individual consumers may value different product attributes in different degrees. For instance, most consumers will learn that for men's socks, the attributes of durability, construction, materials, and appearance are highly relevant. Different consumers will learn to value each of these attributes differently. The sum of these evaluations for relevant attributes represents the total affect (or feeling) associated with that product. The more positive the affect, the more positive is the attitude toward the product. Similarly, the more negative the affect, the more negative is the attitude toward the product.

To apply this logic to consumer deception, we must first recognize that most promotional strategies are designed to alter beliefs about a product and/or brand by (1) changing an existing belief, (2) introducing a new belief, or (3) making an existing belief more salient (a larger weight for that attribute) or more important (a higher characteristic score). In addition, we must be aware that the receiver of advertisements may be dealing with attributes not cited in the advertisement by either using them or "adding" them by the process of veridical perception. We repeat: it is not what the communication contains, but what the receiver does with it. Therefore, it seems probable that deception can occur in either of two ways:

1. The promotional communication influences the probability that a receiver associates a particular belief (regarding a given attribute) with a brand;
2. The promotional communication influences the weights the receiver attaches to a particular attribute.

For example, an advertisement could attempt to increase the probability of a belief about "safety" being associated with a particular brand. Or, an advertisement could seek to increase the importance assigned to a belief regarding safety.

It seems inappropriate to focus primary attention on the attitudes toward Product A (the overall quality score) because this represents a cumulative sum of products (which, in turn, equal the multiplication of weights times beliefs about the attributes). It assumes that consumers, because of deception, hold an excessively favorable attitude toward a product. Even here, it would be necessary to pinpoint the deception by showing how deception affected beliefs about specific attributes or the evaluation of these attributes.

An important assumption of the proposed research technique that follows is the classification of product attributes into two categories, (1) objective and (2) subjective.[45] Objective attributes are those that relate to design, wear, performance, guaranties, and the like. Subjective attributes relate to style, appearance, aesthetic qualities, and the like. Attributes that have typically been classified as "psychological" or "well-being" fall potentially into either classification.

This two-way classification is important because of the absolute necessity of allowing advertisers freedom in the area of *subjective* attributes. These merely influence affect (feelings), but add nothing otherwise to factual product evaluation. Advertisers should be free to introduce new subjective attributes and to work toward a more positive evaluation of existing subjective attributes.

If an objective, positively valued attribute has acquired a high probability of being associated with a specific brand when, in fact, objective evidence (1) is to the contrary, or (2) needs qualification to be true, then deception has occurred. Similarly, if consumers are persuaded to view a subjective attribute as an objective attribute, then deception has occurred.

Normative Belief Technique. Gardner has developed a "normative belief technique" as a means of operationally detecting deception in advertising.[46] As a first step, it is necessary to establish norms for attributes within product classes. This is a delicate process, beset by many problems. Within this approach, it is first necessary to identify *salient* product attributes.[47] In this task, a variety of structured and unstructured questionnaires might be used to identify product attributes that seem salient to a wide variety of users of the product. These data would be supplemented by similar information collected from

[45] [Gardner used the terms "functional" and "nonfunctional" to denote "objective" and "subjective" attributes, respectively. We altered his usage to conform to our earlier usage in Chapter 3.]

[46] David M. Gardner, "Deception in Advertising: A Conceptual Approach," *Journal of Marketing* (January 1975), pp. 40–46.

[47] As reflected in a recent paper by Wilkie and Weinreich, techniques to measure salient product attributes are in a state of flux. See William L. Wilkie, and Rolf P. Weinreich, "Effects of the Number of Attributes Included in an Attitude Model: More *Is Not* Better," Institute Paper, Institute for Research in the Behavioral, Economic and Management Sciences, Herman C. Krannert Graduate School of Industrial Administration, Purdue University (June 1972).

"experts" on this product category. The advantage of the information supplied by the experts is that it is less likely to be contaminated by consumer attitudes and expectations.

As a second step, the product attributes thus identified would be classified as objective or subjective. In carrying out this classification process, the views of both consumers and experts would be relevant.

The third step would be to establish acceptable ranges of probabilities of associating various attributes to a particular product [in our usage, "specimen"] and to establish acceptable ranges of evaluation. The reason for establishing ranges of evaluation becomes clear in the next step.

The fourth step is to show advertisements for various brands within a product class to consumers and have them (1) estimate the probability that they would associate each attribute with the particular brand being advertised and (2) give their evaluation of each attribute [that is, state the characteristic score they would assign].

Advertisements that produced probability estimates and evaluative estimates within the acceptable range for objective attributes would be deemed nondeceptive.

Using this *normative belief procedure,* an advertisement could be judged deceptive for several reasons. First, it could be judged deceptive because consumers rated the probability of an objective attribute being associated with the specimen as highly probable when, in fact, the product possesses none or insignificant levels of that attribute. Similarly, it could be judged deceptive if, either individually or collectively, objective product attributes are evaluated more positively than warranted by product class norms. This second reason is highly speculative and warrants careful research before it is accepted as a definite criterion for deception.

Consumer Impression Technique. A second method, also proposed by Gardner,[48] centers on *consumer impressions.* This is not a sophisticated technique. However, it is practical and could be implemented quickly with only a short period devoted to the development and testing of questionnaires and procedures. In this approach consumers would be shown advertisements and then asked to state, in response to carefully constructed questionnaires and data-recording procedures, what they believed the advertisement was "telling them." Some questions would be quite general. Others would be specific, for example, a question regarding whether information provided in an

[48] Gardner, op. cit.

advertisement was backed up with a safety claim. Consumer impressions gained from advertisements would be compared with both the data and claims presented in the advertisement to determine if any necessary qualifications are understood. This leads directly to a determination that an advertisement is either deceptive or nondeceptive. Roughly speaking, this corresponds to procedures currently used by many advertisers for pretesting particular advertisements.

Expectation Screening Procedure. A third approach recognizes that, cognitively, consumers exposed to an advertisement are engaged in a comparison process. At a minimum, consumers are comparing what they perceive the advertisement to be saying with expectations of what they anticipate seeing for a given product, brand, or usage combination. If norms could be developed for expectations and evaluative frames of reference, then responses to a given advertisement could be compared with norms for a given product class. If the responses to a given advertisement were significantly different from the norms, that advertisement should be singled out for a very specific and thorough investigation to determine if the total advertisement is interacting in some way with existing belief structure of consumers to produce a deceptive impact.

An Afterthought. One issue that has not been dealt with is the whole issue of selective exposure and relative attention. Any understanding or measurement of deception must take this issue into account. If the potential receiver does not expose himself or pay attention to an advertisement, it complicates many issues. As Sherif, Sherif, and Nebergal point out, responses to communications also vary with the level of involvement in the topic of the communication.[49] Undoubtedly, future research into deception in advertising will take into account these two issues—the matter of exposure/attention and involvement.

CONCLUSION

Because of the simple fact that deception is in "the eye of the beholder," deception in advertising is always going to be with us. *Some* advertisements will always be deceptive to *some* consumers.

[49] C. W. Sherif, M. Sherif, and R. E. Nebergal, *Attitude and Attitude Change: The Social Judgment-Involvement Approach* (Philadelphia: W. B. Saunders Company, 1965).

The critical questions facing governments and advertisers, therefore, are 1) how deception in advertising is to be detected and 2) what level and what kinds of deception are to be tolerated. Most important of all, this paper should have made clear that lying in advertising is too narrow to be an appropriate criterion for deception. In assessing deception in advertising, it is absolutely essential that the reactions of the receiver of the message be taken into account as the most important element in the process.

*　　*　　*　　*　　*

Deception without Lying: A Case Study. Look at Exhibit 1 and *then* answer the following questions.

1. *What interest rate does the Faithful Savings and Loan Association pay on most savings accounts?*

If you—and a "large" number of other viewers of this advertisement answered "6 per cent," then the advertisers would have achieved deception without lying. And the deception thus accomplished would be a perfect example of David Gardner's thesis that it is the *perception of an advertisement,* not the correctness of its facts, that is crucial in deciding whether an advertisement is deceptive.

If you answered, "6 per cent *for saving certificates issued in denominations of $2,500 or more and for terms of 2 years or more,* you would have been exactly right. Deception would not have been accomplished. And our exercise in inoculation may have helped.

2. *Why is the "$2,500–2 yr." qualification printed in such small type?*

Those of a more cynical or suspicious frame of mind are likely to answer that the advertiser hopes to convince receivers of this message that 6 per cent is the rate paid on *all savings accounts* and not just on a particular class of savings certificate.

Others, more trusting or more pragmatic, may answer that the advertiser simply wishes to emphasize the attractive 6 per cent rate. This goal is achieved, of course, by printing a very large "6" and a very small "$2,500–2 yr."

But the example illustrates one of Gardner's main points. To assess the deceptiveness of an advertisement itself may require an excursion into the almost impossible realm of evaluating the *intentions* of the advertisers. To Gardner, intent is irrelevant. What is required is an empirical test in which the message actually communicated is validly measured. If more than some minimum number of a sample of viewers is left with an erroneous impression of the interest rates paid on savings at the Faithful Savings and Loan, then deception has occurred.

EXHIBIT 1
DECEPTION WITHOUT LYING

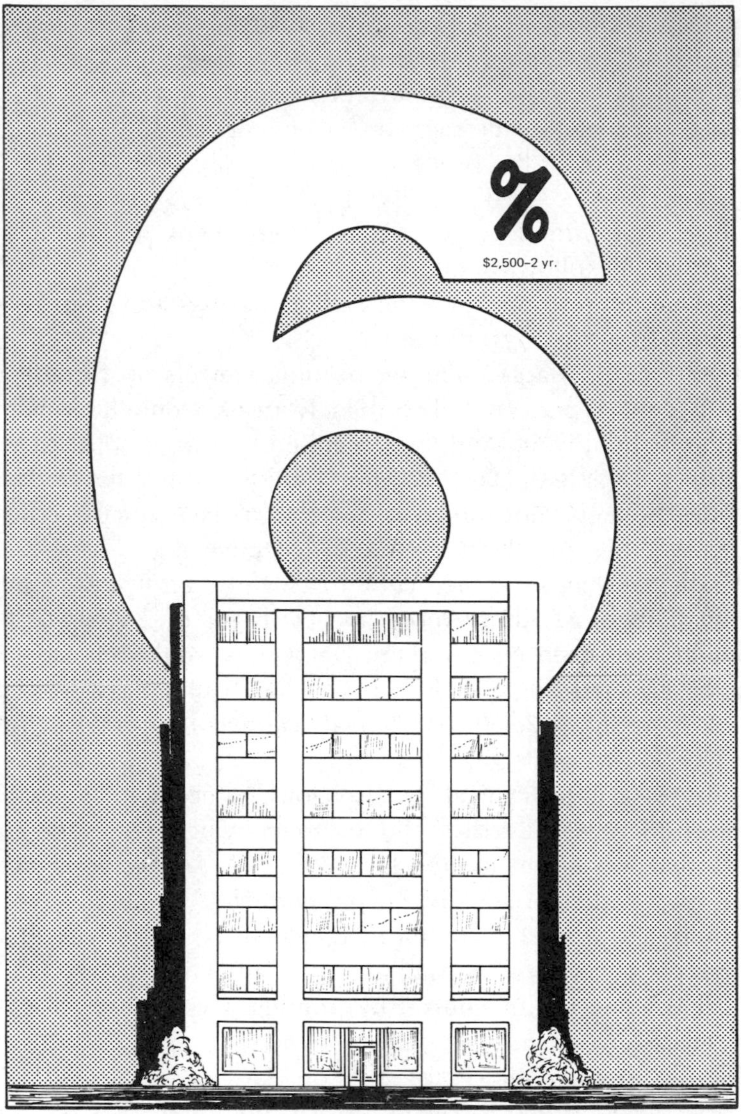

THE FAITHFUL SAVINGS AND LOAN ASSOCIATION

333 Pomfret Ave., Benevolence, California

CHAPTER 5

Product Testing and Consumers Union [1]

Two independent, nonprofit consumer product testing organizations exist: Consumers' Research, Inc., which publishes *Consumers' Research Magazine,* and Consumers Union of U.S., Inc., which publishes *Consumer Reports.* What renders these two organizations unique is their use of laboratory tests to obtain and publish *brand-by-brand* ratings of quality. But more and more, laboratory tests are not the only sources of information. The organizations also rely on controlled-use surveys to pool members' experiences with various products and services, again on a brand-by-brand basis. The surveys provide frequency-of-repair data for automobiles, washing machines, and television sets; readers' ratings of movies; factual data and reported satisfaction with new-car dealer service; records of members' experience, and satisfaction with movers.

Of the two organizations Consumers Union is by far the larger and the more influential. In 1975, *Consumer Reports* had a circulation of 2.2 million and generated an income of $16.2 million compared with a circulation of 111,000 and estimated income of $900,000 for *Consumers' Research Magazine.*[2] Consumer Union's expenditures for the generation of consumer information came to about $3.9 million

---

[1] Since this chapter deals extensively with Consumers Union, the reader is entitled to be reminded that the author has been a member of the board of directors and the executive committee of the board of Consumers Union since 1968. Neither the board nor the executive committee deal directly with the details of product testing that are reviewed here. The views expressed in this chapter are those of the author and do not necessarily reflect the opinions of Consumers Union.

[2] Sources: Consumers Union's budget estimates from *Consumer Reports,* p. 752; Consumers Union's circulation: *1975 Buying Guide Issue,* p. 447; Consumers' Research's circulation from *Consumers' Research Magazine* (November 1974), p. 35.

whereas those of Consumers' Research were commensurately smaller. Consumers Union's efforts resulted in the publication in 1974 of 545 pages of test information, derived from 108 tests of 2,031 varieties of products.[3]

In addition to product testing, both organizations publish articles providing nontest consumer information or dealing with issues of public policy that affect consumers. Examples of nontest consumer information from *Consumer Reports* include articles dealing with breast cancer, buying beef, cold remedies, the cheapest way to fly to Europe, "obsolete" diseases and why people catch them, and, for renters, how to read a lease.

Policy-type articles are exemplified by discussions of state lotteries, the economics of milk (beef, oil) production and distribution, credit reform, the safeness of public water supplies, consumer class action suits, and advertising and the Federal Communication Commission's "fairness" doctrine.

Nonetheless, for both organizations the collection and publication of brand-by-brand quality information, mainly from laboratory tests, continues to be their central function.

Because of the predominance of Consumers Union, our discussion —once we get beyond the history of product-testing organizations— focuses on it exclusively. Because of similarities in the techniques and objectives of the organizations, much (although not all) of the discussion of Consumers Union will apply to Consumers' Research. The great reliance of many consumers on Consumers Union is sufficient reason for the discussion to go beyond that required to evaluate Consumers Union as a source of consumer information.

History of Consumer Product-Testing Organizations.[4] Consumers' Research and Consumers Union are linked in a curious and revealing way. Consumers' Research was formed as a nonprofit organization in 1929 in response to the ferment created by the bestselling book, *Your Money's Worth,* by Stuart Chase and Frederick J. Schlink.[5] In this book,

[3] Author's tally.

[4] A fascinating account of Consumers' Research's first seven years is given in Sybil Schwartz, "The Genesis and Growth of the First Consumer Testing Organization" (Master's Thesis, Columbia University, 1971). For a detailed and authoritative review of product-testing organizations in the U.S. and Europe, see Hans B. and Sarah V. Thorelli, *Consumer Information Handbook*: Europe and North America (New York: Praeger, 1974).

[5] If *Your Money's Worth* is taken as the intellectual antecedent of consumer product testing, then Henry C. Harap's book, *The Education of the Consumer* (New York: Macmillan Publishing Co., Inc., 1924) may be viewed as the intellectual forerunner of consumer economics and consumer education.

the authors sought to show how difficult it was—given fraud and misrepresentation—to "get your money's worth." They also discussed possible institutional remedies. The upshot was the formation of Consumers' Research, which was organized to serve as a clearinghouse of consumer information. At the outset and to this date Schlink has remained the leading spirit in Consumers Research.

Consumers' Research grew modestly and then was caught in a crisis symptomatic of the 1930s: its employees sought to unionize, a move that was fought vigorously and successfully by Schlink. A striking result of this fight was the formation by the striking employees and their supporters of a competitive product-testing organization, Consumers Union. Since the time of the strike—1935—Consumers' Research's ill-begotten offspring, Consumers Union, has far outdistanced its "parent" both in circulation and in influence. And the gulf in both dimensions seems to be growing.

In term of control the two organizations differ greatly. Although a nonprofit organization, Consumers' Research is controlled by a self-perpetuating five-person board, two of whom are the president and his wife. By contrast, Consumers Union is guided by a 21-person board elected through a mail ballot by its subscribers. In 1974, 236,000, or about 1-in-9 subscribers, exercised their right to vote.[6] Despite the "competing biographies" nature of the mail ballot and the fact that incumbents have a heavy advantage, this voting procedure has produced a vigorous, hardworking, and independent board with a substantial annual turnover. The nature of the board and the ability of subscribers to change it constitute an important channel by which the desires of subscribers are fed back to the organization.

The increasing acceptance by individual consumers of product test results as a source of consumer information is mirrored by the increase in the circulation of *Consumers Reports,* the Consumers Union publication, since its inception:

1936	3,000
1937	40,000
1942	80,000
1947	175,000
1952	480,000
1957	780,000

[6] The 1974 vote was smaller than usual because of problems with mailing.

1962	800,000
1967	1,100,000
1972	2,200,000
1975	2,200,000

This record also signals, especially for recent years, the growth in Consumers Union's capacity to influence market practices and legislative developments. In view of Consumers Union's adversary relation to much advertising, it is ironic to note that Consumers Union's growth is linked to its "discovery" of advertising. Since 1966 between 24 and 34 per cent of Consumers Union's income has been devoted to advertising and promotion.

Socially speaking, Consumers' Research's greatest contribution has undoubtedly been to demonstrate the feasibility of conducting product tests and selling the resulting brand-by-brand quality information in a monthly publication. This idea was carried first from Consumers' Research to Consumers Union. More recently, with the technical and financial assistance of Consumers Union and other testing groups, 38 consumer product-testing organizations have been established in 32 countries.[7] All of these organizations are members of the International Organizations of Consumers Unions (IOCU), established in 1960 with headquarters in The Hague.

The Information That Consumers Union Provides. As noted earlier, Consumers Union in 1974 published 545 pages of product test information, based on 108 tests of 2,031 models. This information appeared in 11 monthly issues of *Consumer Reports,* along with about 250 pages of nontest consumer information. Much of this information is reproduced in condensed form in the 448-page annual *Buying Guide Issue,* which every member receives as the December issue of *Consumer Reports.*

The scope of Consumers Union's product information is restricted both by the limitations of product testing technology and by budget constraints. (Its 1970 budget of $13.6 *million* was minuscule as compared with the $67 *billion* [8] business spent on informing and persuading consumers, and the $616 *billion* U.S. consumers spent for all goods and services.) Briefly, Consumers Union focuses on widely purchased, nationally or regionally distributed, testable products. This means that

[7] Sources: *Consumer Review,* April, 1975, pp. 54–55, and Thorelli and Thorelli, op. cit., pp. 518–519.

[8] The assumptions for this conceptually difficult and admittedly rough estimate are spelled out in Footnote 15, Chapter 11.

a substantial fraction of the products consumers purchase are not covered by Consumers Union. Among categories that are largely excluded are the following:

1. Services. Notable exceptions: life insurance, automobile insurance, moving services.
2. Smaller local or "house" brands.
3. Nonstandard products, for example, ladies dresses or furniture. Exceptions: sofa beds, carpeting.
4. Products purchased by a small number of people, for example, musical instruments of the less common variety.

Those who enjoy ironies may take amusement from the symbiotic relationship between Consumers Union and advertising. If there were no advertising, there would be no standardized, nationally distributed brands. With no national brands, the information produced by Consumers Union would be of little help to the consumer.

The Type of Information Provided. For each set of product tests published, Consumers Union presents the following types of information:

1. *The identity of models/brands/manufacturers,* some of which the consumer may not have hitherto been aware. Consumer Union does *not* provide the address of local retailers. Indeed, *Consumer Reports* may list brands or models, which, to the frustration of its readers, are unavailable in their locale.
2. *A discussion of what characteristics are desirable* in the product tested. This is the problem of weights that we encountered in Chapter 4.

As compared with model ratings, such general information possesses a longer "life." Subscribers to *Consumer Reports* find general product information and the model ratings to be of about equal importance in leading them to renew their subscriptions.[9]

---

[9] A 1970 survey of subscribers to *Consumer Reports* identified the following as the most important reasons for continuing to subscribe:

	Per Cent Selecting:
"It tells me what to look for in a product."	31
"The test reports help me choose the specific products that are best for me."	29

Of a list of possible responses, these were the most frequently chosen. The sample consisted of 350 randomly selected subscribers. A follow-up survey confirmed that nonrespondents in the original survey did not differ appreciably from those responding. Source: Benson and Benson, "Survey of Present and Former Subscribers to Consumer Reports" (Mount Vernon, N.Y.: Unpublished Report, 1970), Table T47.

3. Information on the *extent to which particular varieties possess the desired characteristics.*

Consumers Union provides variety-specific quality information in two forms: 1) a table ranking varieties (first, second, and so on) or placing them in rating groups ("Acceptable," "Unacceptable") on the basis of their overall quality scores; 2) discussions of the desirable and undesirable properties of particular varieties of products.

The headings used by Consumer Union to designate rankings or rating groups are not standard. The following rankings are in current use: 1) "Acceptable," "Conditionally Acceptable," "Not Acceptable"; 2) Under the general heading of "Acceptable," the following were judged approximately equal in overall quality; listed in order of increasing price; 3) "Very Good," "Good to Very Good," "Good," "Fair," and so on; 4) listed, within types, in order of estimated overall quality; differences among closely ranked products were judged slight.

If justified by the quality scores in a particular set of tests, two standard accolades are awarded in the rating tables:

Check-Rated (√). In Consumers Union's words "Models are check-rated when the test samples prove to be of high overall quality and significantly superior to those of other models tested." [10]

Best Buy. This designation "is accorded to models which are not only rated high but also priced relatively low, and should give more quality per dollar than other Acceptable models." [10] In terms of our Chapter 3 discussion, "a Best Buy" would lie on or close to the perfect information frontier on its rightmost, or high-quality, side.

Consumers Union describes the test methods it employed and, in words, the weights, or importance, it assigned to each characteristic. This explanation should enable the careful reader whose weights differ from those of Consumers Union to modify, in a rough way, the ranking of particular varieties tested to suit his tastes.

As noted previously, Consumers Union has begun to experiment with the publication of overall quality scores; however, it publishes neither its weights nor its characteristic scores.

4. Rough *price* information. *List* price is usually supplied with the

---

[10] *The 1975 Buying Guide Issue, Consumer Reports* (December 1974), p. 6.

notation that discounting is widely practiced. For some products, Consumers Union publishes the range of prices its shoppers encountered. This may help the consumer estimate the possible range of discounts available to him. But the range is limited in two respects. First, it pertains to national, not local markets. Second, the price obtained by the Consumers Union shopper is not a "bargained" price.

Using Consumers Union's Product Quality Information. Should you rely on Consumers Union's model ratings or should you take the time to digest the entire article? Your answer will depend upon how well you want the variety purchased to "fit" *your* preferences. If you are particular about this, you must digest all the information to increase the chances of getting the variety that will stand your test of time. But if you prize nonshopping activities (such as working and tennis), or if past experience with Consumers Union's highly recommended models has left you highly satisfied, then the ratings should be sufficient.

In two types of circumstances Consumers Union provides no information on product characteristics that may be important to you: 1) where no valid test can be devised, for example, the durability of certain products; 2) where "tastes" are important and are likely to vary greatly from person to person.[11] In the case of omitted characteristics, the consumer should first recognize the existence of the problem. Then he is in a position to search elsewhere for the needed information. Once he has obtained it, he can perhaps "adjust" Consumers Union's ratings to compensate for the omitted characteristics.

For one omitted characteristic, durability, Consumers Union sometimes provides substitute information in the form of frequency-of-repair records. This information is useful under two assumptions: 1) that current models are substantially similar in durability to those for which data on repair frequencies were obtained, and 2) that the manufacturer has not altered his quality control program. In particular cases, Consumers Union often comments on the appropriateness of applying past frequency-of-repair records to current varieties of the product.

As noted earlier, all of the numbers in Consumers Union's quality assessments are translated into rankings, ratings, or words. The reader

[11] Where tastes are *not* expected to vary greatly from person to person—perhaps the case with rosé wine—useful information can be obtained from taste tests with panels of experts, or from surveys of consumers of the product. For an example, see "Rosé Wines," *Consumer Reports* (January 1972), pp. 52–54.

of *Consumers Reports* never—with one exception—sees any of the following numbers: the weights assigned to various characteristics, the characteristic score for a particular variety, or (and this is the possible exception) the overall quality score assigned by Consumers Union's technical staff to a particular variety.

What does this mean to the consumer of Consumers Union's testing information? If he is quantitatively apt, it means that he is receiving less precise information and fewer details than if complete numerical data were published. This assertion is based on the assumptions that 1) it is extremely difficult to match words to numbers with precision, and 2) the greater space required to describe a set of numbers verbally will prevent all details from being reported. For the quantitatively less apt, Consumers Union has performed a service by translating possibly difficult-to-comprehend numbers into more readily understandable words. For both types of consumers, however, the nonpublication of numbers implies that the consumer must accept, *on faith,* Consumers Union's delineation of rating groups as "meaningful." Except as gleaned from past favorable experience with the use of Consumers Union's ratings, the consumer has no means of knowing how "large" or how "important" the differences between rating groups are. Nonetheless, in terms of experience with its "recommendations" (on all matters, presumably), almost all subscribers have found Consumers Union to be "generally right" or "right more often than wrong." [12]

For those who plan to purchase a model highly recommended by Consumers Union, it is prudent to select several candidates from the top of the list. The reasons for making multiple selections are several. First, retail outlets in your area may not handle a particular *brand* or, if they do, they may not stock the recommended *model.* Because of limited resources, Consumers Union does not usually test

[12] A probability sample of subscribers to *Consumer Reports* was asked, "Based on your overall experience with *Consumer Reports,* how would you describe their recommendations?" The responses selected by subscribers were as follows:

Generally right	56%
Right more often than wrong	33
Wrong more often than right	..
Generally wrong	..
Not enough experience with recommendations to judge	11
Total	100%

Sample size About 350

Source: Benson and Benson, op. cit., Table T27.

all the models in a manufacturer's line, however, its Marketing Department does invest considerable effort in seeking to identify, *in advance of* the model year, those models as candidates for testing that are most likely to be purchased by consumers. In addition, models change frequently, and, unhappily, as Consumers Union proclaims, "a rating of a given model should not be considered a rating of other models of the same brand, unless noted." [13] That is to say, the quality of a "successor" model or a "sister" model may differ considerably from that tested. Again unhappily, even the trained engineer, much less an ordinary consumer, may find it difficult to try to assess intra-family differences in quality by casual examination. The older the set of ratings, the greater is the number of names you will need. If you do not need to see a model before purchasing, the telephone will afford a handy check on whether a store has the model you want.

At the point of purchase, you will need the model name and identification number. If you lack total recall and do not mind being identified as an aggressive consumer, then carry *Consumer Reports* or the annual *Buying Guide Issue* so that you have complete information on the spot. If you wish to be less conspicuous, you can carry notes with the relevant names and numbers.

The Validity and Reliability of Consumers Union's Test Information. The two questions that new acquaintances ask most frequently about Consumers Union and its ratings are: How can I be sure that Consumers Union is honest? How can I be sure that its ratings are "reliable," especially when the organization tests only one of a kind? Honesty first, then reliability.

The strongest evidence of Consumers Union's honesty is its continued existence after 40 years. The publication of brand comparisons is a legally and financially hazardous activity for the testing organization. Erroneous ratings, stemming from either dishonesty or incompetence, could result in legal damage suits, and given the vast resources of the typical billion dollar corporation, the financial contest would be lopsided indeed. Thus, in view of Consumers Union's 40-year history and several thousand product tests, the absence of any successful lawsuits against it is strong evidence indeed of both its integrity and competence. In this now fairly long history, less than 10 such suits have been initiated; no such suit has been won by a business complainant.

Consumers Union's organizational structure and policies further

[13] *The 1975 Buying Guide Issue*, op. cit., p. 5.

lead to a belief in its honesty. As mentioned earlier, its board is elected by subscribers from candidates who are carefully screened to avoid possible conflicts of interest. And, of course, subscriber-voters perform their own screening on the basis of the candidates' biographical sketches.

A number of Consumers Union's policies are designed to protect it from possible threats to its integrity. Lest there be any suspicion of bias, Consumers Union accepts no advertising. For the same reason, Consumers Union prohibits any citation of its test results by producers and sellers and invests considerable efforts in policing this policy. Consumers Union's legal right to prohibit the commercial use of its test results was upheld most recently in a 1970 court decision.[14] Similarly, Consumers Union has invested its not-inconsiderable cash reserves in low-yielding government securities rather than expose itself to any suspicion, however remote, that its interest in a particular corporation might influence its published test results.

The following challenge to its detractors has regularly appeared in the annual *Buying Guide Issue:*

> If you ever hear that any CU rating has been influenced by *anyone,* ask whoever says it to write it down and sign his or her name to it; then please send the document to us. Consumers Union takes full responsibility for the integrity of its work. We think it fair to ask anyone who impugns that integrity to assume responsibility for doing so—and the consequences.[15]

As far as the author knows, no one has ever accepted this challenge.

For whatever reasons, the overwhelming majority of subscribers believe in the incorruptibility of Consumers Union. Ninety-four per cent of its readers disagreed with the assertion that "pressure from a manufacturer can get Consumers Union to alter their test reports."[16]

We turn now to the second question posed: How can I be sure that Consumers Union's ratings are "reliable," especially when the organization often tests only a single specimen of most varieties of products? Again, the answer comes in several parts.

[14] Consumers Union versus Theodore Hamm Brewing Company, Inc., Civil No. 13600, District of Connecticut, June 29, 1970. In upholding Consumers Union's non-commercialization policy, Judge Robert C. Zampano declared: "Through the years it [Consumers Union] has been scrupulous in avoiding the slightest affiliation with any commercial interest. Its most important asset is its good name for independence and accuracy. Its reputation is the foundation upon which the public confidence rests."

[15] *The 1975 Buying Guide Issue,* p. 7.

[16] Benson and Benson, op. cit., Table T44.

In the first place, Consumers Union takes several steps to ensure that its samples are *not* unrepresentative. A first step is that samples are purchased just as the public purchases them. Were it to accept manufacturers' samples or "borrow" sample items from sellers, it is only too probable that such a sample selection process would yield a test item that was superior to the typical production item. A second step that Consumers Union takes, upon receipt of the test item, is to check to see that they conform to the manufacturer's *intentions*. Do they match the manufacturer's specifications? Are they adjusted properly? Consumers Union notes failures on either count and makes appropriate corrections. Where corrections cannot be made, a new sample is purchased. Thus, in product lines where it is appropriate, Consumers Union, in effect, operates a quality control program on the sample it tests.

But, suppose, after these steps have been taken, that the sample is still "unrepresentative?" How do Consumers Union's test engineers recognize and take account of this?

First, recall an idea discussed earlier. For many characteristics in which the consumer is interested, the extent of sample-to-sample variation is of negligible practical importance. In effect, *every* sample is "representative" of the specimen the consumer might purchase. For example, the sample-to-sample variation in the weight of the engine of the Volkswagen "Beetle" is unlikely to affect the overall conclusion that the Volkswagen is prone to turn around when it is braked on snow or ice or a curve.

A second consideration is that the primary concern of Consumers Union and consumers alike is with "big" differences. For example, the difference in gas consumption (on a standardized trip) between the 1974 Toyota Corona and the Fiat 128 4-door sedans is 24 versus 26 miles-per-gallon. Hardly anyone would judge this difference to be "important." This is not so regarding the 24 versus 31 miles-per-gallon difference between the Corona and the Datsun B-210. Happily, sampling theory assures us that the larger the difference the smaller is the size of the sample required to detect it. Unhappily, we cannot be sure that a sample of one—no matter how carefully selected—will detect all large differences. Nor can we be sure that differences of the size just cited (24 versus 31 miles-per-gallon) will be close estimates of the "typical performance" of each car. It is the consumer's destiny to be left with some uncertainty, with the knowledge that Consumers Union will occasionally be wrong, and with the hope that, as time passes and its budget grows, larger samples will become a reality.

But there exists a major factor that reduces the probability that the *interpretation* of test results will be wrong. This is the application of Consumers Union's considerable technical expertise and cumulative experience. Morris Kaplan, the technical director of Consumers Union for 25 years, stated:

> all data obtained, but particularly data obtained on small samples, should be interpreted with an awareness of the degree to which the sample is likely to be representative of the product the consumer will buy. Understanding how the product performs its functions, how it is made, the variability in performance associated with variations in manufacturing, the significance to the consumer of measured differences in performance of the product all contribute to the necessary awareness.[17]

In practice, the application of this approach works as follows. The test engineers form judgments as to whether a result is "unexpected." Before accepting an unexpected result, Consumers Union's testers will seek a theoretical explanation for the "deviant" test outcome. Suppose a test shows that an appliance inflicts an electric shock on its user under certain circumstances. Is this a fault of that particular sample item or of all of its kind? If the Consumers Union engineers can construct a satisfactory explanation of why the appliance is shock-prone, then they will accept the initial test result as being characteristic of other specimens of a particular model. If not, a second sample may be purchased and tested.

We turn now to the appropriateness of the test actually performed. Naturally, the Consumers Union test engineers seek to devise valid tests. Their cumulative experience contributes to success in this task. Nonetheless, the consumer of test information must be aware of the possibility that the test actually used may not be adequate. Consider high-fidelity speakers. An important characteristic from the listener's viewpoint is that the speaker "uniformly" reproduces sound over as wide a frequency range as possible. In the past, Consumers Union asserted that this characteristic was validly and sufficiently measured by a frequency response curve. However, some sellers of high-fidelity equipment questioned this. Without stopping to explain or to evaluate frequency-response curves, we note that the Consumers Union test of this characteristic in the past consisted of the measurement of this "family" of curves. The usefulness of its

[17] Morris Kaplan, "Sampling," *The International Consumer*, No. 415, 1966, pp. 12–14.

ratings of speakers depended upon whether Consumers Union was correct in asserting a positive relationship between a "smooth" power response curve and fidelity of sound reproduction. In more recent tests, Consumers Union adopted more stringent standards, insisting that a high quality rating depend upon *both* its frequency response curve as measured (plus a variety of other technical considerations) and the judgment of a panel of listeners. In this case there was a close correspondence between the objective laboratory measurements and the listening panel's assessment.[18] Still, there is the lesson in all this: the test must be appropriate to the characteristics evaluated.

The reader who likes to "get to the bottom of things" will ask if official Consumers Union statements exist regarding such fundamental problems as the conceptualization and measurement of quality or the validity problem just discussed. At this writing no such statements exist, and for this Consumers Union is at fault. It is also true that the several academic disciplines that should be concerned with the two problems mentioned—Economics, Human Ecology (a new name for Home Economics), Statistics, Quality Control—are only beginning to accept the intellectual challenge posed here.

The Proper Mix of Product Test Information. It is useful to ask what types of product tests will serve consumers best, even though different individuals will come up with different criteria and assign different weights to each criterion. The author suggests the following, and, in so doing, makes again a distinction between individual payoffs, where benefits accrue to the individual user of test information, and social payoffs, where benefits accrue to nonusers as well.

A. *Suggested Criteria for Individual Payoffs.*
1. *Test Information That Will Be Used.* Only when consumers use the information can there be individual payoffs. Whether readers use the information is likely to depend, in part, upon the method and quality of communication.

Where data on past usage is unavailable, it is necessary to try to anticipate likely usage. The next four criteria should be helpful in determining, in advance, which tests are most likely to be used.
2. *"Big-Ticket" Rather Than "Small-Ticket."* Purchasing a better-quality variety is a means of reducing the "true" price. The greater the money price, therefore, the greater is the payoff from information on quality.

[18] *Consumer Reports* (July 1972), pp. 417–427.

(However, big-ticket products tend to be purchased with lesser frequency. And Consumers Union faces the problem of selling a *monthly* publication. For this reason, it "seeks to try for a balance between large single-purchase items such as automobiles and smaller everyday items such as foods and household supplies." [19]

3. *Products with Greater Quality Variation.* If there is little quality variation, then the ill-informed shopper will do fairly well by concentrating on the money price. The greater the variation in quality, the greater is the payoff to product test information. An example is the single-lens reflex cameras discussed in Chapter 3.

4. *Lack of Test Information Results in Grievous Harm.* This criterion asserts that it is important to know about potentially unsafe products.

5. *Products That Are Significantly Innovative or Are So Touted.* Examples: Polaroid's color picture-on-the-spot cameras—the SX-70—and the rotary-engine Mazda automobile. Both embody significant technical advances and both were highly advertised. (Polaroid claimed that the SX-70 was "an invention so radically new, it actually changes the way we live our lives.") [20]

B. *Criteria for Social Payoffs.*

6. *Tests That Contribute to Product Improvements* as manufacturers correct deficiencies detected by testing.[21]

7. *Tests That Identify and Assess the Environmental Impact of Products.*

8. *Tests That Result in New Laws or Regulations* that in turn result in better products or the elimination of hazardous products. For example, Consumers Union's tests of children's toys probably led to new legislation that has tended to keep unsafe toys off the market.

This is the primary justification for most of Consumers Union's food-testing program.

In addition to these criteria, a product testing organization must take into account at least two other factors:

---

[19] *Consumer Reports* (November 1971), p. 689.

[20] Ibid. (May 1974), p. 380.

[21] *Business Week* commented (December 23, 1967, p. 86): "Countless manufacturers have improved their products because of a Consumers Union rating. Some examples: Clevite eliminated a shock hazard in a stereo headphone. Remington corrected a tendency for its electric knife to jam, and Westinghouse improved the design of its electric broiler. 'Smart manufacturers,' says Dr. Robert Entenberg, professor of Marketing at the University of Denver, 'use *Consumer Reports* to see if they can improve their products.' "

9. *The Cost of the Test.* Formally, Consumers Union seeks to maximize the usefulness of its test program subject to its budget constraint, $17.1 million in 1974. This condition implies that in choosing between two tests of equal "usefulness," it will select that least costly to perform.

Consumers Union can also adjust marginally by reducing the sample of varieties tested.

10. *Tests That Satisfy "Most" of Its Subscribers.* To maintain its circulation and hence its income, Consumers Union must satisfy most of its current and would-be subscribers.

Tests performed should be of use to a greater rather than a lesser fraction of its subscribers. No matter how useful tests of harps are likely to be to individuals, Consumers Union is unlikely to undertake them since few subscribers are likely to find this information useful.

Consumers Union's Selection Procedures. Consumers Union first tallies suggestions from three sources: readers' letters (4,000 per month), its annual questionnaire (a sample of 20,000), and its staff. A master list of the most popular candidates is then circulated to the relevant test divisions (Food, Appliances, Automobiles, and so on) along with information stating when a product was last tested. The head of the division then screens the candidate products, commenting in each case on 1) Consumers Union's ability to test the item, 2) how the tests fit into the division's program for the year, and 3) the usefulness of the information. The resulting division lists are then submitted to an "operations committee" consisting of the directors of Consumers Union's technical, editorial, marketing, and library departments and their key assistants. The operations committee then approves or modifies the division list. As this discussion suggests, the selection process is highly participatory.

Consumer Reports' actual product test mix is summarized in Table 1. Is it optimal or otherwise? One step toward answering this question is to ask how well it conforms to the criteria suggested previously. If it is assumed that most products in the leisure-time, automobile, major appliance, and life insurance categories are "big-ticket," then 86 per cent of *Consumer Reports'* pages and 80 per cent of Consumers Union's tests meet this criterion. Unfortunately, there is no easy means of assessing the extent to which Consumers Union's test program meets some of the other criteria listed.

Table 2 reveals how well satisfied the subscribers to *Consumer Reports* are with its existing coverage of products. On balance, most

TABLE 1

Consumers Union's Product Test Information for 1974: Distribution By Type of Product [a]

Per cent of:

Type of Product	Pages in Consumer Reports	Models Tested	No. of Tests
Automobile and Accessories:	24%	4%	13%
Automobiles	21	2	10
Accessories	3	2	3
Major Appliances (refrigerators, washing machines, room air conditioners, de-humidifiers, etc.)	11%	10%	11%
Leisure-Time Products:	37%	51%	51%
Electronics (hi-fi, TV, etc.)	7	6	10
Recreational Equipment, Sports, Outdoors	14	12	22
Photography, Photographic Equipment	4	4	4
Do-It-Yourself: Home Workshop, Gardening, Paint; Floor Coverages	12	29	15
Everyday Products:	7%	14%	11%
Foods, Beverages	3	6	4
Home, Office, Kitchen Supplies, Luggage	2	3	4
Cleaning, Soaps, Toiletries	2	5	3
Child Care, Baby Supplies, Toys, Cosmetics	0	0	0
Health-Hygiene:	1%	1%	2%
Small Appliances (mixers, irons, coffee makers, under $50)	3%	5%	3%
Clothing, Textiles, Fabrics, Footwear	1%	1%	1%
Information on Services: [b]	16%	14%	8%
Frequency of Repair	2	8	3
Life Insurance (sophisticated estimates of prices) [c]	14	6 [c]	5
Total	100%	100%	100%
Total Number of Pages, Models, or Tests	545	2,031	108

[a] Source: Author's tally of the January to November, 1974, issues of *Consumer Reports*.
[b] Counts only services for which quantitative information was published.
[c] For life insurance, each company for which policies were priced was counted once. Actually, up to 40 prices were estimated for each type of policy.

TABLE 2

Subscribers' Views on Topics Covered in Consumer Reports for 1970 [a]

A. Coverage of Different Product Classes

Product Class	Too Little	About Enough	Too Much	Total
Medical and Health Information	42%	54%	4%	100%
Clothing, Footwear, etc.	39	58	3	100%
General Consumer Information (credit, warranties, insurance how to buy, protective regulations, etc.)	35	63	2	100%
Home Furnishings (furniture, floor covering, etc.)	35	64	1	100%
Everyday Products (detergents, polishes, foods, room deodorants, etc.)	33	60	7	100%
Leisure-Time Products (camera, high-fidelity, camping, sport, etc.)	18	69	13	100%
Small Appliances (mixers, irons, coffee makers, etc.)	14	83	3	100%
Major Appliances (refrigerators, washing machines, etc.)	13	86	1	100%
Automobiles	11	76	13	100%

B. Coverage of Types of Information

Type of Information	Too Little	About Enough	Too Much	Total
How to Use and Maintain Products	41%	57%	2%	100%
Price, Availability, and Discounts	33	66	1	100%
What to Look for in Selecting a Particular Model	29	71	0	100%
Product Defects and Deficiencies	22	76	2	100%
How the Test Was Conducted	14	78	8	100%
Comparative Specifications Table	12	83	5	100%
Safety Information	12	85	3	100%

[a] The question asked was: "Please indicate whether you think *Consumer Reports* devotes too much, about enough, or too little attention to each of the following types of products (types of information?)" Source: Benson and Benson, op. cit., Tables T11–T19.

subscribers are satisfied with the extent of coverage in leisure time products, automobiles, and appliances. They would, however, like more coverage of medical and health information (much of it nontest), clothing-footwear, home furnishings, and everyday products.

As to *types* of information, the evidence of Part B of Table 2 suggests that subscribers are satisfied with the amount of product test information ("comparative specifications tables"), but want more general information—on the use and maintenance of products, market information (price, availability, discounts), and what characteristics are desirable or undesirable.

Another test of satisfaction is the extent to which consumers use the information provided. Here the record, as displayed in Table 3, is impressive. Except for hair shampoo (a small-ticket item), 65 to 87 per cent of subscriber-shoppers said they consulted *Consumer Reports*. Of those who purchased these products, 51 to 75 per cent reported buying a "top-rated" model.[22]

In two important ways subscribers are frustrated by Consumers Union's product test information. Thirty-six per cent complain that the "auto issue comes out too late to do you much good,"[23] whereas 65 per cent agree that "after you pick a model to buy you often can't find that model in the stores."[24] The second complaint could arise from the passage of time, sometimes considerable, since the last tests of this product. For this reason the suggestion has been repeatedly made that, for frequently purchased products, Consumers Union should produce and sell updated tests and rating charts for an additional fee. The suggestion for the publication and sale of "current, or updated ratings" has never been adopted since Consumers Union has taken the position that other "new directions" should have greater priority. This brings us to an enumeration of some new directions in which Consumers Union is moving.

New Directions. From about 1970 to 1974 the burgeoning of activity at Consumers Union matched its rapidly increasing circulation. Within Consumers Union itself a notable development was the establishment, in 1971, of a survey unit. This unit utilizes sample surveys, first, to undertake market research intended to find out what subscribers want and to test their reactions to new programs, and,

---

[22] Similar results were obtained for eight other products. They are not, however, summarized in Table 3 since sample sizes are too small to provide reliable estimates for each product separately.

[23] Benson and Benson, op. cit., Table T44.

[24] Ibid.

TABLE 3

Subscribers' Use of Consumer Reports in Shopping [a]

Product	Per Cent Who Shopped for This Item [b]	Per Cent of Shoppers Who Consulted Consumer Reports	Per Cent of Purchasers Buying "Top-Rated" Model	Other Model
New Automobile	38%	74%	[c]	[c]
Hair Shampoo	58	44	81%	19%
Color TV Set	29	87	75	25
AM/FM Radio	25	65	48	52
TV or FM Antenna	19	69	51	49
Coffee Maker	15	71	77	23
Sewing Machine	15	76	64	36
Record Changer	13	72	62	38

[a] Source: Benson and Benson, op. cit., Tables T21 and T22.

[b] Includes both purchasers and nonpurchasers.

[c] Not asked for automobiles. However, Table T20 shows that 39 per cent of purchasers indicated that Consumers Union's reports helped them "a great deal" in arriving at a decision, whereas an additional 44 per cent stated that the reports helped them "a fair amount." See Table T20, op. cit.

second, to "mine" the collective experience of member consumers. An example of the first type was a survey designed to measure the likely response of subscribers to a separate automobile publication. Frequency-of-repair data on various products—automobiles, cameras, sewing machines, television sets—are examples of the second type of surveys directed toward mining subscribers' collective experiences.

Another new development was the establishment, in 1972, of the Consumer Interests Foundation (renamed the Consumers Union Foundation in 1975). Its objective was to undertake research in the consumer interest that does *not* result in product tests of interest to individuals. It was expected that its existence would enable both subscribers and nonsubscribers alike to contribute to research in the general consumer interest. The first project undertaken by the Consumer Interest Foundation was the development of criteria for deciding whether advertising claims in the automobile industry were appropriately "substantiated." Unfortunately, the foundation's first fund-raising efforts proved monumentally unsuccessful and the foundation now lies dormant (not dead) awaiting more propitious times for another try.

A third development was the fathering, in 1972, of *Media and Consumer,* a monthly publication designed to serve as a focal point and seminal influence for consumer journalists in all the media—television, radio, and newspapers. The audience for this publication consisted mostly of journalists and consumerists. Its contents featured examples of successful consumer journalism its subcribers could emulate. As an example, an early edition featured a series of stories, developed by *The Minneapolis Star,* on the nutritive content of hamburgers and the sanitary conditions of hamburger "joints" in the Minneapolis area. Subsequently, many other media undertook their own hamburger stories. Although launched by funds provided by Consumers Union, *Media and Consumer* was controlled by its own board of consumer journalists. By early 1975, its circulation had reached 15,000 with an influence vastly exceeding its circulation.

Unfortunately, this story has an unhappy ending. In mid-1975, *Media and Consumer,* ever so close to financial self-sufficiency, went into bankruptcy and ceased to exist. Despite its untimely demise, some felt that this venture had made a long-run contribution to both the quantity and quality of consumer journalism.

Two other developments in Consumers Union merit our attention—the establishment of a Washington office and its excursion into television programming.

The Washington office, established in 1969 with a single lawyer and expanded in 1973 to five lawyers, is Consumers Union's voice in Washington. The office *seeks remedial actions* against consumer abuses (for example, airline overcharges, household moving abuses, and inadequate test standards for microwave ovens); it *petitions* government agencies for positive actions on behalf of consumers (for example, to require posting of octane ratings, to require disclosure of side effects in advertisements of over-the-counter medications); it *testifies* on consumer legislation (when invited); it *comments* on prospective government regulatory actions (again, when invited); and it *sues* on behalf of the consumer interest. One of the most attractive aspects of this enterprise, which accounts for about 1 per cent of Consumers Union's expenditures, is that its actions *could* result in the saving of lives and money many, many times the size of its budget.

Some of you, perhaps as a result of being too much caught up by outrage, the excitement of the fight, and the attention the fight receives, may overrate the benefits of such activities. You should remember that the war is won when real change occurs, not when a headline writer chalks up a victory. Consumers Union's "victory" over American Express is a case in point. As a result of an out-of-court settlement, in May, 1974, American Express, without admitting any violation of federal antitrust laws, agreed to notify merchants honoring its credit card that they *no longer were required* to charge the same price for cash and credit card purchases.[25] "Chalk up" a battle won by Consumers Union on behalf of consumers. Unhappily, a check of 20 Detroit merchants a month later showed that none were granting discounts to cash purchasers.[26] Pending further evidence, we conclude that consumers have won a battle, but not a war. The war will be won only when real change occurs, and all cash purchasers are accorded a discount as compared with credit card users.

And now we turn to television. In 1974, Consumers Union sold three-minute spot features, incorporating consumer information and advice, to more than 50 television stations commanding 25 per cent of the nation's potential television viewers. For both Consumers Union and the television stations, this experiment was a new departure. For Consumers Union it represented its first major venture beyond the printed word, opening a vast new audience, presumably less educated and less affluent than readers of *Consumer Reports*. For participating stations it represented the first time that they had passed control of news items to an outside organization, namely Consumers Union. By the end of 1975 this venture had yet to become self-sustaining financially. Nor was its future assured. But it did represent a bold move, something to be watched.

The Social Contributions of Consumers Union. Perhaps it is a sign of the times that all of Consumers Union's new departures, except for the Survey Unit, represent *social* contributions. That is, their benefits to nonsubscribers exceed by far their benefits to current subscribers, and now the large circulation and considerable prestige of Consumers Union make it possible for the product-testing program as a whole to improve the lot of nonsubscribers. As noted earlier, this improvement can occur when a bad rating by Consumers Union induces manufacturers to improve their products. It also may occur when publicity according to particularly dramatic test outcomes conveys the essential information to nonsubscribers and to government regulators, as well. Consider the case of microwave ovens when Consumers Union labeled as "Not Acceptable" all of the microwave ovens it tested and reported on in April, 1973. It did this because, in its words, "we are not convinced that they are completely safe to use." [27] The reason was possible radiation hazards. The resulting publicity conveyed this message to some nonsubscribers who might

---

25 *Consumer Reports* (June 1974), p. 432.
26 *Detroit Free Press*, May 2, 1974, p. 114.
27 *Consumer Reports* (April 1973), p. 221.

otherwise have purchased microwave ovens. Although the relevant government agencies did not accept Consumers Union's view of the matter, the discussion will probably lead to ultimately greater safety in the kitchen.

Summary. For the individual consumer, there is not the slightest doubt that an $11 subscription to *Consumer Reports* (or $27 for three years) will repay a typical purchaser of consumer goods many times over. Nor would most people doubt that nonsubscribers, too, have benefited substantially from the existence and activities of Consumers Union.

CHAPTER 6

Negotiating the Purchase

In marketing circles a generation ago, it was customary to hail the American one-price-to-all system of retailing as a great invention: it economized on the time and effort of both seller and buyer.

Whatever its merits or demerits, it is clear that in our time discounting and bargaining have eliminated the one-price system for a vast array of products. And it is also clear that multiple pricing opens up vast opportunities to consumers—for profit, or for loss. This chapter focuses on techniques of corralling these "profits" in direct buyer-seller contacts. As such, it is the natural sequel to Chapters 2 and 4. Locating new opportunities for consumer profit and assembling the necessary information are prerequisites to securing consumer profits, but in many cases such gains only materialize through direct buyer-seller negotiations.

It is useful to distinguish between discounting and bargaining.

Discounting is "the charging of a lower than 'normal' price." Usually there is a single discounted price offered uniformly to all purchasers receiving the discount. For some products discounting is so prevalent that the "normal" price, for example, a "list price," proves to be fictional.

Bargaining, by contrast, consists of "a series of concessions and counterconcessions, converging finally toward mutually agreeable terms and a sale, or resulting in an agreement that agreement is not possible."

Because bargaining is more complex and hence more interesting, we focus initially on it. Nonetheless, as we proceed, it will be apparent that some of the discussion is equally applicable to discounting.

WHEN ARE PURCHASE TERMS NEGOTIABLE?

The pooled experience of many people suggests that discounts are obtainable in the most unexpected quarters: accommodations in luxury resorts, doctors' fees, car rentals, fashionable dress shops, large department stores, apartment rentals. This suggests that, if you do not want to miss a discount, you should test the negotiability of prices widely. The question, "What discount do you offer?" is likely to uncover more discounts than the more timid question, "Do you offer discounts?" Or, if you wish to be less aggressive, you might offer, quietly, after learning the posted or quoted price, "I'd buy that for $_____." Fill the blank in with an amount about 3/4 or 4/5 of the quoted price.

Rather than casting your discount net just anywhere in the sea of goods, it may help to know where the fishing is best. The following list is suggestive:

Class of Product	Chance That Price and Other Terms Are Negotiable
Unique goods, such as a particular home or a painting	Almost always
Used items, or new purchases, involving trade-ins	Most of the time
New automobiles	Most of the time
New appliances	Most of the time
Home repairs, improvements (contracting, plumbing)	Most of the time
Professional services	Some of the time
Mail order	Almost never
Small-ticket items	Almost never

Better than a list, which is necessarily incomplete, is an understanding of the analytical principles that lie behind it. We turn now to these.

In general, there are two reasons why prices (and other purchase terms) may be negotiable: 1) sellers find it profitable to practice price discrimination, and 2) the price contains subjective elements.

Under price discrimination, you will recall, sellers find it profitable to charge different prices to different purchasers, when 1) a lower price is the only way to make a sale to a particular customer,

2) the price received covers at least the selling costs of the seller, and 3) the seller does not have to generalize the lower price to all purchasers. If this still sounds unfamiliar, the reader should retrace his steps and review pages 23–24 in Chapter 2.

Several additional comments are made here that are particularly relevant to point-of-purchase negotiations. First, not all sellers practice price discrimination eagerly. The tone and content of your discussion must convince the seller that you will be *his* customer only at a discounted price. Second, not everyone in a retail establishment has the authority to offer a discounted price. Hence, you should try to deal with someone who does possess the authority—the owner or a department head, depending upon the size of the establishment. Third, a low voice and discreet approach to the seller may get you a discount when a loud, aggressive approach will not. The reason: a seller will usually feel that less profit is forthcoming when he has to generalize discounts to many sellers. Quiet negotiations enable him to confine his discount to the informed consumer.

"Beauty is in the eye of the beholder." So, too, is the worth of unique goods. Thus, one individual on viewing a particular house may proclaim that it is worth $45,000 whereas another stoutly maintains its worth as $55,000. The absence of any standard formula by which a "true" price can be determined leaves scope for such disagreements and hence scope for negotiation as well.

And the extent of the unique goods category is greatly expanded by the fact that every used good is unique. Although the "Blue Book" (of the National Association of Dealers of Automobiles) can provide car dealers and consumers alike with average prices for used cars of a given make and vintage, the differential experiences of each car makes it impossible for everyone to arrive at a single, unique price. About 70 per cent of all new car purchases involve a trade-in.[1] And since the value of the trade-in is subject to negotiation, this means, by extension, that for 70 per cent of new car purchases, the overall price is open to negotiation.

It is worth repeating: wherever 1) sellers find it profitable to practice price discrimination, and 2) wherever a purchase involves a unique good (or trade-in), there are likely to be opportunities for the consumer to negotiate favorable terms.

[1] Lewis Mandell, et al., *1971–72 Surveys of Consumers* (Ann Arbor: Institute for Social Research, University of Michigan, 1973), Table 3–4, p. 37.

BARGAINING [2]

To Bargain or Not to Bargain. Bargaining—or seeking discounts—represents a conflict process. You are trying to advance your own interest at the expense of the seller. In cases where bargaining is not accepted as customary or where you have bargained hard and successfully, you may wind up on less friendly terms with the seller. This need not be a necessary outcome, however. Sometimes competent bargaining on the part of the consumer induces both respect and friendliness on the part of the other party. But the possibility of winding up on less friendly terms with the seller is a cost the serious bargainer must be prepared to accept.

It is also possible that bargaining leaves you uncomfortable, possibly because it conflicts with early learned notions that sellers are to be trusted, not questioned. Or, because you feel less than perfectly confident about your bargaining ability. Or, simply, because you feel vaguely that bargaining is "cheap" or "in bad taste." Malaise from any of these sources is also a cost of bargaining.

If, for you, these costs are great, then perhaps you should forego bargaining and achieve "peace of mind." The price of your peace of mind is the more favorable terms you might otherwise have achieved. But before you decide to eschew bargaining, bear four things in mind: 1) bargaining is widely practiced and widely accepted these days by individuals in widely different socioeconomic circumstances; 2) bargaining is an art that most can master; 3) the potential payoffs to successful bargaining are considerable; [3] 4) correspondingly, the negative payoffs to nonbargaining are also considerable in situations where bargaining is usual, for example, the purchase of an existing home.

The Nature of "The Game." As a starter, let us assume that the price of a new car is the only purchase term being bargained.

[2] For a humorous, anecdotal approach to bargaining, see Frank B. Gilbreth, Jr., *Innside Nantucket* (New York: Thomas Y. Crowell Company, 1954). The author and his wife, seeking to purchase a New England summer "inn" match wits with shrewd small town real-estate brokers and bankers.

[3] In a small city in the Southeast, owners or managers of 86 per cent of all home appliance stores acknowledged that they charged different prices to different customers for identical items. For one-third of the sample stores, owners reported the maximum difference in price as 30 per cent or more. Almost one-half of the firms charging different prices cited the "bargaining strength and knowledge of customers" as the primary reason for offering a lower price. See Walter J. Primeaux, Jr., "The Effect of Consumer Knowledge and Bargaining Strength on Final Selling Price: A Case Study," *Journal of Business* (October 1970), pp. 419–426.

At the outset of bargaining, both buyer and seller are assumed to have in mind a range of acceptable prices, such as those depicted as follows:

Seller's
Range

$4,400

4,000

3,600

Buyer's
Range

$4,000

3,600

3,200

Except for the list price of $4,400, which the seller gives in response to a direct question, neither buyer nor seller knows the other's range. From the buyer's viewpoint, the object of the game is to get the seller to reveal his entire range of acceptable prices while concealing his own—the buyer's. And, if the seller's lowest acceptable price is within the buyer's range, to purchase at that price—in the example, at $3,600. It is contrariwise for the seller. For him, total success would be a sale at $4,000. Ordinarily, neither buyer nor seller achieves total success. But this fact alters the objectives of each not one whit. Nor does it alter the nature of bargaining: what one gains, the other loses. Of course, there exist limits to gains or losses. If the final offers are not *minimally* acceptable to both parties, no final bargain will be struck.

In bargaining, beliefs matter. The seller's *beliefs* regarding the prospective actions of a potential buyer determine the actions of the seller himself. More specifically, the seller's beliefs at any point regarding the knowledgeability and determination of the buyer will be formed on the basis of his total impression of the buyer. He will take into account the buyer's demeanor, the accuracy and the depth of knowledge his discussion of the product reveals, the quickness of his arguments and observations, and his financial background as revealed by his appearance and speech. All of these aspects of the buyer will help the seller decide whether a higher price will suffice or whether he must offer a lower price.

Bargaining, though, is a dynamic process meaning that both seller and buyer may revise their beliefs regarding the other as the discussions continue. In the course of bargaining, certain moves on the part of the buyer will convey the notion that he is both knowledgeable and determined and will accept only the lowest possible price. It is to these bargaining tactics—sometimes called gambits, ploys, or strategems—that we now turn.

The Tactics of Bargaining. Everything the buyer does is aimed at convincing the seller, first, that the buyer knows or will get to know the seller's entire range of acceptable prices, and, second, that the resolve of the buyer is sufficiently firm and his bargaining skills sufficiently great so that a purchase will be made only at the lowest possible price.

In bargaining, knowledgeability encompasses technical information regarding the product, knowledge of the local market including the identity of other sellers and what they offer, knowledge of a particular seller's costs, and, finally, knowledge of the techniques of bargaining.

Technical knowledge of a product may be firsthand or secondhand. Some of us, because of our hobbies, may be auto buffs, high-fidelity fans, or the like. The knowledge we personally possess will save us in bargaining from accepting the substitution of an inferior brand, or variant, for a superior brand, or a higher-priced variant that we really do not want for the lower-priced variant we do. But for most of us, reliance must be placed on some outside source—*Consumer Reports,* a knowledgeable acquaintance or friend, or a professional—an auto mechanic, a house appraiser. It makes sense to let the seller know somehow—by carrying *Consumers Reports* or by conversation—that you are either personally knowledgeable or will rely, or have relied, upon some expert source.

By all means let the seller know that you are aware of competitive brands and competitive dealers. You may wish to tell the seller that you plan to contact other dealers—if you have not already done so. If you have other price bids in hand, you may wish to tell the seller that these are the prices he has to *beat.* You would not accept the *same* price from the seller to whom you are now speaking. (After all, the dealer you visited first was very helpful, and spent a lot of time with you.)

But bear in mind that individual responses to bargaining tactics are not uniform. Indeed, it is this factor that makes bargaining an art rather than a science. The approach of "bidding one seller off against another" could produce a strongly negative response. The seller may feel "used" and react by refusing to deal at all. The verbal and non-verbal reactions of the seller to each bargaining move should help guide you in deciding on your further moves.

We now come to the question of the accuracy of information. In bargaining, as in poker, bluffing is commonly accepted. *Bluffing*,[4] as most of us know, consists of "the proffering of false information about present possibilities or future intentions." In terms of what we have just discussed, the buyer may assert—falsely—that Seller X (a different seller) will sell him the particular automobile in question for $3,900, a figure $100 less than X's actual offer. If the bluff is successful, the seller to whom the bluff was addressed will offer a price of $3,900 or lower. (If the bluff is not successful, the buyer may have to be prepared to rationalize his acceptance of the $4,000 figure!) On the other hand, if the seller finds this price not credible, he may tell the buyer this and advise that he buy from X. Remember that a bluff of this sort is potentially less embarrassing if you already have a moderately acceptable price in hand.

Bluffs, of course, are no monopoly of the buyer. A common seller's gambit is to tell the potential buyer that *this* (favorable) *price* or *this particular car* (specific body type, engine) will not be available "tomorrow" or "next week" or "next month" and that purchase today is necessary. Usually—but not invariably—this is a bluff. The buyer's defense against the bluff consists of common-sense inference as to whether the seller's supporting arguments are plausible. (For example, in July in a high-demand year, it is plausible that a particular car model will be unobtainable later, because of the imminent end of the model year.)

Accurate information on the seller's wholesale costs gives the buyer a good notion of the region in which the seller's lowest acceptable price will be found. In the case of cars, *Edmund's 1975 Car Prices,* cited in Chapter 2, gives wholesale prices for new cars whereas the *NADA Used Car Guide* gives both average wholesale and retail prices for used cars. But the information on new car wholesale prices is never wholly reliable as a guide: manufacturers may grant discounts at the end of model years, or conduct contests for salesmen that lead dealers to sell cars at less than normal prices. The alert buyer will thus always "test" for the possibility of lower prices.

The mutual testing of wills by both seller and buyer is a central feature of bargaining. There are several things the buyer can do to convey the idea to the seller that he will hold out for the lowest price. First, he should display just enough enthusiasm for the product to maintain the salesman's interest and to show he is 'serious" about buying. No more. Second, he must wait—patiently. Long pauses are

[4] See pp. 160–161 for a discussion of "Ethics and Bluffing."

characteristic of competent bargaining. Impatience is usually a signal to the seller that the buyer will pay more.

But perhaps the ultimate test of a price is the walkout. When the potential customer moves toward and out the door, the seller may accept this as conclusive evidence that a lower price must be offered if the sale is to be made.

As in other phases of bargaining, it is the quality of the acting that is crucial. The words, the form of the "leavetaking," and other matters may vary from person to person. But to be effective, the performance must "ring true."

The walkout ploy is not without possible awkwardness. If the seller calls the retreating customer back and offers him a better price, there is no problem. The walkout has succeeded.

But when the walkout establishes, with a high degree of confidence, that the seller's lowest price has been reached at the previous stage, retreat to the previous price offer may be somwhat awkward. The buyer may feel that he has to work out a plausible reason for returning and accepting a price that he had said before was "unacceptable." Or, substantively, the seller may (correctly) interpret the buyer's return as evidence of a willingness to pay more, and withdraw his (seller's) last offer.

Should the buyer give the seller his name and telephone number? To do so facilitates renewal of contract after a walkout. On the other hand, it may reveal a stronger interest in the seller's product than the buyer would prefer to disclose. Then, too, it probably lengthens the time required for a walkout to establish the seller's lowest price.

In general, the length of a walkout necessary to establish the seller's lowest price will vary. Usually, the smaller the price of the good, the shorter is the required walkout. And the reverse is true. In the case of houses, days and possibly even weeks may be needed.

Bargaining: Unique Goods. Some goods are truly unique—greatly different in important respects from all others. Paintings or particular houses come to mind. To a much lesser degree, used items of any product are unique to a degree. Your five-year-old Chevrolet station wagon will resemble others of the same vintage and type in specifications, but its condition may differ because of the particular pattern of use and care to which you have subjected it.

Truly unique goods pose greater opportunities and greater hazards for the bargainer. In contrast with nonunique goods, the price cannot be reached by a well-defined process such as adding a given percentage markup to a known (and given) wholesale price. Instead, *both* seller and buyer must grope for an unknown subjective price.

With regard to a house—and some other items as well, such as a boat, the buyer can command outside help from a professional house or boat appraiser. The house appraiser aids the purchaser in several ways. Most obviously, he provides the purchaser with an estimate of the market value, reckoned by the conventional (though deficient) methods that other appraisers and lending institutions apply. Equally important, the real-estate appraiser provides a mass of bargaining arguments for the would-be purchaser: prices paid in recent neighborhood sales of similar houses, information on taxes, a critical appraisal of the structure including weaknesses and likely repairs, plus an evaluation of the neighborhood. All this the buyer can use to intimate that the house is worth much less than the asking price. At the same time, there is no need for the buyer to reveal the appraiser's estimate of value to the seller. Since the buyer paid for it, the estimate is his property. And he can imply—perhaps a bluff—that his low bid reflects the result of the appraiser's investigation.

The hazard of "hard" bargaining for unique goods is that in making a low bid—that is, testing for the seller's lowest acceptable price—the unique good in which you are interested may be sold out from under you. You can avoid this untoward outcome by being sure that the seller knows where you can be found. Or, to the same end, you can inform the seller that before selling it to anyone else, he should contact you. There are costs to these hedges. Both moves, the second more than the first, reveal to the seller a greater interest on your part than you may like to disclose. You have traded off some of your bargaining strength in order to reduce the chance of losing something you really want.

When Not to Bargain. Although the prices of all unique goods are, in principle, bargainable, occasions arise when it is appropriate to buy at once and forswear bargaining. Such would be the occasion when a seller, through error or for personal reasons, offers a unique good on terms that are so favorable that "almost any" potential buyer would recognize it as a "bargain" and snap it up. The crucial element in correctly identifying such a bargain is information. The individual possessing the background information about that class of product and the particular information about the particular item placed on sale will be in the best position to discriminate between a true bargain and a potential "lemon" (whose offer price is justifiably low). Has a house truly worth $60,000 been offered for $45,000 for "innocent" reasons—an error of judgment by the seller or his agent, or the seller's urgent need for funds? Or is the price properly low—perhaps because of the discovery of an infestation of termites, news of plans for a new close-by highway, or a change in zoning? The would-be buyer must balance the costs of being wrong (and purchasing a lemon) against the possible loss of a bargain while information is being checked out. It is evident that an important consideration in purchasing such an item is the buyer's capacity to absorb a serious loss.

Price Plus Other Terms. We have thus far assumed that price was the only purchase term being negotiated. Let us change that. With regard to a car, other terms might include who is to finance a credit purchase and at what rate, whether the car purchased comes from the dealer's on-hand stock or has to be ordered, and the timing of contract signing and delivery. In the case of a house purchase, the range of terms is even greater, especially for existing houses: timing of occupancy, terms of financing (such as the possible takeover of an existing mortgage or the seller's willingness to accept a second mortgage), including items such as stoves as part of the house, and deciding who is to pay the current year's taxes.

Multiple terms greatly enrich the possibilities of gains, or losses, from bargaining. The "game," as before, is to obtain as many concessions as possible from the seller while making minimal concessions yourself. The new element is that buyer and seller will probably attach differing importance to various terms. Thus, from the buyer's viewpoint, he is out to extract maximum concessions from the sellers on the terms *he* views as most important while making, on his part, larger concessions with apparent reluctance on terms he believes less important and smaller concessions with true reluctance on terms he views as more important.

The more complex situation demands more forethought. The buyer should, as far as possible, determine beforehand what is important to him. At the same time, he should think out what terms are likely to be of greatest importance to the seller. Thus, he will be prepared to offer "sweeteners" at the appropriate time.

All of our discussion of bargaining thus far has seemed to assume that bargaining takes place in a single session. This need not be so. Indeed, it is common and useful for bargaining, especially where large sums are involved, to take place in more than a single session. Intervals between sessions give the buyer time to rethink both possibilities and tactics. Also, a long wait or walkout helps make manifest the firmness of the seller's last offer as well as telling the seller something about the resolve of the buyer.

Single-Phase "Bargaining." For those who strongly dislike bargaining, single-phase bargaining offers an alternative. In this approach, the buyer declares his distaste for bargaining and asks the seller to give his single, lowest price. Given this single bid by the seller, the buyer will then make up his mind. The case of Mr. B in Chapter 2 provided a detailed example of this ploy in practice.

The advantages of single-phase bargaining are clear; it economizes on time and effort. The disadvantages are equally clear. Since there is but one contact between buyer and seller, everything rests on the ability of the buyer to convince the seller in this single contact that he—the buyer—is knowledgeable and determined.

The Displacement of Price. The point is simple, but often forgotten: gains from adept bargaining on particular terms can be frittered away by inept bargaining on other terms. As a specific example, the buyer may bargain well and successfully on the price of the "basic" car, but then give up much of his gain by purchasing accessories at list price. Or, alternatively, suppose the entire purchase price is well-bargained, but the buyer accepts the dealer's first-proffered (and costly) arrangements for financing. The lesson to be learned from this is that bargaining should take into account all aspects of a purchase transaction.

The Contract That Binds. In examinations students are usually warned: "Read the questions carefully!" Invariably, some fail to do so, and, instead of answering the questions actually asked, they provide answers for questions they believe the professor *should* have asked. For such students, there is no recourse. They have answered the wrong question and must pay the penalty. This is also true in the case of written contracts. Consumers have been warned *ad nauseam* to read them before signing. Yet many do not, some to their later regret.

The case for reading a contract is overwhelming. In law, it is the written contract that normally binds the signatories. Knowing this and knowing too that some consumers will not wish to appear "fussy" or "unsophisticated," some sellers will write a contract that does not conform to the terms verbally agreed upon. Such a seller may word the agreement ambiguously—and thus make it difficult to enforce, or he may put down ("by mistake") incorrect terms, or he may fail to include terms actually agreed upon (again, "by mistake").

Ex post efforts by the purchaser to enforce a verbal agreement that differs from the signed, written contract are unlikely to succeed. The reasons are straightforward. First, the law of contract is greatly biased in favor of those who write the contract, almost always, the sellers.[5] Second, for most consumer transactions, the legal fees needed to achieve redress are likely by far to exceed the possible gains.[6] Third, agreements reached in bargaining are often unwitnessed, or witnessed by persons of dubious legal credibility, for example, one's spouse.

The wronged consumer does have some forces—and they are increasing—on which he can rely.[7] A "small" business heavily dependent upon advertising can sometimes be influenced through complaints to the media in which he advertises. A second source of help is the "consumer complaint" television programs and newspaper columns now conducted by many local television stations and newspapers. These programs derive their effectiveness from the fact that they can provide unfavorable publicity—a sort of "negative" advertising—for businesses that have wronged their consumers. For the same reason, the newly appearing state consumer agencies—consumer counsel offices or consumer protection divisions operated by the attorneys general of various states—can help. Finally—two traditional avenues of redress—the Better Business Bureaus and small claims courts—may be helpful, especially in the case of grievances involving "establishment" businesses or individuals.

What the foregoing discussion underlines is the great merit of prevention. It is better to be somewhat embarrassed, awkward, and perhaps fussy and see that all the gains of bargaining are accurately embodied in the written contract you sign. It is useful to remember that the professionals in bargaining—businesses, governments, institutions—are extremely circumspect about the contracts they sign, paying lavishly for lawyers to draft and check all contracts before signing. Most of these strictures on contracts apply equally to all contracts, whether they are the result of bargaining or not.

Some contracts are so complex that their full implications are evident only to lawyers. Such is the case when a house or a business is being purchased. An ounce of prevention surely calls for legal review before signing (and, in the case of the house, before signing the "earnest money" or down payment contract).

Ethics and Bluffing. As noted earlier, the proffering of false infor-

[5] For documentation on this point, see "Translating Sympathy for Deceived Consumers into Effective Programs for Protection," *University of Pennsylvania Law Review* (January 1966); also Philip G. Schrag, "Consumer Rights," *Columbia Forum* (Summer 1970).

[6] Schrag, op. cit.

[7] Means to individual consumer redress are discussed at length in Chapter 7.

mation or false intentions—bluffing—is a widely practiced and widely accepted feature of bargaining.[8] And, much more important, buyers must recognize and be prepared to deal with the fact that many sellers will use the bluff when it is advantageous for them to do so.

In deciding whether to bluff yourself, it is also worth noting that the contest between buyer and seller is usually unequal, with superior experience and knowledge as well as survival-of-the-fittest considerations being on the side of the seller.

Although dishonesty in the form of bluffing is widely accepted, there is a presumption that agreeable terms, once reached, will be honored by both buyer and seller.

Common Seller's Gambits. In medicine, knowledge of the disease is helpful in developing cures. Similarly, in bargaining, the development of counterploys is aided by familiarity with sellers' ploys. We discuss a few of those most commonly employed.

Lives there a man whose ears have not been assaulted by the salesman's insistent assertion?—"You'd better buy *now*. You won't be able to get it later at this price!" Supporting arguments are numerous: a contest (real or imagined) among salesmen, the end of a formal sale, the model's being closed out. The difficulty for the buyer is that the salesman may be right. As suggested before, the only resource for the buyer is the exercise of common sense and logical inference. It is highly likely that all prices in a large department store will rise to their "normal" level when a preannounced storewide sale ends. It is unlikely that used car prices in a particular used car lot will rise on any car "tomorrow." Given the uncertainty involved in the pricing of unique goods, a "low-priced" house may well be sold by tomorrow. The recognition of a genuine bargain is indeed a payoff to knowledgeability. Given such circumstances, it may be truly said that the knowledgeable, not the meek, will inherit the earth.

---

[8] Albert Z. Carr in a provocative article in the *Harvard Business Review* (February 1968) asserts that business ethics differ from personal ethics. Bluffing is acceptable under business "rules of the game." Not only is it proper for businessmen to bluff, but it is necessary. In Carr's own words:

Most executives from time to time are almost compelled, in the interests of their companies or themselves, to practice some form of deception when negotiating with customers, dealers, labor unions, government officials, or even other departments of their companies. By conscious misstatements, concealment of pertinent facts, or exaggeration—in short, by bluffing—they seek to persuade others to agree with them. I think it is fair to say that if the individual executive refuses to bluff from time to time . . . he is ignoring opportunities permitted under the rules and is at a heavy disadvantage in his business dealings (p. 144).

Some sellers "bait" potential buyers by advertising immensely attractive bargains, which, when the buyer appears, are no longer available for a variety of reasons. The inevitable sequel to the "bait" is the attempt to "switch" the would-be purchaser to a different model, offered on much less attractive terms. The identification of "bait" tactics should immediately result in the posting of "buyer beware" signals in the potential buyer's mind. What counts, of course, is the effective use of the buyer's time to obtain the specimen and the terms he wants, not what got him there in the first place.

It is common practice for some sellers to advertise inflated list or "normal" prices in order to convey the notion that they offer larger discounts or trade-in allowances than their competitors. What counts for buyers is not the size of the supposed discount or trade-in but the total he must pay (in addition to any trade-in) to purchase the good of his choice, and it is the reasonableness of this sum that he must evaluate.

The "low-ball" is intimately related to "baiting." Again, the salesman quotes an impossibly low price as though he is about to honor it. In the meantime the buyer becomes psychologically "hooked" on the purchase as details of the purchase are discussed and made specific—the color of the car, the upholstery. At the last moment the salesman may announce that the "manager will not allow the price" or "there was a small clerical error (of $200) in the price quotation." This is an instance where courage is important. In my judgment the buyer should demand that the original price be honored or he should walk out, taking care to inform the relevant government agency or Better Business Bureau of this seller's actions.

The Prebargained Price. Bargaining imposes heavy time-effort costs, especially on those who find it distasteful. Nonetheless, the payoffs resulting from effective bargaining are substantial. Thus, many will find it surprising that few businesses or institutions are organized to negotiate better terms than the average individual consumer could obtain on his own.

There are exceptions, but they are relatively minor. Real-estate agents often render valuable services in searching out houses and negotiating terms on behalf of their clients.[9] But usually the real-estate agent operates under instructions from his principal and not as an independent, professional bargainer. Further, since houses are non-standard items, there is no possibility that the real-estate agent can exploit the mass purchasing power of a large group of consumers.

[9] It is more usual for real-estate agents to be hired by and to work on behalf of sellers of homes rather than buyers.

Some credit unions and some cooperatives have undertaken to negotiate favorable prices from new car dealers. Mostly these efforts have been experimental or small-scale. The organization approaches a dealer and ascertains whether he is willing to sell to the organization's members at lower prices. Often the organization finds the seller willing to do so. The advantages from the seller's viewpoint are threefold: 1) this may be viewed as a peculiarly effective promotional device, yielding him new customers at low cost, 2) since the price is pre-bargained, none of the salesman's time is "wasted" on bargaining, and less salesman time is "wasted" on persons who are just "shopping around," 3) acceptance of some low-margin customers may enable him to sell to more high-margin customers. (If the dealer overfulfills his sales quota for the year, the manufacturer often grants him a rebate on overquota sales.)

Credit unions and cooperatives arranging prebargained prices must monitor two aspects of car sales—price and service. The former requires a sampling and checking of purchasers' invoices, whereas the latter can be effected by telephone or mail surveys of past purchasers. If post-purchase service is not satisfactory, then the "low" prebargained price turns out to be low in appearance only.

A number of profit-making firms advertise prebargained prices.[10] The one firm with which the author is familiar caters to unions, credit unions, and fraternal associations. It purports to sell new cars at $100 over the "dealer's wholesale costs." An investigation disclosed, in the case of this firm, that the dealer's cost it listed did not correspond to those actually paid. Hence, the $100 margin was a hoax.

The foregoing discussion may explain why no long-lived business or institution has developed to bargain collectively on behalf of the consumer. The essential problem is credibility, and here most profit-making organizations are automatically, although perhaps unjustly, suspected of a conflict of interest. Although credit unions, cooperatives, and other consumer organizations may face a lesser credibility problem, they often suffer from a lack of enterprise, imagination, or resources. Hence, to date, relatively few have ventured in this direction.

AFTER-PURCHASE EVALUATION OF THE PURCHASE

Experience from past purchases and past bargaining constitutes the lowest-cost reservoir of consumer information obtainable. A

[10] For a journalistic account of the operations of several such firms, see the *New York Times*, December 26, 1971, p. 1.

modestly discriminating review of your past buying experience may provide you with large amounts of information relating to:

Particular *brand* (a *Grumman* canoe)
Generic types (an *aluminum* canoe or boat)
A particular seller:
    Service
    Adjustments
    Financial arrangements
Your own approach to:
    Securing discounts
    Bargaining

Several examples may illuminate the possibilities of feedback from one's own experience.

In 1946, the author purchased a 17-foot Grumman lightweight aluminum canoe for $170. Over 20 years its use has yielded an enormous amount of recreational satisfaction. What is more, physical depreciation of the canoe was near-zero and repairs were negligible ($4 for two holes incurred while shooting rapids). Moreover, the financial depreciation was negative; its secondhand value exceeded the price originally paid for it.

Thus, when this canoe was stolen in 1966, the author knew at once from his experience that an *aluminum* canoe would be perfectly satisfactory and that the Grumman (which had changed little) suited him well. What is more, he knew that, except for cosmetic considerations (scratches, the sheen), a used model would be as satisfactory as a new one, and a good deal cheaper. Given the durability of such canoes, it mattered little from which dealer he purchased. Finally, casual exchanges with fellow canoeists gave him a general knowledge of used prices. Thus, when a quick want ad and telephone search of dealers revealed that one was selling a used 17-foot Grumman lightweight canoe for $185, he was able at once to recognize this as a good "deal"—especially in view of the time of year (the July 4th weekend). Personal inspection confirmed the "good" condition of the canoe. The author purchased this used canoe on the spot.

Sometimes the "message" from past experience pertains to the sellers themselves. Accumulated experience has identified for the author's family two large discounters who will permit a purchaser to return almost any merchandise without question. Similar experience has confirmed that a particular large department store will truly service appliances purchased from it up to the point where the customer is completely satisfied.

THE PRINCIPLES AT WORK—EXAMPLES OF
BARGAINING [11]

The Purchase of a Bicycle. Mr. D has cycled for many years and many miles and is knowledgeable about bicycles. The bicycle he wishes to purchase will be used by him on weekdays during the summer—to ride to work—and on weekends by his wife, carrying a child behind her. A careful consumer, Mr. D prizes the notion of "value for money."

Given this background, it takes little time for Mr. D and his wife to agree on a high-quality bicycle, a Raleigh. Mr. D's objective is to buy the Raleigh at the lowest possible price.

Of the several sellers of Raleighs in town, the Rolling Wheel Cycle Shop is the natural one to approach first. Rolling Wheel is the largest seller of Raleighs and Mr. D knows the store is reputable, having purchased bikes from it before.

At the Rolling Wheel, Mr. D talks with the chief salesman. After a discussion on the merits of alternative generator-light combinations, frame sizes, and the like, Mr. D declares that he knows exactly what he wants, and lists it. Then he tells the salesman, "I plan to go to several bicycle shops, including City—your competitor. So I want you to give me the best price you can on the whole business."

At this the salesman motions him to a side counter. "We'll see what we can do. Of course, you know, City doesn't handle Raleighs."

(The salesman was right. Mr. D's friend had told him that City has the lowest prices in town on "English bikes.") With that, the salesman wrote down the following:

Ladies 26 inch Raleigh	$71.95
less trade-in [a]	7.20
	64.75
Baby seat	8.95
Miller generator-light	6.95
Lock	1.95
Two elastic straps	1.50
	$84.10

[a] Both the salesman and Mr. D understood that the trade-in was fictitious, and that this was a covert means of giving a discount.

[11] Again, facts become quickly obsolete. The numbers here pertain to 1969. Not so the principles, which are as pertinent now as they were in 1969. Similarly, the citation of brands is intended to convey realism. Most emphatically, the mention of a particular brand does *not* constitute endorsement, either positive nor negative.

Mr. D noted that the 10 per cent discount applied to the bicycle itself, but not to the accessories, but he did not mention it. Instead, he asked the salesman: "How much time after I give you the word will the bike be ready?" The salesman: "Two days." With this, Mr. D left.

Several hours later Mr. D telephoned Rolling Wheel. (He had not visited City Bicycle.) The conversation went something like this:

Mr. D: "I looked over that price quotation you gave me. The price on the bike looked OK, but you didn't knock anything off from those high-margin accessories. Let me make a suggestion. I like 'round' numbers, like $80. The total you quoted me was $84.10. For $80 even, I'm your man."

Salesman: "I'll have to check the figures . . . [after a pause] I think I can see my way to that, $80 plus sales tax."

When Mr. D returned two days later, his new bike and bill were ready. He paid the $80 and left the shop, highly pleased. The total payoff to his bargaining was thus $11.30 on a purchase involving $80–90. The first $7.20 came easily in response to the buyer's asking for a good price and saying that he expected to look elsewhere. The second-stage payoff of $4.10 came in response to the telephone call and the positive suggestion as to what an acceptable price would be.

Tactically, the departure of Mr. D from the Rolling Wheel Cycle shop was important. It perhaps convinced the salesman that Mr. D would look and, perhaps buy, elsewhere. Similarly, Mr. D gained in credibility by phoning from his own home rather than coming to the store. Coming to the store would have revealed to the salesman too great an interest on the part of Mr. D in Rolling Wheel's Raleigh. Further, for Mr. D, the time-money cost of the phone call was trivial. This would not be so for an in-person visit to the Rolling Wheel.

Toward a New Car. Mr. and Mrs. E have done most of their "homework." They have read *Consumer Reports,* they have visited automobile showrooms, and have even driven the two models they were most interested in. As a result, they have settled on a particular make of station wagon and set of accessories that they now wish to buy. Further, Mr. and Mrs. E have some accumulated savings. Since they know that the interest rate on borrowed money is 9 or 10 per cent given their credit rating and the interest rate on saving is 5 per cent, it is cheaper to "borrow" from their savings than to finance the purchase. They are confident they have the discipline to rebuild their savings fund. Now, to purchase.

The E's decided long ago that they would buy from a "large" dealer in the "outer" downtown area. A dealer with a large sales volume, they reasoned, could afford a lower profit margin per car. Unlike the heart-of-downtown dealer, the outer area dealer would focus on sales to individuals and not on fleet or business sales. They decided to eschew the dealers who advertised the most flamboyant deals, figuring that these dealers' behavior on other points may be as doubtful as their advertising. On this, the E's may have been wrong, but the testing of the proposition could be costly.

This line of reasoning led them finally to New World Motors,[12] a large, near-downtown dealer in their quadrant of the city. They told the salesman that they had pretty much decided on the particular combination of body type, motor, transmission, and accessories they wanted. Just to be sure, they went over them again with the salesman who wrote them down. They told the dealer that they were interested in getting a good price, but also in dealing with a company that would honor its warranty. "Before we buy," Mr. E said, "we expect to get price quotations from several dealers, so give us your best price. The station wagon we're trading-in is outside." The car appraiser got into the old car, started its motor, listened for 15 seconds, got out, and wrote down a number for the salesman.

After five minutes of figuring, the salesman announced, "$2,518 plus your old car will get you the model that you want." Up to this point, there had been no talk of financing.

So Mr. E asked, "What about financing?"

The salesman replied: "We can arrange it or you can get it yourself, either way." From the neutrality of this reply, the E's concluded that this dealer did not get a rebate from the finance company.[13] Otherwise, the dealer would have been eager to arrange the financing. The cash price and time price were thus the same in this case.

Mr. E asked the salesman to write up the price formally. This the salesman did, presenting it complete with the manager's initials to Mr. E. Mr. E thanked the salesman for his consideration and told him that if the E's decided to purchase from New World, the salesman would hear from them within the week. The E's had spent an hour and a half at New World.

Crossroads Cars (another fictitious name) was the nearest dealer

---

[12] This is a fictitious name assigned to a real-life automobile dealer.

[13] Frequently, car dealers and other sellers of consumer durables will enter an arrangement with a finance company by which the durables seller shares in the profits from the financing. The arrangement is mutually advantageous. The finance company gets more business since the durables seller now has a monetary incentive to steer credit purchases in its direction. The durables dealer, if he is aiming at a standard profit per sale, can elect to take his profits from either the credit rebate or the sales of the durable good. From the consumer's viewpoint, the rebate arrangement makes it possible that the seller will offer a lower price on the car if he anticipates a credit sale.

of the same make, and it was the proximity of Crossroads that led the E's to go there next. With the salesman Mr. E was quite direct. "We know just what we want. I'll write it down for you. . . . We've already got one price quote and we'll buy from the company that gives us the lowest price. But we also want a dealer who will honor the warranty." Mr. E deliberately did not mention the price quoted by New World. He figured that if he did not know New World's quote, the Crossroads salesman might believe it to be lower than it really was.

Again, an appraiser examined the old car briefly. Then the salesman said, "We can give you what you want for $2,506 plus your old car."

Mrs. E. intervened at once: "That's exactly $12 less than the other dealer. On a $2,500 transaction, it's about the same. We might as well go back to New World. The salesman there was very nice and put in a lot of time helping us."

The Crossroads salesman took the bait: "How much would it take to switch you?"

"$100," replied Mr. E quickly.

The salesman demurred, "I'll have to talk with the sales manager."

After five minutes he returned. The manager suggested splitting the $100: Crossroads would knock an additional $75 off the price and the E's would pay $25 more." "No!" interjected Mrs. E, the more determined of the two. "It's $100 or nothing, Let's go, E."

At this the salesman backed down, "I'll talk to the manager and see what he says."

As he was about to leave, Mr. E added, "You can tell him, that with the $100 off, we'll sign up today." The manager accepted, and the E's gambit was a total success.

The salesman wrote up the sale and the E's made a down payment of $100. Since the car they were ordering would not be delivered for three weeks and since they had bargained hard on price, Mr. E was worried that the seller might try to alter the trade-in allowance when the old car was finally brought in. He accepted the salesman's assurance that this would not happen. And it did not. But Mr. E acted incorrectly. He should have insisted that a sentence be written in the contract saying that the contract was void if the trade-in was not accepted at the price stated.

For the E's the trip to Crossroads cost them 45 minutes of travel and bargaining time. This gave them a "profit" of $100 for 45 minutes' work. Assuming that the E's pay 30 per cent of taxes on additional income earned, this profit from bargaining was equal to $143 of addition income. ($143 less $43 of taxes leaves $100 for spending.)

Bargaining for a House. With a new baby due in six months, Mr. and Mrs. F knew they needed a larger house. Since they both enjoyed water sports, they wanted to be near the large lake in the center of their city. In price, they felt they could pay as much as $40,000, but would be happier at $30,000. Mrs. F, who enjoyed such things, had made a Sunday "hobby" of looking at houses near the lake.

On this particular Sunday they had both looked, fruitlessly. One last want ad listing was a house on the very fringe of their search area, well away from the lake. When they saw the house, they almost decided not to go in. It looked to them like a $45,000 house. It lay at the end of a short street with houses on only one side. On the other hand, next to the house lay a railroad spur, well-fenced off, but very real nonetheless.

Finally they entered. Several other parties were also going through the house. The neighborhood was evidently in demand and the F's were impressed by the house. Built in the 1920s, care had been lavished in its construction, as was evident in the casement windows, the copious number of electrical outlets, the tile block construction, and the coved corners and ceilings. There were four bedrooms (just right), the living room was light and spacious and had a fireplace, and the basement—though undeveloped—had possibilities. Not all was favorable: there was only one bathroom and it was old-fashioned, the kitchen could use remodeling, and there was a single rather narrow garage.

But when the F's sat in the living room, they were sold on the view. The owners were acting as their own agents in selling the house. The owners' asking price turned out to be $33,000, a number considerably less than the F's had anticipated. For perhaps an hour the F's talked with the owners, the owners extolling the virtues of the house and the location, while the F's sought to abstract relevant information. The owners were selling because the husband had been transferred to a different city. (This reassured the F's since it seemed unlikely then that they were selling because of some defect in the house or the site.) How much were their heating bills?

The owners said about $400 a year.

Taxes?

About $800.

Schools?

The relevant elementary school was almost a mile away, but was supposed to be "very good."

Was it true that a new highway would be put in about a block from the house?

"They've been talking about it for years," said the owner, "but they haven't done anything, and I don't think they will."

Were there children in the neighborhood?

Yes, next door. And it turned out that the ages of the children were right.

What was the condition of the roof? The furnace? Was there a mortgage on the house?

Yes, for $18,000 at 6½ per cent, the owners thought.

$18,000 isn't very much.

Did they know what the bank might do for a new mortgage?

The answer was "No."

The number and quality of questions as well as the length of the F's stay clearly told the owners that the F's were strongly interested. Before they left, Mr. F asked if the owners would mind if the F's had a house appraiser look at the house. The "did not mind" answer was important because it indicated to the F's that the owners were not trying to cover up something negative about the house.

At the F's home animated discussion ensued. This was, they agreed, the house they wanted. They did not need an appraiser to be quite confident that this house was a good buy at $33,000, but both felt that it might be purchased for $30,000.

If the F's thought the house was worth $33,000, how about others? At this point Mrs. F did a bit of research. Digging through a pile of discarded newspapers, Mrs. F discovered that "their" house had been advertised for the last ten Sundays. (They also decided that if they had been selling the house, they would have put in a more conspicuous ad for so nice a house.) The season, too, was on their side. Ordinarily, houses do not move fast in the middle of winter. These factors along with the owner's impending move to another city —he had been quite specific on this point—suggested that the owners might be amenable to a bid below their asking price. The F's too, would feel more comfortable with a lower price. They decided to offer $30,000. In order to keep the house from being sold out from under them, they decided they would act quickly.

Mr. F phoned the owner at midmorning on the next day. Mr. F said that the F's were seriously interested in the house. However, upon weighing their finances, they felt they could afford only $30,000. The owner said that he felt the house was definitely worth $33,000, but he would discuss the F's offer with his wife.

Later in the day the F's talked further about the house. They discovered to their dismay that neither could recall accurately the location of closets in the bedrooms. They decided that Mrs. F should telephone the owners later and ask if she could have another "look-through."

Their attention also turned to the matter of financing. With mortgages going at 7½ per cent, Mr. and Mrs. F decided that the owner's existing mortgage at $18,000 at 6½ per cent looked most attractive. In response to their questions the previous day, the owner had indicated that he would be willing to take a contract for deed [14] for $2,000 or $3,000 if it were necessary. The F's reviewed their resources —including a possible loan from Mrs. F's mother—and decided that with the latter they could raise as much as $15,000 of their own money. Added to the existing $18,000 mortgage, they would have $33,000, enough to cover the $30,000 they hoped to get it for, and still allow $3,000 or more for moving and other expenses associated with buying a new house.

The F's also pondered what concessions they might make, if necessary, to "sweeten" their offer in the eyes of the seller. One possibility was taxes. In their state the payment of property taxes lags: owners can pay their property taxes in the year after they are incurred. But when properties are transferred, all taxes due must be paid. The seller is legally responsible and usually makes the payment. The F's guessed, however, that the owner might be short of liquid funds, and that an offer to pay the taxes (some $800) might be viewed most favorably by him.

As for the F's themselves, they had the problem of selling their old home and moving if they bought the new house. In view of this, the later the time of transfer, the better it was for them. Especially since a winter move in a northern state is bound to be difficult.

That evening Mrs. F visited the house again. She checked the bedroom closets and found them sufficiently large. She checked the basement, discreetly looking for any watermarks, something that had worried her. (The presence of watermarks would suggest that the house was susceptible to seepage during the spring thaw and flooding during rainstorms.) There were none.

As she left the house, the owner's wife told her that she and her husband could not accept the F's offer of $30,000. Mrs. F explained that $30,000 was as much as they could afford, unfortunately, and left.

The F's decided to wait at least another day before making another move. The time of year—February—and the ten weeks the house had been on the market convinced them that their chances

---

[14] A *contract for deed* is a type of mortgage debt in which the title of ownership remains with the seller until the debt is fully repaid. This contrasts with the usual mortgage in which the title passes to the buyer at the time of sale.

of their losing it to another buyer were small. Another day might make their bid look better to the seller.

On Tuesday there was no contact between seller and buyer. But on Wednesday, as planned, the F's decided to try their "sweetener" on the owners. Mr. F phoned the owner, expressed the F's continued interest in the house, but also emphasized the F's feeling that they were "pushing against their financial ceiling." The F's had talked it over and decided that they could scrape enough to take over the owner's mortgage. This would make it a cash deal as far as the owner was concerned and would simplify the sale. "There is one other thing we could do that should make it more attractive for you, continued Mr. F. "We could pay the taxes due for this year. I believe you told me they run about $800." (In so offering, the F's were increasing the price they would pay by $800.) The owner said that he and his wife would consider this and let Mr. F know.

The owner called back an hour later. His message was the F's bid was accepted. The talk then turned to the "earnest money" contract. Mr. F asked, "How much do you want as down payment?" The owner mentioned $750.

Mr. F said, "Why don't we round that to $1,000?" (Given the F's success in negotiating the basic price, they felt it prudent to be generous in working out subsidiary terms. All kinds of annoyances could crop up in the transfer if the former owners felt too negatively about the terms and the buyers.)

The F's then suggested that their lawyer draw up the "earnest money" contract. "We'd want him to go over it anyway, so we might as well have him draw it up." The owners were agreeable. And this pushed both parties to remove ambiguities that might have clouded the later transfer. The lawyer urged them to make up their minds whether the stove would be left in place. (The F's decided they didn't want it.) He also wished to know when the transfer would take place. (Both parties agreed to one-and-a-half months later; they also agreed that the F's could move their things in two weeks early without paying rent.) The final contract to buy would be binding if the mortgage holder would permit the F's to assume the owner's mortgage or if the F's could arrange financing elsewhere. But if neither of these worked out, the purchase agreement would be abrogated and the F's down payment would be returned.

The verbal agreement was reached on Wednesday and the earnest money contract signed on Thursday. The F's were pleased with themselves and their new home.

The Patience That Pays Off. Again, the subject is automobiles, the central issue is the testing of wills between seller and buyer, and the lesson is that patience pays.

Mr. and Mrs. H were savvy buyers. They knew what they wanted —a certain compact with a certain set of accessories. And they had done their homework. They knew that the late Fall of 1970 was an apt time for car-buying. Demand was slack and a recession was coming on. With little money in the bank, financing was important. Investigation revealed that 10 per cent was a good rate for a new car loan. And they checked and had their creditworthiness confirmed by the biggest bank in their small town.

As to price, the H's wanted to pay no more than $125 to $150 over dealer cost. This would give the dealer what they regarded as a "fair" profit and they would not be overpaying. In addition, they expected to get 36 months' financing at 10 per cent. And they stood ready either to make a cash payment of $350 or to put $50 cash down and offer their old car as a trade-in. Some calculations showed that all this was consistent with monthly payments of about $115 per month, an amount they could afford.

With these numbers in hand they approached North American Cars and were assigned a salesman. They showed him the typed-out specifications of the car they wanted with the accessories they wanted. They told the salesman that they were aware that sometimes car dealers made their profits from the sale of the car itself and sometimes from their share of the financing. It didn't make any difference to them what the stated price was as long as the monthly payments came to $115 per month for 36 months.[15] Could he do it?

The salesman got out some thick looseleaf books, containing dealer and retailer prices for components and accessories. He listed what they wanted on the back of an envelope with the list price next to it. Then he performed some more calculations, this time on *his* pad. For $115 per month for 36 months, he announced, they could have the car they wanted, subject of course "to the approval of the manager."

---

[15] It implied that the amount they initially owed the dealer was about $3,565, subject to the errors of all manual calculations. (This was before the era of the hand-held calculator.) In addition, the dealer would receive either $350 as a cash down-payment or $50 in cash plus their old car.

The $119 monthly payment cited on page 174 corresponds to an initial amount owed of about $3,690.

The H's were unusual in their knowledge of loan payment tables and in their desire to bargain in terms of monthly payments. They thought that this mode identified them as financially knowledgeable consumers. And it probably did.

This was just what the H's wanted, so they were pleased. The car that they were getting was somewhat unusual. Their taste for accessories was such that the cost of the accessories would come to about one-half of the price of the car itself. (The usual is probably about one-quarter.)

They asked the salesman how long it would take for "their" car to be delivered. "About three weeks," he answered. And that was that. No papers were signed. But—looking back—the H's were clear in their minds that a deal had been made.

Just about three weeks later, the salesman telephoned to tell them that their car had been shipped that day from the factory. He asked them to come in within two or three days to make the final arrangements and pick up their car.

The H's came to the salesman's office, tingling with pleasure at the idea of driving off in their new car. Their euphoria was replaced with disgust and anger when the salesman told them that he had talked with the sales manager and the manager would not accept the $115 monthly payments. He set $119 as the lowest acceptable. That, the salesman pointed out was only $4 a month more.

It took the H's only a moment to calculate that $4 a month would come to $144 over 36 months. And that was $144 they did not wish to pay. The H's were not entirely surprised by what had happened. They knew about the sales manager-won't-go-along ploy and they were determined not to be victims of it.

They told the salesman that they were disappointed that North American Cars did not keep its word. They were still ready to buy the car at the $115 per month originally agreed upon, but not for more. And with this statement they left.

Back in their living room, disappointed and angry, the H's reviewed their situation. They didn't need a car right away. Their old car would hold up for quite a while. On the other hand, North American had a car on their hands which would not be easy to sell: too many extras! The thing for them to do was to wait.

And wait they did. But not for long. No more than two days had passed before the salesman from North American phoned, urging them to reconsider. Even at $119 a month, he argued, they would have a good buy. The H's were immensely gratified by this contact. The phone call told them graphically that the salesman expected to have a hard time selling "their" car. They would wait, and wait confidently, for him to offer better terms.

Over the next two weeks this scene was reenacted at two-day intervals to the accompaniment of an improvement in terms offered.

And the "message" of these encounters was the same, but stronger each time: North America was having a tough time in selling "their" car. The denouement came exactly two weeks later when the salesman called to capitulate: "I talked it over with the manager again. He says that the car is yours for $115 per month."

The upshot was that the H's went in to North American. After checking the papers with appropriate caution, they found them satisfactory and signed.

*   *   *   *   *

Mr. I also ran into the "sales manager-won't-go-along" gambit. But his case differed from the H's in several illuminating particulars. First, Mr. I was ready to purchase a car standing in the dealer's lot. Second, Mr. I had been dealing with a salesman who identified himself as the "Assistant Sales Manager."

It was the second reason that Mr. I was somewhat surprised when the salesman, after ostensibly consulting the sales manager, stated that the sales manager would not let him sell the car for the $125 above cost that Mr. I thought they had agreed upon. Instead, the manager insisted on getting $200 above cost. Mr. I's reaction was immediate: he walked out, after telling the salesman that he would only buy at the price they had agreed on. (Like the H's, he was not in urgent need of a new car at that particular time.)

In Mr. I's case there was no contact with the salesman for a week, which by chance encompassed the July 4th weekend. And then it was Mr. I who initiated contact with the opener (after identifying himself to the salesman): "Have we got anything to talk about?" Salesmen hardly ever being at a loss for words, a conversation ensued. In it Mr. I expressed the view that he had been misled by the salesman. "When you told me," he said to the salesman, "that you were the Assistant Sales Manager, I took your acceptance of my $125 offer seriously, figuring that approval by the sales manager was routine." The salesman explained that the "Assistant Sales Manager" title was nominal, given to lure him away from another automobile dealer. Then he said, "Wait a minute. I'll talk your case over with the manager." There ensued two minutes of silence before the salesman came back to the phone: "You've got yourself a deal!" And so, Mr. I, like the H's, achieved the terms he had originally been offered and the "sales-manager-won't-permit-it" gambit failed.

The lessons of these episodes? If you can, be in a position to wait! If you can, don't get yourself too emotionally attached to the object you wish to buy.

Though we cannot be sure, it is probably true that the waiting periods in these two episodes communicated important information to both sellers and buyers. They showed the sellers that these two buyers were determined, not malleable. And the lack of alternative buyers during the waiting period increasingly underlined, for the seller's benefit, the unlikelihood of finding another buyer who would buy at a higher price. In Mr. I's case, this point was reinforced by the passage of the Fourth of July weekend, traditionally a good week for automobile sales.

The waiting period was more encouraging to the H's than to Mr. I. For the H's the initiation of contacts by the seller and their frequency strongly revealed the salesman's interest in them as purchasers. Mr. I was less favored. But his action in re-establishing contact is easily justified: he had little to lose.

The overriding lesson: patience pays off.

CHAPTER 7

The Rules by Which We Decide

Imagine that you are comfortably watching television when, without warning, a voice interrupts: "A tornado is reported to have touched down at ———" (a point two miles from your home). What should you do?

Two possibilities come at once to mind: 1) Stay where you are (and hope), or 2) Go to the southwest corner of your basement. But which to do? A reasonable first reaction is to ask and answer: What is the worst possible consequence of each? The answers come quickly. Stay where you are and the tornado may take *both* your home *and* your life. Go to the basement, and the tornado may take your home, but not your life. Clearly the second is preferable. So off to the basement you go. Know it or not, your choice resulted from the application of what has been called the Minimax decision rule.

Consciously or unconsciously, all of us follow such rules to arrive at decisions. It is the task of this chapter to make sure that we understand decision rules and apply them correctly. For the most part we apply these rules informally in the case of "small" decisions and more formally in the case of "big" decisions.

The rules discussed are generally applicable. The situations in which they may be employed constitute a map of human experience: to marry a particular person or not, to buy now or search further, to major in English or physics in college, to put your savings into a savings account or a mutual fund, to join an organization or not, to commute in your own car or by bus, to vacation here or there, to become a doctor or a lawyer. Expressing the same propositions in terms of principles, decision rules may be applied equally to economic and noneconomic choices, to personal or organizational or business decisions, in situations where we are well-informed or where we are abysmally ignorant, and finally to "big" or "little" decisions (though, as suggested, the formal use of rules is most suitable to big decisions).

If you are innocent of mathematical knowledge or skills, you may view the numbers and calculations of this chapter with misgivings. Fear not! The contents of this chapter have been tested on and mastered by hundreds of the mathematically unsophisticated. On the other hand, if you are mathematically knowledgeable, and even have mastered decision theory, there still remains for you a challenge— how to apply these ideas to personal or family decision-making.

THE RULES: HOW THEY WORK

Examples sometimes teach us more effectively than a discussion of pure principles. Acting on this assumption, we follow Mr. and Mrs. J and their two teen-age children as they react to the tornado threat with which this chapter began. They have just learned from a television report that a tornado is reported to have touched down two miles from their home. The decision they must make is 1) to stay where they are in the living room, or 2) go to the basement.

For convenience, the essential "facts" of the J's decision problem are set down in Table 1. A casual glance at Table 1 reveals some unfamiliar concepts. Before we turn to the discussion of decision rules themselves, we must be clear about the meanings and sources of the numbers in the table.

Basic Concepts. Row 1 in Table 1 lists the *alternative actions* among which the J's must choose. In this case the choices are two: 1) stay where they are, or 2) go to the basement.

There is no general rule regarding the number of alternative actions to be considered. However, the J's, like most of us, avoid complexity wherever possible. So, intuitively and without formal analysis, the J's have ruled out several alternatives not listed here. After all, the consideration of more alternatives would make their decision-making more time- and effort-consuming.

Often the number of alternative actions to be considered can be reduced by being sure that you are considering *only one stage* of a choice problem *at a time*. For example, the choice presented to the J's in Table 1 of 1) staying where they are, or 2) going to the basement really represents a collapsed version of a two-stage choice problem: Stage 1: *whether* to move; Stage 2: *where* to move (assuming the J's decide that moving is appropriate).

Similarly, some actions are such "long shots" in terms of their

TABLE 1

A Tornado Threat

Background: The J family is aware that tornado-producing conditions exist in their general area. But just a moment ago they heard on their television set that a tornado funnel was observed to touch down at a lake about two miles from their home. Their choice: A) stay where they are, or B) go to the basement.

	A			B	
1. Alternative actions	Stay where they are			Go to the basement	
2. Outcomes	I	II	III	IV	V
3. Subjective probability of outcome	0.950	0.049	0.001	0.950	0.050
4. Utility:					
a. Objective component	$0	−$3,000	−$10,000	$0	−$3,000
b. Subjective component	$0	−$10,000	$-\infty$ [a]	−$25	−$5,000
5. Net utility	$0	−$13,000	$-\infty$ [a]	−$25	−$8,000

Description of Outcomes:

A Outcomes
- I — No damage, storm passes.
- II — No injuries to people; house suffers damages of $10,000 of which $7,000 is covered by insurance.
- III — An occupant of house killed; house demolished.

B Outcomes
- IV — No damage, storm passes.
- V — No injuries to people; house suffers damages of $10,000.

---

[a] Infinity—a number larger than any other you can possibly imagine is denoted by ∞. $+\infty$ ("plus infinity") would be shorthand for the most heavenly outcome imaginable. By parallel reason, minus infinity ($-\infty$) signals the worst imaginable disaster.

possibility that they can be eliminated out-of-hand without formal analysis. For example, the J's quickly dismissed the possibility of getting into their car and trying to drive out of the tornado-threatened area. They feared they might not be quick enough. What is more, they might inadvertently drive *toward* rather than away from the tornado's funnel. This is a type of action that would obviously be rejected by *any* plausible decision rule.

Possible outcomes resulting from a particular action are listed in Row 2, three outcomes for the "stay where they are" action and two for the "go to the basement" alternative.

Again, there exists no general rule regarding either the number of outcomes to be considered or the detail in which each outcome is specified. The desire to economize on time and effort will lead most people to consider only those outcomes that are different in "important" respects. Each person will have to decide for himself what differences are important.

A *probability* expresses the likelihood that a particular outcome will occur. When the television weatherman makes the statement that "tomorrow there is a 4-in-10 (or 40 per cent) chance of rain," he is expressing a probability. In what follows we assume that only the outcomes listed could occur. This means that the sum of the probabilities associated with each action will be 1.00. For example, the "stay where they are" subjective probabilities are 0.950 + 0.049 + 0.001 = 1.000. This assumption, as we presently show, simplifies our arithmetic.

Subjective probabilities (Row 3) are those assigned by the decision-maker himself. And this at once raises the question as to how the decision-maker arrives at a particular probability. The answer is that the decision-maker will draw on, in varying degrees, logical inference, personal experience, the experience of others, and formal statistical data to form a judgment as to the probability of an outcome. An example may clarify the problem. Suppose one wishes to form a judgment regarding the probability of becoming ill from drinking unboiled water from a river while on a canoe trip. In forming this judgment, it would be most helpful if someone had contacted the last 500 canoeists who had drunk unboiled water from this river, and counted the number who had become ill. But would this be enough? Of course not. It would be crucial to know the illness rate for those who *customarily* drank unboiled river water and for those who do not —in view of the possibility that partial immunity arises from repeated exposure. Further, one would need to know with considerable precision, in just what section (or sections) the drinker had sampled the river's waters, and so on.

There are other factors that would help in forming a judgment: knowledge of the sources and extent of pollution in the river, the rate at which rivers purify themselves for various water depths, rates of flow, by seasons, a knowledge of the means by which various diseases are transmitted from one victim to another. But not one of these is sufficient by itself. The lesson of the example: "judgment" is indispensable, and there exists no formula for making the judgment.

The role of experience in forming subjective probability assessments deserves comment. This is a case where the old adage, "Practice makes perfect," is not correct. What is probably more correct is a modified maxim: "Practice, *with feedback*, makes perfect." Those wagering on football games, for example, are likely to improve their success if they carefully review their past record and the presumed reasons for their success or failure. In many areas of consumer decision-making, it is impossible to learn from one's experience: events tend not to be repeated under similar circumstances.

Utility (Rows 4a, 4b, 5) is the total satisfaction associated with a particular outcome. It is convenient, for purposes of making calculations, to express utility in dollar units. When we say, as in Row 5, that the net utility of Outcome II is —$13,000 (minus $13,000), we are saying that for this individual this outcome affords as much loss of satisfaction as the loss of $13,000.

It is possible to assign utility to an outcome in a single step. But for many of us, it is probably easier to divide net utility into two parts and to assign utilities separately to the two parts. This is what has been done in Table 1.

Under Outcome II, Item 4a. represents the "objective" component—that for which dollars are actually gained or lost. Item 4a. is analogous to the "objective gross payoff" that we encountered in Chapter 2. As the description of Outcome II explains, the —$3,000 represents the $3,000 of financial losses *not* covered by insurance. This represents an actual financial loss. It is the J's best estimate of the amount they would have to pay out to restore their home.

By contrast, Item 4b. represents the *"subjective"* component of utility, which, in this case, comes to —10,000. By way of interpretation, we can say that the anguish that the J's would experience as a consequence of this outcome is equivalent to the distress that the loss of $10,000 would induce, given their financial position.

Together, the objective and subjective components sum algebraically to give us the *"net utility"* shown in Row 5—$13,000 for Outcome II.

Several lessons are embodied in this example. Whenever subjective and objective components are both present, the objective components should be assigned dollar values *first,* because dollar values for the objective components come from the real world. If this procedure is followed, the dollar equivalents of the subjective components will bear correct relationships to the objective components. In other words, the dollar values assigned will correctly indicate the extent of remorse (in this case) or satisfaction (when dollar values are positive).

In following these examples, the reader should not try to second-guess the author and say whether the values assigned to various components are "correct." Only the decision-maker himself can determine whether they are correct since they represent *his* view of the situation. Nonetheless, it may be instructive for the reader to review the reasoning behind the assignment of values in the example.

For Outcome I, both the objective and subjective components were 0. This figure implies, in the case of the objective component, that this outcome had neither dollar rewards nor dollar costs, and, for the subjective component, neither satisfaction nor dissatisfaction. (You may feel that the sigh of relief following the passing of the tornado should be followed by a sigh of relief, to be reflected in a positive subjective component. But Mr. J's satisfactions are Mr. J's, and we will accept them as such.)

This example also constitutes a first encounter with "disaster" and its symbol, $-\infty$ (minus infinity), a convenient numerical device for representing "disaster," or something so terrible that it is totally unacceptable. If, in the mind of the decision-maker, something is bad, but not *that* bad, it should be represented by a negative number smaller than minus infinity.

As the description of the outcomes indicates, the objective component for Outcomes II, III, and V consists not of the aggregate damage to the house and persons but of the net cost born by the decision-maker himself—that is, the amount of economic damage not covered by insurance. This is why the numbers are not larger.

Despite the identical objective components for Outcomes II and V, Outcome no. II has a larger subjective component than Outcome V, because when the decision-maker kept his family "where they were," he would have regretted later that he had not taken all possible precautions.

For Outcome IV, minus $25 represents the annoyance that the decision-maker felt in having to spend an hour in the basement.

We are now ready to make our acquaintance with the rules themselves.

MAXIMAX: The Optimist's Rule. The operation of the rule is straightforward.
First, list for each action the outcome with the *highest net utility.* Disregard subjective probabilities.
Second, ask which of these two outcomes has the greatest net utility. Take the action yielding the highest net utility.

Selecting data from Table 1, we can summarize the choice dictated by Maximax as follows:

Action	A	B
Outcome	I	IV
Net Utility	$0	−$25

Maximax leads us to choose Action A, as the "frame" around A indicates.

The observant person will note that Step 1 was superfluous: it would have been simpler to just scan Row 5 for the largest positive number (although in this case the "largest" number was 0). However, the two-step process helps us to decode the nickname for this rule. Maximax (from the Latin *maximum maximorum*) is a shorthand way of saying, "Choose the best-of-the-best."

Maximax is, of course, the rule of the naïve. You may recall Voltaire's character Candide,[1] who always anticipated the best (even when encountering successive disasters) in this "best of all possible worlds." Candide, although blissfully unaware of it, consistently applied the Maximax rule.

Alas! The real world is not always beneficient; less desirable outcomes do indeed occur. A rule that fails to acknowledge and take account of that fact is deficient. Therefore, with some regret, we discard Maximax.

BEST OF THE MOST PROBABLE. This rule works as follows:
First. For each action list the *most probable* outcome.
Second. Of those just listed, select the outcome with the highest net utility. Take the action associated with this outcome.

Again we extract data from Table 1 to illustrate the rule.

Action	A	B
Subjective Probability	0.950	0.950
Outcome	I	IV
Net Utility	$0	−$25

The Best of the Most Probable rule would lead to a choice of Action A.

The Best of the Most Probable is clearly an improvement over Maximax since it does take into account some of the data on subjective probabilities. However, it does not take notice of some outcomes that might actually occur. In this example no account whatsoever is taken of the fact that the tornado might touch down and destroy the

---

[1] If you are not familiar with this classic, see Voltaire (François Marie Arouet), *Candide and Other Stories,* trans. by Jean Spencer (London: Oxford University Press, 1966).

J's home and their lives as well. This omission does not imply that the Best of the Most Probable is a totally unacceptable rule. In a discussion yet to come, we see that for certain types of choice situations it may be the preferred rule.

Meanwhile we may ask ourselves whether it is a rule that we have used, though perhaps unknowingly. The author's personal answer is that this is the exact rule he and his wife have followed in determining how much life insurance they need for their family.

Minimax: The Best of the Worst. In terms of simplicity this rule matches its predecessors. To follow this decision rule:

First. For each action, list the *worst* possible outcome, that is, that with the lowest net utility.
Second. Of those just listed, select the best, that is, the one with the highest net utility. Take the action associated with this outcome.

For example, from Table 1:

Action	A	B
Outcome	III	V
Net Utility	$-\infty$	$-\$8,000$

Thus, Minimax leads to Action B.

The "decoding" of the nickname for Minimax reveals the fact that most of these rules were devised originally for application to business decisions. Thus, Minimax decodes to: "Take the action that will MINImize the MAXimum (business) loss." This is, of course, logically equivalent to Maximin, which is decoded as "Take the action that will MAXImize the MINimum business profit."

What these nicknames fail to tell us is that this rule is an appropriate recipe for disaster prevention. If one action—and only one—is viewed as "disastrous" by the decision-maker, then—regardless of subjective probabilities—the action yielding *that* outcome will *not* be chosen. In the light of this interpretation it is amusing to learn that a chain of supermarkets in Argentina has adopted "Minimax" as its name. Presumably the owners believe that potential customers like the technical sound of the name and do not realize its correct interpretation as the "best of the worst!"

As a decision rule, Minimax has two virtues: 1) it is simple and easy to apply; 2) under some circumstances it will avoid decisions that may possibly lead to disasters. More specifically, if some—not all —actions have outcomes that the decision-maker regards as disastrous, the use of the Minimax rule will keep a possibly disastrous choice from being made.

The defect of Minimax, like Maximax, is that it fails to take into account what the decision-maker believes he knows regarding the probabilities of various outcomes. Thus, although this rule will prevent the selection of a potentially disastrous outcome, it may still fail to point to the optimal choice if there remain two or more actions among which to choose.

Minimax has been identified as the pessimist's rule. The identification is correct. For Minimax gives its full attention to the worst outcomes associated with each action and pays no attention whatsoever to the best outcomes.

It is these defects in Minimax that lead economists and statisticians to recommend our next rule—the Highest Expected Value—as "best."

Highest Expected Value. This rule, too, requires two steps.

First. For each action calculate the expected value of net utility. As illustrated for the data of Table 1, the expected value is obtained by 1) for each outcome, multiplying the subjective probability by the net utility, and 2) summing these products. Specifically:

$$\text{Action A: } (0.950 \times \$0) + (0.049 \times -\$13{,}000) + (0.001 \times -\infty) = (\$0 - \$637 - \infty) = -\infty$$

$$\boxed{\text{Action B: } (0.950 \times -\$25) + (0.050 \times -\$8{,}000) = -\$23.75 - \$400 = -\$423.75}$$

Second. Take the action with the highest expected value, in this case, Action B.

Please note that $-\infty$ is a number smaller than any number of which you can conceive. Thus, it is impossible to make "minus infinity" any less.

You may observe that these calculations closely resemble those for obtaining arithmetic averages, or means. If you have done so, you are correct. The only element missing is the denominator, which is equal to the sum of the "weights,"[2] which here are the subjective probabilities. Since they sum to 1.0, they must be omitted. If you are better versed in mathematics or statistics, you will identify the calculation as an estimate of the mathematical expectation of the mean. This is also correct.

In meaning, these formulas may be interpreted as averages. Were we able to take Action A again and again under identical conditions —this is practically impossible, of course—the net payoff would be minus infinity for Action A and —$423.75 for Action B.

This interpretation underlines the great virtue of this rule in the eyes of economists and statisticians. It utilizes *all* of the information in Table 1 regarding subjective probabilities *and* net utilities. Its disadvantage is equally obvious. Most consumers find arithmetic calculation tedious and perform such calculations with a high error rate.

It is our intention to discuss the conditions under which various rules are equivalent and also to say which rule is "best" for particular choice conditions. First, however, we expose the reader to several other examples of the rules in action to show how the format may be adapted to different types of decisions.

EXAMPLES OF THE RULES AT WORK

Purchasing a House. Mr. and Mrs. K have found a house they think they want to purchase. The decision they must make is whether to buy now or to wait and consult an appraiser before taking further action.

As a first step, we accept the "facts" of this choice as given in Table 2. This will enable us to check our understanding of the mechanics of applying each rule. As before, the correct choice for each rule has been placed in a box.

---

[2] The arithmetic average of three numbers—4, 5, and 6—could be written this way:

$$\frac{(1 \times 4) + (1 \times 5) + (1 \times 6)}{3} = \frac{4 + 5 + 6}{3} = \frac{15}{3} = 5$$

The 1's in this example correspond to the subjective probabilities. In ordinary calculations we omit the 1's because they do not affect the outcome of the calculation.

In the expected value calculations in this chapter, the subjective probabilities differ so they must be introduced explicitly. Since they add to 1.0 (corresponding to the "3" in the example), the sum of the weights need not be written down explicity.

TABLE 2
Purchasing a House

Background: Mr. and Mrs. K have already located a house they would like to buy. The sellers asks $30,000. The K's choice: (a) to buy now or (b) obtain an appraisal and then decide to buy.

	A Buy Now			B Wait, Get Appraiser			
1. Alternative actions							
2. Outcomes	I	II	III	IV	V	VI	VII
3. Subjective probability	0.5	0.4	0.1	0.4	0.1	0.3	0.2
4. Utility of outcome:							
a. Expected $ saving as compared with I	$0	$0	−$5,000	$0	$0	$5,000	$0
b. Objective costs	0	0	0	−$50	−$50	−$50	−$50
c. Subjective satisfaction	$2,000	−$3,000	−$4,000	$3,000	−$10,000	$3,000	−$4,000
d. Subjective costs	0	0	0	−1,000	−1,000	−1,000	−1,000
5. Net utility (4a + 4b + 4c + 4d)	$2,000	−$3,000	−$9,000	$1,950	−$11,050	$6,950	−$5,050

Description of Outcomes:

A Outcomes

I   K gets the house for $30,000, everything works out satisfactorily.

II   K gets the house for $30,000, afterwards finds at house was overpriced and could have been purchased for $25,000; but in other respects the house is satisfactory.

III   K gets the house for $30,000, has to pay out $5,000 for repairs that the appraiser would have spotted.

B Outcomes

IV   Appraiser reports: the house is worth $30,000; K bids and gets the house; everything satisfactory.

V   Before appraiser reports, the house is purchased by someone else.

VI   Appraiser reports: the house is worth $25,000; K bids and gets it for $25,000; everything satisfactory.

VII   Appraiser reports: the house is worth $25,000; K's bid of $25,000 is not accepted. Continues search for a house.

Maximax:

Action	A	B
Outcomes	I	VI
Net utility	+$2,000	+$6,950

Maximax leads to a choice of Action B.

The Best of the Most Probable:

Action	A	B
Subjective Probability	0.5	0.4
Outcome	I	IV
Net utility	+$2,000	+$1,950

The Best of the Most Probable leads to Action A.

Minimax:

Action	A	B
Outcome	III	V
Net utility	−$9,000	−$11,050

The Minimax rule dictates the choice of Action A.

Highest Expected Value:

Action A: $(0.5 \times \$2,000) + (0.4 \times -\$3,000) +$
$(0.1 \times -\$9,000) = \$1,000 - \$1,200$
$-\$900 =$
$= -\$1,100$

Action B: $(0.4 \times \$1,950) + (0.1 \times -\$11,050) +$
$(0.3 \times \$6,950) + (0.2 \times - \$5,050)$
$= \$780 - \$1,105 + \$2,085 - \$1,010$
$= \$750$

Following the Highest Expected Value rule, we decide on Action B.

The layout of the house purchase problem in Table 2 is instructive. As compared with the layout for the tornado problem, this table presents considerably more detail, because the house purchase problem is more complicated. Like the J's in the earlier case, the K's find it easier to consider separately the objective components (items 4a. and 4b.) and the subjective components (items 4c. and 4d.) of utility. But thinking about the utilities was also eased for the K's by dealing separately with payoffs and costs. We discuss costs first.

Costs consist of that which is undergone or foregone to attain a given end. For Action A the *objective costs,* item 4b., were $0, but for Action B they include $50, the appraiser's fee. Note that the *same costs* are common to all the outcomes associated with a particular action. The reason for this is that costs are incurred at the time the action is taken: the commitment is made before any outcome is known.

The *subjective costs,* item 4d., represent the money equivalent of the expected anxiety born by the K's as a result of awaiting the appraiser's report. Stated frankly, the K's are afraid that they might lose a house that greatly attracts them. The anxiety is an unpleasant feeling and hence carries a negative sign. The $1,000 in this particular illustration is the amount the J's would be willing to pay (but do not literally pay) in order to avoid this anxiety.

And now to the payoffs (items 4a. and 4c.). The objective utility components (payoffs) are those for which there corresponds an actual dollar gain of dollar cost. To avoid unnecessary calculation, the gross objective payoff is zero unless a dollar payoff greater or less than Outcome I was anticipated. This was the case in Outcome III where the K's would incur $5,000 of unexpected expenses (a negative saving as compared with Outcome I) and in Outcome VI where, as a result of the appraisal, the J's would succeed in purchasing the house for $5,000 less than the price in Outcome I.

Item 4c., subjective satisfaction (or payoff), represents the K's expected reaction to each outcome. As the numbers reveal, the J's are most pleased—apart from the objective payoff—with Outcomes IV and VI. In both cases, Action B—waiting to consult an appraiser—turned out to be correct. The positive $3,000 figure shows how pleased the J's were. Correspondingly, the other subjective payoffs reveal less pleasure and in some cases, substantial remorse regarding the outcome. All of these are proper ingredients in arriving at a correct solution.

One might properly ask about this framework for decision: why are these particular outcomes considered? Why are not others of the infinitely large number of possibilities considered? The answer is that the K's, like most of us, value their time. They also find decision-making mildly painful. This leads them to restrict the number of alternative outcomes they consider. The outcome in Table 2 represent what in the K's judgment are the several basically different outcomes they can envision. The numbers in the table are those that they are most likely to encounter. How realistic they are will depend on their knowledge, experience, and intelligence.

Having drained this example of its lessons, we are ready to turn to an example from a quite different domain—an individual's deciding to attend college or not.

College or No? In this example, a young man, Mr. L, is making

TABLE 3
College or No?

Background: Mr. L, a high school senior at about the 50 per cent ranking in his class, is deciding whether to attend college. The choice, somewhat simplified, is between A—attending college, and B—taking a selling job now (and not attending college).

1. Alternative actions	A Attend College			B Take Job	
2. Possible outcomes	I	II	III	IV	V
3. Subjective probability	0.60	0.35	0.05	0.60	0.40
4. Utility:			Thousands of Dollars		
a. Expected real income over earning life—1969 dollars	($20,000 × 45 yrs.) $900	($15,000 × 47 yrs.) $705	($10,000 × 48 yrs.) $480	($13,000 × 50 yrs.) $650	($13,000 × 50 yrs.) $650
b. Subjective component	500	300	−100	400	−200
c. Objective costs	−16	−16	−16	0	0
d. Subjective costs	−2	−2	−2	0	0
5. Net payoff	$1,382	$987	$362	$1,050	$450

Description of Outcomes:

A Outcomes

I Completes college successfully, takes job, everything works out well..

II Completes two years of college; drops out after attaining a marginal record; gets position as computer programmer.

III Flunks in first year; takes lower-paying job than under outcome IV.

B Outcomes

IV Takes selling jobs, does well in it, and is satisfied with it.

V Takes selling job, does well in it, but is eternally dissatisfied because he knows he could have done better.

an important choice—to attend college or take a job now. Table 3 provides the facts.

Accepting the numbers as representing Mr. L's view of his own situation, we again rehearse our understanding of the mechanics. The correct choice is that in the "box."

Maximax:

	A	B
Action		
Outcome	I	IV
Net utility	$1,382	$1,050

The Best of the Most Probable:

	A	B
Action		
Outcome	I	IV
Subjective probability	0.60	0.60
Net utility	$1,382	$1,050

Minimax:

	A	B
Action		
Outcome	III	V
Net utility	$362	$450

Highest Expected Value:

Action A:
$$(0.60 \times \$1,382) + (0.35 \times \$987) + (0.05 \times \$362)$$
$$= \$829.20 + \$345.45 + \$18.10 = \$1,192.75$$

Action B:
$$(0.60 \times \$1,050) + (0.40 \times \$450) = \$630 + \$180 = \$810$$

The particulars of this example deserve some comment. Note how small the costs are as compared with the other elements of the payoff. Some decision time would have been saved and little accuracy lost had they been omitted.

Some purists will argue—and be technically correct—that the expected future income stream should have been discounted to obtain a present value. (*Present value* is defined as the sum, presently possessed, which when invested at a reasonable rate of compound interest would yield the stream of future incomes that the decision-maker expects to receive.) The present value concept reflects the important idea that a dollar possessed today is worth more than a dollar received in the future because of the fact that the presently possessed dollars begin to earn interest immediately.

A number of factors account for the failure to undertake discounting. Although tables exist in which "present values" may be looked up,[3] Mr. L—like many of us—lacks easy access to such tables and being unfamiliar with both tables and the concept fears that he will make a serious mistake in using them. Finally, since the estimates of expected income are necessarily very rough, Mr. L feels that it is inappropriate to apply refined statistical concepts to *very rough* estimates of lifetime income flows.

THE RULES AND REAL LIFE

Problems Encountered in Using the Rules. Suppose there is a "tie" where the net utilities of the outcomes being used as the basis for choice are identical. What should the decision-maker do? The first step is to review the net utilities assigned to each outcome. If, upon review, the tie continues, the solution is simple: flip a coin.

The rules presented take no account of the degree of certainty the decision-maker feels with respect to either the subjective probabilities or the utilities he has assigned. On some matters, the decision-maker may believe that his estimate of subjective probability is rather precise whereas for another outcome, his estimate may represent a wild guess. Decision rules exist that take account of the degree of certainty one attaches to subjective probabilities. Here we have chosen to exclude them on the grounds that *consumer* decision-makers will not, in practice, use rules more complicated than those already presented.

Aside from modifying the decision rule, the decision-maker saddled with a high degree of uncertainty always has the possibility of considering a new action—searching for more information. Indeed, this was precisely the possibility that was being considered in the house purchase example earlier in the chapter.

This brings us to the effect of the general knowledgeability of the decision-maker on the quality of choice-making. In general, the more knowledgeable the decision-maker, the better is the quality of decision-making. The person who is familiar with and understands the decision rules of this chapter is likely to organize the making of his choices more effectively. The person whose factual knowledge of his environment and whose capacity for forming "shrewd judgments" is greater will utilize subjective probabilities, payoffs, and costs that correspond more closely to reality.

[3] *Handbook of Tables for Mathematics*, 4th ed. (Cleveland: Chemical Rubber Co., 1970).

Equivalences and the "Best" Rule. Earlier in this chapter we stated that economists and statisticians regard the Highest Expected Value rule as "best," because it utilizes all the information in the decision table, both subjective probabilities and net utilities. This conclusion is correct as long as the time- and effort-costs of making decisions are disregarded. In fact, some rules are easier to apply. To be specific, once the "facts" of the decision table have been worked out, any of the first three rules—Maximax, Best of the Most Probable, and Minimax —can probably be worked "in your head" without resort to writing on paper. And, under certain conditions, these rules yield approximately the same result as the Highest Expected Value. When is this? If either 1) the subjective probabilities of the less probable outcomes are very "small," or 2) the net utilities attached to various outcomes are not greatly different, then the Best of the Most Probable and the Highest Expected Value rules will give similar results. As suggested, the saving of time and effort will recommend the use of the simpler rule under these circumstances.

You can also verify the proposition that Minimax and the Highest Expected Value give the same result when only one action has *no outcome with a net utility of minus infinity.* In such a case, both Minimax (without calculation) and Highest Expected Value (with calculation) imply that you select the action with no potential disaster. One caution: if several actions have "disastrous" outcomes, one should pause and ask "really" whether all the outcomes are disastrous. If on second thought any action is not disastrous, it should not be assigned the "minus infinity" value.

Even when it fails to give equivalent results to the Highest Expected Value, Minimax can claim two situations in which its application may be highly desirable. The first is for persons who, for reasons of their own, may not care to take the trouble of making the optimal decision, but for whom it is highly important to avoid very bad decisions. Minimax will help achieve this goal, though imperfectly.

Another recommended application is for "small" decisions where the gain from more careful decision-making cannot justify the "work" involved in the Highest Expected Value. Again, Minimax helps avoid the worst.

Are Decision Rules for Real Life Use? Is the message of this chapter that we should use decision rules *formally* for most decisions? Emphatically not. As we have stated many times, decision-making is time- and effort-consuming. For the myriad "small" decisions most of us make, the payoff to formal decision-making is not likely to justify the effort. But what this chapter should have done is acquaint you with the important elements of each decision: the identification and evaluation of alternative outcomes, the assignment of subjective probabilities, and the identification of the rules you have been implicitly using.

It may lead you to ask quickly about contemplated alternatives; Will any result in a "disaster?" Or, are the chances of that outcome occurring small enough so that it may be ignored?

THE RULES IN PRACTICE

Tornadoes, Minimax, and Grades. The tornado in the example with which this chapter began was not a creation of the author's imagination. It actually occurred. In early June, 1965, the tornado in question cut an ugly swath across Minneapolis and its suburbs from the southwest to the northeast. The unhappy toll: 7 people killed, 40 injured, and 200 homes damaged or destroyed. By chance, most of the students in the author's course in consumer economics at the University of Minnesota that year actually faced the choice posed at the beginning of this chapter: to stay where they were or to go to the basement. By intent rather than by chance, these students had been exposed to the decision rules of this chapter. And, by chance rather than by intent, the final examination for the course took place several days after the tornado's lethal passage.

These events set the stage for a "natural" experiment that should engage your interest: an opportunity to find out to what extent students, actually confronted by a harsh choice, followed Minimax and went to the cellar, or used some other principle and stayed where they were. At the course examination, students were asked to state—not for a grade, of course, what they had done: whether (1) they had gone to the cellar, (2) stayed where they were, or (3) had been unaware of the tornado threat.

After the examinations had been graded and course grades assigned, the author cross-tabulated student choices and course grades. So, lay your bets! Was there (1) no relationship between grade and reaction to the tornado threat, (2) a positive relationship (students with the highest grades going to the cellar more than others), or (3) a negative relationship?

The numbers have been lost to time. But the results were emphatic: the higher the grade, the more likely it was that the student followed Minimax and went to the basement.

Was this result a fluke? Was it applicable only to this class or only to this event? Not at all. A considerable body of research findings attests to the fact that people with higher educational attainments tend to behave in a risk-avoiding way. And it is our view that risk avoiding squares best with the use, knowingly or unknowingly, of the Minimax rule.

The studies we consider identified different actions as "risk-avoiding." Two of them formed risk-avoiding indexes by assigning points to risk-avoiding acts. The risk-avoiding actions and the points assigned to them are summarized as follows:

Table 4

Study	Risk-Avoiding Action	Points Assigned
1 [a]		
	1. *Seat belt usage:* head of family reports that family uses seat belts *all of the time*	Only action considered
2 [b]		
	2. *Seat belt usage:* head of family has seat belt fastened *all or part of time* while driving	1
	3. *Use of new products:* head of family says that family does *not* try new products when they first come on the market	1
	4. *Polio vaccination: all family members have had* polio vaccine (data collected in 1965)	1
	5. *Medical insurance:* family is covered by medical or hospitalization insurance	1
	6. *Financial reserves:* family has liquid reserve funds equal to two months or more of take-home pay	1
	7. *Family planning:* head of family is married and family has used some method to limit the number or plan the spacing of children	2
	head of family *not* married (this was done to neutralize those ineligible for family planning)	1
	Total possible points	7
3 [c]		
	8. *Seat belt usage:*	
	No belts in car	1
	Have belts:	
	head of family uses all of the time	2
	head of family uses some of the time	1
	head of family uses none of the time	0

Study	Risk-Avoiding Action	Points Assigned
	9. *Financial reserves:*	
	Reserves equal to two months or more of take-home pay	2
	Some savings now or in recent past	1
	No savings now or in recent past	0
	10. *Medical insurance:*	
	Whole family covered	2
	Some covered, but not all	1
	None covered	0
	11. *Automobile insurance:*	
	All cars insured	2
	Some insured, but one or more not insured	1
	None insured	8
	Total possible points	8

[a] James N. Morgan, "Who Uses Seat Belts," *Behavioral Science* (November 1967), pp. 463–465.

[b] James N. Morgan, Ismail Sirageldin, and Nancy Baerwaldt, *Productive Americans, A Study of How Individuals Contribute to Economic Progress* (Ann Arbor: Survey Research Center, University of Michigan, 1966), Chap. 18.

[c] Al Arterburn, "Correlates of a Risk Avoidance Index," in Greg J. Duncan and James N. Morgan, eds. *Five Thousand American Families—Patterns of Economic Progress, III* (Ann Arbor: Survey Research Center, University of Michigan, 1975), pp. 351–382.

Table 5 illustrates the results of Studies 1 and 2. The picture is clear. For both a single type of risk-avoiding behavior, "buckling up," and for an index taking account of several types of risk-avoiding behavior, Americans with higher educational attainments are more likely to behave in a risk-avoiding way. For *this* example, at least, the author's class at the University of Minnesota was a "microcosm" of the United States.

But life is often more complex than it seems. And so it is with the relationship between education and risk-avoiding behavior. Study 3, a more recent and a more sophisticated analysis by Al Arterburn,[4] confirms the education-risk-avoiding relationship using a somewhat different index of risk-avoiding behavior. But it also sheds light on what is really going on. When the effects of income *and* education on risk-avoiding behavior are taken into account simultaneously along with other variables, income has a far more powerful influence on risk-avoiding behavior than education (although the effect of education is still important even when income is held constant).

So we arrive at this reinterpretation. High-income people act in

[4] Arterburn, op. cit.

TABLE 5

Education and Risk Avoiding, 1965 [a]

Education of Head of Family	Study 1: Per Cent of Eligibles Using Seat Belts "All of the Time" [b]	Study 2: Mean Value: Index of Caution and Risk Avoiding [c]
Zero to 8 grades	21%	2.51
9 to 11 grades	25	2.87
12 grades	24	3.28
12 grades and nonacademic training	34	3.53
College, no degree	39	3.70
College, bachelor's degree	40	3.87
College, advanced or professional degree	44	4.36

[a] Data are taken from the 1965 Survey of Consumer Finances, conducted by the Survey Research Center of the University of Michigan.
[b] Morgan, op. cit., "Eligibles" were families owning cars that were equipped with seat belts.
[c] Morgan, Sirageldin, and Baerwaldt, op. cit., p. 301.

a more risk-avoiding way than lower-income people, presumably because they have more to lose and possibly because they have larger resources from which to pay for risk-avoiding. (Automobile and medical insurance cost money; it is easier to save if your income is higher.) Higher incomes, of course, are highly correlated with more education.

But even after all this is said, education still has "its own" effect: something associated with the educational experience leads persons with higher educational attainments to be more cautious and risk-avoiding than people with lesser educational attainments.

FOR FURTHER STUDY

This chapter has sought to introduce you to those decision rules that could be used by intelligent consumers in making typical consumer choices and that do not require extensive calculation. As you probably suspect, there exists a vast literature on decision theory "out there," and if you wish to conduct further explorations into unknown territory, the author recommends:

> *Accessible to everyone:*
> > David W. Miller and Martin K. Starr, *The Structure of Human Decisions* (Englewood Cliffs, N. J.: Prentice-Hall, Inc., 1967), chapts. 1–5.
> *Accessible to anyone understanding high school algebra:*
> > D. V. Lindley, *Making Decisions* (New York: John Wiley & Sons, Inc., 1971).
> *Somewhat more detailed and more difficult:*
> > Robert O. Schlaifer, *Analysis of Decisions Under Uncertainty* (New York: McGraw-Hill, Inc., 1969).
> > In this book decision theory is applied to problems of business administration.
> *A "basic" review article:*
> > Leonard J. Savage, "Elicitation of Personal Probabilities and Expectations," *Journal of the American Statistical Association* (December 1971), pp. 783–801.

CHAPTER 8

Individual Redress:
The Righting of
Consumer Grievances

At one time or another almost all of us have suffered from "consumer grievances," as a reaction to:

—the product whose performance fails to match reasonable standards, or worse, fails to work at all;
—the purchase on which we were "overcharged";
—the order paid for, but not received;
—the service promised, but not provided;
—misleading or deceptive selling claims.

This chapter is intended as a consumer's guide to the minimization and correction of these and other consumer grievances.[1]

The chapter begins with the enumeration of a comprehensive catalog of consumer grievances. Next comes a discussion of the steps a consumer may take by way of prevention. The object is to avoid grievances before they occur and to minimize their seriousness if and when they occur. After this the reader is acquainted with the levers he or she can activate vis-à-vis sellers in seeking redress of grievances. Finally, the chapter describes the existing avenues for redress and assesses their effectiveness.

As its title suggests, this chapter is addressed to the actions the individual consumer can take in seeking redress of *his* or *her* grievances. It does not deal with the actions society might take to ameliorate the grievance problem. This topic is reserved for Chapter 11.

[1] We distinguish between grievances and complaints. A *consumer grievance* is an instance of consumer dissatisfaction, whether communicated or not. By contrast, a *complaint* is a grievance that has been voiced.

A CATALOG OF CONSUMER GRIEVANCES

In the following list grievances are classified under four major headings: delivery failures, performance failures, communications failures, and misrepresentation-deception-fraud. It is important to note that in the last class failure is *intentional* on the part of the sellers whereas in the first three classes failures are not intentional.

A. *Delivery Failures*
   1. Good or service ordered, but:
      a. Delivered or provided tardily;
      b. Not delivered or provided at all.
   2. Good or service ordered, but not as specified.
   Examples: A car is delivered minus the power steering that had been ordered. Or, the garage performed a "major" tune-up rather than the "minor" tune-up that had been requested.
B. *Performance Failures*
   1. Production failure: design acceptable, but the particular specimen is defective and fails to perform as might reasonably be expected.
   Example: A worker on the automobile assembly line installs a gasket improperly and the radiator coolant leaks out. A teak dining room table bears a conspicuous scratch because of inadequate crating in transit.
   2. Design failure: all specimens of this variety of product exhibit the same deficiency.
   Example: The brake design on a car permits water to seep into the brakes and hence they operate unreliably during rain.
   3. Quality of service less than might be reasonably expected.
   a. Because of incompetence of those providing service.
   Example: Mechanic lacks sufficient knowledge of brake alignment machine, hence front wheels vibrate despite the wheel alignment and wheel balancing performed.
   b. Because of carelessness in provision of service.
   Example: A competent mechanic performs the same wheel alignment and balancing operation as in 3 a., but does it carelessly. So the front wheels still vibrate after the servicing.
   4. Seller fails to correct fault in product after it is called to his attention.
   Example: The car in 3 b. is returned to the service station. But the manager disclaims any responsibility, suggesting that the

wheels had been thrown out of alignment after the car left the service station.

5. Product is unsafe (an extreme form of 2 or 3).

C. *Failure of Communication*

1. Seller and buyer have different understandings of what the seller (buyer) promised with respect to:

a. The characteristics the good or service possesses;

Example: The buyer understood that power brakes were "included" in the price quoted whereas the seller understood that power brakes were an "extra."

b. What services the seller promised to provide (what the buyer promised to do).

Example: The buyer understood that the seller would deliver and install the washing machine whereas the seller expected the buyer to arrange for both.

c. Price.

Example: The buyer believed himself eligible for a new car loan at 9 per cent even though the seller's literature indicates clearly that this rate applies only to those paying 30 per cent or more in cash, a class to which this buyer does not belong.

d. Other sales terms.

Example: The buyer of a high-fidelity system believes that the agreed purchase price includes a cartridge whereas the seller's understanding is that it does not.

D. *Misrepresentation, Deception, Fraud* (clear, deliberate intent to deceive)

1. Seller does not intend to deliver the goods (services) promised.

2. The seller deliberately misrepresents the price or other terms.

3. The seller deliberately asserts that the good (service) has characteristics it lacks.

Examples: Sellers of some brands of aspirin claim that it will "work" better than other brands even though scientific evidence supporting the claim is lacking.

4. Seller asserts that the product is safe, when he has evidence that it is unsafe.

After viewing the list, you might reasonably ask: how often does the typical consuming family experience a grievance? Once a year, twice, five times, ten times, or higher? And what are the most common grievances that families encounter? We do not know, and, as yet, no one has undertaken the systematic survey of consumer grievances that would yield the answers to these questions.

Nonetheless, all consumers can take preventive steps to forestall the occurrence of grievances in the first place. And there are also preventive steps that the consumer can take to minimize the seriousness of any grievance that may occur. It is to these steps that we now turn.

The Prevention or Minimization of Grievances. The case for prevention, as opposed to the "cure" of consumer grievances, is particularly strong for two reasons. First, the correction of grievances tends to be a costly and uncertain process, and it is especially costly in terms of time and frustration. Second, grievances are seldom resolved to the complete satisfaction of the complaining consumer. Third, as letters to consumer complaint columns suggest, even presumably knowledgeable consumers are "taken" from time to time. For these reasons it behooves us to review possible preventive procedures.

In matters of prevention, as in so many other aspects of consumer choice, the "marginal" principle holds: the more "serious" the possible grievance the greater your preventive efforts should be. Thus, suppose that carelessness led you to purchase thumbtacks that bend too readily. Your grief (and grievance) would not be too great. This would not be so if the new roof on your home leaks, or lasts five rather than ten years. The roof—to mix metaphors—merits pounds, not ounces of prevention.

Easy-Return and High-Service Sellers. As we saw earlier (Chapter 2), retail sellers will find it advantageous to practice product differentiation, and some will develop a justified reputation for postpurchase servicing. If you buy a washing machine from them, they will see to it that it works well, no matter how many no-charge service calls are required. The lesson to the intelligent consumer is straightforward. In purchasing goods whose need for postpurchase adjustment or repairs is high—television sets, automobiles, and high-fidelity equipment come to mind as examples—deal with a seller who "specializes" in postpurchase service, other things being equal.[2] This should minimize possible grief.

Some retail sellers, however, have differentiated their outlets in

---

[2] The purchase of a specific postpurchase service contract is an alternative. In this case you will want to know about the record of the firm providing the service. This information, however, is not easy to obtain.

a "low service-easy return" direction. In such stores you may have difficulty locating a salesperson. But, on the other hand, exchanges or refunds are accomplished easily with almost no questions asked. This then (again, other things being equal) is the type of outlet in which to purchase goods that are at once portable and susceptible to early breakdowns. Examples might be cheap watches, small appliances, and mechanical toys. You could also purchase goods on a tentative, trial basis—clothing for children at home or decorative items whose suitability to your home you wish to test.

Your own experience or the "borrowed" experience of friends and acquaintances should enable you to identify both high-service and easy-return retailers.

Purchase from Reputable Sellers. This bit of advice may seem rather "empty." How, you may ask, do I assess the reputation of a seller? There is no simple, definite answer to this question, but the following suggestions should be helpful.

First, before dealing with an unknown seller on a major purchase, a call to the Better Business Bureau (hereafter BBB) to check on the firm's complaint record is in order.

But the consumer should be clear as to what the BBB's record will and will not do for him. A "bad" record with the BBB usually identifies an unreliable firm, one worth avoiding. On the other hand, a "good" complaint record with the BBB is no guarantee that the firm is honest or reputable. (The discussion of Better Business Bureaus on pp. 214–19 shows why this is so.) What is more, even the "honest and reputable" firm may not serve you *best* with respect to both price and the quality of goods and services. In short, the BBB check will—at most—screen out some of the "bad" firms with which you should not deal.

Obtaining and "testing" information relating to the reputation of a seller is simply a special application of the general rules for acquiring and testing information. So a second major suggestion is that you review the section in Chapter 4 on "Obtaining and Evaluating Consumer Information." Nonetheless, a particular step should be singled out for attention here. Probably the best "bank" of information regarding the reputation of sellers is the accrued experience of you and your friends and acquaintances, especially those whose information and judgments have proved useful in the past. A consensus of past experience and judgments should help greatly in identifying sellers who will serve you well and in avoiding those who will serve you poorly.

For some kinds of sellers—particularly providers of "big-ticket" goods or services with whom you deal infrequently—it is appropriate to ask the seller himself to supply you with information regarding the financial reliability of his firm and a list of his past customers whom you may wish to consult. Alternatively, where it is appropriate, you might wish to inquire of the relevant regulatory agency regarding the financial stability and service record of the firm in question. This action would certainly be wise in determining the reliability of, say, a small insurance company or a charter air line.

Specify the Purchase Terms. An analysis of our "catalog" of grievances reveals how central the communication process is to both the birth and assessment of consumer grievances. Delivery failures are judged "failures" because delivery performance does not conform to the terms agreed upon (communication) or with "normal" delivery performances for that product in that locale. Performance failures, too, will similarly be judged "failures" because they do not meet standards agreed upon (communications, again), or promises made in advertising or promotional literature (and again, communications), or the norm for that product and industry. Similar observations apply to fraud-misrepresentation-deception with the important difference that in the case of fraud, it is the *intention* of the seller to deceive. And, of course, our remaining grievance category—failure of communications—centers, by name, on the problem of communications.

What does this imply for prevention? In the first place, it behooves the grievance-avoiding and grievance-minimizing consumer to seek and then to keep all documents relevant to the purchase. The collection would include advertisements, leaflets, and other documents that record the claims of sellers on behalf of their products or services. The consumer should also keep contracts embodying the terms of sale agreed upon.

Since the written word is presumed to be the enemy of ambiguity and misunderstanding, the intelligent consumer should try to record all purchase agreements in writing.

But a written agreement is not enough. It must be clear to both the seller and to others. It is worth repeating: it is usually the *written contract that binds.* And when the contract offered is a "standard" contract, drafted by the seller's lawyers, the consumer can usually rely on two things: 1) its prose will often be close to impenetrable; 2) it is likely to embody provisions favorable to the seller and unlikely to embody proconsumer provisions. When proffered a contract by a seller, the knowledgeable and grievance-avoiding consumer should take the time to verify that the contract represents *his* understanding of the agreement and embodies provisions that are acceptable to him. Where it does not, he should insist that the agreement be modified and that the modification be validated by initialing. Again, the marginal principle applies: be most careful when the potential grievance is greatest.

In some cases, sellers refuse to provide written confirmation of prices quoted in advance. Here the recommended preventive course is to record both the price quoted (or other terms quoted) as well as the name of the informant, and, if the purchase is a major one, the consumer may wish to obtain an independent check of the price from another informant, along with the name of this second informant.

The Preacceptance Check. The point at which you accept a good as "yours" is a pivotal point in any purchase transaction: at that point any malfunctions or problems built into that particular specimen tend to become your responsibility. Up to that point they unquestionably belong to the seller. After acceptance by you, however, it becomes increasingly difficult, even with warranties and guarantees, to identify a fault as the seller's responsibility rather than yours. It becomes even more difficult to persuade the seller to accept responsibility for correcting the fault.

For these reasons it is a proper exercise in prevention to check a good before accepting it, if this is at all possible. In the case of a car, check the operation of all instruments, accessories (radio, air conditioning, heater) and as many adjustments as you can (coolant level, oil level, tire pressures) *before you drive the car away.* The purpose of such a check is twofold: 1) to identify faults at a time when your leverage vis-à-vis the seller is maximal, and, more important, 2) to ascertain that the seller's agents have verified the functioning and adequacy of systems you cannot check and of whose existence you may be unaware.

If such a check appears to disclose either poor preparation on the part of the dealer or serious malfunctions, then you should refuse delivery. If small faults are disclosed, this is the time to specify them and to make arrangements for their correction by the seller.

Preventive Leverage. In a later section we identify and assess the leverage through which the consumer can exert pressure on sellers in the event of a dispute. At least two actions can be taken in advance to strengthen your leverage.

First, and obviously, you can and should develop over time a status that will increase your weight in any dispute. Your personal reputation for honesty and probity, your (good) credit record, your affiliations—where you work, your church, the recreational, civic, fraternal, and other organizations in which you are active—will all add to your bargaining weight.

Second, wherever it is costless to you, you should purchase on credit. If credit is obtained from an organization other than the seller, then you have enlisted an ally in the case of any dispute. It may be presumed that the seller has a strong and abiding interest in the sales the credit-granting organization makes possible. By extension he—and the credit organizations, too—are concerned that credit-using customers be satisfied. Thus, financing a purchase through a credit organization—BankAmericard, Master Charge, American Express, your local bank or credit union—is a prudent preventive action, especially when the cost of short-term financing is zero or negligible.

Similarly, when you finance your purchase through the seller himself, you have created a lever of use in case of a dispute—your unpaid balance. It is possible and reasonable for you to notify the seller: "When you have set things straight, I will resume [complete] my payments."

So much for prevention. We now turn briefly to the nature of redress.

THE NATURE OF REDRESS

No matter how extensive our preventive efforts, most of us will sooner or later be the victim of some grievance as consumers. It is proper to ask what constitutes acceptable redress of a consumer grievance.

Assuming that the grievance was entirely attributable to some failure on the part of the seller, it seems reasonable that the seller should bear the full costs arising from the grievance. It would follow then that, ideally, redress of grievances would involve:

1. The correction of the condition giving rise to the grievance, *plus*
2. Cash or in-kind compensation sufficient to offset the inconvenience, the lost time, as well as the cost of secondary damages arising from the grievance. (As an example of secondary damages, consider the case where a brake failure on a newly purchased

car resulted in damage to a second car. The damage to the second car would represent "secondary damage.")

In practice, in the author's judgment, the best that can realistically be expected is the correction of the condition giving rise to the grievance. Nonetheless, it is appropriate for consumers to make at least a small investment in seeking full redress (including compensation for costs), especially in "serious" grievances. Consumers suffering grievances will want to consider which, or which combination, of the following forms of redress is preferable in the light of their particular circumstances and grievance.

1. Replacement of a defective specimen (or service) with a satisfactory one;
2. Repair;
3. Refund of purchase price;
4. Provision of substitute good (or services) during the repair period;
5. Cash or in-kind reparation.

LEVERAGE IN SEEKING REDRESS: THE CONSUMER'S ARSENAL

There are certain concerns that, when activated, give the consumer leverage in obtaining redress. Knowledge of these concerns will help the consumer to select that combination of pressures that is likely to be most effective in his particular case.

Seller's Desire to Deal Fairly and Honestly. Many sellers derive great personal satisfaction from their reputation for fair and honest dealing. The concern of such sellers for their reputation will *per se* lead them to deal favorably with genuine grievances.

Seller's Interest in Long-Run Profits. Some cynics would argue that even if you cannot bank on the seller's basic desire to deal fairly and honestly, the one factor you can count on—if the firm is not simply "fly-by-night"—is the seller's interest in long-run profits. The variety of factors on which long-run profits depend arms the consumer with many weapons in his quest for redress.

First is the seller's interest in *you, individually, as a future custo-*

mer. If your grievance is with a business that relies heavily on repeat sales to the same set of customers, then the seller's stake in you as a future source of sales provides a potent force in seeking redress for your current grievance. Rationally, he has to weigh the cost of providing redress in a particular instance against the whole series of future sales that might be lost if you remain dissatisfied.

Second, the seller is likely to be interested in *groups* to which you belong as *future customers.* Thus, your declaration—"When I tell the people I work with at the university [substitute any other work group] how shabbily I have been treated by you in settling my insurance claim, they may think twice about dealing with you"—is likely to have force, especially if the group is big and the seller has reason to believe that you have influence within the group. Of course, to be effective, this threat has to be credible.

An attractive aspect of this particular lever is its versatility: it can be applied by reference to any of the groups of which you are a member—your work group or the clubs and voluntary organizations to which you belong.

Third, the seller is necessarily concerned with the *public image of his business,* and the adverse effects any negative publicity might have on it. Thus, the possibility, if real, that your grievance might receive a public airing affords a compelling argument for redress. Publicity need not be negative, of course. Sometimes, generous settlements of grievances receive favorable publicity. And this, too, is a possibility to which the seller may respond positively; indeed, spreading praise of good service where no grievance is involved is a useful consumer tactic in the long run.

Sellers are concerned not only with their public reputation but also with *their reputations among other businesses* with which they deal—the seller's suppliers, his business customers, and businesses who have referred customers to him. Thus, the complaining consumer is well advised to communicate his complaint not only to the offending seller but also to the businesses that have a supply, customer, or referral relationship to the offender. The desire to please *them* may induce him to redress the grievance.

Similarly, a business' long-run profits will depend heavily on *its access to markets.* As suggested in the discussion of prevention, the seller may be dependent upon credit-granting businesses. He will also be dependent upon advertisers. In certain lines, his continued operations may depend upon renewed accreditation or licensing. The lesson to the complaining consumer is clear: communicate your complaint to those on whom the seller depends for his continued access to markets—the advertising media he uses, relevant accreditation or licensing agencies, and credit grantors.

To sum up, anything that threatens the seller's long-run profits constitutes a potential force for achieving redress.

Seller's Concern for Short-Run Profits. But long-run profits are not everything. Some steps taken by the redress-seeking consumer will force the seller to ask himself: which will cost me more *now*—to fight, or to redress the grievance?

The consumer can take certain steps that will increase, or *appear* to increase, the cost to the seller of fighting the consumer's claim. In the first place, the consumer can voice his claim so noisily and so publicly that it will be obvious to the seller that the costs of his resistance are very high in terms of adverse publicity. Secondly, the consumer can *threaten* a lawsuit. The threat of a lawsuit is cheap as compared to the actuality. And, often, the threat is sufficient to convince the seller of the seriousness of the complainant's intentions.

The Seller's Aversion to Potential or Actual Regulation. Quite naturally, sellers dislike regulation. It is costly to them in terms of restrictions on their freedom of choice, in terms of diverting their efforts from what they view as their chief function, and in terms of the actual cost of compliance.

Obviously, the nonresolution of consumer grievances can become the basis for the institution of regulation in a previously unregulated line of business or for the institution of more rigorous regulation. The complaining consumer can utilize the aversion of the seller for regulation by threatening or actually communicating the substance of his complaint to incumbent legislators, aspiring politicians, and existing regulatory bodies. The desire to avoid regulation should provide the seller with a strong incentive to settle a valid consumer grievance.

AVENUES FOR REDRESS

Considerations of Strategy. In seeking redress, the marginal principle (again!) holds: take (additional) steps to achieve redress as long as the expected marginal gain exceeds the expected marginal cost of that step. Go further if you wish to make a *social* contribution, such as occurs when the success you achieve in redress enables another less energetic and less skillful consumer to achieve redress with less resistance on the part of a particular seller or class of sellers.

As noted earlier, full redress consists of the correction of the condition giving rise to the grievance plus compensation for secondary losses resulting from the grievance. Since what constitutes full redress is likely to remain relatively fixed in a particular situation, the consumer's strategy should be first to use low-cost means of obtaining redress and then, as necessary, to escalate to higher cost means. Different people may correctly have a different view of which means are "low-cost." For example, persons for whom verbal communication is easy and letter-writing painful would view personal contact as a "low-cost" means and letter-writing as "high-cost."

A starting point in any effort to seek redress is to analyze the position of the particular seller with a view to identifying the pressures to which he is likely to respond. Then the consumer must decide which of the following avenues of redress will provide the best vehicle for applying leverage. In so deciding, he should be aware that several means or avenues for redress can be actuated simultaneously, often at reduced cost. He should also be aware that successful redress may require escalation of leverage over several stages.

Let us now review critically specific avenues or means that aggrieved consumers may utilize in seeking redress.

Personal Contact with the Seller. This is a natural first step. It is particularly appropriate where the grievance is of "modest" proportions. When seeking redress by personal contact, always try to deal with persons of maximum authority—the owner (where the business is small) or the head of the department. Such persons are likely to consider your problem as an individual case rather than relying on "rules" (which may not fit your case) to deny redress.

Face-to-face meetings usually favor the seller. He is experienced, you are inexperienced. (Although this may be your first complaint of this sort, he may have handled thousands like it.) In personal contact your weaknesses stand revealed: any lack of will, any lack of education or knowledge, any lack of verbal facility, any inability to react quickly to arguments or proposals. Further, since you are on the supplicant's side of a desk in the seller's complaint office, you lack weapons you might otherwise possess—exposure of the seller to publicity or help from outside agencies.

A realistic appraisal of your capacities in pursuing redress on a face-to-face basis may lead you to eschew this approach with good reason, especially if it imposes heavy travel and inconvenience costs.

In seeking face-to-face resolution of grievances, you should be aware that some sellers reward their complaint departments not for settling disputes in a way that satisfies their customers but rather for minimizing costs to the sellers. And you should always bear in mind that you have the option of following other avenues for redress. Indeed, it is sometimes appropriate to inform the seller that you may consider other avenues of seeking correction of your grievance.

Letters. As compared with personal contact, a letter of complaint may dramatically shift the initial advantage from the seller to the complaining consumer. Any quickness in verbal argument and any disadvantage in personal appearance is irrelevant. The experience of the seller (or his representative) is now a less pronounced advantage. The consumer can take time to organize and present his case without fear of interruption (untoward or otherwise). Finally, the consumer now has initiative in proposing an acceptable solution for the complaint.

There are a number of steps a complaining consumer can take to maximize the effectiveness of his letter-writing. Status and appearance count when communicating by letter. If he is affiliated with an organization by virtue of employment, officeholding, or membership—the consumer can "borrow" some of the status of that organization by using its letterhead for his letter of complaint.[3]

Also a letter of complaint should be addressed to the highest officer in the company, unless circumstances dictate otherwise. The reason is that the owner or chief executive will usually tend to take a longer and broader view of the firm's interests. In many cases the correction of a particular consumer grievance will seem like "small potatoes" compared to the firm's long-run reputation, or even the longer-term goodwill of a particular customer. Finally, the "chief" can countermand petty rules whose strict interpretation might forestall the correction of the grievance.

In writing letters of complaint, be sure to send copies and *keep originals* of relevant documents—purchase orders, receipts, canceled checks, advertisements, warranties, and correspondence. Organize your message carefully and, if possible, type neatly. Be sure to identify carefully relevant dates or times, the relevant good (model) and parts, and the terms.

The addressees, the contents, the organization, and the destination of carbon copies should all reflect your analysis of the leverage that might be applied to this particular seller. For example:

[3] Unless the organization is an appropriate party to the grievance, either the form or the substance of the communication should make clear that the consumer is writing on his own behalf, and not on behalf of the organization with which he is affiliated.

Many of the people who work with me at _____ are insured with _____ (the addressee firm). If they should ask me about my experience with _____, naturally I will tell them about my experience, as accurately as I can.

Another example:

I am sending a copy of this letter to the State Insurance Commissioner and to Senator _____, Chairman of the Senate Committee on Insurance.

Still another example:

I am sending a copy of this correspondence to the American Express Company (substitute any other credit card system) through whom I financed this purchase.

Frequently the pursuit of redress will give rise to a series of letters. If your first letter does not achieve the desired results, then it is appropriate to escalate successive letters in terms of form (politeness to curtness to credible threats) and addressees. The first letter may be addressed only to the seller at whom the complaint is directed. A second letter still with the seller as the main addressee might be sent in carbon copy form to leverage parties, for example, the Better Business Bureau, regulatory agencies, legislators, Consumers Union. If necessary, a third letter might be *addressed* to the regulatory agency (or the other leverage party) with a *carbon copy* to the business complained against.

An effective second-stage addressee or carbon copy destination is

Office of Consumer Affairs
Executive Office of the President
The White House
Washington, D.C.

This Office headed by the special assistant to the president on Consumer Affairs is a focal point in initiating new consumer legislation or in determining the administration's reactions to consumer legislation originating outside the administration. Almost universally, businessmen-sellers are loath to provide a "case" in the form of unresolved consumer complaints for further regulatory legislation. Hence, a letter or carbon copy directed to this office may activate a potent force for redress.

Newspaper Complaint Columns ("Action Line") or Television Programs. If personal contact with or a letter to the seller is a natural first step in the redress process, then the use of a media complaint column is a natural second step for two reasons: it is low cost and it is effective.

In recent years many television and radio stations, as well as newspapers, have introduced complaint or problem-solving programs or columns. "Action Line," the complaint column of the *San Diego Evening Tribune,* is probably typical of the genre. (Unfortunately no systematic data is available on the number and effectiveness of such programs.) Its proclaimed purpose is "to cut red tape, solve problems, get answers, and stand up for your rights." Although its scope extends beyond consumer complaints, content analysis of "Action Line" columns on a small sample basis suggests that consumer complaints make up about 40 per cent of the problems dealt with.

Access to a consumer complaint column is simple. You telephone or write to the newspaper or station, tell them your complaint, and send in copies of documents where relevant. They take it from there, using their "clout" as necessary.

The program's (column's) objective is to increase the station's (newspaper's) audience (circulation). Their lever in seeking resolution of consumer complaints is to provide negative publicity for offending sellers and positive publicity for firms offering generous corrective actions. Operationally such programs report both the complaint and the settlement and then let each member of the audience decide whether the episode changed his attitude toward the firm in a favorable or unfavorable direction.

Some programs identify all sellers involved, others identify only some of the sellers involved, and still others use no firm names at all. Regardless of which practice is followed, the possibility of negative publicity is without doubt the lever that leads most sellers to offer redress. Indeed, the motive seems so strong that sellers sometimes offer redress in instances where many in the audience may feel that the complaint was not valid. For these programs, redress almost invariably consists of the correction of the complaint and almost never extends to reparations for secondary damages. The success record for published (televised) complaints is extremely high, perhaps on the order of 90 per cent. In the absence of a systematic investigation, the fraction of unpublished complaints and their success rate is not known. By the same token, without a careful investigation one cannot know whether some sellers, large advertisers in the sponsoring media, are immune from adverse publicity.

Better Business Bureau. The nation's 139 Better Business Bureaus (BBB's) operate the only nationwide consumer complaint system.[4] In 1970, the BBB's handled 8 million telephone and personal contacts, of which about 22 per cent represented complaints and the remainder inquiries regarding the firms' complaint records.

In view of the BBB's long history (the first was established in 1912), their reputation, and their accessibility—they are to be found in most large cities—it is only natural that many consumers in seeking redress turn first to the local BBB. The important question is whether they should.

In the case of *modest grievances involving "establishment" busi-nesses,* it is the author's opinion that the BBB's constitute a helpful ally, and should be used. *A modest grievance* is one requiring neither a change in the retailer's general policies nor "large" costs to correct the condition giving rise to the dispute. An *establishment business* is a business that has been and expects to be in the same line for the indefinite future. The consumer can usually identify it from its long past history or the permanence of its quarters.

In the case of *serious grievances,* it is the author's judgment that the BBB's complaint system is not likely to succeed in producing a satisfactory resolution of the grievance. Indeed, to the extent that the use of the BBB complaint system precludes reliance on a more effec-tive channel of redress, the BBB complaint system may be actually detrimental of the consumer's efforts to achieve redress. A *serious* grievance is one whose correction would impose large costs on the seller or require a change in his policies.

In the author's view, the ineffectiveness of the BBB's in serious grievances stems from an insurmountable conflict of interest built into their financing and organization. The stated purpose of the BBB's is the correction of consumer grievances. The rub is that these grievances arise from actions or nonactions on the part of the very businesses who furnish the BBB's funds and who populate the boards of the local BBB's.

Since these partially negative judgments of the author pertain to the only national consumer complaint service, the reader should

---

[4] A list of BBB's may be obtained by writing to the Council of Better Business Bureaus (845 Third Avenue, New York, N.Y. 10022).

examine carefully the basis of these judgments and form his own regarding the effectiveness of the BBB's.

Some Qualifications. BBB's are locally organized, controlled, and financed. Thus, there may be differences among BBB's with respect to the degree and energy with which they pursue the consumer's interest. Although BBB's may differ in zeal, considerable uniformity among them exists in terms of the character of members, the composition of their boards, as well as the rules and procedures they follow in handling consumer complaints. It is this uniformity of procedure that makes it both possible and meaningful to form judgments regarding the average BBB's effectiveness in resolving consumer complaints.

Although the BBB's are primarily local, a national organization—the Council of Better Business Bureaus—was founded in 1970.[5] It has sought to further several praiseworthy reforms: the recruitment of consumer representation as a minority on local BBB boards, the establishment of a consumer arbitration service on an appeals basis, the monitoring and reviewing of national advertising in all media, and the improvement and expansion of local services by adding staff and telephones. But it is the local BBB that is important to the complaining consumer; its functioning is now reviewed and evaluated.

The reader is reminded that the judgments expressed here represent *average tendencies.* Thus, there will be individuals whose complaints have been more or less favorably handled. What we focus on is the outcome the average consumer is likely to experience when dealing with the average bureau on an average complaint.

An Analysis of BBB Procedures. As stated earlier, no one has yet conducted the scientific sample survey of consumer grievances and their resolution that would provide a sound statistical basis for assessing the effectiveness of the BBB as a complaint-handling organization. What can be done is to examine BBB rules and procedures and infer the likely effectiveness of the BBB from this process. We are helped by the results of the Rosenthal Report,[6] an investigative report of the BBB undertaken by a law student with the support of Representative Benjamin Rosenthal of New York.

[5] For further details on the proposed program of the Council, see H. Bruce Palmer, "Consumerism: The Business of Business," *Michigan Business Review* (July 1971), pp. 12–17. Palmer was president of the Council of Better Business Bureaus.

[6] Representative Benjamin S. Rosenthal, "Report on the Better Business Bureaus," *Congressional Record,* December 17, 1972, pp. E13764–778.
The author has been unable to locate any "pro-BBB" attempt to assess the effectiveness of BBB complaint procedures.

BBB Complaint-Handling Procedures. Typical steps in BBB complaint procedures are enumerated as follows, along with clarifying or critical comments, where relevant.

1. The consumer complainant states his grievance and the settlement he considers fair either on a BBB complaint form or in a letter. Complaints may be made either by telephone or in person.
2. The BBB's exclude certain complaints as being beyond their scope:

    a. Complaints of "high" or "excessive" prices;

    b. Complaints regarding fit, wearability, or durability;

    c. Complaints regarding the inefficient operation of appliances, whenever this is not covered by a written guarantee;

    d. Disputes already adjudicated or in process of adjudication.

    Comment: Complaints regarding product durability or efficiency in operation could constitute valid consumer grievances.
3. BBB forwards the complaint to the relevant, usually local, business, asking it to deal with the complaint and to inform the BBB of actions taken or not taken as well as its reasons.
4. The business may elect:

    a. Not to answer the complaint. The fact of "nonanswering" will be entered on the "record" of this business with the BBB.

    b. Reply to the BBB, but decline to adjust the complaint, stating its view that the complaint was unwarranted or was not its (this firm's) responsibility.

    c. Reply to the BBB, stating the corrective action it proposes to take or has taken.
5. If the business "declines to adjust" the complaint, the BBB forwards the refusal to the complaining consumer with a letter in which the BBB steps out of the picture. The following form letter is a typical BBB disclaimer in this situation:

> Per the enclosed copy of correspondence received from the captioned firm, this has obviously become a *controversial matter.* As you may know, the Better Business Bureau is a public service organization voluntarily maintained by hundreds of business firms to foster accurate advertising, informative selling, and fair competition. And at the same time, to protect both business and public against unfair and fraudulent practices. Firms interested in customer good will usually give prompt attention to complaints forwarded by the BBB, and do

everything within reason to satisfy them. The Bureau fights fraud and customer abuse with facts. It has no way of forcing any firm to make an adjustment and, consequently, can be of no further assistance to you in this instance. If you seek further assistance in this matter, we suggest you consult legal counsel.[7]

Comment: The dismissed complaint may or may not have been valid. But its validity has been judged by neither the BBB nor any neutral body. In the meantime the complaining consumer has invested effort and patience in a system that refuses to judge the correctness of his complaint.

Certainly one inevitable effect is to dampen his efforts to seek further redress. This would especially be true—if he believes, as many do—that the BBB does in fact judge both the validity of his complaint and the action of the seller. (BBB literature is careful to state that no such judgment is made.)

6. If the business "adjusts" the complaint, BBB forwards the report of the firm's "adjustment" to the consumer, asking him to get in touch with the BBB if he is still unsatisfied. The following letter from the Metropolitan New York BBB embodies this approach:

> If this complaint has not been adjusted to your satisfaction, please let us know. If we don't hear from you, we will assume that it has been adjusted.

a. As the quoted paragraph states, this will be counted as a satisfactorily settled complaint *unless the consumer notifies the BBB of his dissatisfaction.*

Comment: Note that no evaluation has been made of the fairness of the "adjustment." Yet failure of the consumer to take positive action by writing to or telephoning the BBB to voice his continued dissatisfaction will result in the "adjustment" being counted as "satisfactory" by the BBB.

It seems plausible that many consumers, still unsatisfied, may "give up," having exhausted their quota of protest efforts or having concluded that further efforts to seek redress will be fruitless. Some may conclude, erroneously, that the BBB as well as the seller views the proposed adjustment as "fair."

---

[7] This form, used by the BBB of Greater Seattle, is widely employed by other bureaus.

b. If the consumer registers his continued dissatisfaction with the seller's proposed "adjustment," then he will be informed, as in No. 5, that this has become a "controversial matter" in which the BBB can be of no further help.

In compiling the firm's complaint record, this episode would then be accounted as an "unadjusted complaint." [8]

Summing up, the BBB's are indeed "paper tigers." In their procedures the BBB's deliberately eschew levers that our analysis suggests would be helpful in seeking consumer redress. A comparison of the BBB's complaint service with an "ideal" agency is revealing in this respect.

First, an ideal complaint agency would form judgments regarding both the existence of a legitimate complaint, the allocation of responsibility for its correction, and the fairness of the corrective action. The judges would have some claim to impartiality, and an appeals mechanism should be provided. The BBB's offer none of these procedures.[9]

Second, an ideal agency would publicize the true record of businesses in generating and resolving consumer complaints, naming names. Except in bulletins to member businesses, the BBB's do not take steps to publicize the complaint records of firms, although they do furnish information regarding the complaint records of firms in response to individual enquiries. However, such reports, based on the unreliable "accounting" scheme described previously, and sketchy as well, may conceal rather than reveal a genuinely "bad" complaint record.[10] To the extent that this is true, the net effort is to hurt rather than help the consumer.

Third, when actionable fraud or deception is uncovered, an ideal

---

[8] An article in the December 10, 1973, issue of the *Christian Science Monitor* reports on a different set of complaint categories. But there is no evidence to suggest that the new system of classification would require modification of the conclusions given.

[9] An exception for which success is claimed is the consumer arbitration system operated by the Metropolitan BBB. According to its executive officer, Stan Gibell, a four-year trial has made arbitration a standard and successful part of the BBB program in New York City. Of some 150,000 complaints per year, about 1 per cent go to arbitration. See "Arbitrators Aid Consumers Here," *New York Times,* August 25, 1974, p. 51.

[10] In the past, the BBB's have justified their lack of specificity and aggressiveness in circulating a firm's complaint record on grounds of possible libel suits. This fear was reduced in 1972 when the Council of Better Business Bureaus obtained a master insurance policy that protects its members from slander and libel cases. See *American Council on Consumer Interests Newsletter* (March 1972), p. 1.

agency would either 1) undertake legal action against the alleged wrongdoer itself, or 2) urge the appropriate government agency to do so, by cooperating with it. The BBB's undertake no legal actions themselves. According to the Rosenthal Report, they hardly ever urge legal prosecution arising from the acts of deception or fraud their complaint service uncovers. The BBB's do, however, cooperate in giving government agencies access to BBB files.

Fourth, BBB's might use expulsion from their own membership [11] as an instrument to encourage better firm behavior in terms of both initial behavior and the resolution of consumer complaints. In fact, the expulsion rate in 1970 was 0.1 per cent.[12] Moreover, according to the Rosenthal Report,[13] "membership rosters in Chicago and Washington contain a disproportionately high number of firms that have been the subject of disciplinary action by the Federal Trade Commission."

Finally, the ideal agency would have strong (dominant?) consumer representation on both its controlling board and its complaint evaluation committees. As of 1975, consumer representation within the BBB's is almost nonexistent.

Small Claims Courts

The small claims courts, or conciliation courts, as they are sometimes known, represent a higher level of escalation in the redress process. As contrasted with the means thus far considered, small claims courts invest a third party with an active role in seeking to resolve the dispute.

The small claims courts provide the consumer with "small" grievances—typically claimed damages under $300—with an informal court where, at best, he can get his grievance adjudicated cheaply and swiftly. At worst, the seller may refuse to abide by the decision of the small claims court, and the complaining consumer must then undertake a formal lawsuit if he is to pursue his complaint further.

From the viewpoint of the consumer, the small claims court has some appealing characteristics. In most states, judges do not insist on formal procedures or strict legal rules of evidence. Also, in most states, lawyers are not needed in small claims court proceedings although they are permitted to appear. The proceedings are usually brief with a decision usually rendered at a single session. A small filing fee is

---

[11] About 2 to 4 per cent of all businesses, including most large "establishment" firms, are members. Rosenthal Report, op. cit., p. E13767.

[12] Rosenthal Report, op. cit., p. E13764.

[13] Ibid., p. E13764.

charged, usually on the order of $5 or $10. If the consumer is successful, he can often recover this fee.

Procedures. The complaining consumer files a statement of his grievance, indicating his estimate of the dollar amount of damages he has suffered. A summons is served on the seller against whom the grievance was filed, ordering him (or his representative) to appear in court on a given date. In many states, the seller if he is incorporated must appear through an attorney.

In some cases this summons alone may be sufficient to induce the seller to correct the grievance to the satisfaction of the consumer before the "trial" takes place. If the case is not settled or resolved, the trial takes place. If the seller appears, the judge will hear the consumer's story and render his judgment. If the seller fails to appear, the judge will declare a "default judgment," by which the consumer is awarded the entire amount of damages claimed.

Unfortunately, a favorable judgment or default judgment may not be the end of the consumer's problem: 1) the seller may appeal the favorable judgment to a higher court or 2) the seller may refuse to pay the amount of the judgment. Either action may necessitate a formal lawsuit with counsel and strict rules of evidence, and, as we see in the next section, the costs of a formal lawsuit are likely to exceed the dollar value of damages suffered in the typical consumer complaint. To the extent that sellers refuse to pay small claims court judgments or appeal such judgments, the effect is to deny the fruits of the judicial system to consumer complainants with "small" grievances.

Advantages and Limitations

Aside from the overriding limitation of small claims courts just mentioned, it is worth summarizing their advantages and limitations as avenues for consumer redress. On the advantage side, they are cheap and quick, and an analysis of a 1970 sample of small claims cases suggests that the odds of a favorable judgment favor consumers by two to one.[14]

Foremost among the limitations of small claims courts is the low limits on maximum claims eligible for adjudication via the small claims route. The maximum award is $300 in many states (perhaps half) and $500 or less in most states.

---

[14] See "Buyer versus Seller in Small Claims Courts," *Consumer Reports* (October 1971). The article discusses these courts in some detail.

In small claims courts, as in most other avenues of redress, sellers appear to have the advantages arising from experience. Some sellers appear in court frequently, hence are more likely to be familiar with its procedures and rules. Sellers are often familiar (perhaps even too "friendly") with court personnel. Finally, they can purchase the services of counsel at "wholesale" prices as we see in the next section.

But the greatest disability of the small claims courts is the "escape route" via nonpayment or appeal they provide to determined sellers. The lesson for consumers is that small claims courts are likely to be applicable chiefly to "small" grievances with establishment sellers. In clear-cut cases of fraud it is likely that sellers will refuse to pay, forcing an unacceptably expensive lawsuit on the consumer. In cases involving major policies, for example, the provision of warranty repairs in automobile sales, it is likely that the seller will probably fight any judgment, thus also requiring a lawsuit. All of which brings us to consideration of lawsuits in the regular courts.

Individual Lawsuits in the Regular Courts

For the complaining consumer, the *threat* of a lawsuit is all advantage whereas an *actual* lawsuit is all disadvantage. The difference hinges on cost, the cost of an actual lawsuit usually far exceeding a dollar estimate of damages sustained in the typical consumer grievance.

A potential lawsuit imposes three types of additional expected costs on the seller. First, there are the legal costs of preparing the case and actually appearing in court. Even though sellers can typically purchase legal services at more favorable rates than consumers, the preparation and conduct of any lawsuit is costly. Second, there are hidden costs to the seller that could be substantial, such as the diversion of some of the firm's personnel from their usual tasks. For example, employees may have to spend some time rummaging the files for data requested by the plaintiff's (consumer's) lawyers in making their case. Third, the firm's public image may be tarnished. In some cases knowledge of the suit will be confined to court personnel, or to businesses in related lines. At worst, the case might be publicized in the media. Either instance imposes very real costs in terms of the firm's reputation. Obviously, a lawyer representing a complaining consumer would do his utmost to expand the public's knowledge of the case.

To be effective in achieving redress, the consumer's threatened lawsuit must be credible. He should be able to name an actual law firm that will prosecute his suit. Indeed, he may choose to push the threat right up to the point of a letter declaring an intention to sue for damages. The credibility of his threat—hence, the likelihood of success—will depend on the determination exhibited in the consumer's personal behavior and on the realism of the steps he takes in apparently moving toward a lawsuit.

In summary, the threat is advantageous to the consumer because the expected cost to the seller is high whereas the cost to the consumer is low. *Actual* lawsuits are all to the disadvantage of the consumer for the following reasons. In the first place, as noted before, there is the cost barrier. In 1970, according to Philip Schrag,[15] experienced lawyers charged from $40 to $100 per hour. Even in a simple case, the necessary steps—verifying the facts, checking out and arranging for witnesses, checking the law, preparing briefs—would take at least eight hours. Thus, the cost of research would be at least $300. As if this were not bad enough, one should note that in consumer damage cases the consumer pays for his own legal costs if he wins, and for both his own and the seller's court costs if he loses. (Violations of the Truth-in-Lending Act constitute an exception to this rule.)

There is also a time barrier, comprised of the often long lag between the initiation and the conclusion of a suit. And finally there is a fear barrier in terms of the willingness to undertake a lawsuit when it is appropriate. Most consumers are unfamiliar with and fearful of dealing with lawyers and the law. This prevents them from suing for damages even when it is appropriate.

Again, the legal contest between seller and consumer is unequal. The contracts consumers sign have been usually drawn to protect sellers, and the seller's access to legal services is more favorable than that of the consumer. He can hire lawyers on a salary or a retainer basis, obtaining "bulk" discounts for a large volume of similar cases. The seller's lawyer, too, can increase his effectiveness and profit by settling with the small percentage of consumer claimants who fight. This latter point, however, provides an opening of which the individual consumer may be able to take advantage.

Government Agencies. During the last five years a spate of "consumer" agencies have come into existence in federal, state, and local

---

[15] Philip G. Schrag, "Consumer Rights," *Columbia Forum,* Summer 1970. However, lawyers in small towns and rural areas often charge less. And legal costs may be made manageable through the contingent fee. Under this arrangement the lawyer receives an agreed per cent of any award, typically a third. Thus, if the case is lost, the consumers pay nothing.

governments. Created as independent agencies or lodged in the attorney general's office, they combine, in varying degrees, a number of functions:

1. They seek to regulate the structure of markets and firm behavior in a generally competitive direction;
2. They seek to curb unsafe products and unsavory commercial practices;
3. They engage in consumer "education";
4. They act as consumer advocates in both regulatory and legislative matters;
5. They operate either formal or informal consumer complaint systems.

It is the last function we consider here.

For the complaining consumer, government agencies, whether federal, state, or local, represent relatively weak channels for individual redress. There are reasons for this state of affairs.

First, for many government agencies with a consumer interest— the Food and Drug Administration, the Federal Trade Commission, the Interstate Commerce Commission, the Federal Power Commission, and state public utility commissions—the complaint resolution function is relatively minor.

A second reason is that these complaints are labor-intensive; even if these agencies were well-manned, they would have difficulty in dealing effectively with the large volume of consumer complaints. In fact, most government agencies are relatively undermanned and hence are unable to cope effectively with individual consumer complaints.

Third, since most consumer complaints do not involve violations of existing laws, many government agencies dealing with consumer complaints have adopted procedures and stances remarkably similar to those of the BBB's. They summarize the consumer's complaint, forward it to the seller, and ask the seller to deal with the complaint and to report his actions to the agency. Ordinarily, the process stops when the seller responds, unless the inquiry discloses actions thought to be illegal.

Where a consumer believes that his complaint involves an illegal act on the part of the seller, then a government action is a highly appropriate channel for seeking redress. In other cases it is the author's judgment that consumers would do best to seek redress from the seller either in person or by mail. And if he chooses to do so by mail, the consumer would be well advised to send carbon copies of his complaint to the relevant government agency. The forces lurking behind the scene are obvious: the possibility of legal action now or of restrictive laws or regulations in the future.

INDIVIDUAL REDRESS IN REAL LIFE: EXAMPLES

For Whom Do the Regulators Toil? The gut reaction of most of us, when confronted by an instance of market failure or merchant mischief, is that "there ought to be a law" to correct the particular kind of consumer injury we have just sustained. But a law usually involves a government agency to administer it. Before you charge off in advocacy of a new law, ponder on the experience of the moving industry. The trailer-truck rental do-it-yourself part of the industry is unregulated. The long-haul moving van part of the industry is regulated by the Interstate Commerce Commission "in the public interest."

To sample service and attitudes, the author inquired about prices and access to credit from (1) trailer-truck rentals and (2) long-haul moving companies. We look first at trailer-truck rentals.

The author's city of 100,000 offers relatively little choice for trailer rentals: there is one national firm and six outlets. So, there is a single price unless one goes outside the city. For truck rentals, the situation is more favorable: four national firms quoting different prices and 12 outlets. For both trailers and trucks, credit is no obstacle. One makes a deposit and then pays the remainder when the equipment is returned. Both deposit and final payments can both be made by a personal check, any national credit card, or, of course, cash.

For long-haul movers where consumers are "protected," the number of competitors *is* favorable; seven national firms offering ten outlets. But all of these movers quote from the identical price schedule ("tariffs") established by the Interstate Commerce Commission (ICC). But differences do arise with respect to estimates of the size of your load and promises with respect to loading and arrival times for your belongings. With respect to credit, the world of the long-distance movers is shockingly different. Inquire about credit to a moving company and the clerk will tell you firmly: "You may pay by certified check, money order, or cash. And you must pay *before* your goods are unloaded." No credit cards. And she may add, righteously, "This is an ICC requirement." For whom do the regulators toil? *Not* for you and for me.

We pursue the subject of long-distance moving further by looking at a modest grievance of the author arising out of the billing practices of movers, as mandated by the ICC.

The author's household goods were moved from Minneapolis to Ithaca, New York, where they were put in storage. (This is why payment prior to unloading was not required.) Subsequently the author received a bill for $580.48 with the following notice enclosed from Minneapolis Van and Warehouse Company, an Allied Van Lines affiliate.

July 19, 1974

SUBJECT: New Interstate Commerce Commission Regulation Regarding the Payment of Charges of Household Goods Carriers (49 CFR Section 1322.1 (c))

Gentlemen:

The Interstate Commerce Commission has issued an order changing the extension of credit regulation which has been in effect for many years. The new credit regulation is effective for shipments *loaded* on or after July 22, 1974. For those of you that may not be aware of this change, here is a summary of the regulation:

1. The free credit period of seven calendar days (excluding Saturdays, Sundays, and legal holidays) shall automatically be extended to a total of 30 calendar days for any shipper who has not paid the carrier's freight bill within the initial 7-day period.
2. The shipper will be assessed a service charge by the carrier equal to one per cent of the amount of the freight bill subject to a $10.00 minimum charge, for an extension of the credit period.
3. No carrier shall grant credit to any shipper who fails to pay a duly presented freight bill within the 30-day period, unless and until the shipper satisfies the carrier that all future freight bills duly presented will be paid strictly in accordance with the rules and regulations prescribed by the Commission for the settlement of carrier rates and charges.
4. No service charge authorized by these regulations will be assessed in connection with rates and charges on freight transported for the United States, for any department, bureau, or agency thereof, or for any State or territory, or political subdivision, or for the District of Columbia.

We are bringing this change in the credit regulation to your attention in view of the responsibility that carriers and shippers have to comply with the order of the Interstate Commerce Commission regarding payment of freight charges.

Our customers have always cooperated with us in the past and, with this in mind, we feel confident that they will recognize our position and do their utmost to implement the new credit regulations with as little inconvenience as possible.

Very truly yours,

Emil R. Calzaretta
Vice-President—Finance

This was certainly a mouthful. But the author was pleased that the ICC was finally doing something for consumers, namely, giving them the free credit privileges in paying movers similar to those they enjoyed with most other businesses. The author paid his bill in two weeks and washed his hands of the matter.

Thus, he was something less than pleased when the Minneapolis Van and Warehouse Company on October 31 sent him a notice with the following inscription:

This bill was not paid within the allotted 7-day period, therefore we must charge you the fine or item 20 per ICC, or $10.
See attached.

And the "attached" turned out to be another copy of the July 19 letter that he now reread with care.

When one considers the value of time, $10 is scarcely worth fighting for. But principles are. And the author decided to use this protest as a test bed to see what it might reveal regarding the character and capacity of various agencies for redress. Hence, the following letter and its "harvest" of replies.

November 7, 1974
Interstate Commerce Commission
Washington, D. C.
Attorney General Warren Spannous
State of Minnesota
Action Line
Channel 4—WCCO, Minneapolis

Column 1
Minneapolis Star

Gentlemen:

Two months ago, after moving from Minneapolis to Ann Arbor, Michigan, I was duly billed for my moving expenses by the Minneapolis Van & Warehouse Company. I paid their bill within 15 days.

Enclosed with the bill was an explanation of a new ICC regulation issued under the signature of Vice-President Calzaretta of Allied Vans. Paragraph 1 of this letter (which I enclose) reads:

> "The FREE credit period of seven calendar days . . . shall automatically be extended to a total of 30 calendar days for any shipper who has not paid the carrier's freight bill within the initial seven day period." [Capitalization mine.]

I was pleased to note that the ICC was finally extending to consumers-movers the privilege of 30 days' free credit, which they receive from most commercial organizations—Sears, American Express, BankAmericard, most department stores.

Imagine my anger when I received the enclosed bill for an additional $10 which I am asked to pay "per order of Interstate Commerce Commission." Upon rereading Mr. Calzaretta's "explanatory" letter, I found it to be hopelessly vague. Specifically, the "credit period" referred to in Paragraph 2 is *not* defined. If "the extension of the credit period" refers to a period of 8 to 30 days after billing, then Paragraph 2 contradicts the phrase "free" in Paragraph 1 and gives lie to that phrase. For Mr. Calzaretta's information "free" means "without charge or cost."

Truthfully, I was misled by Mr. Calzaretta's long, legalistic letter. And I must add that many other people to whom I have shown this "explanation" of the ICC regulation have been similarly confused. (Is there no one at Allied Van who can write simply and clearly?) Having been misled, I refuse to pay the $10 "fine" which Minneapolis Van seeks to extract.

Turning to the substance of the ICC regulation (which I know only from Mr. Calzaretta's letter), I would urge the ICC to require moving companies to grant the same 30-day free credit (genuinely "free") period to consumers-movers which is accorded them by most commercial organizations.

When is the ICC going to begin to deal with both consumers and carriers in an even-handed way?

I would urge the other addressees of this letter to note and to publicize the ICC's action or inaction on this matter.

Sincerely,

E. Scott Maynes
Visiting Research Scientist
cc: Minneapolis Van & Warehouse Co.

Over the next few months the author's mailbox was periodically filled with replies to this letter. What annoyed him was the view, so often expressed in these letters, that "a rule is a rule" and the absolving of ICC and Allied Van from responsibility for the misunderstandings that their turbid prose had produced.

Emil Calzaretta of Allied Van was one of the first to reply:

December 5, 1974

Dear Mr. Maynes:

Constant involvement in a comprehensive 1975 budget plan for Allied Van Lines has prevented my replying sooner to your November 7 letter to Minneapolis Van & Warehouse Company, regarding a new Interstate Commerce Commission regulation.

I am sorry that you believe you were misled by my July 19 letter explaining the service charge for late payment of your bill. That letter was designed specifically for traffic managers and corporate officials who have the day-to-day responsibility for relocating their employees, and who should be familiar with the governmental rules and regulations governing our industry. Perhaps, to a degree, my attempts to clarify a rather comprehensive credit regulation were not as clear and simple as I had originally intended. Additionally, for use by our agents, we prepared the enclosed "sticker" about the new ICC regulation, that was to be attached to invoices. I assume this sticker was not used on your particular invoice.

Here is the government regulation (49CFR Section 1322.1 (c)):

"Except as provided in paragraph (b) of this section, motor common carriers of household goods must also provide in their tariffs that (1) the aforestated credit period of 7 calendar days shall automatically be extended to a total of 30 calendar days for any shipper who has not paid the carrier's freight bill within the aforesaid 7-day period, (2) such shipper will be assessed a service charge by the carrier equal to 1 per cent of the amount of said freight bill, subject to a $10 minimum charge, for such extension of the credit period, and (3) no such carrier shall grant credit to any shipper which fails to pay a duly presented freight bill within the 30-day period, unless and until such shipper affirmatively satisfies the carrier that all future freight bills duly presented will be paid strictly in accordance with the rules and regulations prescribed by the Commission for the settlement of carrier rates and charges. Provided, That no service charge authorized herein shall be assessed in connection with rates and charges on freight transported for the United States, for any department, bureau, or agency thereof, or for any State or territory, or political subdivision thereof, or for the District of Columbia."

Obviously, as you are now aware, if freight bills are not paid within seven days, a one per cent ($10) must be assessed by the carrier. Under the law, we have no choice in the matter.

Again, my apologies for not having acknowledged your letter sooner and for the confusion that my letter may have caused you.

Sincerely,

Emil R. Calzaretta
Vice-President–Finance

The red sticker mentioned in paragraph 2 was indeed clear:

NOTICE

Under a new I.C.C. regulation, a service charge of 1% of the freight bill amount (subject to a $10.00 minimum) will be assessed unless this invoice is paid within seven (7) days (excluding Saturdays, Sundays, and legal holidays) from the first 12:00 o'clock midnight following mailing or presentation of the freight bill. The assessment is included in the larger charge on this invoice.

Failure to pay within the 30-day calendar credit period may cause revocation of credit privileges.

But this had not been attached to the author's bill.

But notice Mr. Calzaretta's dogged insistence that the author should pay the $10 fine, whether misled or not. And notice, further, how the ICC is employed as a shield for the regulated: "Under the law, we have no choice in the matter."

A chief of interpretations for the Interstate Commerce Commission signed in at about the same time:

Bureau of Operations
Interstate Commerce Commission
Washington, D. C. 10423
December 6, 1974

Dear Mr. Maynes:

This is in reply to your letter of November 7, 1974, concerning the new regulation of the Commission under which you were billed by Allied Van Lines for an additional charge of $10 for failure to pay the carrier's freight charge within 7 days (excluding Saturdays, Sundays, and legal holidays).

I agree with you that the explanation of the new regulation which accompanied the bill for the original charges was somewhat misleading. The first paragraph gives the impression that the extension of the credit period to a total of 30 calendar days is "free" as well as the initial seven-day period. The second paragraph could have corrected this impression by the use of the word "such" or "that" in place of "an." As written, the paragraph may well be understood to mean that the $10 charge is for "an extension" of the 30-day period referred to in the first paragraph. I am sending a copy of this letter to Mr. Emil R. Calzaretta, Vice President–Finance of Allied Van Lines, Inc., over whose signature the explanation was made.

The reason for this added charge is that the requirement of payment within the mentioned 7-day period was being ignored by many commercial shippers. Usually household goods carriers allow credit only to commercial shippers. Prompt payment of freight charges is essential if carriers are to avoid extensive borrowing of working capital, the cost of which would be reflected in increased rates for all who use the services of the carriers. It seems to be a fair arrangement that those who take the additional time to make payment should stand the additional cost rather than assessing a proportion of that cost against all shippers, even those who pay in cash upon delivery.

Very truly yours,

T. J. Delaney, Chief of
Interpretations
Section of Motor Carriers

The author was pleased to see that Delaney, "Chief of Interpretations" for the ICC, found Calzaretta's letter "somewhat misleading." But he looked in vain for Delaney to express the view that the fine was out of order in view of the misleading character of the "explanatory" letter. And most consumers would be taken aback at Delaney's apparent approval of the movers' practice of granting credit to commercial shippers while denying it to ordinary consumers. For whom does the ICC toil?

The Attorney General's Office of Minnesota disclaimed jurisdiction. They wrote: "Your complaint has been referred to the Interstate Commerce Commission as it has primary jurisdiction over trade practice matters of this type." And the ICC—except for the Delaney letter —was never heard from again.

Action News of television station WCCO apparently contacted Allied Van, with the result that they were sent a copy of Calzaretta's letter of December 5. Action News then wrote to the author:

The enclosed letter was sent to Action News.
We would appreciate any comment, suggestion, or answer you may have.
We'd be grateful if you would return the letter . . . or a copy of it . . . along with your remarks.

By this time the author had become tired, and his words had begun to be unquotable.

Column 1, the Consumer Action column of The Minneapolis *Star* wrote as follows:

Dear Mr. Maynes:
Thank you for writing Column 1 about your disagreement with Minneapolis Van & Warehouse Co. Unfortunately, it appears that the firm was correct in charging you the $10.
The regulation seemed confusing, until we were told by an

ICC official that prior to the regulation carriers were not allowed to provide credit at all. This was an attempt to prevent them from using credit to attract the business of larger, corporate clients, at the expense of persons like yourself.

The new regulation allows seven days before payment is required. Previously, bills were to be paid on delivery. The extension to 30 days requires a finance charge if the bill is paid after the initial seven days. The minimum charge, as in your case, is $10.

I hope this answers your question. If you care to pursue the matter any further, I suggest you contact the ICC office nearest you.

The author found Column 1's response annoying. It dealt not at all with the question of whether Calzaretta's letter of July 19 was misleading. And he thought that Column 1's logic was less than impeccable. Is not the central issue the right of consumers to have 30 days in which to pay? Are consumer customers of the truck rental companies affected adversely because the rental companies also grant corporate clients credit? It seems doubtful.

And so we come to the end of this account of a consumer protest. The lesson, if there is one, is that it is much more difficult to pursue a grievance against a regulated firm on an issue that is not crystal clear. And it seems appropriate to ask once again: for whom do the regulators toil?

The Price of Rights. Mr. J and his sister planned somewhat unusual arrangements for their trip to Washington, D.C. Instead of flying from Hartford, Connecticut, to convenient but nondescript National Airport in Washington, their destination would be Dulles International where they would experience for the first time Dulles' different airplane-to-terminal buses and the terminal's distinctive architecture.

Imagine their consternation when the counterman at Hartford Airport informed Mr. J: "Sorry, sir, we can take you to New York (the intermediate stop for their flight) but you will have to take a different flight from New York."

"But," expostulated Mr. J, "my sister and I are traveling together to Washington."

The counterman was adamant: "Sorry. We can take both of you to New York. And we can take her to Dulles. But we just haven't enough seats to take you from Kennedy to Dulles. We'll see that you get another flight from New York, though."

Mr. J's indignation and blood pressure began to rise. "See here.

I made this reservation three weeks ago. And, your people in Washington told me that my reservation was in order."

The counterman: "All I know is that I can't give you a seat through to Washington. Here, I'll check your bag to New York though."

By this time Mr. J was seething and his sister was embarrassed.

His sister urged: "Come on, George, we can both change in New York and go to National."

But Mr. J was unrelenting. To the counterman: "I will *carry* my bag on. And I want you to tell your New York people that if they want my seat, they will have to carry me off the plane! And I mean that." He shouted this in a loud and angry voice that drew considerable attention.

The flight to New York was an uneasy one for Mr. J and his sister. He was angry, determined, and anxious. She thought that he was in the right, even though she would not have protested so volubly herself. She commented, "If they overbooked, I would have thought that they would have bumped someone who had just got his reservation. You had yours three weeks ago."

At Kennedy Airport the New York passengers debarked, leaving a small number of Washington-bound passengers lounging. But Mr. J remained firmly in his seat, resolute. They would *not* dislodge *him* from *his* seat. . . . After a time, they heard a hubbub of foreign-sounding voices. As seats filled up and a large number of "Alitalia" labels passed, the mystery unraveled: the new passengers were Italian tourists. The reservations picture cleared too: the airline had block-booked almost an entire planeload of Italian tourists, fresh from Rome. This was why Mr. J had been bumped.

Still, Mr. J remained in his seat, apprehensive. Mentally he rehearsed the argument to come. But the argument never came: the plane engines started. And the seat situation became clear: the airline had bumped a more pliant passenger than Mr. J. Or, perhaps, some of the tourists did not show up. An hour later the Italian visitors and the J's deplaned at Dulles. And now it was a lovely day and a worthwhile sight.

Mr. J thought that the lesson of this episode was plain: making a fuss pays. But even he was ready to acknowledge that you couldn't afford an episode like this very often: too much adrenaline used up, too much wear-and-tear on the nerves. But both the J's blamed the airline.

His sister stated it this way: "If we had been told in Hartford that they wanted our seats so that some Italian visitors could see Dulles, we would probably have been willing to give them up. But in Hartford they didn't say a word about that." From such partial understandings, many consumer grievances arise.

*Legal Fees: An Ounce of Prevention.** When the N's sold their home without benefit of a real estate agent for $50,000, they paid their lawyer $225 for handling the legal aspects of the transfer. The transaction was not wholly routine, since it involved the bureaucratic complexities of a Veterans Administration-guaranteed mortgage and a "closing" at which they, as sellers, were not present. Their lawyer was experienced, sound. They thought that his fee was reasonable.

So when they began to investigate housing, and thus closing costs, in the smaller, five-bank town to which they were moving, they were not prepared for the unpleasant surprise that awaited them. In Littletown, according to representatives of all five banks, the "customary" fee paid to a lawyer was 1 per cent of the price. For the $70,000 house they had their eye on, this would mean $700, or more than three times as much as they paid their city lawyer for essentially the same job. This thought left them exceedingly unhappy. But what were they to do?

The N's racked their imagination. Should they seek a lawyer in the nearest large city 50 miles away? They quickly dismissed this idea. For one thing, they would not know what lawyer to approach in a strange city; for another they had doubts whether many lawyers from another city would come out to work for them in Littletown. . . . The N's decided to ask the various real estate agents who had been showing them houses whether there was any way of avoiding the 1 per cent fee. Not unexpectedly, the answer given by all the real estate agents was the same. One per cent of the price was the going rate and all their customers paid it.

In the meantime further negotiations made it almost certain that they would buy the house at 250 South Cherry, Littletown, for a price in the vicinity of $68,000. In the process of negotiation they came to know the sellers, the Ames, and found them very congenial. They spoke of what the Ames would leave behind when they moved out— drapes, some bookcases, and the like. It became clear to the N's that it would be an amicable transfer with a minimum of fuss. Still, with $68,000 involved, they thought they needed a lawyer to assure that the legal aspects of the purchase were handled correctly.

And then Mr. N had a brainstorm. They had learned from the

---

* In this example—as with most in this book—the events are real while the names are fictitious.

Ames that a man named Ed Barrow would act as the Ames' lawyer. Perhaps the N's could use the same lawyer. And, perhaps, since the seller's interest and the buyer's interest called for checking the same items, they could purchase Barrow's services for a lower fee. They checked out Barrow's reputation with people at the company where Mr. N would work in Littletown. The reactions were affirmative: Barrow was viewed as honest and competent. Some of Mr. N's fellow employees had used him on real estate transactions.

That satisfied the N's. They would see whether the Ames would be willing. Before broaching the matter to the Ames, they discussed what terms might be acceptable—for the Ames, for Barrow, and of course for themselves. Working alone for the Ames, Barrow would receive 1 per cent of the price, unless the Ames had some special arrangement with him. So the N's decided that together they and the Ames should offer to pay him 1 1/4 per cent of the price. They (the N's) would pay 5/8 of 1 per cent and the Ames would also pay 5/8 of 1 per cent, making a total of 1 1/4 per cent. That way each of them would save 3/8 of 1 per cent and Barrow would get 1/4 of 1 per cent more than if he worked for the Ames alone. The 3/8 of 1 per cent they would save would come to $255 when applied to $68,000. That was worth a little effort.

The N's "tested" this gambit on their friends. The Ames would be willing, their friends thought, but Barrow would never agree.

And the Ames were willing. Now "all" that remained was to convince Barrow that he should accept. At Barrow's office the N's stated their proposition. They wanted him to handle the legal aspects of the transfer of 250 South Cherry for *both* them and the Ames. They had talked with the Ames, they told him, and the Ames were willing. Their relationship with the Ames was cordial and the transfer seemed routine. They proposed that, as a fee, they pay him 5/8 of 1 per cent, or $425 and the Ames pay him 5/8 of 1 per cent, too. Thus, he would earn more for about the same work. And both they and the Ames would pay less than usual. If Barrow did not accept, they would engage another lawyer from a different firm. Did he see any problems?

Barrow replied that the arrangement was somewhat unusual. He went on to note that, if any dispute should arise between the Ames and the N's, he would withdraw as agent for the N's. But otherwise he was willing as long as the Ames were.

And that is the way it went. The N's and the Ames each paid $425 (instead of the "customary" $680). The N's and the Ames each saved $255. (And, of course, for a 4-person family with a before-tax income of $25,000, this saving would be equivalent to $435 (= $255 × 1.75) of additional income. See Table 2 in Chapter 1.) And, by representing both buyer and seller, Barrow earned $850 instead of $680.

A Legal and Economic Footnote. On June 16, 1975, the United States Supreme Court ruled that minimum legal fee schedules (for representing clients in house transfers, for example) violate the price-fixing prohibitions of the antitrust laws and hence are illegal. Does this render the previous example obsolete? Not at all. As we noted in Chapter 2, tacit agreements by which lawyers (or real estate agents or other professionals) charge "customary" fees may fix prices just as effectively as a minimum fee schedule adopted by a bar association.

One additional word of caution is in order. It is possible that a lawyer representing *both* parties to a real estate transaction may not pursue the interest of either party with the same vigor as a lawyer representing a single interest. In this situation more than most, a client places his greatest reliance on the competence and integrity of the lawyer he employs.

Reparations, Anybody? The Q's long day started pleasantly in Paris, the last day of their European trip. Under a bright, blue sky they boarded a bus at 9:00 a.m. for Luxembourg where they would take a 1:30 p.m. flight on Icelandic Airlines to New York. The first problem of the day occurred when they discovered that Icelandic had sold their reservations out from under them. (Instead of reconfirming 72 hours before flight time, the Q's had reconfirmed 68 hours in advance.) This meant a later flight. Instead of arriving at Kennedy at 7:30 p.m., they would arrive at 10:30 p.m.

The Q's second crisis started at 11:00 p.m. at Kennedy Airport, New York, when they rented a car from Hertz. It reached a nasty climax when they ran out of gas on an interstate highway in Connecticut at 1:15 a.m. It is on this grievance that this case centers. Mr. Q's letter to Hertz recounts the episode.

July 31, 1970
Hertz Corporation
P. O. Box 2856
Grand Central Station
New York, New York 10017

Re: *Rental Agreement No. 7235114-4*

Gentlemen:

On Sunday evening, July 19, I rented a car from your JFK office. Two aspects of the rental were highly unsatisfactory:

1. *Most important, the car given me had an almost empty gas tank.* The result was that I ran out of gas and was stranded at 1:15 a.m. on a superhighway—extremely awkward and possibly hazardous.

2. On the *phone your agent said I could drop off the car in Meriden, Connecticut,* my destination. At the parking lot I was told that New Haven and Hartford were the nearest drop points. [Each is 20 miles from Mr. Q's destination.]

Let me fill you in on the details.

(1) *Meriden, Not Hartford*

I approached the Hertz counter at the International Arrivals —East Wing—at 11:05 p.m., July 19, and phoned (there being no attendant) to ask whether they had a car which I could drop off in Meriden, Connecticut. After I told your representative that Meriden lies halfway between Hartford and New Haven, he said it would be possible to drop off the car in Meriden. When I arrived at the Hertz parking lot, however, the clerk informed me that Hertz has no agency in Meriden. She offered to have my wife and I drive back to Avis, which has a Meriden station. Having been awake continuously for 23 hours, we declined. The net effect was to involve us in an unnecessary trip to Hartford and an unnecessary mileage charge.

(2) *Running Out of Gas*

At various times I have rented cars from Hertz, Avis, National, and Budget. In every case the car rented was delivered with a full tank of gas. Thus, it seemed understandable that neither my wife nor I thought to look at the gas gauge. The fact that we had been awake for 23 hours straight and were just emerging from the confusion of JFK did not add to our alertness. (Your Hartford desk man seemed to think that any sane person would check the gas gauge under these circumstances. He seemed further to believe that any car renter would be aware of the possibility that JFK might run out of gas on a Sunday night. We found this man to be rude and unsympathetic, one of the best ads for *Avis* that we've encountered.)

We ran out of gas about 6 miles south of Wallingford on the Wilbur Cross Parkway at 1:15 a.m. Fortunately, a passing motorist was willing to take us to my parents' home in Meriden where we got my sister's car, picked up a can of gasoline, drove back to the North Haven entrance, and finally retrieved your car. As you can imagine, it was not a pleasant experience for people, then 26 hours awake, at that hour of the morning (3:30 a.m.)!

Aside from the unpleasantness of the experience, these two mistakes on your part produced unnecessary expenses for us as follows:

Sister's car to North Haven and back, 40 miles at $.15 per mile (your rate)	$6.00
Two extra highway tolls	.30
Extra mileage charge—Meriden to Hartford 20 miles at $.12	2.40
Total	$8.70

It seems fair that Hertz bear this additional expense.

I hope that the next time "I rent a corporation" my experience will be more favorable.

Since the rental charges were placed on my American Express credit card, I am sending them a copy of this letter.

Sincerely,

A month passed with no reaction whatever from either Hertz or American Express. Mr. Q thought that an establishment business such as Hertz might respond to a prod from the Better Business Bureau. So he sent the following letter to the local Bureau.

September 2, 1970
Better Business Bureau of Minneapolis, Inc.
701 2nd Avenue South
Minneapolis, Minnesota 55402

Gentlemen:

See the enclosed letter of complaint that I sent to the Hertz Corporation on July 31.

Since I have as yet received no answer from them I am asking for whatever help you can give me.

Sincerely,

Two days after Mr. Q had mailed his "reinforcing" letter to the Better Business Bureau, Hertz paid up. Their letter:

September 3, 1970

Dear Mr. Q:

I am in receipt of your letter dated July 31, in regard to rental agreement number 7235114-4.

Please be advised that I have notified our adjustment department in accordance with the $7.50 deduction from your billing. As calculated by yourself, I have deducted the personal expense in concern with your sister's car allowing for the 20 per cent discount which is applied to our mileage charge and therefore deducted from your calculation.

Your American Express account will be credited in the amount of $7.50.

I am sincerely sorry for the inconveniences you encountered. It is my personal hope that you might on your next occasion when a rental car is necessary, give us the opportunity to redeem ourselves in your eyes and prove to you why we are the leader in our industry.

Very truly yours,
The Hertz Corporation

L. A. Strouse
City Manager

If you appreciate gamesmanship, you will appreciate the ploy of the Hertz city manager in deducting the 20 per cent discount!

So a letter was sent and $7.50 gained. But Q's wife was only partially satisfied. Being stranded on an interstate highway at 1:15 in the morning was entirely disagreeable. And it was her view that they should have tried to get Hertz to pay "reparations" for the very real anxiety and discomfort they had suffered. What do you think? How much should they have sought? $10? $25? $50? Would Hertz have paid?

But the wheels of large organizations grind slowly. The episode was closed when the Manhattan office of Hertz wrote on October 21 to tell the Better Business Bureau that the city manager at Kennedy Airport would write them regarding the Q matter!

A Fraudulent Tire Repair, or, What the Consumer Does Not Know Might Hurt Him. The financial damage in this episode was small, only $5. And the odds are that, undetected, the loss of $5 would have been the end of it. But, there was also the long-shot possibility that this fraud, compounded by inept workmanship, could have resulted in a serious automobile accident or even death for Mr. P and his family.

The story is best told in the letter Mr. P addressed to the Minnesota Attorney General's Office:

August 10, 1969

Consumer Protection Division
Attorney General's Office
State of Minnesota
St. Paul, Minnesota 55101

Gentlemen:

Let me report an automobile service complaint for possible action by your office. It involves the installation of a *defective, used* tire tube instead of the new one requested. Had it not been discovered, it could have resulted in considerable peril to the lives of my family.

The story was this. The tire on the left rear wheel of my 1963 Chevy II had a slow leak which no service station was able to repair. To eliminate the problem, I was advised to install a *new* tube in what had been originally a tubeless tire.

On Friday, August 1, 1969, my work took me to the Greenland section of the Twin Cities. It seemed convenient to leave my car at a gas station, have them install the tube while I completed my business in the Greenland area, and then to pick up the car with the work completed.

I phoned the Mobil Greenland Service Station, 2277 Green Avenue.[16] They said they could do the job. Accordingly, I left my car and they completed the work. I picked up the car and paid the bill. (The bill read "new tube $3.25, tax $.14, labor $1.50.") I had no reason whatsoever to suspect that a *new* tube of the appropriate size had *not* been installed.

The next day the tire in question went flat, apparently the result of picking up a tack. It was a "lucky" flat. When the tire was taken off the wheel, it revealed that Mobil Greenland instead of installing a new tube, had put on a used, faultily patched tube. This was the judgment of the mechanics at the Crest 66 Service Station, at 1822 Hennepin Avenue, Minneapolis, who removed the tire and tube.

On Tuesday, August 5, I returned to Mobil Greenland, and showed the defective tube to the manager. His comment: "You

[16] Since the business in question has become defunct, there is no point in using its correct name or address. Ironically, the business was a consumer cooperative.

can't keep your eye on them [the mechanics] all the time." He refunded my money. He offered to have a genuinely new tube installed. For reasons you can imagine, I declined.

What action of a corrective nature can be taken? I have both the Mobil Greenland receipt and the tube in my possession.

I am sending a copy of this letter to (1) the District Office of the Mobil Oil Company, and (2) the Better Business Bureau of St. Paul.

Sincerely,

In composing this letter, Mr. P knew what corrective action *he* would have proposed: a fat fine of (say) $100 on Greenland Mobil to encourage its managers and other service station managers to avoid fraudulent shortcutting of the type illustrated in this episode. Despite the disgust the episode triggered in Mr. P, he was realistic enough to have only modest expectations regarding the "possible corrective actions" mentioned in the next-to-last paragraph of his letter. In this he was not disappointed.

Consider the reactions by the various parties involved:

The Manager of Greenland Mobil managed nothing more than a refund of Mr. P's $4.89 and his sour comment on his mechanics: "You can't keep your eye on them all the time." No mention was made of disciplinary action for the mechanic in question.

The Attorney General's Office responded in a letter whose first paragraph suggested that it was composed for a different, but recurring problem with Mobil:

We are in receipt of your letter to Mobil Oil Gift Headquarters regarding the credit card which was issued in your name.

Thank you for bringing this matter to our attention. We will retain this information for our files and possible legislation in this area.

The letter was signed by a "Special Assistant Attorney General, Consumer Division." Presumably the letter still rests in his file.

Mobil Oil Corporation expressed what seemed to Mr. P genuine, if ineffectual concern, in two ways. First, it sent a St. Paul company lieutenant to Mr. P's office to express the company's concern [17] and

---

[17] After discussing Mr. P's problem and expressing Mobil's inability to control its "independent dealers," this gentleman gave Mr. P a coupon authorizing him to receive ten gallons of gasoline, free!

the Mobil customer relations manager in New York wrote to Mr. P as follows:

August 25, 1969

Dear Mr. P:

The copy of your August 10 letter to the Consumer Protection Division of the Minnesota Attorney General's Office has been referred to me. I was sorry to learn of the difficulty you had experienced with the tube installed by Greenland Mobil, in Saint Paul. Please accept our sincere apologies for the concern and inconvenience you were caused.

Although all Mobil dealers are independent businessmen, Mobil is definitely interested in the quality of service rendered to the motoring public. A great deal of effort is expended in counseling with our dealers on the importance of courteous, reliable service at all times. Whenever anyone is not treated in a proper manner, we wish to know about it so that we can specifically point out the dissatisfaction to the dealer toward the end of avoiding future occurrences.

A copy of your letter is being forwarded to our Twin Cities District with the request that they discuss your experience with those concerned. You may be sure that this will receive a high priority, and that they will be in touch with you.

We deeply regret the reason for your letter, but wish to thank you for bringing this matter to our attention. You understanding and goodwill are very important to us.

Sincerely,

For its part, the Better Business Bureau of St. Paul forwarded to Mr. P a copy of the same letter from Mobil with this note:

Attached is

AN ANSWER TO YOUR COMPLAINT

filed with your Better Business Bureau recently. We know you would like a copy.

We sincerely hope the answer is satisfactory to you. Should you not be satisfied with the company's side of the story, you are privileged to pursue your complaint through other channels.

Please think of the Bureau's informational services *prior* to doing business with individuals and firms about which you know little.

After reviewing these outcomes, Mr. P stated his own disposition of his case: grievance *un*resolved!

The Plaint of the Old Cyclist. An old friend, the old cyclist, puts his case better than we can:

April 6, 1970
Chairman
Raleigh Industries, Ltd.
Nottingham, England

Dear Sir:

I wonder how many people have been killed when—come rain or freezing conditions—the caliper brakes on their Raleigh bicycles failed to stop them!

I write as a cyclist of some experience. I have owned and used Raleigh bikes in England and Scotland during World War II, in India, and in the U.S. The brakes on the Raleigh I purchased last summer are just as defective and dangerous in the rain as the first Raleigh I purchased in England 27 years ago.

This fault is not exclusive to Raleigh cycles. Rather, it is shared by the entire "family" of Raleigh cycles and other makes as well, indeed by all bikes equipped with caliper brakes. My message is addressed to you because I am the owner of a Raleigh and because Raleigh, in most respects, enjoys a reputation as the "Rolls Royce" of bicycles.

I am sending copies of this letter to *Which,* to *The Times,* and to *Consumer Reports* (the American counterpart of *Which*). It may be that I am not a solitary complainant.

I look forward to the time when my Raleigh will be equipped with brakes which are effective in all kinds of weather.

Sincerely,

I. C. Clearly, Cyclist

This was a complaint, finally given voice, because the feelings and exasperations of the old cyclist were rubbed raw each time when, with wet rims, he squeezed and his brakes failed. He had few illusions that his letter would do anything. But he felt better at having composed and sent it.

As it turned out, Mr. Clearly was never to discover whether he was a "solitary complainant." This letter yielded the following "bag" of responses:

Raleigh Industries: no reaction whatsoever.

Which (the British equivalent of *Consumer Reports*): a letter from the head of membership services observing that "we have not heard of trouble with caliper cycle brakes before" and informing Mr. Clearly that "the Home Office has the power either to exert pressure on a manufacturer, or to have dangerous goods modified and even withdrawn." (Mr. Clearly, drained of his protest energies by this letter, did not contact the British Home Office.)

The Times of London responded in classic form:

Dear Sir:

I am asked to acknowledge your letter of April 6, which has been carefully noted.

Sincerely,

Hercules Grytpype Thynn

And perhaps it was. But as far as Mr. Clearly could discover, this was the sole reaction of *The Times* to his communication.

Consumer Reports: no reply.

Summing up: It was a good thing that the writing of this letter made the Old Cyclist feel virtuous. As far as he could see, the stone he had thrown into the pond had disappeared below the surface, strangely, with no discernible ripple.

With the bicycle boom of the 1970s—according to the *New York Times,* 58 million bicycles were pumped into the market in the 1970–75 period [18]—Consumers Union started to test bicycles. And their tests confirmed what Mr. Clearly's experience had uncovered a long time ago. *Consumer Reports* stated it this way (with reference to three-speed bikes): "But calipers have severe limitations in wet weather—our riders experience an almost total loss of brake response in our braking tests when wheel rims were wet." Their suggested solution was drastic: "If your bike has caliper brakes, when the rims are wet, go extra slow and *walk* your vehicle down hills." No investigation was reported as to how many reader-cyclists followed this advice.

[18] *New York Times,* June 29, 1975, Business Section, p. 3.

One year later, in reporting on ten-speed bicycles, *Consumer Reports* [19] confirmed its earlier findings, but also reported some progress: [20]

> Our previous experience with caliper brakes led us to expect a substantial decrease in stopping power—and we sure experienced it on this go-around. More than half the bicycles took more than 70 feet to stop. You probably can do better than that by dragging your feet. And some bikes used up as much as 150 feet, with an almost total loss of brake response. The ratings record wet-braking performance in percentages of normal braking in dry conditions. Note that the best was only 35 per cent.
>
> There are some signs, though, that manufacturers have been working on the wet-braking problem. The "all weather" *AW* blocks on the *Itoh* have holes on the sides, presumably to distort the rubber surfaces during hard braking and make channels for water to escape. Stopping distance for the *Itoh* with wet brakes was 60 feet. [There follows favorable references to the SMF Roadmaster Pursuit, the Murray Phoenix, The Peugot U08 and Mixte U018, which stopped in 50 feet.] The best wet-brake performers were the three Schwinn racers, all giving stops of about 45 feet.

Mr. Clearly found it unsurprising that the three Raleighs were among the *worst* when it came to braking performance when wet. (Of 39 bikes tested, four retained only 10 per cent of their braking performance when wet; 12—including four Raleighs—retained only 15 per cent of their dry braking performance.)

Thinking it over in 1975, Mr. Clearly was pleased that cycle manufacturers in the 1970s were finally beginning to respond to his long-standing complaint.

[19] *Consumer Reports* (January 1974), pp. 18–28.
[20] Ibid., p. 21.

PART TWO

THE PERFORMANCE OF THE ECONOMY FROM THE CONSUMER VIEWPOINT

CHAPTER 9

Consumer Sovereignty: An Overview of the Issues

"Consumption," Adam Smith declared 200 years ago, "is the sole end and purpose of all production."[1] And by way of emphasis, he declared: "the interest of the producer ought to be attended only so far as it may be necessary for promoting that of the consumer."[2] Thus did Adam Smith, the "father" of economics, establish the conventional wisdom that was to prevail for 190 years—the notion that consumption is the main goal of all economic activity.

It was only in 1965 that the publication by Gary Becker of "A Theory of the Allocation of Time"[3] signaled the ultimate obsolescence of this view. (We say "ultimate" because, as in the case of any new idea, Becker's innovation will gain ascendancy only after the passage of some time.) Becker's theory holds that satisfaction arises from activities in general and not solely from "consumption" activities. Thus, people will derive satisfaction not only from dining, playing tennis, sleeping, and contemplating—all examples of consumption— but also from "working." Can anyone deny that many professors, business executives, welders, and performers in the arts, entertainment, and sports realms gain satisfaction from the "work" activity itself and not merely from the consumption their salaries make possible? The main point is that it is satisfaction and not just consumption that justifies economic activity.

---

[1] Adam Smith, *The Wealth of Nations*, 3rd ed. (London: J. Dove, 1826), Book IV, chap. VIII, p. 620.

[2] Ibid.

[3] Gary S. Becker, "A Theory of the Allocation of Time," *Economic Journal* (September 1965), pp. 493–517.

In a seminal article 25 years ago, Kenneth Boulding argued for the *minimization* of consumption. But Boulding's article did not achieve the same attention as Becker's. See Kenneth E. Boulding, "Income or Welfare," *Review of Economic Studies*, Vol. 17, No. 2 (1950), pp. 77–86.

The reader will recognize that he has encountered these thoughts earlier in this book, at the beginning of Chapter 2. They are repeated here because they are essential background for the discussion of *this* chapter.

Nonetheless, it still remains true that consumption activities comprise a large proportion of all the activities that yield satisfaction. For this reason we still find it appropriate to pose and seek to answer the central question of "consumer sovereignty": how well does our economy serve the consumer?

The discussion of consumer sovereignty is organized into two parts. First, we deal with the meaning of consumer sovereignty at some length. Second, we go on to an overview of the "big questions" relating to consumer sovereignty as well as a catalog of obstacles to its attainment. Perhaps not surprisingly, the criticisms of our economy by professional economists have almost zero overlap with the complaints of consumerists. This provides a convenient division of labor. Thus, Chapter 10 deals with the criticisms of economists whereas Chapter 11 is devoted to the plaints of consumerists.

THE MEANING OF CONSUMER SOVEREIGNTY

Most simply, if we assert that "the consumer is king" in a given economy and mean it, we are asserting the doctrine of consumer sovereignty. More carefully, *consumer sovereignty* [4] may be defined as a condition under which "all economic processes are ultimately focused toward satisfying wants of ultimate consumers." [5] An alternative definition would specify consumer sovereignty as "production in conformity to the preferences of consumers."

Thus far economists have been able to identify only one market arrangement guaranteeing the achievement of consumer sovereignty: perfect competition. A listing of the requirements of perfect competition may help us understand the concept of consumer sovereignty and some of the mechanisms that make its achievement possible. The assumptions of perfect competition are:

[4] The term "consumer sovereignty" was coined by W. M. Hutt and first appeared in his book, *Economists and the Public, A Study of Competition and Opinion* (London: Jonathan Cape, Ltd., 1936).

[5] This definition comes from the definitive essay on "Consumer Sovereignty" by Jerome Rothenberg in David Sill, ed., *International Encyclopedia of the Social Sciences, Vol. III* (New York: Macmillan Publishing Co., Inc., 1968, pp. 326–35). See also the insightful paper by Abba P. Lerner, "The Economics and Politics of Consumer Sovereignty," *American Economic Review* (May 1972), pp. 258–266.

1. Many producer/sellers, so many that no single seller can perceptibly influence industry price or output;

2. Many consumers; again, so many that no single consumer can exert a detectable influence on industry price or output.

3. Perfect information. Each actor in the economic arena—the producer/seller of final products, the seller of inputs, and the consumer—obtains at zero cost the complete and accurate information he needs to act effectively. He also possesses perfect understanding of relevant concepts as well as perfect foresight.

4. Perfectly mobile resources. Inputs such as labor, natural resources, capital, and entrepreneurial capacities are assumed to move freely and at low cost from one usage to another.

5. Homogeneous products, that is, products of uniform quality.

When buttressed by further assumptions regarding the objectives of the economic actors, consumer sovereignty is achieved. The assumptions regarding the actors' motivations and the ultimate results of these assumptions are as follows:

Producers/sellers of final products seek to maximize profits. They are successful when, with respect to:

1. *Product mix and output level:* they are unable (try though they may) to alter their product mix or output level in any way that would enable them to increase their profits. (Remember that prices are given by the market; the individual seller is unable to affect them.)

2. *Purchase of inputs:* they are unable to alter their use of labor or other inputs in any way that would decrease their costs.

3. *Profit level:* they are receiving just that level of profits that will keep themselves and their capital in their present employment.

Sellers of inputs seek to maximize their utility (satisfaction). They are successful when, with respect to:

1. *Work/leisure choice:* for labor inputs, they are unable to find a work/leisure combination that would yield greater utility.

2. *Sale of inputs:* they are unable to find another use for the inputs they own that would yield a higher return.

Consumers seek to maximize utility. They are successful when, with respect to:

1. *Spending/saving choice:* they are unable to alter the division of income between spending and saving in a way that would yield greater utility.

2. *Purchase mix:* they are unable to alter their mix of purchases in any way that would yield greater utility.

The result of all this is consumer sovereignty, whereby each consumer obtains the quality and kind of goods and services that satisfy him most at the lowest possible costs.

It is self-interest constrained by a competitive market structure that makes this consumer sovereignty engine run.

In these sunlit uplands of perfect competition the air is clear and sweet. There are no rip-offs of the types deplored by either economists or consumerists. The would-be monopolist desirous of restricting output in order to raise prices is thwarted by the existence of a multitude of competitive sellers of the identical product. Should he post a higher price, he will sell nothing; should he be stupid enough to restrict his output, he will reduce his profits.

In this happy environment consumers need *not* beware: they *know.* Being perfectly knowledgeable, they detect and avoid unsafe products and fraud. In this world of homogeneous products, they are spared the frustrating task of assessing the quality of different specimens of products. Thus, they need not compare various specimens of air conditioners, because all (of a given size) are identical. But they are *not* excused from the presumably easier task of deciding between different products, such as between air conditioners and attic fans.

At this point two matters deserve further comment. First, consumer sovereignty should be regarded as an objective toward which an economy is (one hopes) moving. Second, economists and consumers stress different outcomes of consumer sovereignty. Economists dwell almost exclusively on the composition of output and its conformity (or nonconformity) to the preferences of consumers. Consumerists, on the other hand, place their emphasis on conditions surrounding purchase transactions.

THE "BIG QUESTIONS"

Having completed our visit to the never-never land of perfect competition, we seek to further our understanding of consumer sovereignty by spelling out the "big questions" of consumer sovereignty and assessing the answers given to each by actual economies in the real world. The biggest of the big questions receives detailed treatment in Chapters 10 and 11.

Whose Wants? How Registered? When consumer sovereignty is defined as a condition "under which all economic processes are ultimately focused toward satisfying wants of ultimate consumers," two questions immediately come to mind. The first is 1) What importance is to be assigned in a given economy to satisfying the wants of different consumers (the young versus the old) or different types of wants ("necessities" versus "luxuries," for example). This may be termed the question of weights, or of relative importance. And the second is 2) How are the wants of consumers to be registered or transmitted? We discuss each of these questions in turn.

On the weights question, the answer given by all market economies is that individual consumers have weights proportionate to their incomes (and, perhaps secondarily, proportionate to their accumulated wealth since this too can be applied to purchases). In discussions of consumer sovereignty *per se,* the prevailing distribution of income and wealth is not usually questioned. (You should bear in mind that all societies modify the initial distribution of income and wealth through the taxes and transfer payments systems they adopt.) Only in the almost-never economy of pure communism do all individuals have equal weights.[6]

In most economies, the preferences of several groups are almost invariably accorded either lesser or zero weights: young children, the (obviously) mentally ill, drug addicts, and similar persons. For these groups the objective of lesser or zero weights is achieved either by keeping money out of their hands or by sellers refusing their proffered purchases. Correspondingly, certain classes of goods may be viewed as socially unacceptable and their distribution is restricted or prohibited—for example, some drugs, the services of prostitutes. Prohibition, of course, is tantamount to a zero weight when it is effective.

Mention the registration of wants and you at once raise the question of the extent to which expressed preferences represent the "true" wants of the individual. The main body of economists, while acknowledging the power of advertising, tend to take the view that, by and large, such expressed preferences do, in fact, represent what consumers really want. Not so, says John Kenneth Galbraith, the profession's most articulate "inside" critic. Galbraith argues that, for many

[6] Some Israeli kibbutzim are examples. See Kenneth E. Boulding, *The Economy of Love and Fear* (Belmont, Calif.: Wadsworth Publishing Co., Inc., 1973) for an analysis of nonmarket transfers.

products, sellers are successful in using advertising and salesmanship to manipulate the tastes of consumers. The result is that producer sovereignty replaces consumer sovereignty. Instead of producing what consumers "really want," the economy satisfies the wants that producers synthesize!

The Radical Economists take a long-run view and are more sweeping in their criticisms. They contend that a capitalistically oriented education system and the lifelong habituation of individuals to a capitalist economy together fatally bias the transmission of economic "values" [7] from one generation to another. [8] The biased values so transmitted are not those that would come from exposure to what they regard as a more enlightened economy. And so the expressed preferences for goods, biased by these capitalist values, do not represent the "true" wants individuals would have expressed had they been nurtured in a better economic society, presumably a Marxist one.

A detailed exposition of the views of Galbraith and his critics is found in Chapter 10.

This still leaves the problem of how individuals' preferences for particular goods are transmitted from consumers to producers. Three possibilities exist. First—and the one on which we concentrate—is via dollar "voting" through the familiar market mechanism. Second, preferences may be transmitted as an expression of opinion or influence through some political process. In this case we assume that those possessing power sincerely wish to respond to the preferences of consumers. Third, an economic "czar" by some intuitive or magical process may claim to "know" what consumers really want or, alternatively, what is "good for them." In effect, the latter has been the assumption of all Eastern European economies, excepting the Yugoslav, up to the recent past.

What Is to Be Maximized? There is general acceptance of the

---

[7] *Values* may be defined as "criteria of desirability." See Robin Williams, Jr., "The Concept of Values" in David M. Sills, ed., *International Encyclopedia of the Social Sciences* (New York: The Free Press, 1968). As such, they may be viewed as higher-order preferences over an abstract domain, for example, "the importance of conservation of the physical environment," the "importance of the individual," and so on. The word *preference* has usually been reserved for a more specific domain, for example, the "preference" for a particular good. Values are important because they may be influential in determining one's preferences for particular goods and services.

[8] To learn more of the Radicals' views on consumer sovereignty, see Herbert Gintis, "Consumer Behavior and the Concept of Sovereignty: Explanations of Social Decay," *American Economic Review* (May 1972), pp. 267–278.

view that *all* firms seek to survive as independent entities. And, in a market economy, this requires the securing of a minimum level of profits. But beyond that, the issue is whether firms seek to maximize profits or sales.

In the half of the economy that might be described as workably competitive—where sellers and buyers are relatively numerous and the degree of product differentiation is small—this issue is no issue at all. Profit maximization and sales maximization will give the same result.

But in the oligopolistic half of the economy the issue is worth posing. To be clear, oligopolistic firms are few and usually offer differentiated products. Further they are interdependent: the actions of one firm in altering price, output, or the characteristics of its (variety of) product will affect the demand for another firm's product. There are two major questions to be posed in the oligopolistic sector:

1. Do profit maximization and sales maximization give clearly different results for the behavior of oligopolistic firms?
2. If they do, what is it that most firms seek to maximize—profit or sales?

Galbraith's answers to these two questions are clear and emphatic. Sales maximization does, as the very term suggests, lead to greater output. And he constructs a veritable catalog of arguments to support his view that those in control of oligopolistic firms have adopted sales maximization as their primary goal. His overall conclusion with respect to consumer sovereignty is that it is *not* achieved in the oligopolistic sphere of our economy. Quite the contrary. Consumers get *too much of what they do not truly want* (since their wants were created by sellers).

The main body of economists—to the extent that they have considered Galbraith's arguments—hold grave doubts as to his position on both questions. They are not sure that under real life conditions profit maximization and sales maximization do yield clearly different results. But they are of almost one voice in accepting profit maximization as the goal of oligopolistic firms. In summation most economists would hold that oligopolistic firms prevent the achievement of consumer sovereignty *because they produce too little,* as compared with the norm of perfect competition.

In Chapter 10 we grapple in detail with the problem of what is maximized.

Obstacles to Consumer Sovereignty. Our review now turns to the obstacles to consumer sovereignty posed by the realities of the 1970s as articulated by consumerists. Six are singled out for attention: 1) the problem of consumer information, 2) the problem of consumer grievances, 3) the underrepresentation of the consumer interest, 4) time as a scarce resource, 5) environmental effects and other interdependencies, 6) neighborhood effects.

The Problem of Consumer Information. In terms of consumer information, consumer sovereignty is achieved when the relatively uninformed and little-searching consumer succeeds in purchasing a specimen lying on the perfect information frontier; that is, he gets the quality he wants at the lowest possible price. Two issues are central here: 1) To what extent do uninformed, little-searching consumers actually purchase specimens from the perfect information frontier? 2) What are the factors that account for purchases at higher than frontier prices?

You are likely to recognize this issue as the Part I discussion turned upside down. In Part I of this book the economic environment was taken as "given" and we asked what rules and procedures would help the consumer to make effective purchase decisions. Here we evaluate the informational effectiveness of the economy and its determinants. It is "effective" when it gives all consumers the quality they prefer at the lowest possible price.

The Problem of Consumer Grievances. This discussion, too, is a turnabout from Part I. There we dealt with the steps the individual might take in avoiding grievances or in seeking redress of those that occur. Here we deal with the problem from the social viewpoint. We investigate the extent to which our economy "produces" consumer grievances, and why, and how well redress of grievances is achieved.

Obviously, the economy in which consumer sovereignty is completely achieved would have no grievances whatever: all consumers would be completely satisfied with both their purchase transactions and their postpurchase use of products.

The Underrepresentation of the Consumer Interest. Government intervenes in the private sector in many ways: by setting the "rules of the game" (the law of contract, the determination and regulation of acceptable competitive behavior); by prohibiting or regulating specific acts (misleading advertising), the distribution of specific goods (automobiles that fail to meet pollution standards), specific terms (maximum interest rates as specified in usury laws); by granting subsidies (price support payments to farmers) and imposing taxes (special taxes on alcoholic beverages). If the consumer interest is underrepresented in government, it seems highly likely that the outcomes of government actions will not be "focused toward satisfying the wants of ultimate consumers." Instead of being neutral or favoring consumers, laws, regulatory actions, and regulations are likely to favor producers.

An example should make the problem clear. Consider the regulation of interstate moving by the Interstate Commerce Commission (ICC). The fact that the ICC pays greater attention to prompt payment of moving bills than to ensuring the accuracy of premove estimates of moving costs suggests the predominance of producer versus consumer influence.[9] It may also be subversive of consumer sovereignty.

Time As a Scarce Resource. The issue here is straightforward. If individuals fail to take the scarcity of time into account in deciding upon the activities of their lives and the purchases needed to undertake these activities, then they may schedule "too much," feel "harried," and be surrounded by a multitude of unused goods. This is scarcely a condition where "all economic processes are ultimately focused toward satisfying wants of ultimate consumers," and hardly one to be characterized as consumer sovereignty.[10]

Since the problem is newly recognized and conceptually difficult, the discussion is necessarily conjectural and amorphous, factors that do not affect the reality of the problem discussed in Chapter 10.

Environmental Effects and Other Interdependencies. In a well-behaved market economy, the prices of goods reflect *all* the benefits conferred by the good and *all* the costs imposed by the production of the good. Usually all the benefits accrue to the purchaser—the person who buys and eats the steak—and all the costs are borne by the producer of the good—the wood-carver who paid for his wood and did the carving himself. But this is not always the case, and it is the exceptions that concern us here.

The benefits of the tulips in my front yard will be shared, without charge, by all who pass my house. Had I been able to collect a pay-

---

[9] The moving bills of consumers must be 1) prepaid, 2) paid by a certified check, or 3) billed to an employer before belongings are unloaded at their destination.

[10] Some might argue that we are indicting the economic system for a flaw that consumers themselves can correct. But do they really possess the necessary insight—that time is a scarce resource? Or is the difficulty really chargeable to two products of the system?—1) affluence, and 2) a deficient economic education that has not dealt with time as a scarce resource?

ment for these *external economies,* I might have been induced to plant more or better. If on a camping trip I dispose of my wastes carelessly, the cost of this *external diseconomy* may likewise be shared with those who follow me in the use of that campsite. Had I been forced to pay for a proper cleanup, I might have foregone or cut short that camping trip. The major point is that when the benefits to *all* individuals and the costs imposed on *all* individuals are *not* reflected in prices, too little will be produced of goods that are subject to external economies and too much will be produced of goods that are subject to external diseconomies. Consumer sovereignty will *not* be achieved.

These examples are in contrast to the case of the automobile that failed to make a curve and demolished someone's living room. It is not an "external diseconomy," although the explosion of the car into the living room did come unexpectedly from an "external" source. But, if an effective automobile insurance system was in operation, the costs imposed on the owner of the house and the occupants of the living room would be borne by the driver's automobile insurance company. And, in deciding how much automobile insurance to purchase and how much to drive that automobile, the careless driver would have taken into account the cost of his auto insurance. Thus, the cost would have "internalized." In the case of true external diseconomies, such costs are *not* taken into account.

With but little effort, each of us could compile an extensive list of external economies, some of which are important and some frivolous. For example: the pleasures conferred by an architecturally pleasing building; the lower price and better service you may receive as a result of the aggressive, contentious actions of activist, price-comparing consumers; the improvement in your day occasioned by the passage of a beautiful woman or handsome man; and the greater supply of honey the beekeeper gains as a consequence of his neighbor's flower gardens. And there are diseconomies, too: pollution (air, noise, water, privacy), someone else's smoking or halitosis, the other person's contagious disease (his cold, hepatitis, influenza, leprosy), congestion (highways, subway, air travel, bikeway). Some things may enter as both external economies and diseconomies. Your cat may be a boon to the neighbor otherwise afflicted by field mice and a bane to the neighbor who is a bird-watcher.

You will probably recognize that most of the environmental concerns to which our generation has become so strongly sensitized in the last ten years are simply a special kind of external diseconomy.

One might reasonably ask why these kinds of benefits and costs have not become purchasable property rights and thus taken into account by other producers and consumers.[11] The answer is that like many consumer interests, these benefits and costs are 1) disperse, 2) difficult to trace or measure, and 3) sometimes transient. The unpleasant aroma emitted from a malt mill amplifies these observations. The affected area extends downwind probably one to two miles, the "effect" diminishing with the distance. Just how offensive the odor of barley mash (and thereby how costly) is a judgment that will vary from one affected individual to another. Since winds shift, the effect of this odor is a transient one.

Such an external diseconomy could be "internalized" by the imposition of a tax on malodorous emissions or by regulations prohibiting such emissions above some technically defined level. Such corrective actions would correctly place the costs of these odors on malt consumers.[12]

The politics of regulation make this device difficult to apply in practice. First, it requires recognition of the problem. Next it requires the political mobilization of a large enough body of citizens, amateurs in politics, to offset the concentrated interest of the malt producers in continuing their lower-cost, polluting methods of production.

Such is the typical nature of representation on opposed sides of environmental issues: the numerous, amateur, marginally affected consumers versus the highly focused, professionally represented, knowledgeable polluters.

Externalities deal with the effects of someone else's *actions* on me. The "neighborhood effects" to which we now turn focus on the influence my perception of my neighbor may have on my utility.

Neighborhood Effects. Ordinarily, economists assume that the utility functions of different individuals are independent. Translated, this means that the satisfaction from possessions, income, or activities is the same regardless of anyone else's possessions, income, or activities. A moment's reflection will reveal that this is unrealistic. The

[11] Abba Lerner declares that the genius of a market economy is its capacity to convert a set of rights, or negative rights (prohibitions) from something that was fought over into a purchasable commodity. The problem with respect to some environmental "rights" in the 1970s is that they have yet to be converted into property rights, for example, a ticket for "breathable air." See Abba P. Lerner, "The Economics and Politics of Consumer Sovereignty," *American Economic Review* (May 1972), pp. 258–259.

[12] The case for this treatment of an externality is made in William J. Baumol, "On Taxation and Control of Externalities," *American Economic Review* (June 1972), pp. 307–321.

more sensitive among us may feel their overall satisfaction (utility) from their economic position may be diminished because they feel they are living in great luxury in a generally poor society. Such has been the experience of many American professionals who have lived in India. In such a case the perceived utility of other people directly enters the utility function of the person whose satisfaction we are evaluating.

In a second kind of case, my neighbor, or someone else, enters my utility function indirectly through the level of living or particular goods he possesses. Specifically, the utility I derive from my possessions, income, or activities depends upon my possessions, income, or activities *relative to his*. This notion gives rise to "snob" or "bandwagon" effects. An example of a "snob" effect would be the "extra" utility conferred by the ownership of an "exotic" automobile, such as, a Mercedes-Benz. Some of the satisfaction afforded by it results not from possibly better performance but rather from the fact that relatively few, and presumably only discriminating, people own such a car.[13]

The term *bandwagon* effect denotes the tendency of individuals to strongly desire things that others in their group have. For example, if others in his group have air conditioning, then the bandwagon consumer "must" have air conditioning, not for its own sake but so that he can keep up with other members of his group—who happen, of course, to be named "Jones!"

For consumer sovereignty to be completely achieved, these and other neighborhood effects must be taken into account. To date, economics has identified the problem, but has yet to develop techniques capable of analyzing the problem posed by such interdependencies.

CONSUMER SOVEREIGNTY AND THE PUBLIC SECTOR

The application of the consumer sovereignty concept to the public sector does not come easily. There are two reasons for this. First, some of the "products" of the public sector tend not to be recognized at all as "products." Second, the mechanisms by which users of government services signal their demands for these government services are ill-defined and uncertain in terms of results. Both of these ideas require elaboration.

---

[13] "Antisnob" effects can also be identified: the person who owns less house or less automobile than that usually associated with that person's income.

One major and often unrecognized product of government consists of the laws, institutions, and regulations that govern all manner of economic activities. Examples are the law of contract, the Federal Reserve System (the placement of control as well as the policies and regulations the system adopts and enforces), the Civil Aeronautics Board (again, the placement of control and the policies and regulations it adopts and enforces). Actions by legislatures to alter laws and institutions, and regulatory actions by government agencies may aid or impede the goal of satisfying the wants of ultimate consumers. Only to the extent that such actions further the satisfaction of such wants are they consistent with the notion of consumer sovereignty.

A second, unrecognized product of government consists of systems for redistributing income and wealth: systems of taxation (income, sales, estate, corporation income, Social Security) as well as of transfer payments (Social Security and veterans' benefits, Medicare, unemployment compensation). The *operation* of these systems is related to consumer sovereignty; to the extent that they collect and dispense monies quickly, accurately, and without disputes, they promote consumer sovereignty. Consumer sovereignty is also involved in the judgment as to whether the kind and extent of redistribution implicit in these systems contributes maximally to the satisfaction of the wants of ultimate consumers.

We turn now to a consideration of the mechanisms by which the demands of users of government services are transmitted. For the relatively small number of government services or products for which prices are charged familiar market mechanisms signal demand.

But most government goods are not sold on a market.[14] In such cases political devices are used to communicate the demands of users for these services: voting for legislators, voting in referendums, letter-writing, complaining, making contributions (termed "bribes" when the relationship between the thing demanded and the "contribution" becomes too immediate), lobbying, attending meetings, urging, protesting. These efforts may be directed toward elected representatives

---

[14] The Musgraves point out that in the case of goods that are 1) nonrival or 2) not subject to the exclusion principle, markets fail to some degree and, therefore, these goods tend to be produced by government. A good is *nonrival* if A's participation in its benefits does not reduce its benefits to others. An example would be an uncrowded bridge.

The second category consists of goods where it is impossible or inefficient to exclude nonpayers from using them. An example would be a city street.

For reasons why these goods tend usually to be provided by the public sector, see Richard A. and Peggy B. Musgrave, *Public Finance in Theory and Practice* (New York: McGraw-Hill, 1973), chap. 3, "The Theory of Social Goods."

or government employees charged with providing the service ("bureaucrats" is the pejorative name). Even without further analysis, it is clear that the processes by which the demand for nonmarket government goods are registered are ill-defined. It is also clear that the relationship between registration of particular demands and changes in quantities produced is uncertain. From this observation comes the immediate conclusion that the assessment of the extent to which economic processes in the public sector satisfy the wants of ultimate consumers will be neither precise nor certain. The best we will be able to do is to identify tendencies and their causes.

In Chapter 11 we analyze carefully the processes by which users of government services, consumers in particular, seek to influence government actions. And, in the same chapter, we examine the possibility that bureaucrats may be motivated by other objectives than simply serving voters.

CHAPTER 10

Consumer Sovereignty: The Views of Economists

Three issues claim our attention in this chapter: 1) the extent to which producers/sellers manipulate demand, 2) what it is that firms seek to maximize, and the difference it makes, and 3) the extent to which consumers find themselves harried by their failure to recognize time as a scarce resource.

PREFERENCES IN AN AFFLUENT SOCIETY: JOHN KENNETH GALBRAITH'S CRITICISMS

John Kenneth Galbraith stands almost alone among economists (although not among *consumer* economists) in stressing the role of advertising in creating and managing the preferences of consumers. Given the almost instinctive antipathy of many students and many consumerists to advertising, this stance of Galbraith's is by itself enough to assure him an interested hearing and perhaps an excessively ready acceptance. We respond to these inclinations of our sovereign readers by assigning Galbraith's views a central position in our discussion of consumer sovereignty.

Galbraith's views are summarized and criticized here. But students who wish to sample his highly readable prose for themselves are advised to consult *The Affluent Society* and *The New Industrial State*.[1]

[1] John Kenneth Galbraith, *The Affluent Society*, 2nd ed. rev. (New York: Mentor Books, 1958, 1969); John Kenneth Galbraith, *The New Industrial State*, 2nd ed. rev. (New York: Mentor Books, 1967, 1971). For a compilation of criticisms, see Charles H. Hession, *John Kenneth Galbraith and His Critics* (New York: Mentor Books, 1971). Galbraith's book, *Economics and The Public Purpose* (Boston: Houghton Mifflin Company, 1973) introduces new emphases, but leaves his major themes unaltered. For this reason we have cited the two earlier volumes where his positions are argued more extensively.

Galbraith's Challenges and Their Application. In attacking the received doctrines of economics, Galbraith stresses two major themes:

1. *Producers, Not Consumers, Are Sovereign.* Through successful advertising and salesmanship, producers/sellers "manage" the preferences of consumers. Thus, it is producers, not consumers, who ultimately determine the volume and composition of output.
2. *Many of the Wants Being Satisfied in Our Economy Are Nonurgent,* Even Frivolous. This follows from the notion that many wants are contrived by sellers and are not original with consumers themselves.

We should be clear about the domains to which Galbraith's analysis and criticisms apply. They do *not* apply to the world of small firms and atomistic competition. Instead they apply to the oligopolistic sector—what Galbraith terms "the industrial system." The industrial system accounts for most output and is composed of the 2,000 or so technically dynamic, massively capitalized, highly organized corporations that dominate our economy.

Galbraith's analysis is restricted further in that it focuses almost exclusively on the manufacturing stage of production and the producer-controlled aspects of marketing and hardly at all on the functioning of retail markets. (Retail markets, too, may be characterized by oligopolistic structures. But they do not receive Galbraith's attention.) In thus restricting his view Galbraith is wholly conventional, wearing blinders shared by most members of the economics profession.

Galbraith on Technology and the Large Corporation. Understand modern technology and its requirements, Galbraith argues, and you will understand the structure and motivation of both the New Industrial State and its dominant institution, the giant corporation.

In a brilliantly selective parable, Galbraith contrasts technology and its imperatives in 1900 and in the 1960s. He compares the development of the first Ford automobile in 1903 with that of the Mustang 66 years later.

In the case of the first Ford, only five months elapsed between the formation of the Ford Motor Company and the delivery of its first car. The capital invested was modest: $100,000, only $28,500 of which was in cash. And the labor force required in that first year consisted of 125 men.

The planning and production of the Mustang in the 1960s offered a vivid contrast. There, *three and one-half years* elapsed between conception and delivery of the first car. In addition to the $6 billion of capital utilized by Ford Motor Company in turning out its multitudinous products, the company expended $59 million on tools and equipment usable only on Mustang production. In 1964, the first year the Mustang was marketed, employment at Ford stood at 317,000.[2]

For Galbraith, this parable and its supporting discussion etch the following characteristics of modern production:

1. An increasing span of time between conception and quantity production;
2. The commitment of immense quantities of capital;
3. The increasing specialization of physical equipment and manpower to the achievement of particular tasks, for example, the production of the Mustang.

And, when they consider these factors together, large corporations feel compelled to avoid large errors and the large, possibly fatal, costs associated with them.

The highly capitalized, bureaucratically controlled corporation seeks to avoid such large errors by "planning." As in socialist theory, it concentrates on the *ex ante* avoidance of mistakes rather than on *ex post* correction. Since markets are a rich source of uncertainty—and hence of undesirable outcomes—the giant corporation seeks to insulate its activities from market uncertainties by internalizing them or by controlling markets. The following devices are the most salient manifestations of this motivation:

1. On the matter of product lines, the large corporation may *diversify into or conglomerate* many substantially different product lines so that a failure in one line will be offset by successes in others;
2. It seeks to assure its supply of capital *by relying on retained earnings and depreciation-generated funds* and—as a backstop—by establishing cordial relations with lending institutions;
3. To assure its supplies of raw materials or parts, it may *integrate backward to produce its own supplies,* thus ensuring availability and avoiding unfavorable prices; where integration is not possible, it *seeks to establish long-term contracts and cordial relations* with suppliers, its size proving helpful in this;

---

[2] Galbraith, *The New Industrial State,* op. cit., pp. 30–31.

4. With regard to labor costs, it seeks to avoid surprises *by entering into long-term contracts with unions* that are renegotiated only at predetermined intervals;

5. Similarly, *with respect to business and government customers* for its products, *it enters into long-term contracts and seeks cordial relations* with customers.

6. *On the selling side, it "manages" the consumer by inducing him, through advertising or salesmanship, to buy what the corporation wants to sell at the price it wishes to charge.*

It is the last of the features from this portrait of the industrial firm on which we now focus. Some of the other features receive attention later in this chapter.

Galbraith on the Management of Consumer Demand. "The purpose of demand management," Galbraith declares,[3] "is to insure that people buy what is produced—that plans as to the amounts to be sold at the controlled prices are fulfilled in practice." And, according to Galbraith, this is what giant corporations usually achieve.

Affluence makes possible the management of consumer demand. In a poor society, individuals' wants will be grounded in urgent, physical need for such things as food and shelter. They need not be contrived by someone else; they will be "original with the individual." But, as incomes rise, the individual will begin to satisfy less urgent wants. And here the possibility of manipulation by sellers arises. In Galbraith's words: "The further a man is removed from physical need, the more open he is to persuasion—or management—as to what he buys."[4] And Galbraith identifies the manager—the giant corporation—and the means—salesmanship and advertising.

Serving the giant corporations is an entire industry devoted to the control and/or management of demand. It consists of a huge communications network embracing television, radio, periodicals, newspapers, billboards; a large array of merchandising and selling organizations (of which Sears, Woolworth, K-Mart, General Motors dealers, Macy's might be examples); nearly the entire advertising industry; and numerous ancillary research, training, and other related services.

All of these agencies are mobilized by the corporation in a massive effort to minimize the chances of product failure. And an entire panoply of management actions is orchestrated toward the

[3] Ibid.
[4] Ibid.

same end. Not just advertising, but the devising of a sales strategy, the design of a product embodying salable features, the conception of model changes, decisions as to packaging and performance—all are designed to ensure that the product sells in the expected quantity at the expected price. And, by Galbraith's assertion, they achieve success.

What is more, Galbraith argues, they may succeed without consumers ever becoming aware of it: "It is true that the consumer may still imagine that his actions respond to his own view of his satisfactions. But this is superficial and proximate, the result of illusions created in connection with the management of his wants." [5] Galbraith's thesis, then, is that producers/sellers manage consumers so well that the consumers themselves are unaware of their puppet status.

This line of argument has important implications for our view of the functioning of our economy. In short, it replaces *consumer* sovereignty with *producer/seller* sovereignty. The chain of causation is reversed.[6] The Accepted Sequence—Galbraith's phrase—by which consumers ultimately control the composition of output through their dollar votes is replaced by the Revised Sequence, under which oligopolistic firms reach forward to reduce uncertainty by controlling markets. By advertising and salesmanship *they* determine what consumers will "demand." The chain of causation is closed as these same firms "respond" to the demand they have created. They do this by producing the goods they originally planned to produce at the prices they selected.

The Revised Sequence is not all-conquering. In that part of the economy characterized by small units, the Accepted Sequence will still prevail. It is in the sector of the giant corporations that the Revised Sequence predominates, and, even within this domain, one will find many individual consumers capable of resisting persuasion. However, the Revised Sequence will describe the central tendency of this sector.

If accepted, the Revised Sequence biases the composition of output in three important ways:

1. *More Urgent versus Less Urgent Wants.* Galbraith's general thesis is that a contrived want is, by definition, a nonurgent want. Since, according to the arguments, most of the wants satisfied by

---

[5] Ibid., p. 214.

[6] Since Galbraith is an inveterate and skillful phrasemaker, the student of Galbraith almost needs a glossary. In *The Affluent Society*, Galbraith terms this reversal of causation the "Dependence Effect" since consumer demand is "dependent" upon the manipulation of producers. See Galbraith, *The Affluent Society*, op. cit., chap. 11.

the giant corporation sector are contrived (or managed), that sector is satisfying many less urgent or even frivolous wants.

The application of this idea to other sectoral comparisons yields the biases listed under No. 2 and No. 3.

2. *Oligopolistic Sector versus "Competitive" Sector.* If 1) giant corporations do successfully manage consumer demand for their products, and if 2) these corporations seek to maximize growth rather than profits (a contention of Galbraith discussed in the next major section), then Galbraith argues the giant corporation sector will account for an inappropriately large proportion of total output. In particular, the output of the giant corporation sector will exceed that which would result from genuine consumer sovereignty.

3. *Private Sector versus Public Sector.* In the contest for resources between the demand-synthesizing private sector and the public sector, it is Galbraith's famous contention in *The Affluent Society* that the private sector will invariably win. From this emerges the graphic contrast of shining new cars (private sector) versus dirty, ill-lit, hole-filled urban streets (public sector); brand new television sets (private sector) versus old, dingy, ill-maintained public schools (public sector). In terms of popular appeal and political influence, this assertion of the "social imbalance" has been immensely influential. For example, the emphasis in the French 4th long-run Economic Plan (1961–1965) on investment in schools and other public buildings was traceable, in part at least, to Galbraith's pleadings. What is crucial in evaluating this hypothesis is an explanation of how citizen wants for public goods can be accurately gauged and transmitted. We return to this in Chapter 11.

The Management of Consumer Demand: Counterevidence. By any interpretation, the successful "management" of consumer demand should imply two outcomes: 1) large corporations should seldom experience failure in the launching of new products, and 2) a successfully launched product should command customer loyalty, that is, brand-switching should be minimal.

Although both are empirically testable propositions, Galbraith eschewed statistical testing, relying instead on casual observations, the plausibility of his arguments, and even on a debating trick.[7] By contrast, we have sought out, rather than avoided, statistical evidence.

---

[7] As to the debater's trick consider the following from *The New Industrial State* (p. 206, footnote 10): ". . . this disaster [Ford Motor Company's failure with the Edsel] is cited (by those who are made unhappy by those ideas) to prove that planning of

And the evidence on both of these points contradicts Galbraith's contentions. We turn first to the launching of new products.

Success and Failure in the Launching of New Products. The collection and interpretation of evidence on product failures is beset by two types of ambiguity:

1. Differences in what constitutes a "new product";
2. Differences in what a "failure" means, for example, withdrawal of the product from the market, or sales lower than predicted.

Despite possible discrepancies resulting from the factors just cited, the data in Table 1 are fairly congruent, pointing toward a single conclusion. They suggest an average product failure rate on the order of 30 per cent to 40 per cent. The digestion of these results is aided by a summary statement by Thomas S. Robertson, perhaps the most careful of scholars on this subject. Robertson writes: [8]

> As already argued, large companies are likely to market fewer failures than small companies and sophisticated, market-oriented industries are likely to market fewer failures than unsophisticated, production-oriented industries.
>
> While it is difficult, therefore, to provide an average new product failure ratio which will apply uniformly, documentation has shown this failure rate can be quite high. To say that a *majority* of new products fails is probably fair, although it would be more meaningful to present standardized figures by industry if such figures could be obtained.

To add frosting to the cake, one might ask whether the reasons given for the failure of new products in Part B of Table 1 evoke the image of Galbraith's market "managing" corporation, or, alternatively, of companies often thwarted by a market they cannot manage.

---

consumer demand by giant corporations will not work. It proves what I unhesitatingly concede, which is that it doesn't work perfectly. Its notoriety owes much to its being exceptional." End of footnote, end of discussion.

The doubter might ask: Does the Edsel fiasco owe its notoriety to the fact that new products almost always succeed, or to the fact that this was a fiasco of enormous proportions—following an investment of $5 billion of 1958–61 dollars by Ford?

The citation of a single instance, either pro or con, is, of course, no substitute for a careful sifting of statistical evidence.

[8] Thomas S. Robertson, *Innovative Behavior and Communication* (New York: Holt, Rinehart, and Winston, Inc., 1971), pp. 18–19.

Finally, after looking at Part C of Table 1, one notes that the companies fathering the "conspicuous losers" on *Business Week's* list would appear to many as prototypes of the demand-managing oligopolist.

TABLE 1

Evidence on Launching of New Products

Part A: Estimates of Failure Rates

Population	Criteria: Per cent failed of products actually introduced on market	Failure Rate
1. Booz, Allen & Hamilton, 800 client assignments in 200 firms noted for their product development programs[a]		
All Industries:		37.5%
Chemical		41
Consumer packaged goods		37
Electrical machinery		37
Metal fabricators		29
Nonelectrical machinery		41
Raw materials processors		41
2. Buzzell and Nourse:[b] 123 "distinctly new" products in the food industry	a. Discontinued after test marketing	22%
	b. Withdrawn following regular introduction	17%
3. Cochran and Thompson[c]	Per cent "failed" of products introduced to market	30%

Part B: Reasons for New Product Failures[d]

Reason	Per Cent
Inadequate market analysis	32%
Deficiency in the product	23
Higher costs than anticipated	14
Poor timing	10
Competition	8
Weaknesses in marketing efforts	13
Total	100%

Part C: Conspicuous "Losers" [e]

Firm	Brand Name/Product
Campbell	"Red Kettle" soups
Lever Brothers	"Vim" tablet detergent
Best Foods	"Knorr" soups
Colgate	"Cue" toothpaste
General Foods	Post cereals with freeze-dried fruit
Bristol-Myers	"Aerosol Ipana" toothpaste
Scott Paper	"Babyscott" diapers
Sylvania	"Colorslide" TV viewer
Gillette	"Nine Flags" men's cologne
Hunt-Wesson	"Suprema" spaghetti sauce
Warner-Lambert	"Reef" mouthwash

[a] Booz, Allen & Hamilton, Management Consultants, *Management of New Products* (New York: Booz, Allen & Hamilton, 1968).

[b] Robert D. Buzzell and Robert E. M. Nourse, *Product Innovation in Food Processing, 1954–1964* (Boston: Divsion of Research, Harvard Business School, 1967).

[c] Betty Cochran and G. Clark Thompson, "Why New Products Fail," *The National Industrial Conference Board Record* (October 1964), pp. 11–18.

[d] Ibid.

[e] *Business Week*, March 4, 1972, pp. 72–77. *Business Week* asked several "new product specialists" to look over the past decade and identify "failures" in that 1) they did not meet their marketing goals and were withdrawn from the market, or 2) they were relegated to "fade-out" status, or 3) both.

Whatever the difficulties of interpretation, the data of Table 1 give no support to Galbraith's assertion that large corporations manage consumer demand.

Brand Loyalty and the Management of Demand. If advertisers were successful in managing demand, one would expect that:

1. Consumers' attitudes toward particular brands would be stable over time;
2. In purchasing, consumers would remain loyal to a particular brand and *not* shift from one brand to another.

Evidence on these two propositions comes from a national survey in which respondents answered questions regarding their attitudes toward and purchases of 19 brands in 7 product classes that most people would view as highly amenable to advertiser manipulation: analgesics (such as aspirin), cigarettes, coffee, denture cleansers, hair sprays, mouthwash, and peanut butter. Data were obtained from a national probability sample of 2,000 women responsible for purchasing these items in their households. Respondents were interviewed three times over a six-month period.[9]

Data on consumers' attitudes toward the 19 brands are summarized

TABLE 2

Changes in Consumers' Attitudes Toward Particular Brands Over Six Months

Part A: Stability in Attitudes Toward Brands: Nineteen Brands in Seven Highly Advertised Product Categories [a]

Expressed Attitude [b]	Wave I	Wave II (3 months later)	Wave III (6 months later)
Excellent	21%	21%	21%
Very good	27	25	28
Good	33	36	34
Fair	14	13	13
Not so good	3	3	2
Poor	2	2	2
Total	100%	100%	100%
Number of respondents	About 2,000	About 2,000	About 2,000

Part B: Extent of Change in Attitude Toward a Particular Brand Over Six Months [c]

Change in Attitude		
No change		48%
Changed:		52%
Once	34%	
Twice	18%	
Total	100%	
Number of respondents	About 2,000	

[a] The product categories were: analgesics, cigarettes, coffee, denture cleansers, hair sprays, mouthwash, peanut butter.
Achenbaum, op. cit., Figure 1, p. 5. Reprinted from the Journal of Advertising Research. © Copyright (1972), by the Advertising Research Foundation.
[b] The table reads: "Twenty-one per cent of the ratings of the 19 brands by the 2,000 respondents were 'excellent,' 27 per cent were 'very good,' etc."
[c] Achenbaum, op. cit., Figure 7, p. 7.

[9] For a detailed analysis of this survey see Alvin A. Achenbaum, "Advertising Doesn't Manipulate Consumers," Journal of Advertising Research (April 1972), pp. 3–13.

in Part A of Table 2. At first blush, the data of Part A seem strongly supportive of Galbraith's thesis: respondents' perceptions of the quality of particular brands change *not at all* (after taking account of sampling errors) over the six-month period. But Part B of Table 2 quickly dispels any illusions: after six months more than half the respondents had shifted from their initial attitude toward the brand, some viewing the particular brand more favorably, some less favorably. What is more, 18 per cent of respondents changed their rating twice, hardly what one would expect of a "loyal," well-manipulated consumer.

So far the discussion has centered on attitudes; but our main concern is with *purchase* behavior. Data from Table 3 reveal a very strong relationship between changes in attitudes toward a particular brand and repeat purchases of that brand. If attitudes toward a brand shift—and they do—then these shifts in attitudes will result in a shift

TABLE 3

The Relationship Between Changes in Attitudes Toward a Brand and Repeat Purchases [a]

Initial Attitudes (as expressed in Wave I):

Change in Expressed Attitudes [b]	**Very Good**	**Good**	**Not So Good**		**Poor**
	Per Cent of Wave I Purchasers Buying Same Brand:				
Much more favorable (by 2 classes)	Inap.	Inap.	83%		
More favorable (by 1 class)	Inap.	78%	48%	Too	Too
Unchanged	86%	62%	52%		
Less favorable (by a class)	64%	35%	22%	Few	Few
Much less favorable (by 2 classes)	36%	15%		Cases	Cases

[a] The table reads (Column 1, starting with Row 3): "Of those whose initial attitude toward the brand was 'excellent' and whose initial attitude was 'unchanged' between Wave I and II, 86 per cent brought the same brand; of the 'excellents' in Wave I whose attitude became 'less favorable,' 64 per cent bought the same brand; and of the 'excellents' whose attitude became 'much less favorable' only 36 per cent bought the same brand."

Source: Achenbaum, op. cit., Figure 9, p. 7.

[b] "Much more favorable" denotes that their Wave II attitude was two classes more favorable than their Wave I attitude, that is, a change from "good" to "excellent."

of purchases from one brand to another. It would be our judgment that the data presented here and other data not reproduced here fully justify the author's summary statement: [10]

> Consumers' attitudes vary as widely and frequently as does purchase behavior. Consumers rarely stick to any one brand. If advertising affects their attitudes, it hardly mesmerizes them.
> Product experience is also an important influence on future purchase. People do not rely on what they see or hear.

Thus, Achenbaum's investigation strongly suggests that—for this set of products—brand loyalty is *not* the order of the day and sellers have *not* successfully "managed" demand. The restriction of the conclusion to *this* set of products is important. On the one hand, these products seem like "natural" targets for the creation of synthetic demand. On the other hand, these are "experience goods," involving repetitive purchases and such small outlays that the consumer may feel that he can reliably test their usefulness himself. What of non-experience goods?

Achenbaum's interpretation of how advertising works merits our consideration. He writes: [11]

> If communication of information alone is not the way consumer behavior is affected by advertising, how is it? The data suggest that the process works something like this.
> Information about one or more product attributes which are *salient to consumers* is communicated in a persuasive context by national advertising. These attributes can be sensory, evaluative, or emotional.
> If the communication is persuasive enough to improve consumers' attitudes on that attribute, their attitudes toward the overall brand will improve as well. This improvement in overall brand attitudes will concomitantly increase the probability of purchase.
> But some product attributes have more clout than others. The more salient the attribute—i.e., the more correlated a change in attitude is with the change in overall attitude, the larger the effect on future brand share.
> This is why the advertiser wants to know what is salient to the consumer. Unless he can support his claim on a salient factor and unless he can communicate it in a persuasive manner, he

[10] Ibid., p. 13.
[11] Ibid., p. 12.

will have done nothing to enhance his market position. There is nothing manipulative about this process. Advertisers either consider the consumer wants and cater to his wants, or face market failure. We [Achenbaum is in advertising research] are all too well aware of the myriad of well advertised new products which have failed to meet this market standard.

The Management of Consumer Demand: A Caution. The evidence just presented suggests that large firms cannot create and maintain brand loyalty for small-ticket, experience goods at will. The earlier evidence similarly suggests that giant firms often fail in their efforts to launch new products. But we must be careful. From this negative evidence we must not conclude too quickly that the advertising and salesmanship efforts of large firms are without influence; quite the contrary is true. The dramatic example of highly advertised Bayer's aspirin selling year after year at a price three times that of equivalent unbranded aspirin, the statistical fact that many new product launchings are successful, and our own personal reactions together suggest that advertising and salesmanship are sometimes successful in altering our preferences. The frustrating fact is that we do not know exactly how effective advertising is. (Nor, do advertisers themselves usually know, if that is any comfort.)

And if large corporations are even moderately successful in influencing consumer tastes, then we must deal with some of Galbraith's other assertions regarding consumer sovereignty. Here the issues are philosophical and statistical evidence is inappropriate.

When Are Our Preferences "Our Own?" Galbraith's answer to this question is straightforward: individual's preferences are "their own" when they have a physical basis or are otherwise original with the individuals themselves. Otherwise, they are contrived and their fulfillment does not represent the achievement of consumer sovereignty. Note well the flatness and the lack of any qualifying conditions in Galbraith's position.

We consider two major criticisms of Galbraith's views. The first line of criticism, that of Friedrich Hayek, is summarized trenchantly in the following declaration of Hayek's: [12] "To say that a desire is not important because it is not innate is to say that the whole cultural achievement of man is not important." By way of elaboration, Hayek

---

[12] Friedrich A. Hayek, "The Non-Sequitur of the Dependence Effect," *Southern Economic Journal* (April 1961), pp. 346–348.

points out that the preferences of individuals for "great" literature or "great" music are not original with individuals, but are usually cultivated by the producers of such works. And he thrusts home his attack by asserting that ". . . *in Galbraith's words, the process of satisfying the wants* [such as great musical works] *creates the wants."* [13]

A second line of criticism, original is these pages, would assert that the central issue is not the *source* of preferences, but rather their stability. Realistically, both the values of individuals [14] and their preferences for specific products may be influenced by diverse agents: physiological needs, religion, formal education, parents' teachings both formal and informal, Consumers Union, and salesmen and advertising. In determining whether the purchase of particular goods represents an example of consumer sovereignty, the crucial test is whether the purchase has stood the test of time or experience. The test calls on the individual to look back on a particular purchase and say—after the product has been consumed—whether the purchase was a good buy, an average buy, or a bad buy. In forming this judgment the individual can take advantage of any experience with the good or any knowledge of the good or its substitutes coming his way since the purchase was consummated. But he must apply any revised view of the purchase to his financial circumstances *at the time of purchase.*

An example may clarify this thought process. In December, 1945, the author, then interested in purchasing a canoe, saw some advertisements of a sporting goods store, extolling the virtues of a new aluminum canoe. The aluminum canoe, the advertisement claimed, was lighter and more durable than its canvas competitor, yet it matched the handling properties of the canvas canoe. After inspecting it, the author purchased the aluminum canoe. Now, almost 30 years' of experience later, the author feels that this was one of the best purchases he ever made. *Ex post,* the consumer's surplus [15] embodied in this purchase was positive and large.

Ordinarily, the look backward will be over a much shorter period, for example, today's view of last night's meal. But the logic of the appraisal poses the same question: in the light of possibly greater information, was the choice that was actually made one that the

[13] Ibid.

[14] As noted earlier in this book, *values* are higher order preferences that serve as "criteria of desirability," useful in choosing among more specific actions or goods. Thus, the person who prizes or "values" being "up" on things is more likely to purchase a first-night ticket to a new play.

[15] The *consumer's surplus* consists of the difference between the maximum price an individual would have been willing to pay and the price he actually paid.

individual would like to repeat? The answer would be "yes" where the consumer's surplus, viewed *ex post,* was either zero or positive. And consumer sovereignty would be served in this case. On the other hand, consumer sovereignty would be subverted if the *ex post* consumer's surplus was negative.

Some may note that this procedure calls for an intertemporal comparison of satisfaction. And this they will find logically inadmissible. The argument would be that, with the passage of time and experience, the individual is no longer *the same;* hence, his judgments will necessarily be different. The counterargument would be that it is an individual's beliefs that count, and that even illusions yield satisfaction—especially *if* they are not shattered.[16]

A second example may offer additional amplification. Consider the individual who buys an amulet (a tiger's tooth) for protection. If his illusion of protection lasts until his death (even at the hands of a tiger), then his consumer's surplus will remain zero or positive, and consumer sovereignty will have been served *as far as preferences go.*

The relationship of this criteria to the characteristics of consumers is of some interest. Presumably, the more knowledgeable consumer, having explored alternatives more carefully, is less likely to experience an unpleasant surprise. It is more difficult to evaluate the probability of an unpleasant surprise for the unintelligent consumer. Being less intelligent, he may be more likely to make a poor choice initially; but then, not being as sensitive to his environment, he may be less likely to realize that his choice has served him ill rather than well.

The Satisfaction of Nonurgent Wants: Criticism. It is Galbraith's assertion that as average affluence increases, individuals satisfy wants of decreasing urgency. With this proposition there can be little quarrel. Common observation and even the crudest interpretation of rationality confirm that individuals will tend to satisfy their most urgent wants first before turning to wants of less urgency. The crucial issue is the degree of the urgency of those wants that are currently being satisfied in America.

Galbraith's contention that consumers are satisfying wants of low urgency contrasts starkly with the sentiments of consumers, as re-

---

[16] To learn more about psychological mechanisms that tend to protect existing illusions and to create new, protective illusions, see the discussion of cognitive dissonance in Robert B. Zajonc, "Cognitive Theories in Social Psychology," in Gardner Lindzey and Elliot Aronson, *The Handbook of Social Psychology,* 2nd ed. (Reading, Mass.: Addison-Wesley Publishing Co., Inc., 1954, 1968).

vealed by their behavior. Let us examine the arguments and the evidence.

The first piece of evidence comes from data on individuals' contributions to charitable and civic organizations. If individuals believe that their income is being devoted to purchases of goods and services of low urgency (low marginal utility), it seems plausible that they would be willing to contribute "generously" through charitable and civic organizations to less fortunate individuals. Furthermore, as their affluence increases, one would expect them to become more "generous."

The fact is that in 1950 individuals devoted 1.62 per cent of their income to contributions.[17] By 1972 the corresponding figure was 1.76 per cent despite the fact that *real* family income had almost doubled in the interim.[18] And in 1973, 49 per cent of families made contributions of less than $100 to all charitable and civic organizations.[19] This is to be compared with a median family income of $12,000. You will have to decide for yourself whether contributions of this size are "generous," reflecting a low marginal utility of income. It is the author's judgment that they are not.

A second argument is rhetorical: how many individuals have you encountered lately who were *not* resistant to increases in *their* tax bill?

Even if the behavior of consumers reveals a favorable disposition to things material, there remains the possibility that this preference for "materialism" represents a perversion of their value system and hence is invalid. We now turn to a discussion of this problem.

Materialism: Valid or Invalid? If individuals have been widely exposed to divergent views on the desirability or undesirability of materialism, then it would be our view that the position they finally adopt on this issue is *valid*. If this interpretation of validity is accepted, then the question to be answered is whether individuals have, in fact, been widely exposed to divergent views on materialism. Let us review the current situation.

In our economy there scarcely exists a major opinion-influencing institution that lacks either a "natural" position or an ardently com-

[17] From Table 2, "Contributions by Individuals As a Per Cent of Income" in Allen H. Lerman, "A Survey of Charitable Contributions by Income" (Washington, D.C.: Office of Tax Analysis, Department of The Treasury, mimeographed, October 1974).

[18] *Ibid.*

[19] Based on tabulations from a report on the National Survey of Giving, conducted in 1974 by the Survey Research Center of The University of Michigan for the Commission on Private Philanthropy and Public Needs.

municated, highly explicit position on the issue of materialism. Think, for example, of advertisers and salesmen, labor leaders, professors from diverse disciplines (philosophy, marketing, economics), professional Christians (substitute any other religion), leaders of the Sierra Club. Advertisers and the salesmen have a vested interest in selling *material* goods and services; labor leaders represent employees with a vested interest in producing *material* goods (and thus, jobs and union members); professors presumably have a vested interest—though they may deny it—in gaining acceptance of their perhaps diverse analyses of the issue; professional Christians—it would seem—possess a doctrinal, vested interest in *nonmaterial* or "spiritual" goods; finally, Sierra Club leaders have a vested interest in gaining adherents to their religion of conservation and *nonmaterialism*.

In real life all of these agents—and others, too—urge their claims. Not so in Galbraith's discussions. There the spotlight is focused exclusively on the actions of advertisers and salesmen. He writes as though these other agents in value formation do not exist. And the consequence is clear. The materialism urged by advertisers and sellers prevails with predictable results: material wants are given undue precedence over nonmaterial wants. And this is done to such an extent that the material wants being satisfied are nonurgent and increasingly so; many are even frivolous.

In deciding whether the present values of Americans are valid, the crucial issue is whether all claimants have had sufficient access to channels of communication so that their views have had a "fair" hearing. Unfortunately, systematic evidence on this point is totally lacking. This means that you and I will have to form a judgment ourselves, on whatever basis we can, as to whether different views of the materialism/nonmaterialism issue have had a fair hearing.

In so judging, however, it is perhaps instructive to reflect that in 1960 The Environment—a code name for nonmaterialistic values—had few adherents and certainly none of those institutions usually considered powerful. Yet, by the mid-1970s, The Environment has become a powerful political cause and one encounters discussions in many places of such related topics as zero population growth and zero economic growth.

Galbraith also focuses on the subsidiary issue of the satisfaction of private material wants versus public material wants. As noted earlier, he asserts the existence of a "social imbalance" by which nonurgent private wants are met while urgent public wants go unfulfilled. Here Galbraith's arguments suffer the same defect: he has lavished much attention on the means by which preferences for private goods are stimulated and none at all on the corresponding devices for stimulating a demand for public wants.[20]

Summing up, we can note that the behavior of consumers betrays no evidence whatsoever of felt satiation with material goods. The "low" rate of charitable contributions and of people's strongly communicated distaste for paying taxes seem to reflect a high marginal utility for material goods. To the extent that proponents and opponents of materialism have had a fair chance to communicate their claims, then individuals' preferences for things material must be considered valid and Galbraith's criticisms on this point invalid.

Galbraith's contention that oligopolistic firms account for too large a share of total output as compared with competitive firms rests on two cornerstones: 1) his belief that large firms successfully "manage" consumer demand for their products, and 2) his view that large firms maximize sales rather than profits. We have just dealt at length with the management of demand and values. We now consider just what it is that firms maximize.

SALES VERSUS PROFIT MAXIMIZATION

Both sales maximization and profit maximization presuppose that large firms possess substantial "market power" to affect the prices and level of their own sales. Before we turn to the issue that divides Galbraith from most mainstream economists, we pause to deal with the sources of monopolists' "market power." Because this is the stuff from which many courses in Economics are made, our brief discussion is in the nature of an outline. The student who seeks an exposure to the larger literature is referred to Frederick M. Scherer, *Industrial Market Structure and Economic Performance* (Chicago: Rand-McNally & Co., 1971); W. G. Shepherd, *Market Power and Economic Welfare* (New York: Random House, Inc., 1970); and Roger Sherman, *The Economics of Industry* (Boston: Little, Brown and Company, 1974).

Sources of Market Power. Given the familiarity of the subject to you, perhaps the best way to approach the subject is to ask you to "test" yourself by constructing your own list of factors contributing to market power. Then compare your list with that of the author, yours could be better. Yet both are likely to be incomplete and to contain overlapping categories.

---

[20] This defect is partially corrected, however, in *Economics and the Public Purpose* in which Galbraith analyzes the mechanisms by which the demand of the government for military equipment is stimulated. See pp. 141–145.

"Economies of scale" will probably be on everyone's list. It should come as no surprise that a "large" firm, operating efficiently, can produce a given automobile for (say) $2,000 per unit whereas a "small" firm might have to spend up to $10,000 or $15,000 or more per unit to produce the identical car. Given the economies of large-scale production, it seems only natural that the automobile industry should be populated by very large firms. And, as we all know, it is.

Of course, economies of scale may exist for financing and selling as well as for production. With respect to financing, large firms by reason of diversification of product lines may appear less risky to lenders and hence command a lower interest rate than smaller, non-diversified firms. The same holds for selling. In this era of television, an hour of prime time purchasable for (say) $200,000 may command an audience of 10 million, giving a unit cost of $.02 per viewer. It takes no deep analysis to note that only large companies are in a position to make advertising outlays of this order of magnitude.[21]

Another basis for monopoly and hence market power consists of *barriers to entry* into an industry. These include large capital requirements (which in turn may arise from economies of scale); lack of access to the necessary technology because of patent controls, the high time and dollar costs of research, and a possibly small pool of trained technicians; control of essential raw materials by existing competitors; government regulation that aims to conserve the competitors rather than competition;[22] aggressive pricing by existing firms with a view to discouraging new entrants.

Location is still another source of market power. As most of us can attest, high prices, slack service, and poor-quality food are usual in airport (or railroad, bus terminal, or toll-road restaurants) reflecting no doubt the absence of competitors. The extent to which locational advantages confer market power often depends upon the size of the market—for example, a supermarket that is one among several in a

[21] *If*—and it is a big "if"—potential new entrants possess access to large quantities of capital, then, according to a sophisticated analysis by Richard Schmalensee, established firms will have no advantage over new entrants in attracting customers. See Richard Schmalensee, "Brand Loyalty and Barriers to Entry," *Southern Economic Journal* (April 1974), pp. 579–587. This means that entry is possible, on equal terms, to large firms, but not small firms.

[22] A case can be made that the Civil Aeronautics Board has acted to conserve competitors rather than competition. Consider the fact that despite a 3,400 per cent increase in air travel from 1945 to 1971, not a single new trunk air carrier was certified. In several route cases, routes were awarded on the basis of their financial weakness rather than on evidence relating to the quality of past and prospective performance: the award of a New York-to-Miami route in 1964 to Northeast and the award in 1974 of a Tokyo-to-Saipan route to Pan American, by then a financially distressed firm. Things like this are covered in Clair Wilcox and W. G. Shepherd, *Public Policies Toward Business*, 5th ed. (Homewood, Ill.: Richard D. Irwin, Inc., 1975).

very large shopping center versus the single supermarket in a small town.

Collusion, either overt or tacit, provides still another route to market power. Consider the automatic car washes in a large city. In terms of outcomes, it matters little whether the various car washes sign a formal agreement to set prices—overt collusion—or just tacitly achieve the same goal by following the prices charged by "Car Wash Number One." Of course, collusion may be applied to facets of market behavior other than prices. For example, there may be an agreement to divide markets so that the number of firms serving a given area is reduced, perhaps even to a single firm. Or, the collusion may call for the sharing of technical or other information, but only within the colluding group.

Sometimes *firms grow "naturally"* from a competitive status to one where they can exert market power. But *acquisitions* of other firms or *mergers* with other firms also provide a means by which market power is enhanced.

The final item in this catalog of devices yielding market power is an old friend, *product differentiation.* By contriving varieties of products that *are* different or appear to be different, some producer/ sellers achieve market power they might otherwise lack. As noted earlier, this process is facilitated by the technical complexity of modern products and by the shortage of search time from which most consumers suffer.

These then are the devices for achieving monopoly status and market power. Once achieved, market power confers on its possessor the possibility, to a degree, of dictating prices and quality to the market rather than being dictated to by the market. Both Galbraith and mainstream economists agree that large oligopolistic firms possess market power. But they differ in their interpretation of what such large firms do with the power they possess. We turn now to this issue.

Profit versus Sales Maximization: The Difference It Makes. Since Adam Smith (1776) [23] and even before, economists, and the public too, have known what to expect from "monopolists": higher prices and lower outputs than competition would enforce. Economists came to their prediction from the assumption of profit maximization and the mathematics of maximization. The public achieved its knowledge from experience, often painful.

[23] Adam Smith, *The Wealth of Nations,* 3rd ed. (London: J. Dove, 1826), Book IV, Chap. VIII, p. 62.

Now we encounter Galbraith and others who proclaim sales maximization as the dominant goal of large firms. To the question of whether sales maximization gives greatly different results, we answer: we believe so.[24]

By a strange irony, we find that the sales-maximizing possessor of market power to restrict output. To this result Galbraith would add produce at a price level and output level that yields a "normal profit." (A *normal profit* is just enough to ward off possible takeovers by other firms and to keep the firm's capital in its current employment.) As everyone knows, the competitive price is lower than the monopoly price (where the monopolist seeks to maximize profits). And the competitive output is higher than the monopoly output. A second irony is that the sales-maximizing large firm is following the economist's prescription for such natural monopolies as local public utilities. Public utilities commissions try to ensure that regulated monopolies set their rates, or prices, at levels that yield a "reasonable" level of profits,[25] and what the regulators seem to view as "reasonable" profits corresponds to normal profits.

Thus—advertising aside[26]—Galbraith's sales-maximizing large firms would produce at the competitive level instead of using their market power to restrict output. To this result Galbraith would add the alleged effects of manipulated demand. Successful manipulation implies that the *aggregate* demand for a given product is increased

[24] The difference is emphatic for the simple models presented here. But some recent work with more realistic models of firms suggests that the differences implied by sales maximization and profit maximization may not be so great. See footnote 56 on p. 295.

[25] Actually, an alternative solution is suggested by some theorists—that regulated monopolies should produce at the level where price equals marginal cost. This "solution" is not operationally feasible because of 1) difficulties in ascertaining marginal cost, and 2) the fact that this rule would condemn firms with declining marginal cost curves, for example, transit systems, to chronic operating losses. See Sherman, *The Economics of Industry*, pp. 358–360 and pp. 372–374.

[26] Genuinely competitive firms face horizontal demand curves, implying that they can sell all they produce even without the benefit of advertising. Large firms with market power never face this situation and hence usually find it profitable to engage in advertising.

When advertising occurs, the location and shape of the demand curve depend upon the amount of advertising undertaken. Profit maximizers will utilize smaller amounts of advertising than sales maximizers. Hence, the demand curves of profit maximizers will be 1) different and 2) lower than those of sales maximizers. It follows that the output of the sales-maximizing large firm will be greater than that predicted for profit maximizers. This line of argument is spelled out graphically in the Appendix to this chapter.

This argument does not, however, involve any "manipulation" effects of advertising.

over the competitive level.[27] Together, these arguments form the basis for Galbraith's contention that the output of large firms is disproportionately large as compared with that of the small firm sector. In this manner, too, is consumer sovereignty alleged to be thwarted.

The Same Argument, Graphically.[28] Figure 1—already familiar to many of you—clarifies the difference between sales maximization and profit maximization pictorially.[29]

Figure 1 depicts the demand and costs of a large firm producing a single product.[30] If you are unfamiliar with Figure 1, some explanations are in order.

First, the *average revenue* curve is the demand curve—the number of units of the product that persons exposed to the profit-maximizing dose of advertising would purchase at various prices over a given time period. A competitive firm—one among many sellers—can sell all it wants at a given price. But a large firm with market power faces a falling demand curve: it can only increase sales by decreasing its price.

Marginal revenue is the increment in total receipts (="revenues") associated with a given reduction in price.

Average cost is almost self-explanatory: the total cost per unit of a given level of output. Average cost is the sum of 1) average *fixed costs* and 2) average *variable costs.* Fixed costs consist of those costs that are incurred regardless of the level of output, such as property

[27] Galbraith maintains that successful manipulation implies increased aggregate demand for the advertised product. A situation where Firm A gained at the expense of Firm B, leaving aggregate demand for the product unchanged, is inconsistent with Galbraith's hypothesis.

[28] This section seeks to make the analysis of the previous section more explicit by the use of graphic analysis. But it introduces no new material and no new ideas. Hence, it may be omitted without a loss of coverage.

[29] For a clear and detailed explanation of price and output setting by a monopolist, see Richard F. Leftwich, *The Price System and Resource Allocation,* 5th ed. Hinsdale, Ill.: Dryden Press, 1973), chap. 11.

[30] In the more realistic case of the multiproduct firm, Baumol argues that the firm must opt for revenue maximization rather than sales maximization. The reason is that sales maximization concerns the *number* of units sold whereas revenue maximization deals with the revenues added by each sale. It is inappropriate to add numbers of television sets and refrigerators (with their different sales prices and costs), so the multiproduct firm must concentrate on the revenues added by the sales of either one more television set or one more refrigerator. The additional revenues, expressed in dollars, can be added.

Revenue maximization yields different, though qualitatively similar results to sales maximization. For a detailed analysis of revenue maximization, see William J. Baumol, *Business Behavior, Value and Growth,* rev. ed. (New York: Harcourt Brace Jovanovich, Inc., 1967).

Figure 1

Output and Price Determination:
Profit Vs. Sales Maximization

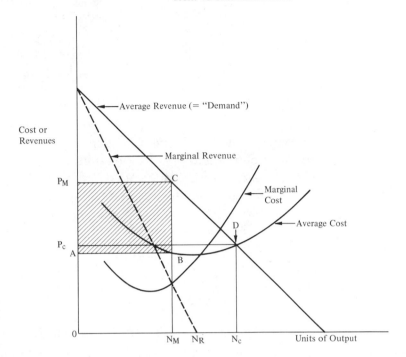

taxes. *Variable costs* are those that are related to the level of output, for example, costs of labor and raw materials. One of the items included in average cost is the normal profit mentioned previously. If normal profit is not achieved, then the firm may be susceptible to a managerial takeover by another firm, or the owners may decide to shift their capital resources to some other activity.

The following assumptions lie behind the demand and supply relationships depicted in Figure 1:

1. The demand and cost curves depicted are given and are known precisely to the managers of the firm.
2. With respect to advertising:
   a. the firm undertakes the amount of advertising consistent with profit maximization; [31]
   b. advertising undertaken by this firm is informative; that is, the "messages" involved consist of verifiable information;

[31] Here it is assumed that profit and sales maximizers engage in the same, profit-maximizing level of advertising. The more complex case where they choose different levels of advertising is analyzed in the Appendix to Chapter 11.

3. In deciding on price and output, this firm and others producing the same product act independently; that is, the actions of a single firm are taken without reference to possible responses by other firms.

For profit maximization, the mathematics of maximization call for output and price at a level where marginal revenue = marginal cost. Thus, for this firm profit maximization implies an output of ON_M in Figure 1, a price of OP_M, and greater-than-normal profits of $ABCP_M$.

Sales maximization, consistent with the retention of control by the present management and with the continued deployment of capital in this activity, calls for output and price at the point where average revenue (average price per unit of output) equals average costs (average cost per unit). In Figure 1, this implies an output of ON_C, a price of OP_C, and a zero level of greater-than-normal profits.

And, obviously, sales maximization yields a higher output and lower price than profit maximization.[32]

WHAT DO FIRMS MAXIMIZE?

The Traditional View: Profits. In 1776, when Adam Smith began to establish the foundations of economic theory, it was only natural to identify profit maximization as the objective of business owners. After all, in the small stores, workshops, and farms of that day, the profits of the business owner were the analogue of the wages paid to laborers and the interest paid to the lenders of capital. And it was obvious to Smith, a realist, that all these participants in economic activity were propelled by self-interest.

The first half of the nineteenth century was marked by the invention of the corporation and the second half by the appearance of large corporations, often closely associated with dominant, well-known owners—Andrew Carnegie, John D. Rockefeller, and James J. Hill are familiar names. No one, academic or otherwise, doubted that these leaders and the corporations they dominated aimed at anything but maximum profits.

It was only with the bureaucratization of the corporation that

[32] Revenue maximization, which occurs at the point where marginal revenue is zero or ON_R, in Figure 1, gives an output greater than the profit-maximizing output, but less than the sales maximization output. The revenue-maximizing price—not identified in Figure 1—would also lie between that of the profit maximizer and the sales maximizer.

began after World War I and became prevalent after World War II that economists began to doubt that corporations were aiming solely to maximize profits. The seeds of doubt were first planted in the classic study of *The Modern Corporation and Private Property* by Berle and Means in 1932.[33] The authors asserted and documented their contention that control in the large corporation was shifting from the owners (stockholders) to the management. From this point it was only a short step to assert that the managers—whoever they were— might have different objectives than the owners. And the objective usually assigned to managers was that of maximizing sales, not profits. William J. Baumol, the most conspicuous mainstream economist to espouse this view, states it clearly: ". . . the typical oligopolist's objectives can usefully be characterized approximately as sales maximization subject to a minimum profit."[34] We recommend Baumol's book to the student interested in a careful, analytical treatment of sales maximization. However, in our discussion we stay with Galbraith as our protagonist of the sales maximization viewpoint.

Galbraith's Case for Sales Maximization. According to Galbraith, power in the large corporation lies with The Technostructure, meaning the individuals manning the important committees in the corporation. And The Technostructure uses its power, Galbraith asserts, to make decisions consistent with its chief objective—sales maximization.

Lying behind Galbraith's assignment of power to The Technostructure in an arresting hypothesis woven out of economic history, which may be designated as the "scarce factor" hypothesis. We let Galbraith explain it in his own words:

> Power in the corporation goes to the factor which is hardest to obtain or hardest to replace at the margin . . .[35]
>
> Until about two centuries ago, no perceptive man would have doubted that power was decisively associated with land.[36]
>
> Later with the factory system and large-scale production, capital was what counted. So power over the enterprise passed to capital. And so did prestige in the community and authority in the state.[37]

[33] A. A. Berle and Gardner C. Means, *The Modern Corporation and Private Property* (New York: Harcourt Brace Jovanovich, Inc., 1932).

[34] William J. Baumol, *Business Behavior, Value and Growth,* rev. ed. (New York: Harcourt Brace Jovanovich, Inc., 1967).

[35] Galbraith, *The New Industrial State,* op. cit., p. 70.

[36] Ibid., p. 86.

[37] Ibid., p. 55.

Then a new factor entered—organized intelligence, whose alias is "The Technostructure":

> Given a competent business organization, capital is now ordinarily available. But the mere possession of capital is now no guarantee that the requisite talent can be obtained and organized. One should expect, from past experience, to find a new shift of power in the industrial enterprise, this one from capital to organized intelligence.[38]

It is the complexity of the decisions made in the modern, large corporation that gives importance and power to "organized intelligence." No one individual has the knowledge to deal with such complex problems himself. Instead, problem solving takes place in committees. In Galbraith's views such corporate committees perform three important functions: 1) they facilitate the pooling of specialized knowledge; 2) they permit the testing of opposing ideas; and 3) they encourage the mutual intellectual stimulation of members. The people who populate the important committees and make the important decisions comprise Galbraith's "Technostructure." To Galbraith, it follows naturally that they determine the overriding objectives of the corporation.

Obviously, The Technostructure includes the chief executive and the top three or top five executives. But Galbraith does not specify how far down the organizational hierarchy of a corporation The Technostructure extends. This is an important oversight. Objectives—and power as well—may differ between the several top executives of a corporation and those further down the corporate hierarchy.[39]

Why the Stockholders Lack Power. Galbraith offers three reasons to why stockholders do not effectively exercise the power that the law accords them. The first is the wide dispersion of stockholding and hence the attenuation of the typical stockholder's interest. To exercise influence on the corporation would require much effort and great expense, far more of each than the typical stockholder's financial interest would justify. Second, even if he wished to exercise influence,

[38] Ibid., p. 75.

[39] Although the outer boundaries of The Technostructure are not defined by Galbraith, it is clear that a "large" number of people are included in The Technostructure. Note this (*The New Industrial State,* op. cit., p. 160): "The Technostructure, to repeat once more, lodges the power of decision with groups. And these involve the participation of a large number of individuals of widely varying rank and position. Thus, a large number of people have access, or the illusion of access, to power."

the stockholder is likely to be thwarted by the information problem—in Galbraith's words, the "incomprehensibility of large corporations" because of their complexity. Third, rather than try to influence the corporation, the dissatisfied stockholder has an easy "out"; he can sell his holdings.

Together, in Galbraith's judgment, these factors account for the inability of stockholders to exercise power. They also account for the observed ability of The Technostructure to follow their own objectives, rather than those of the stockholders.

But the critic would assert that Galbraith overlooks three important factors: 1) the fact that "control" in a corporation can be exercised by the owner or owners of a tiny minority of shares outstanding; 2) the fact that a particular stockholder's interest—even though tiny as compared with the number of shares outstanding—may be of transcendent interest to him; 3) the possibility that large sales of shares by disenchanted stockholders may depress the price of the corporation's stock, thus leaving its management and Technostructure vulnerable to takeover by outsiders.

From this discussion it is not obvious whose objectives will prevail—those of the stockholders or those of The Technostructure.

The Technostructure and Sales Maximization. But, for the moment, let us assume that The Technostructure holds the reins. What are its goals? Galbraith identifies four:

1. Sales maximization ("growth in sales");
2. Survival and autonomy for the firm;
3. Technical virtuosity, a preference for producing technically exotic goods, such as computers;
4. A rising dividend rate.

As survival-autonomy is a goal shared by sales maximizers and profit maximizers alike, and as technical virtuosity and a rising dividend rate are argued by Galbraith to be of secondary importance, we concentrate our attention on sales maximization.

Why should The Technostructure embrace sales maximization as their primary goal? The case that Galbraith makes is both sophisticated and complex. In essence, four considerations commend sales maximization to The Technostructure.

First, a larger organization maximizes opportunities for promotion and for higher salaries as compared with a smaller organization. And Galbraith argues, the same larger sized labor force represents "the best protection against contraction."[40] A small firm with a small Technostructure and a large body of undifferentiated blue-collar workers will not hesitate to lay off employees when faced with a shrinkage in demand. Not so the large firm in which influence is widely dispersed among a relatively large Technostructure.

In addition, three psychological-sociological factors reinforce the preference of The Technostructure for sales maximization. The first is the principle of "consistency" with other goals, in this instance, the consistence of sales maximization in one's own firm with the nationally accepted goal (when Galbraith wrote in 1967) of growth in gross national product. Galbraith argues that the acceptance of a particular goal is facilitated if it is consistent with the goals of other and preferably more important institutions.

A second reinforcing principle is "identification," by which members of an organization tend to accept the perceived goals of the organization as their own. A member of the Technostructure who speaks pridefully of "our company" is more likely to embrace sales maximization as *his own* objective if he becomes aware that this is a company goal. As William Foote Whyte pointed out a generation ago, the individual who identifies completely with his firm may aptly be labeled "the organization man."[41]

Finally, Galbraith argues that the principle of "adaptation" is at work in large corporations. This principle states that individuals will seek to modify the goals of the company so as to conform to their own goals or preferences. Thus, if members of The Technostructure have independent reasons for adopting sales maximization as *their* goal for the corporation, they will seek to have this goal adopted as the commanding goal of the entire organization.

Taken together and applied to different members of The Technostructure in different degrees, these arguments support the notion that the goal of The Technostructure—the group that possesses power in the corporation—will become the goal of the corporation itself.

Sales versus Profit Maximization: the Evidence. Having reviewed the arguments, the time has come to confront them with whatever empirical evidence can be obtained.[42] Two kinds of evidence are

[40] Galbraith, *The New Industrial State*, op. cit., p. 175.

[41] William F. Whyte, *The Organization Man* (New York: Simon and Schuster, Inc., 1956).

[42] To delve deeper into the controversy between proponents of sales maximization and profit maximization, the reader is directed to the extremely witty but incisive series of exchanges between Galbraith, Robert Solow of M.I.T., and Robin Marris of Cambridge University. See Robert M. Solow, "The New Industrial State or Son of

available. The first relates to the profit rates of large firms with monopoly power versus firms lacking monopoly power. The second concerns executive compensation in large corporations and its relationship to profit or sales maximization. We consider each of these in turn.

If large firms *maximize sales* rather than profits, then the profit rate for such firms who possess a greater degree of monopoly power should be no greater than the profit rate for firms lacking such power. Presumably the profit-maximizing firm would seize any opportunity to raise prices, restrict output, and thus increase its profits, whereas the sales maximizing firm would not. In fact, the evidence on profit rates is consistent with profit maximization, *not* sales maximization.

The evidence consists of average profit rates from 1950 to 1960 for a sample 30 "more or less oligopolistic" industries. Following a line of inquiry initiated by Joe Bain,[43] the investigator—H. Michael Mann—classified each industry by the extent of its "barriers-to-entry."[44] If the entry of new competitors is discouraged by very high barriers to entry, then the profit-maximizing firm can seek and presumably obtain a higher rate of return on its capital. (Obviously, a sales maximizer would not want to do this.)

The results are as follows:

Barriers-to-Entry	Average Profit Rate: 1950–60	Number of Industries
Very high	16.4%	8
Substantial	11.3	9
Moderate or low	9.9	13

Affluence," *The Public Interest* (Fall 1967) with a reply by Galbraith and a rejoinder by Solow, pp. 100–119. Also a follow-up comment: Robin Marris, "Galbraith, Solow, and the Truth About Corporations," *The Public Interest* (Spring 1968), with yet another reply by Solow "The Truth Further Refined," pp. 37–52.

But note the dates—1967–1968. As further footnotes reveal, considerable research and discussion have taken place since that scintillating debate.

[43] Joe S. Bain, *Barriers to New Competition* (Cambridge, Mass.: Harvard University Press, 1965), pp. 182–204.

[44] Four criteria were used in categorizing industries by the extent of barriers-to-entry: 1) the importance of economies of scale, 2) the extent of product differentiation (when high, successful entry would require very large promotional outlays), 3) the extent of control of raw materials by existing firms, 4) the amount of capital required for successful entry.

For further details, see H. Michael Mann, "Seller Concentration, Barriers to Entry and Rates of Return in 30 Industries," *Review of Economics and Statistics* (August 1966), pp. 296–307.

Barriers-to-entry are but one manifestation of monopoly power. Mann tightens his test now by confining it to the 21 industries where concentration ratios (for the top eight firms) are 70 per cent or more. These 21 industries not only exhibit high barriers to entry but also are characterized by a small number of powerful competitors. The following results were obtained for a set of industries characterized by even greater monopoly power:

Barriers-to-Entry	Average Profit Rate: 1950–60	Number of Industries
Very high	16.4%	8
Substantial	11.3	9
Moderate or low	11.9%	5
		—
Total		21

The findings are emphatic: firms possessing market power based on either barriers-to-entry or on fewness of competitors obtain higher profit rates on the average. It is difficult to reconcile the findings of higher rates of return, especially over a decade-long period,[45] with anything but profit maximization.

What is more, these results are not unique. The two other major studies in this area—an earlier study by Bain [46] and one by Kamerschen [47]—yield essentially identical results. Their use of different samples of industries, different time periods, and different statistical methods tend to reinforce the strength of Mann's conclusion: that the average oligopolistic firm maximizes profits, *not* sales.

We turn now to a second kind of evidence, relating to the top corporate executives—their power, their compensation, and their goals.

Top executives, despite their obvious dependence upon subordinates for information and advice, can exercise power. And though we have not been able to identify research on this point, a year's worth of *Business Week* documents the exercise of power by the top executives of large corporations: subordinates are fired, mergers are under-

[45] For short periods, it is plausible to argue that sales maximizers may—by accident or otherwise—enjoy higher than average profits. But it seems unlikely that such "accidents" would last a decade.

[46] Bain, op. cit., especially Table XVII, p. 197 and Table XIX, p. 200.

[47] D. R. Kamerschen, "The Influence of Ownership and Control on Profit Rates," *American Economic Review* (June 1968), pp. 432–447.

taken, expenses are cut, new product initiatives are undertaken—usually at the instigation of the top executive(s) or with his active support.

And, in exercising power, it seems possible that such top executives may be following different objectives than those followed by lesser members of the Technostructure.

One thing is clear: the compensation of the top executives of the largest corporations in the United States is geared to the interests of stockholders. There are two bases in evidence for this statement.

The first is descriptive. Data assembled by Wilbur Lewellen show that for the top executives in 50 of our largest corporations [48] stock-dependent compensation (stock options and executive stock) outweighs other compensation (salary, and so on) by a ratio of five to one. Supplementary evidence suggests very strongly that the compensation of the top three or top five executives is similarly weighted in the direction of the stockholders' interest.[49]

The second basis is analytical. The question asked is whether the size of executive compensation is related to the amount of sales achieved or to some measure of profitability, for example, the increase in the net worth of the firm. Two investigations—by Masson [50] and by Lewellen and Huntsman [51]—have used sophisticated econometric techniques to test this proposition. The data pertain again to the 50 largest U.S. corporations for whom earnings histories of executives could be obtained. The data cover eight different years between 1942 and 1963. Despite the use of somewhat different statistical techniques, the conclusions of the two studies are almost interchangeable.

Consider first Masson's interpretation of his findings. The most striking results from this sample of industries are

1. That the firms in these industries do *not* pay their executives for sales maximization;

2. That the financial incentives of the executives do indeed affect firm stock market performance;

3. The coincidence of executive financial return with the stock performance of the firm benefits the stockholders.

[48] See Wilbur G. Lewellen, "Management and Ownership in the Large Firm(s)," *Journal of Finance* (May 1969), pp. 299–322.

[49] See Wilbur G. Lewellen, *Executive Compensation in Large Industrial Corporations* (New York: National Bureau of Economic Research, 1968), pp. 227–228.

[50] Robert Tempest Masson, "Executive Motivations, Earnings, and Consequent Equity Performance," *Journal of Political Economy* (November–December 1971), pp. 1278–1292.

[51] Wilbur G. Lewellen and Blaine Huntsman, "Managerial Pay and Corporate Performance," *American Economic Review* (September 1970), pp. 710–720.

Masson expresses the view that these results are weakened by the nonrandom character of the sample of industries studied, but feels that as a first approximation these results should be relevant to most types of American industry.[52]

Now compare the conclusions of Lewellen and Huntsman with those of Masson:

> Because the results of the study persistently indicate that both reported profits and equity market values are substantially more important in the determination of executive compensation than are sales—indeed, sales seem to be quite irrelevant—the clear inference is that there is a greater incentive for management to shape its decision rules in a manner consistent with shareholder interests than to seek the alternative goal of revenue maximization.
>
> The evidence presented . . . can be interpreted as support for the notion that a highly industrialized economy . . . can in large measure still be characterized by models which are based on the assumption of profit maximization.[53]

To protect the unwary student, we call his attention to several earlier studies that yielded almost opposite results.[54] Unfortunately, these studies suffered from a common and crucial defect: executive compensation was confined to "salaries plus bonuses" and the 80 per cent of executive compensation that is stock-related was not taken into account.

What Is Maximized: A Summing-up. Against Galbraith's wittily argued case for the power and the objectives of The Technostructure, we find arrayed two kinds of hard evidence. The first shows that oligopolistic firms possessing monopoly power have earned higher rates of return over longish time periods, five years or ten years. How else is this to be explained, if not in terms of profit maximization by means of higher prices and restricted output? If The Technostructure in these firms sought sales maximization and possessed power, why

---

[52] Masson, op. cit., p. 1290.

[53] Lewellen and Huntsman, op. cit., p. 718.

[54] J. W. McGuire, J. S. Y. Chiu, and A. O. Elbing, "Executive Incomes, Sales, and Profits," *American Economic Review* (September 1962), pp. 753–761; Arch Patton, "Top Executive Pay: New Facts and Figures," *Harvard Business Review* (September 1966), p. 96; David R. Roberts, *Executive Compensation* (New York: The Free Press, 1959).

was output not expanded and why were prices not reduced sufficiently to yield the same rate of return as firms lacking monopoly power?

The second bit of statistical evidence indicates that the compensation of top executives has depended upon maximizing the stockholder's interest, not on maximizing sales. The evidence from the preceding paragraph suggests strongly that they succeeded.

And so we conclude, with Lewellen and Huntsman, that "a highly industrialized economy . . . can in large measure still be characterized by models which are based on the assumption of profit maximization." [55]

In so concluding, we should be aware that Galbraith's assaults have given burst to a new interest in and new research in this topic. Although it is too early to draw any firm conclusions, some of the current research suggests that sales maximization and profit maximization give, under certain conditions, highly similar results.[56] For this reason an open mind on the subject is to be encouraged.

If firms 1) possess monopoly power, 2) seek to maximize profits, and 3) are unable to manage demand, then their output will be lower than competitive organization would imply. Consumers will be plagued by too few rather than too many of the products of oligopolists. In this respect consumer sovereignty will be thwarted.

SCARCE TIME AND HARRIED CONSUMERS

Contrast the tempo of a small rural town with that of Manhattan. In the small town the pace is leisurely and time may even hang heavy. Quite the opposite is true in Manhattan, where the pace is frenetic and the skyscraper dwellers, especially those with high incomes, are likely to be harried. If the small-towner and the Manhattanite are

[55] Lewellen and Huntsman, op. cit., p. 718.

[56] For a collection of papers on sales versus profit maximization, see Robin Marris and Adrian Woods, eds., *The Corporate Economy* (Cambridge, Mass.: Harvard University Press, 1971).

In one paper in this volume, Robert Solow—Galbraith's critic—concludes on the basis of his model: "in any case, growth-oriented and profit-oriented firms would respond in qualitatively similar ways to such stimuli as changes in factor prices, discount rate, and excise and profit taxes . . . an observer would find it hard to distinguish one kind of firm from the other." (pp. 341–342).

In another study focusing on risk management, Schramm and Sherman conclude that "Market value maximization [after taking account of 'risk management'] no longer collapses into profit maximization, and it can look instead like sales and growth rate maximization." See Richard Schramm and Roger Sherman," Profit Risk Management and the Theory of the Firm," *Southern Economic Journal* (January 1974), pp. 353–363.

tested for "busy-ness" by being asked what their plans are for tomorrow night, the small-towner will probably tell you that he is at home, "free," or engaged in some regular social event. As for the affluent Manhattanite, the chances are that he will have to consult his appointment book before he can answer your question. Few would think of labeling a middle-income small-towner as "harried" whereas many people might assign the high income Manhattanite that label.

What is the relevance of all this to consumer sovereignty? The answer is that most of us, in choosing activities, are accustomed to taking the scarcity of our financial resources into account. But in choosing what to do, some of us may fail to take into account the scarcity of time. Failure to consider scarce time may mean that some "economic processes are *not* focused toward satisfying the wants of ultimate consumers." In other words, the achievement of consumer sovereignty may be thwarted because of a faulty decision framework.

In discussing the relationship between time and consumer sovereignty, we first examine the factors that explain the demands on an individual's time, and then turn to a discussion of time as an unrecognized constraint and finally the conflict time poses for the perfectionist personality.

Activities and the Use of Time. In the short run, all of us are endowed with the same 24-hour day, 168-hour week in which to engage in the activities that yield satisfaction, or utility, to us. Since all of us possess the same "supply" of time, we turn naturally in asking why some are "harried" because of "excessive" claims on their time, to factors influencing the demand for activities, and to the time requirements of these activities.

In this relatively unexplored area [57] it is our hypothesis that the demand for time can be explained by two factors: 1) affluence, which extends the range of one's activities, and 2) urbanization, which vastly increases the number of alternatives among which the consumer can choose.

Each activity we undertake may use up our time in four different ways: 1) choosing—which activity (swimming) to undertake, where, with what equipment, and with whom; 2) preparation for and participation in the activity itself—getting there, the time it takes to swim, eat, to work, or to loaf; 3) the purchase of necessary equipment or

[57] For exceptions see Sebastian de Grazia, *Of Time, Work and Leisure* (New York: The Twentieth Century Fund, 1962) and Staffan Linder, *The Harried Leisure Class* (New York: Columbia University Press, 1970).

rights—for swimming, the admission ticket to the pool and the rental of the snorkel, or, for owners, the acquisition of the pool itself; 4) maintenance and replacement (when appropriate) of the ancillary equipment—in the swimming case, repair of the snorkel and ultimately its replacement, or, for owners, the maintenance of the pool itself.

Affluence in the form of higher real incomes affects both the number and range of choices to be made. Suppose that the average purchase a family makes comes to $10 in 1973 dollars.[58] Using this as the price per purchase, a simple arithmetic calculation shows that between 1947 and 1973 the number of possible purchases increased from 553 (= $5,527 ÷ $10) to 1,112 (= $11,116 ÷ $10). Not unexpectedly, the same twofold increase in real income per family from 1947 to 1972 has been accompanied by a substantial increase in the amount of durable goods owned, as indicated by the following:

Per Cent of Households Owning: [a]

Type of Durable Good	1950	1952	1960	1971	1972
An automobile	59%	NA [b]	77%	83%	NA
Two or more automobiles	7	NA	15	28	NA
Television:					
Black and white	NA	47%	89%	NA	100% [c]
Color	NA		NA	NA	61%
Refrigerators	NA	89	98	NA	100% [c]
Vacuum cleaners	NA	59	74	NA	97
Washing machines	NA	76		NA	97
Clothes dryers	NA	4	20	NA	51
Room air conditioners	NA	1	15	NA	47
Kitchen range (freestanding)	NA	24	31	NA	44
Freezers	NA	12	23	NA	34
Dishwasher	NA	3	7	NA	32
Food waste disposers	NA	3	11	NA	32

[a] For automobiles, the statistic is the "per cent of *families*" who own. For other durables, the table presents the "per cent of *homes wired for electricity.*"
Source of automobile data: *Statistical Abstract of the United States, 1973,* Table 905, p. 549, data from the Survey Research Center. Source of data on other durables: *Statistical Abstract of the United States, 1973,* Table 1174, p. 693, data from *Billboard Publications* and *Merchandising Week.*
[b] Not ascertained.
[c] Rounded.

[58] U.S. Bureau of the Census, Current Population Reports, Series P-60, No. 91, December 1973, *Money Income in 1972 of Families and Persons in the United States,* Table 9, p. 34.

All of us can join with Kenneth Boulding in acknowledging that we are truly "keepers (and maintenance men) of our consumer durables." [59]

And with increasing affluence the range of possible choices has been greatly extended. Three generations ago, someone wanting to go swimming could—in the summer—choose among several local lakes. By two generations ago, the choice had widened to include an indoor pool in the local YMCA or similar institution. By a single generation ago there were usually several public or semipublic pools to choose among. And now, in this generation, children of affluent parents can choose among their own pool and those of their friends.

So with affluence has come the possibility and fact of more purchases. And with more purchases have come more possessions. And, as all of us know so well, with more possessions comes more maintenance and/or replacement. And—to repeat—all four steps—the choice of activities, participation itself, purchases of equipment and rights, maintenance and replacement—all require time.

At the same time urbanization, modern technology, and transportation have vastly increased the set of alternatives among which one could choose. The individual who has moved from a farm or small town to a large metropolitan area may have moved from a one-movie house locale to one where he could choose among 20 movie theaters. At the same time he would have moved from a site with no professional football team, no symphony, no art gallery to an urban environment in which there was one or more of these supremely urban institutions. And, by choosing to grow up in the television era, the individual has succeeded in multiplying his entertainment possibilities many times over as compared with his grandparents and even his parents.

In terms of purchase possibilities, the urban or metropolitan market offers more products, more brand/models, more retail outlets, and more financing agencies among which to choose. The last great inflection point in this process came with the completion of the interstate highway system and similar roads. For the twin cities of Minneapolis and St. Paul the completion of I-94 reduced the driving time between the two downtowns from 30 minutes to 10 minutes, in one stroke doubling the number of retail outlets that were easily accessible to inhabitants of both cities. The same applies to the new shopping areas to which *you* gained access upon completion of such superhighways.

[59] Personal conversation, about 1951.

Thus, affluence has made possible more activities, more purchases, and more maintenance. And urbanization, modern technology, and modern transportation have combined to enlarge and to complicate the set of activities, products, brand/models, and retail outlets among which the consumer may choose.

Time As a Scarce Factor. Although affluence and urbanization have increased the potential demands for time, neither high-income consumers nor urban consumers need be "harried." The prescription for nonharried living is simple: for *all* activities, utilize the "marginal rule" that was applied in Part One to the activity of searching-shopping. The rule: undertake an activity only if the gross payoff from that activity exceeds the incremental cost of the activity. The key to the successful application of the rule is the recognition that no activity is "free" or costless. Any given activity requires the sacrifice of a second-best activity. As suggested in Part One, mental calculation may be facilitated by asking oneself what is the dollar equivalent of the satisfaction that the second-best activity would have yielded.

If with either awareness or unawareness consumers apply the marginal rule correctly, they will not be "harried" and consumer sovereignty in this respect will be served. But the essential question posed by consumer sovereignty is one of fact: to what extent do consumers feel "harried?" Some recent data from the Survey Research Center of the University of Michigan provide at least a tentative answer.[60] Persons comprising a probability sample of the United States population in 1971 were asked this question:

In general, how do you feel about time—would you say that you *always* feel rushed even to do the things you have to do, only *sometimes* feel rushed, or *almost never?*

Our interpretation will be that being "rushed" is equivalent to being "harried" even though some individuals might equate being "rushed" with being "very busy." Table 4 reveals a strong positive correlation between being rushed and family income. On the other hand, a tabulation not reproduced here shows no relationship whatsoever between urbanization and being rushed. Thus, the data in Table 4 are consistent with the notion that high income individuals—the "affluent"—may indeed be "harried," thus marking another area in which consumer sovereignty has not been achieved.

[60] Angus Campbell, Philip E. Converse, and Willard L. Rodgers, *The Quality of American Life* (New York: Russell Sage Foundation, forthcoming in 1976).

TABLE 4

Evidence on the Relationship Between Harriedness and Income [a]

1970 Family Income

How Often Do You Feel Rushed? [b]	All Respondents	Less than $3,000	$3,000– 4,999	$5,000– 6,999	$7,000– 9,999	$10,000– 12,499	$12,500– 16,999	$17,000 or more
"Always"	22%	11%	17%	22%	25%	24%	24%	29%
"Sometimes"	51	34	47	51	50	58	61	55
"Almost never"	27	55	36	27	25	18	15	16
Total	100%	100%	100%	100%	100%	100%	100%	100%
Per cent of sample	100%	14%	13%	13%	18%	13%	16%	13%
Number of cases	2065	291	286	269	365	270	321	263

[a] Source: Campbell, Converse, and Rodgers, op. cit.
[b] The question asked was: "In general, how do you feel about time—would you say that you *always* feel rushed even to do the things you had to do, only *sometimes* feel rushed, or *almost never?* The proportion of the sample not answering the question was 15%.

The Dilemma of the Perfectionist. Some of us have learned too well at the hands of parents or teachers that "whenever you do something (no matter how small or unimportant it is), *you should do it well!*" Unless such a "perfectionist" recognizes the scarcity of time as a problem and makes special efforts to adjust to it, he or she is condemned to eternal frustration. For harried perfectionists—and for harried nonperfectionists as well—three major adjustments are possible:

1. *Reduce the number of activities to be undertaken,* especially those that are time-intensive in any of the aspects mentioned.
2. *Make less important choices on the basis of less information,* or, in other words, make sloppier choices. This solution would, of course, pain the perfectionist.
3. *Try to hire substitutes to carry out less important tasks.*

A little reflection will reveal that all of these suggestions are implied by the marginal rule. It is little wonder that this rule is so beloved by economists!

Appendix to Chapter 10

Advertising: Implications for Profit versus Sales Maximization

       Advertising makes cost and demand curves interdependent. The reason is that advertising affects *both* costs and demand. A "dose" of advertising may be viewed in the short run as a fixed cost and thus affects the average cost curve. To a given level of advertising there corresponds a particular average cost curve (assuming that nonadvertising costs remain constant).

       Similarly, to a particular level of advertising there also corresponds a given demand curve. The reason is that, under imperfect information, advertising will tend to make more customers aware of the offerings of a particular firm. The greater the awareness, other things equal, the greater will be the number of would-be purchasers at any given price. In other words, as advertising increases, the demand curve of the firm shifts to the right.

       These relationships are depicted in Figure 2. We assume that a profit-maximizing or a sales-maximizing management faces the identical set of cost and demand curves. The crucial question is the price, the level of advertising, and hence the level of output each will choose. By definition, the profit maximizing firm will select that pair of AC and D ($= AR$) curves that maximizes profit ($= AR - AC$).

       For the two pairs of cost and demand curves in Figure 2 the profit maximizer would choose:

> Output of ON_{M_1}
> Price of $N_{M_1}L$
> Profit of $IJLK$ ($> ABEF$)

By contrast, the sales maximizer would select:

> Output of ON_{C_1}

Price of NC_1R
Normal Profits Only $(AC = AR)$

In general, we would expect the sales-maximizing output to be greater and the sales-maximizing price to be lower than the profit maximizing levels even when demand and cost curves are made interdependent by advertising.[61]

Figure 2

Advertising: Implications for Profit Vs. Sales Maximization

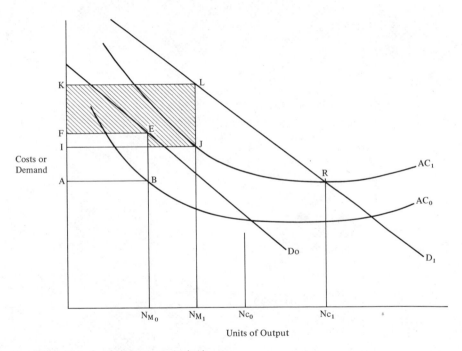

Units of Output

D_0 and AC_0 are demands and average cost associated with
a *lesser* level of advertising while D_1 and AC_1 are
associated with a higher level of advertising.

[61] For a more detailed discussion, see Douglas Needham, *Economic Analysis and Industrial Structure* (New York: Holt, Rinehart, and Winston, Inc., 1969), pp. 63–66.

CHAPTER 11

Consumer Sovereignty:
The Critique of Consumerists

Consumerists and economists observe the same economic landscape, but they use different instruments.[1] The result is that consumerists and economists identify different flaws in the functioning of the economy. And it is with the flaws identified by consumerists that this chapter deals.

But first we pause to examine the difference in viewpoint between economists and consumerists. When economists view the economic world, they employ low-magnification telescopes equipped with special filters. They wish to see the "whole picture," and want not to be bothered by details. Further, they use a strong filter—deductive logic—to screen out elements that their past analysis has "shown" to be unimportant. The consumer information problem, a topic discussed in this chapter, is an example of a problem that the economist's filter has largely screened from view.

Consumerists, on the other hand, use high-powered telescopes so they can get down-to-earth and see details. Their filter tends to screen out complex analysis, leaving feelings and complaints intact. What overwhelms consumerists is their impression that our economy works rather unsatisfactorily, especially for the consumer. Their chief complaints are that the consumer cannot come by the information he requires and that the operation of the economy too often leaves people dissatisfied, complaining. Furthermore, the consumerists' instruments leave them with the strong impression that the system is unfair, failing to give consumers their "say" when it comes to arranging and correcting things.

---

[1] The term *consumerist* and its companion term, *consumerism*, are defined on page 306.

This chapter deals with four major criticisms of consumer sovereignty, raised explicitly or implicitly by consumerists. These criticisms center on four problems: 1) the problem of informationally imperfect consumer markets, 2) the problem of consumer grievances, and 3) the underrepresentation of the consumer interest and 4) the underresponsiveness of government to it.

Before we turn to the substantive discussion, we pause to identify the source of these criticisms. *Consumerism* is the movement from which they spring, whereas consumerists, epitomized by Ralph Nader, are the individuals who populate the movement and espouse consumerism. To give content to the phrase, *consumerism* may be defined as "the articulation of consumer discontent and the furtherance of corrective actions." Or, alternatively, it may be viewed as "a social movement seeking to augment the rights and power of buyers in relation to sellers." [2]

INFORMATIONALLY IMPERFECT CONSUMER MARKETS

Why is it—to repeat the lament of earlier chapters—that single-lens reflex cameras of roughly the same quality can sell in the same local market for prices ranging all the way from $170 to $635? Why is it that prices of (nonparticipating) term life insurance policies sold by reliable companies can range from $1,680 to $3,100?

The culprit is consumer information. It is the thesis of this section that consumers are often unable to obtain the information necessary for the making of effective purchases. Or, sometimes, they fail to act upon the relevant information even when they possess it. The consequence is a reduction of economic welfare as consumers pay higher-than-necessary prices for a given level of quality.

This is the theme written into the activities of the consumer movement's oldest organizations, Consumers Research and Consumers Union. If consumer markets worked well—yielding a high correlation between price and quality—product tests would have been redundant and Consumers Research as well as Consumers Union would have been stillborn.

This theme is also embodied in the initial legislative responses to modern consumerism: unit pricing; nutritional labeling; Truth-in-Credit, Truth-in-Packaging, Truth-in-You-Name-It. Were consumers

---

[2] The first definition is the author's. The second comes from Philip Kotler, "What Consumerism Means for Marketers," *Harvard Business Review* (May–June 1972), pp. 48–57.

able to obtain the relevant information for themselves or if markets functioned so that price was in fact an indicator of quality, there would have existed no demand for this kind of legislation.

The topic, the informational functioning of markets, is the same we met earlier. But the viewpoint has shifted—180 degrees. In Part I we accepted existing market arrangements as given and asked what the consumer needed to know in order to purchase effectively. Here we seek to assess the informational functioning of markets.

Our discussion of the informational imperfections of consumer markets proceeds first by establishing a criterion for assessing the informational imperfection of a market, then illustrates the application of this criterion to particular markets, and, finally, by contrasting consumer markets in 1776 with those of 1976, seeks to identify the causes of informationally imperfect markets in our contemporary economy.

Our exposure to this topic in Part One—Chapters 2, 3, and 4— should enable us to shorten the discussion here.

The Matter of Criterion: The Perfect Information Criterion. Given the subject, it may come as no surprise that we meet price-quality diagrams and the perfect information frontier for a second time. To avoid misunderstanding, the definition of the *perfect information frontier* is repeated here:

> The *perfect information frontier* consists of the positively sloped line segments connecting those points, representing price and quality, for which a given quality may be purchased at the lowest possible price.

At our first meeting, the perfect information frontier served us *as individual consumers* by showing what the market could do for the individual in terms of obtaining a given quality at the lowest price. To partake of these fruits, the individual consumer needed to know the identity of the product varieties on the frontier—the Olympus OM-1, for example—the name, address, and asking price of the retailer with the frontier price.

In this discussion the perfect information frontier shows what an informationally perfect market *could* do for *all* individuals. In such a market all prices, as a first approximation, would be forced to the vicinity of the perfect information frontier. Welfare would be increased because no one would pay more than the frontier price (approximately) to purchase a product of a given quality. Consumers could use the money thus saved for other utility-producing activities.

Turned around, this concept of the informationally perfect market brings us at once to a criterion for identifying informational *imperfections* of a market:

> A local consumer market is *informationally imperfect* "to the extent that prices lie above the perfect information frontier."

And we can further state that consumer sovereignty is thwarted to the extent that a market is informationally imperfect.

It is but several short steps to an acceptable measure of the extent of informational imperfection in a market. Consider Chart 1, which depicts price-quality relationships for single-lens reflex cameras.[3] The highest price quoted is the topmost price for Variety 0, namely $635. For *this particular specimen,* the extent of informational imperfection may be expressed *relatively* as the ratio of $635 to $170, the latter being the frontier price for a quality score of 63.[4] This ratio, 3.74 (= $635/$170), may be interpreted as being 3.74 as great as the minimum price necessary to purchase that level of quality. A frontier price, for example, the lowest price for Variety I, expresses informational perfection.

An overall *index of informational imperfection* could, in principle, be calculated as "the weighted average of such ratios with the weights proportional to the number of items sold at each price over some period." In practice, information on unit sales of varieties by each retailer is usually unavailable and hard to come by, since such data are typically considered "confidential." Hence, a second-best index would be an unweighted average of such ratios. Implicitly, this measure would assume that equal numbers of items were sold at each price.

Summing up, the ratio of the actual price to the frontier price measures, for a particular specimen, the extent of informational imperfection. And the mean ratio measures the extent of informational

---

[3] We review the interpretation of the data in Charts 1–4. On Chart 1 each *variety* of camera is denoted by a letter or double letter (A, B, C . . . AA, BB, CC . . .). Varieties designated by o are not available in this market although they may be available in other markets. Each point (not o) represents the lowest price a local retailer was willing to quote for that variety of camera.

The quality data for cameras are those published by Consumers Union, whereas those for ten-speed bicycles (Chart 2) are the author's quantification of Consumers Union's verbal judgments, as expressed in the ratings table.

Life insurance, gasoline, and shares of General Motors stock are viewed as single-characteristic products (as a first approximation) whose quality is thus uniform.

[4] The frontier price is either the actual or hypothetical lowest price corresponding to a particular level of quality.

Chart 1

Prices and Quality in a Local Market: Single-Lens Reflex Cameras
in Ann Arbor, 1974[a]

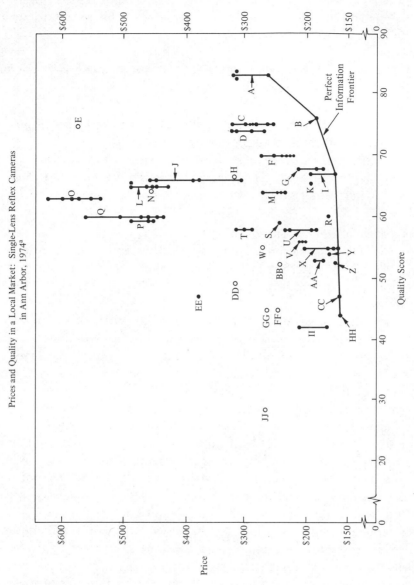

[a]Source: Quality Scores—*Consumer Reports*, November, 1974.
Prices—Collected by Blanche R. Maynes, November 18–26, 1974

The symbol o denotes the list prices of specimens which could not be purchased in Ann Arbor.
The others points plotted represent actual prices.

imperfection for an entire market. The greater the extent of informational imperfection in a market, the greater is the extent to which consumer sovereignty is thwarted.

The Underlying Assumptions and Their Importance. Two assumptions form the foundation of this analysis:

1. *Fully informed consumers make uniform assessments of quality* for different *varieties* of products.
2. *Consumers possess complete and accurate information* regarding the following: the existence of products, varieties of products, and retail outlets; qualities of varieties; prices of specimens.

Some elucidation is in order.

The full information assumption is sufficient to force prices to the vicinity of the perfect information frontier. But it is not necessary; a less strong assumption or a different mechanism may achieve the same result.

One alternative mechanism consists of the reactions of sellers—manufacturers or retailers. With respect to the workings of this possible mechanism, Daniel Padberg's analysis of nutritional labeling, open dating,[5] and unit pricing is instructive.[6] The consumerist proponents of these proposals clearly expected that consumers would assimilate and act on information regarding nutritional content, freshness, and price per unit of size. "Naturally" they would reward makers and sellers on the basis of nutritional content, freshness, and price per unit of size by purchasing the specimens they regarded as optimal on the basis of this information. And, of course, they would not purchase less-than-optimal specimens. In terms of our analysis, prices would tend to be pushed to the perfect information frontier.

Padberg's rather startling results show that this is *not* the way these devices work. Although most consumers approve of these reforms, most do *not* use them. And, of the users, many get the wrong message. Nonetheless, according to Padberg, these reforms may achieve their purpose, in part at least, through their effects on makers

---

[5] "Open dating" calls for the labeling of perishable items so that the purchaser can determine their freshness. Unit pricing prescribes a label specifying the price per unit of size, for example, price per ounce.

[6] Daniel I. Padberg, "Non-Use Benefits of Mandated Consumer Protection Programs," *Proceedings of Workshop II on Consumer Action Research, April, 1975* (Berlin: International Institute of Management, 1975).

and retail sellers of food products. It works this way. The proposal for nutritional labels induces manufacturers to undertake nutritional research so they will not have to face the embarrassment of marketing a product that is nutritionally inferior. Or, by the same token, retailers change their inventory rotation practices so that stale foods are less likely to be found on their shelves. Similarly, retailers revise their pricing procedures so that unit pricing will not disclose anomalies such as a "large" jar of peanut butter costing more per ounce than a "small" jar.

It is also Padberg's contention that consumer activists serve less activistic, less searching consumers by calling attention and giving publicity to the undesirable practices these reforms are designed to eliminate. Thus, the activities of the activists and the responses of manufacturers and retailers to them are two of the mechanisms by which markets may be made more informationally perfect.

We should be careful not to overgeneralize on the basis of Padberg's investigations. Thus far, they are confined to food products and the three devices mentioned previously. Further, Padberg's "non-use" effects may not achieve all of the original objectives. For example, unit pricing is intended not just to eliminate anomalies in pricing between "small" and "large" containers, but, more importantly, to enable consumers to identify the cheapest specimen among alternative brands of the same product.

But Padberg's results are important to us here since they suggest a mechanism by which prices may be pushed to the perfect information frontier without all consumers being fully informed.

Stores that claim they "will never be undersold" suggest another mechanism for achieving the same outcome. Such stores support their claim by meeting the lower price of competitors for any *individual* who shows that he can purchase a comparable item at a lower price in another store. When "enough" individual consumers cite a lower price by competitor stores, then the not-to-be-undersold store will often post a new, lower price that is offered to *all* consumers. What we do not know is how many consumers need to be fully informed in order to induce not-to-be-undersold retailers to lower their prices.

And, of course, the general issue raised by this example is much more important. We do not know how many consumers need to be fully informed in *typical* consumer markets before prices are forced to the frontier. Nor, additionally, do we know the trade-off in effectiveness between anonymous, fully informed consumers and noisy, articulate consumer activists. These are matters for future research. But it seems likely that prices can be forced to the frontier by the knowledge and actions of a minority of consumers.

We turn back to the assumption of uniformity of quality assessments, directing our attention initially to the limitations this assumption poses for our analysis. First, the quality assessments embodied in *our* price-quality charts pertain to *varieties* of products, for example, an Olympus OM-1 camera. Thus, our quality measure takes no account of the characteristics of retail sellers. Were their characteristics taken into account, some points on the price-quality charts might be above-frontier, even under the assumption of full information, whereas some others might shift the frontier downward.

A second limitation is the problem of "intrinsically subjective" characteristics, for example, the aesthetic quality of a painting. Since beauty—in the words of the cliché—is "in the eyes of the beholder," the assumption of uniformity of quality assessments will hold less well for subjective characteristics and hence for products in which subjective characteristics are "important." If this thought is turned around, we arrive at the conclusion that the use of the perfect information frontier becomes increasingly appropriate as the importance of objective characteristics increases.

A third limitation arises from the possible overlap of the product and market sets of different individuals. Recall that both the delineation of the product set and the assessment of quality depend upon the individual's expected use of the product. Thus, recreational photographers and professional photographers might include the identical camera in their product sets, but assess the quality of that camera differently. Differences in the price-to-quality ratio arising from the two usages could not validly be attributed to informational imperfections of the markets. Similarly, market sets are defined for particular individuals. Because of high search costs, one individual's "market" might consist solely of a high-priced subset of specimens in the second individual's market for the same product set. Again, this might produce differences in both the perfect information frontier and in the price-to-quality relationship for reasons not attributable to informational imperfections.

A fourth limitation is the possibility of different quality assessments even for products whose characteristics are predominantly "objective."

Finally, price discrimination based on objective variables—for example, different air fares for individuals of different ages—may give rise to price variations not attributable to informational deficiencies in the market. (Note that such an arrangement is a second-best arrangement to a competitive outcome. But it is likely to be superior to a single higher-than-competitive price.) [7]

Thus, a number of factors exist limiting the validity of inferences based strictly on the perfect information frontier concept. We do not believe that renders the concept useless. We do recommend that the perfect information frontier be estimated. Then the reader should ask whether factors such as those cited could account for the extent of the average price-to-quality ratio. If they cannot, it would be proper to infer that some degree of information imperfection exists. We test this recipe on Charts 1–4 carried forward from Part I.

The Perfect Information Frontier in Practice: Illustrative Interpretations. A first glimpse at Chart 1 on page 309, depicting price-quality relationships for single-lens reflex cameras, conveys overwhelmingly the impression of a zero correlation between price and quality. And statistical calculations confirm the impression.[8] The unweighted index of informational imperfection has a value of 1.90, meaning that the average price of a specimen is almost twice as high as the frontier price for that specimen. Does anything from the foregoing discussion stand between these data and the conclusion that this local market is characterized by much informational imperfection? To telegraph the answer, we believe not. But let us check it out.

Before commencing our checkout, we note that informational imperfections appear to manifest themselves in two forms: 1) a considerable range of prices for identical varieties, Variety 0, for example, being priced from $550 to $635 for a range of $85, and 2) a near-zero correlation between the average price for a variety and its quality.

First, we ask whether the omitted characteristics of retailers could account for the difference. This is a tempting hypothesis. Could it be that the stores quoting the lowest price for a particular variable have poor reputations for service, reliability, and amenities? Alas, of the 11 retailers, none tends to be consistently low or high in price. So the facts give no comfort to this plausible speculation.

What of characteristics of cameras that do not enter the quality scores? The quality scores of Consumers Union are based primarily on "convenience, overall optical quality of normal lens, and freedom

[7] See Armen A. Alchian and William R. Allen, *University Economics,* 2nd ed. (Belmont, Calif.: Wadsworth Publishing Co., Inc., 1967), p. 332; also Basil Yamey, "Monopolistic Price Discrimination and Economic Welfare," *The Journal of Law and Economics* (October 1974), pp. 377–380.

[8] The correlation coefficient, r, is 0.16 when the variables are expressed arithmetically and 0.27 when both variables are entered as logarithms. These values indicate very little correlation between price and quality.

from blur in hand-held use at 1/30 and 1/60 seconds." Durability, though not measured directly, is unlikely to affect the results.[9] Concerning such matters as appearance, prestige of the maker, and weight, you will have to form your own judgment, but it would be the author's judgment that such considerations would not justify the difference between most actual prices and the corresponding frontier prices.

A third consideration is the overlap of product and market sets. As for "product," Consumers Union has assessed cameras for the typical purchaser who uses but one lens and not for the serious hobbyist or professional who is concerned with the "family" of accessories that is compatible with a particular make. Clearly, this could make a difference: the professional/serious hobbyist group might properly be prepared to pay more for a larger family of high quality accessories. But how much more? Would it justify the difference between the frontier price of $170 and the Variety O's *lowest* price—$550, or even Variety J's lowest price—$359? If not, the tentative verdict of an "informationally imperfect" market would still stand.

The "market" set in Chart 1 is incomplete, since would-be camera purchasers might purchase from mail-order sellers whose prices are not charted. If anything, the inclusion of mail-order prices would not affect the informationally imperfect interpretation since, in our judgment, some mail-order prices might be lower but none are likely to be higher than the prices already depicted on Chart 1.

As a fourth consideration, it certainly is possible that a different, fully informed assessor of quality might score the quality of varieties differently from Consumers Union. But how different? There is no way of knowing for sure whether this would alter the general configuration of the price-quality map. But a rereading of the Consumers Union report convinced the author that Consumers Union's assessment was persuasive.[10]

Finally, there exists the possibility of price discrimination based on objective (*not* subjective) factors. Again, this is possible. But we know of no retail camera outlets that follow such a practice, although we are acutely aware that prices are bargainable (representing price discrimination based on *subjective* factors). For this reason we dismiss this factor.

We do not know where *you* arrived in this critical review of Chart 1. The author tentatively concludes that the near-zero correla-

[9] See Chapter 3, page 64.

[10] Note Consumers Union's interpretative statement that "differences of less than about ten points were judged not very significant." *Consumer Reports* (November 1974), p. 798.

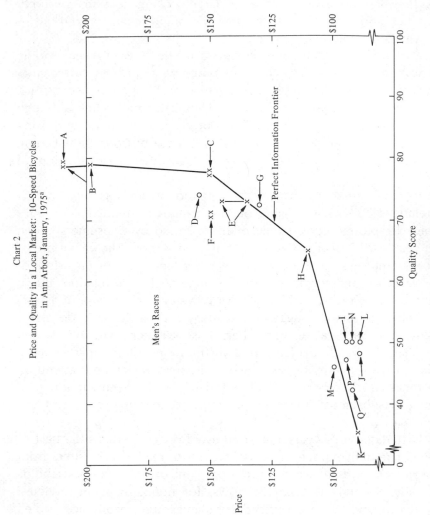

Chart 2

Price and Quality in a Local Market: 10-Speed Bicycles
in Ann Arbor, January, 1975[a]

Men's Racers

Perfect Information Frontier

Price

Quality Score

$200
$175
$150
$125
$100

A
B
C
D
F
E
G
H
I
N
L
M
P
J
Q
K

0   40   50   60   70   80   90   100

[a]Symbols: x denotes *actual* price quotations; o denotes *list* prices published 12 months earlier in *Consumer Reports*. Hence, they are probably lower than current actual prices. Models so designated could not be purchased in Ann Arbor in January, 1975. Sources: (1) Price quotations obtained by Jane Zale; (2) Quality scores represent E. Scott Maynes' quantification of ratings and descriptive materials appearing in *Consumer Reports* for January, 1974.

tion between price and quality is largely chargeable to consumer ignorance and that this market may be validly characterized as informationally imperfect.

Turn now to Chart 2 and ten-speed racing bicycles. Even reading it a second time, you may find this outcome surprising. No calculations are needed to conclude that the relationship here between price and quality is near-perfect. Price *is* an indicator of quality (although the relationship is curvilinear). The outcome is the more surprising since the numerical quality scores are not those of Consumers Union, but rather the author's necessarily less accurate approximation of them.

Is there anything that might cast doubt on this near-perfect correlation? Only one possible blemish comes to mind: the varieties of bicycles plotted consist only of those tested by Consumers Union one year earlier and still on sale in Ann Arbor. The inclusion of successor models to those no longer available or the inclusion of models not tested *might* reduce the price-quality correlation. But it might not. The technical simplicity of bicycles and the ease of assessing their performance suggests that many cyclists can and do assess quality rather accurately. And Chart 1 is consistent with this belief.

Chart 3, which depicts price distributions for nonparticipating and participating term life insurance, is the next to claim our attention. The range of price is considerable and the evidence in support of a verdict of substantial informational imperfections is "hard" and unassailable.

First, data on 20-year-interest-adjusted prices (perhaps the best of several alternative price variants) are most readily accessible from *Consumer Reports* to which only 3 per cent of American households subscribe. Second, as Chart 3 shows, for nonparticipating policies, only two of the 25 lowest-priced companies are "readily accessible" to people in this market. The number is higher for participating policies, 10 of the lowest 25, but includes none of the 4 policies with the markedly lowest prices. Other low-priced companies may be reached only by mail or through general agents, and it is no easy matter to "discover" the general agent for the particular company in which you are interested.[11]

Some doubters may argue that term life insurance is *not* a product

---

[11] To do this, you would have to locate the company's address in *Best's Insurance Manual, op. cit.* (assuming you know it) and then write to ask whether they have a local agent. Or, alternatively, you could make a telephone canvass of numerous local "general agents" to ask whether they represented a particular company. Neither task is easy.

Chart 3

Term Life Insurance: Prices and Access
in Ann Arbor, February, 1975[a]

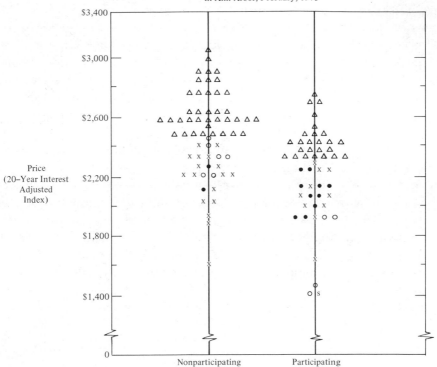

5-Year Renewable and Convertible
Term Policies

Symbols: • Readily accessible (company listed in Yellow Pages)
     x Accessible with difficulty (sales by mail, or company
        has agent in Michigan; *not* listed in Yellow Pages)
     s Special clientele: available only to special class of buyers,
        e.g., teachers
     o No access from Ann Arbor (not licensed in Michigan, no
        agents in Michigan)
     △ Accessibility not investigated.

[a]Source: Price data from *Consumer Reports,* January, 1974, pp. 43–45, accessibility
data from Survey Research Center, University of Michigan.

[b]Price estimates pertain to 25-year-old male in good health assumed to have purchased
face amount of $25,000. The price charted represents the 20-year cumulative cost.

of uniform quality: agents differ in the services they render and in how well they render them. At best, an agent can provide useful counseling on matters of insurance and general financial planning. At worst an agent can provide advice that is wrong. The argument about the role of the agent is correct, but here it is not relevant. The prices quoted are for *varieties* of policies, not specimens. And for varieties (where the characteristics of the agent do not enter), all policies offer a single (and satisfactory) characteristic, protection. It is our conclusion that consumer ignorance keeps the market from enforcing a single price for a product whose quality across companies is uniform.

Finally, we turn to Chart 4 and regular gasoline. Even if we accept the proposition that "gasoline is gasoline," the skeptic could properly note that relevant characteristics of retailers may account for at least some of the price discrepancies depicted here. The omitted character- istics might include differences in convenience (accessibility from a freeway), the range of services provided, ancillary services (windshield wiping, oil check, and so on), and waiting time (the author can attest to lines at the gasoline station with the lowest price). The critical issue for assessing the extent of informational imperfection in this market is whether these differences justify price discrepancies of the order of

Chart 4

Regular Gasoline: Prices in Ann Arbor,
February, 1975[a]

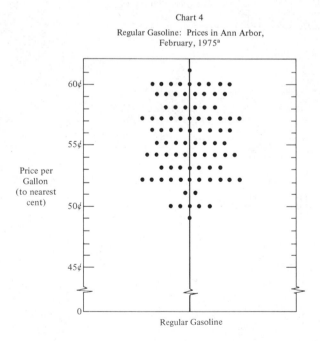

[a]Data obtained by Jane Zale, February 5-9, 1975. Each point represents
the price charged by a different establishment.

magnitude depicted here. Again, each individual must form his own judgment. To the degree that these factors do *not* account for the price discrepancies, then he may conclude that this market is informationally imperfect.

The Perfect Information Frontier: A Summing-up. This discussion suggests that the perfect information frontier estimation and assessment can help us form judgments regarding the degree of informational imperfections in a local market. But the question posed by consumer sovereignty requires a judgment as to informational imperfections of local markets across the economy. Lacking perfect information frontier data and analyses over a large number of products and a large number of local markets, we are unable to use this device (newly introduced on these pages) to assess the informational imperfections of markets on a national scale.

By way of substitute analysis, we propose to undertake a somewhat impressionistic comparison of local consumer markets two centuries ago and now. It is our belief that this comparison will etch rather clearly and accurately a set of factors that produces a considerable degree of informational imperfection in many present-day local markets.

Markets and Consumers: 1776 versus Now.[12] Consider the functioning of retail markets in 1776, notable as the year in which Adam Smith published his *Wealth of Nations,* the first satisfactory analysis of the working of a market economy.

In general, the amount of information required then was much less than it is now. In the rural, small-town markets of that time, the existence of sellers and products, as well as the location of sellers, was common knowledge, available at almost zero cost. What is more, the number of choices to be made was much less than now as a result of smaller incomes and access to fewer products and fewer sellers. "Brands" existed then only in the form of the differential performance of different maker-sellers.

At the same time information was easier to obtain. Products were simple. From common experience, people knew what characteristics of products were desirable and the extent to which particular items

[12] Much of the following section recapitulates, in revised form, an earlier paper of the author: E. Scott Maynes, "Consumerism: Origin and Research Implications," in Eleanor B. Sheldon, ed., *Family Economic Behavior: Problems and Prospects* (Philadelphia: J. B. Lippincott Co., 1973), pp. 270–294. It is reprinted here with permission.

possessed them. Food, for example, was then hardly ever processed, packaged (in the twentieth century sense), or added to. Most people had no difficulty in distinguishing between "good" and "bad" carrots, bread, or meat.

The main defect of the local markets was structural: the small size of the market led to local monopolies. It is thus not surprising to find that this defect has been stressed by economic theory from that time to the present.

Monopoly aside—and this is an important exception—consumers could usually identify good and poor performance on the part of the sellers. Under these conditions, the reward-punishment system at the heart of a market economy worked well. Through an effective market the presumably selfish motivations of sellers were channeled to a constructive end. Markets tended to be cleared by a single, low price.

Two hundred years later the picture has changed drastically. The volume of information that consumers require is now massive for several reasons. First, consumers have *more income to spend.* Second, there are *more products, brands,* and *sellers* (so many that "discovery" of products, brands, and sellers is a problem). Third, not only are there more products and brands but *variants* of brands *have proliferated.* As every car buyer knows, you must decide on body type, "line," transmission, motor size, type of brakes, and numerous accessories. The same phenomenon applies, although on a reduced scale, to other products that were formerly single-variant products. Fourth, *model changes are becoming more frequent,* except (thankfully) for automobiles. Fifth, *prices are now complex,* since separate components of products are often priced separately and discounts are available either explicitly or informally. Finally, given the automobile (and the urbanization, shopping centers, and the supermarkets that are its complements), *each consumer now has access to more specimens.*

On the other hand, the task per se of obtaining price-quality information has become more difficult. The accumulated experience of the consumer and his acquaintances, acquired at near-zero cost, no longer enables the consumer to know prices and qualities. The villain, of course, is the technical complexity of products. To estimate the quality of the single-lens reflex cameras plotted in Chart 1, Consumers Union required a marketing/shopping staff to identify and purchase representative models, technicians to formulate and conduct proper tests, time to perform the tests, and capital to finance staff and material costs. Individual consumers lack these resources.

Aside from the direct costs involved in obtaining information, searching-shopping involves indirect costs—the earnings, recreational, or other opportunities given up to make searching possible. As affluence increases, each hour becomes more valuable. So indirect costs, too, contribute in our times to the greater cost of becoming informed.

But it is not only the cost of obtaining price-quality information that deters many (most?) consumers. It is the lack of a felt need. Too few consumers know how informationally imperfect many markets are and, therefore, underestimate the payoffs to searching. Hence, they undersearch. Contributing to this are many factors: peoples' beliefs in the effectiveness of the "free enterprise" system, a view that is reinforced both by many favorable experiences and by speeches, tracts, books, advertisements of protagonists of free enterprise over a very long period; the failure of economists, until recently, to "discover" the information problem; and the minor role, until recently, of consumerism and consumerists. On the supply side, we reviewed in Part I the reasons why a larger supply of accurate price-quality information was not forthcoming.

The widespread dissemination of price and quality information is not per se sufficient to ensure the effective functioning of markets. Once in hand, information must be put to use.

Everyone "knows" that new automobile (and many other) prices are bargainable, but many consumers find bargaining distasteful or lack the essential skills or the supporting information required to bargain effectively.

The emphatic conclusion to which this review points is that, informationally, local markets performed rather well in 1776 and rather poorly two centuries later. Our judgment on contemporary markets should be checked, however, as suggested earlier, against careful empirical studies of price-quality relationships for many products in many local markets.

The Efficiency of a Seller-Controlled Information Function. In any economy, resources must be devoted to informing consumers regarding products available and the terms on which they are offered.[13] In *any* economy, producers, failing to anticipate consumer needs with perfect accuracy, will devote some resources to efforts to persuade consumers to purchase what they have produced. In our economy,

---

[13] Centrally planned economies have typically assigned lower priorities to the production of consumer goods. Consistent with these priorities, they have underproduced consumer goods. Where shortages are persistent, the resources devoted to the information-persuasion function will typically be less.

this information-persuasion function is carried out by sellers who finance this activity by imposing what is, in essence, an 11 per cent "sales tax" on consumers. In the discussion until now, we have accepted these arrangements as given. Now we review their origins and subject them to critical scrutiny.

Turn back again to 1776. It seemed only natural as markets became larger that sellers, through personal contract, billboards (advertising), "broadsides" (advertising printed on separate sheets), and newspaper or magazine advertisements, should seek to inform consumers of their existence and to persuade them to purchase the advertiser's offerings. Such information-persuasion activities were part of the cost of doing business and hence it seemed only "natural" that these costs should be recovered from consumers in the form of prices sufficiently high to cover such costs in the long run. The recovery of information-persuasion costs by *all* sellers of a given product makes payments to cover these costs unavoidable and thus converts them into a "tax." The consumer is unable to purchase the product without paying "his share" of the information-persuasion costs. This tax has two peculiar characteristics: 1) it may vary as a percentage of sales price from one specimen to another, depending upon how much a particular seller (manufacturer, wholesaler, or retailer) elects to spend on the information-persuasion function; and 2) normally, the size of the tax will not be known to the consumer.

Today, as in 1776, control over expenditures for the information-persuasion function is lodged with sellers, and the expenditures are financed by what amounts to a sales tax.

Two major criticisms are in order concerning the character of the information-persuasion activities of sellers. First, seller-provided information and persuasion tends to be biased by exaggeration and omission. Sellers, being no less human than consumers, tend to put their best foot forward. A salesman for Metropolitan (substitute any other life insurance company) is hardly likely to tell an educator that T.I.A.A.'s (Teachers Insurance and Annuity Association) Five-Year Term Policy is cheaper (even when it is). It is equally unlikely that the seller of a microwave oven, labeled as "unacceptable" by Consumers Union because of possible radiation hazards,[14] will—on his own initiative—warn a potential buyer of this potential hazard. Which of two gas mileage tests will an automobile salesman cite—the one showing the higher or the lower mileage for the car he sells? The answer comes automatically.

[14] *Consumer Reports* (April 1973).

This exaggeration-omission bias, possibly harmless in 1776 when consumers were more likely to "see through" incomplete or inaccurate claims by sellers, seriously short-circuits the informational functioning of consumer markets two centuries later when people are often unable to see through such claims.

But a second defect of seller-controlled information is equally damning from an efficiency viewpoint, if almost unnoticed. Seller control, both in 1776 and now, disperses whereas consumer control concentrates relevant information. If you examine almost any advertisement, or talk with any salesman, you will usually receive information on the offerings of *one firm only*. To collect information on the offerings of other firms, you would have to consult the advertisements/salesmen representing the other firms offering that same product. Contrast this with the concentration of information from any of the consumer publications.

Contrast also the character of information provided by sellers with the results of the Part I assessment that strongly supported the view that the information supplied by consumer controlled organizations is usually accurate and relatively complete.

Information-persuasion efforts are almost completely controlled by sellers rather than consumers. In 1970, seller-controlled expenditures totaled $67 *billion* in vivid contrast to the $13 *million* expended by the two consumer product-testing organizations. To put this difference in perspective, the seller-controlled expenditures exceeded the consumer-controlled expenditures by a ratio of 5,154 to 1!

The seller-controlled expenditures were distributed as follows: [15]

[15] This estimate, necessarily approximate because of the novelty and difficulty of the task, was supplied by Ivan Ross of the University of Minnesota. Sources and assumptions were as follows:

A. Advertising—$21 billion. From S. Banks, R. Reisman, and C. Y. Yang, *Advertising Age,* June 7, 1971, p. 27.

B. Sales promotion—$7 billion. From A. W. Frey and J. C. Halterman, *Advertising,* 4th ed. (New York: The Ronald Press Company, 1970), p. 40.

C. Personal selling—$36 billion. There exists no satisfactory estimate of expenditures on personal selling. However, Brink and Kelley are quoted in Boyd and Levy as asserting the existence of a 3-to-1 or 4-to-1 relationship between expenditures for personal selling versus advertising. Splitting the difference and applying the 3.5-to-1 ratio in 1970, total personal selling expenditures are estimated at $72.8 billion. Assuming arbitrarily that one-half of the efforts of sales personnel are devoted to informing and persuading, one arrives at the $36 billion estimate (0.5 × $72.8 billion). See Harper W. Boyd, Jr., and Sidney J. Levy, *Promotion: A Behavioral View* (Englewood Cliffs, N.J.: Prentice-Hall, Inc., 1970), p. 10.

D. Public relations—$3 billion. The estimate for public relations expenditures is even cruder than those for other components. Ross accepted a forecast by

A. Advertising	$21 billion
B. Sales promotion, including direct mailings	7 billion
C. Personal selling, the information and persuasion efforts of all sales personnel	$36 billion
	3 billion
D. Public relations	$67 billion, or 10.9 per
E. Total	cent of aggregate consumption expenditures.

If we are correct in our assertion that seller-control in-formation-persuasion is 1) biased, and 2) inefficient (because of the nonconcentration of information), then it follows that seller control of information-persuasion efforts contributes to informationally im-perfect markets and thus stands as an obstacle to the achievement of consumer sovereignty.

This chapter has been an analysis of criticisms of consumer sovereignty that are *implicit* in consumerism. One of the ironies posed by the analysis is that consumerists—and most economists, too [16]— have concentrated their attention almost exclusively on advertising, to the neglect of nonadvertising components of seller's information-persuasion activities.

A second irony is that, although some consumerist critics have gone so far as to suggest the abolition of advertising,[17] most con-sumerists and economists have focused their reform efforts on measures designed to eliminate deception in advertising. With only two exceptions, none of these efforts have suggested that resources for information-persuasion be shifted, by means of a tax, from sellers to a consumer-controlled information organization.[18] And yet this is

---

Kalman Druck (*Business Week*, July 2, 1960, p. 42) that public relations, estimated at $2 billion in 1960 could be $6 billion in 1969. He assumed, again arbitrarily, that one-half of public relations expenditures activities are directed toward consumers rather than toward other businesses.

E. Aggregate personal consumption expenditures—$617 billion. Source: *Statistical Abstract of the United States,* 1973, Table 517, p. 320.

[16] Galbraith is a welcome exception. He identifies both "advertising and *sales-manship*" as agents for the manipulation of consumers.

[17] See Joachim Marcus-Steiff, "Economic and Social Effects of Advertising, Some Tentative Conclusions," *Proceedings of Workshop II, Consumer Action Research,* April 1975 (Berlin: International Institute of Management, 1975).

[18] The exceptions are economists. See Max Corden, *A Tax on Advertising,* Fabian Research Pamphlet 222 (London: The Fabian Society, 1961) and Maynes, "Consumer-ism: Origin and Research Implications," op. cit.

clearly the direct (if drastic) policy implication of this analysis. Evidently, seller control of information-persuasion functions has developed so "naturally" and has been sanctioned by such long usage that its analysis and its policy implications are less than obvious.

Information Plus Market Structure: The Competitive Frontier.[19]
The implicit complaints of consumerism—to borrow a biblical phrase—begat the perfect information frontier and, here in this section, the perfect information frontier begets the competitive frontier. Consumerism did not beget the competitive frontier, but it is introduced here because it is highly relevant to consumer sovereignty.

The concept of the competitive frontier takes into account the structure of markets as well as their informational properties. Hence, the definition of the *competitive frontier:*

> The *competitive frontier* consists of "the set of points, and the line of segments connecting them, for which a given quality may be purchased at the lowest possible price, assuming 1) perfect information, *and* 2) *a competitive organization of manufacturing, wholesale, and retail markets."*

Unlike the perfect information frontier, the competitive frontier is a hypothetical construct, not susceptible to direct measurement but useful as a framework for organizing evaluative discussions.

The questions that the competitive frontier addresses and, in principle, answers are the following:

> **1.** What *single, lowest price* would exist for a given quality in a competitively organized local market?
> **2.** *By how much do actual prices* depart from this competitive level?
> **3.** What is the *optimal number of varieties* and what is *their distribution by quality level* in a local market?
> **4.** What is the *optimal number of retail sellers* in a local market?

For each question the evaluation process will call for comparisons of actual with optimal conditions.

Since the competitive frontier represents a grafting of competitive organization onto the perfect information frontier, it retains the assumptions of the perfect information frontier as well as its limitations. Those assumptions (in abbreviated form) were:

---

[19] My formulation of the concept of "competitive frontier" was stimulated by some notes of Udo Beier of Technische Universität Berlin.

1. Fully informed consumers make uniform assessments of quality for different varieties of products.
2. Consumers possess complete and accurate information.

The larger assumption that the market is competitively organized requires the following specific assumptions:

3. *Free entry* exists at manufacturing, wholesale, and retail levels. That is, potential entrants face the same terms as firms already engaged in that activity.
4. *Normal profits* are earned for each variety of a product sold as well as for the entire enterprise at all levels—manufacturing, wholesale, and retail.[20]

The competitive frontier enables us to assess the extent to which the performance of the local market departs from the competitive outcome. Various measures of competitive failure are possible. With respect to prices, one could calculate an *index of competitive imperfection,* estimated as "the weighted average of the ratios of actual prices to prices on the competitive frontier." This would be analogous to the index of informational imperfections introduced earlier. As an *index of optimal variety,* a possible measure might be the ratio of the actual number of varieties of products to the number on the frontier. Similarly, as an *index of the optimal number of retail outlets,* one might estimate the ratio of the actual number of retail outlets to the frontier number. (The diagrams thus far shown would have to be modified to identify retail establishments.) In the case of the last two measures, a market could depart from optimality by having either too few or too many varieties of products or retail outlets.

Although these measures can be estimated, in principle at least, our most likely use of the competitive frontier is as a framework for asking the right questions. We illustrate the possibility by applying the competitive frontier framework to the bicycle data in Chart 3.

Bicycles and the Competitive Frontier. The product is men's ten-speed racing bicycles with list prices of less than $225 and the site for this illustrative analysis is Ann Arbor, Michigan, home of a relatively large population of cycling enthusiasts. In all fairness to bicycle retailers in Ann Arbor, it should be noted that the data do *not* include all their offerings in the relevant product class. They include only

[20] As defined earlier, "normal" profits consist of that level of profits necessary to keep capital in a given employment indefinitely.

varieties of bicycles tested by *Consumer Reports* in January, 1974, and still on the market when these price data were obtained in January, 1975. So our analysis is strictly illustrative.

Suppose that we had access to all the relevant data. *Suppose,* further, that a careful investigation showed entry to be free and firms at all levels—manufacturing, wholesale, and retail—to be making normal profits, no more and no less. Under these conditions there would be no incentive for existing firms to exit nor for new firms to enter this line of activity. In terms of Chart 3, the perfect information frontier and the competitive frontier would be identical. We would conclude that the frontier prices are the correct prices and that actual prices offered do not depart greatly from this optimal level, that the number of varieties offered (seven) is the optimal number with the optimal distribution by quality level, and that the number of retail outlets (ten) is the optimal number. We would conclude further that consumer sovereignty is well served by this market.

For those familiar with the conventional market classifications of Economics, the number of retail outlets in a "competitively organized" local market—seven for bicycles—may be very surprising. The reason is that local markets, realistically, are relatively small, their boundaries restricted by high search costs and (possibly) low payoffs. Perfectly competitive markets are without boundaries since search costs are implicitly assumed to be zero.

As we commented earlier, no direct means exist for estimating the shape and level of the competitive frontier. The best that can be done is to judge the influences of certain factors on its shape and level.

The relationship between the perfect information frontier and the competitive frontier is of interest. If in the bicycle example it could be shown that 1) potential retail entrants were kept out by (say) franchise restrictions, or 2) that potential manufacturer entrants were kept out because of tariffs, *and* that 3) the entrants would have achieved normal profits, then the competitive frontier would probably lie below the perfect information frontier. Normally, we would expect the competitive frontier to be identical with (if competitive organizational requirements are met) or (more likely) to lie lower than the perfect information frontier. In the camera case, to be specific, we would expect the competitive frontier to be the same, or lower than the perfect information frontier. Thus, a verdict of an "informationally imperfect" market will usually yield a verdict of a "competitively imperfect market."

One case where this relationship might not hold comes to mind. In a very dynamic market where demand is expanding quite rapidly—

such as ten-speed bicycles from 1970 to 1975 or hand-held calculators over about the same period—the number of varieties and sellers in a market might expand to higher numbers than is sustainable over a long period. Under such a circumstance, the competitive frontier might lie above the perfect information frontier.

With this tool added to our kit, we are ready to turn to our second major topic, consumer grievances.

THE MATTER OF CONSUMER GRIEVANCES [21]

If it was the consumer information problem that motivated the first wave of consumerism in the 1930s, it is consumer grievances that have propelled the second wave of consumerism in the 1960s.[22] The political response to these new frustrations is seen in newly established "Consumer Counsel" offices or Departments of Consumer Affairs in many (most?) states, many (most?) large cities, and many counties.[23] The journalistic response to this concern, also highly visible, takes the form of "Consumer Action" columns in newspapers and "Action Line" programs on television. In both media these features are accorded choice spots.

Again, this is a Part One subject, inverted. In Part One we asked what steps the individual consumer could take to avoid grievances and to correct those that affected him. Here we treat grievances as a social problem and seek to ascertain the extent to which consumer grievances occur and prevent the attainment of consumer sovereignty.

Our Catalog of Grievances, Reviewed and Expanded. To be sure that we know what we are talking about, we review and add to our

[21] A *consumer grievance,* we repeat, is an instance of consumer dissatisfaction, whether communicated or not. By contrast, a *complaint* is a grievance that has been voiced.

[22] One student of consumerism, Robert O. Herrmann, identifies an earlier "first wave." This occurred in the 1900s and centered on concern for problems of sanitation and safety in food, drugs, and cosmetics. It culminated legislatively in the passage of the Food and Drug Act of 1906. There was no organizational continuity between this wave of consumerism and the one in the 1930s. See Robert O. Herrmann, "The Consumer Movement in Social Perspective," Discussion Paper 88, Department of Agricultural Economics and Rural Sociology, Pennsylvania State University, 1970.

[23] New York was first with both types of organization. The State of New York established the first "Consumer Counsel" office in 1955 when Persia Campbell was appointed to that post by Governor Averill Harriman. The City of New York established the first Department of Consumer Affairs in 1969 when Mayor John Lindsay appointed Bess Myerson as the first commissioner of consumer affairs.

list of the types of grievances consumers encounter: The Part One list: [24]

1. *Delivery Failures.* The good or service ordered is delivered (performed) tardily, not at all, or not as specified.
2. *Performance Failure.* The performance of the good or service fails to match reasonable standards, or worse, fails to work at all.
3. *Failures in Communication.* Seller and buyer have different understandings of what the seller (buyer) promised with respect to characteristics of the good, ancillary services, price, other purchase terms.
4. *Misrepresentation, Deception, Fraud.* These would fall into classes No. 1, No. 2, or No. 3 *except* that they are differentiated by a deliberate intention, on the part of the seller, to deceive the consumer.

To which we add:

5. *Product Is Unsafe.* (An extreme form of No. 2 or No. 4.)
6. *Environmental Effects of Product Not Taken into Account.*

Quantitive Evidence on the Consumer Grievance Problem. To assess the extent and the seriousness of the consumer grievance problem, two pieces of information are required: 1) estimates of the frequency of different types of grievances, and 2) estimates of the mean losses associated with each type of grievance. And, ideally, we would like a historical series of such data so that we could ascertain whether the grievance problem was improving, remaining stable, or —as we suspect—worsening.

The collection of *current* data on consumer grievances poses no insurmountable problems of concept or technique. A well-conceived survey of consumer grievances, utilizing probability sampling along with the validation of a subsample of grievances,[25] could do the job. Unfortunately, no such survey has been conducted or is in prospect. Nor is it possible to reach back, by means of such a survey, to collect such data for some interesting dates in our economic past.

The only hard evidence is that cited earlier, the growth since 1965 and particularly since 1970 of Departments of Consumer Affairs in government and of "Action Columns" and the like in the communica-

[24] For further details regarding this list see Chapter 9, pp. 200–201.
[25] To assure that grievances reported were indeed "grievances" and not merely figments of the consumer's imagination.

tions media. Clearly, politicians and the media are responding to what they perceive to be a swelling of consumer discontent, probably grounded in consumer grievances.

Lacking persuasive statistical data on the volume and seriousness of consumer grievances, we turn as we did in the case of consumer information to a comparative analysis of conditions in 1776 versus two centuries later, hopefully to lay bare the causes of consumer grievances and the trend in such grievances. But, to set the stage and to clothe the problem of consumer grievances with realism, we follow one particularly graphic consumer grievance.

The "Simple" Repair of a Bicycle: Close-up of a Grievance. This consumer epic concerns a family who purchased a three-speed bicycle from a large mail-order retailer. A year and a half after purchase, they experienced a crisis when their son fell from his bike and broke a critical part, rendering the gearshift mechanism inoperative. Since the mail-order repair center was 15 miles away (on the far side of their metropolitan area), their first reaction was to seek a replacement part at the local cycle shop, a large establishment dealing with all sorts of bikes, both simple and sophisticated. "We don't carry *their* parts," the local repairmen told them somewhat condescendingly.

The obvious next move was to contact the mail-order repair center. But a week and a half passed before the parents found it convenient to make the cross-city trip to the repair center.

Since they were unable to locate the repair list for the bicycle, they took the bicycle itself to the repair center, confident that the catalog people would be able to identify and supply the necessary part. But it was not to be. Although the repair center people sought to be helpful, they were unable to identify the missing part, despite much consultation with microfilmed parts lists. And so, after an hour, the parents emerged from the repair center, defeated, unworkable bike in hand.

What to do next? At home they renewed their search for the missing parts list. After three-quarters of an hour, they were successful. With renewed hope, they telephoned the repair center. Imagine their dismay when, an hour later, the repair center people phoned back to say that they could not locate the relevant part in their inventory system. "What are we supposed to do now?" the parents asked, and added sarcastically, "Should we junk it?"

From the telephone came: "I don't know. I'm sorry, but there's nothing more I can do."

The next and final act a few days later was a humiliating trip back to the local repair shop where, after a three-quarter hour search, the local cycle repairman was able, in the spirit of the ingenious Yankee of the last century, to fashion a new "homemade" part that worked.

After four hours of fidgety waiting time, three trips, the bike's being out of service for three weeks (between successive efforts to repair it), 45 miles of metropolitan driving, and $5 of repair expenses, their $40 bike was back in service and their youngster happy again.

To such episodes reproduced thousands of times over (we guess), modern consumerism in part owes its birth. And in the frustration and costs of such episodes we find embodied a significant obstacle to the attainment of consumer sovereignty.

For our purpose, this close-up of a grievance is useful because it communicates so graphically some of the causes of consumer grievances that our more systematic analysis will identify. And now, once again, we contrast markets in 1776 with markets today for purposes of ascertaining what factors in each era tended to produce, or not to produce, consumer grievances.

Consumer Grievances in 1776. We look first at the matter of innocent and not-so-innocent (deception, fraud) failures of communication.

If, as we argued earlier, consumers in 1776 were in a better position than now to "see through" the exaggerations and omissions of sellers and to know price and assess quality, it seems plausible that fewer failures of communication, and fewer performance failures, too, would occur. But other factors probably contribute to the expectation of fewer communications grievances.

The most important was that, under the conditions of 1776, the buyer was likely to have a personal and long-run relationship with the seller. This prompts the question: how many sellers have the temerity to look a personally known buyer in the eye and then to mislead him deliberately?

And what of the instances where deception and innocent failures of communication did occur? Except for the colorful case of the traveling "flimflam man," the placement of responsibility was relatively easy because of the prevalence of small, locally owned, long-lasting retail units whose principal decision-makers were likely to be personally known to the buyer.

And if a dispute should arise between buyer and seller, the "contest" in those days was not likely to be as unequal as it is now. In 1776 it would have been unlikely for a retail organization—even the term sounds alien to 1776—to have a complaint department or staff (more alien concepts!) that specialized in the handling of complaints. At the same time, the less harried, less affluent consumer of 1776 undoubtedly had more time to invest in the prosecution of his complaint. Not the least of the consumer's levers was the need of the seller—unless he was in fact a monopolist—to maintain his reputation in a small, gossip-prone community where bad news traveled fast.

We are now ready to consider performance failures under conditions of 1776. It is worth repeating: given simpler products and fewer products, the consumer was better able to detect and avoid performance failures prior to purchase. But even if he should encounter a performance failure after purchase, he was in a better position to deal with it.

More often a jack-of-all-trades, he could sometimes correct defects himself. If he had to turn to the seller for the correction of a performance failure, conditions were favorable. As noted, he would have no difficulty in identifying a responsible representative of the seller: in many cases, it was the owner, who, in most cases, knew the individual personally. Finally, the seller was often the maker of the good. If not, either the seller could effectuate a repair himself or he could quickly contact the maker of the good who was likely to be close at hand.

Summing up, we may say that in 1776 the relative simplicity of products, the personal relationship between seller and buyer, and the unambiguous placement of responsibility for performance or communication failures contributed to the minimization of consumer grievances and to their satisfactory resolution when they occurred.

Consumer Grievances Today. Unfortunately conditions two centuries later are worse in all three respects. And although we are probably unaware of it, the deterioration in all three conditions stems from the increasing complexity of products. But first we deal with the immediate consequences of complex products.

The technical complexity of modern products by itself is enough to assure a larger number of consumer grievances under the performance failure count. Simply put, the more parts or the more sophisticated the design, the greater is the probability that a product will be delivered to market with some defect. By the same reasoning, the more complex the product, either in technical design or number of parts, the less likely it is that the consumer will identify and hence avoid either a defective exemplar (of a good design) or a poor design.

Not only is the technical complexity of products likely to increase the number of consumer grievances it also is likely to affect adversely the correction of grievances. First, it is now less likely that the buyer can correct the faults himself. Second, it becomes less likely that the retailer—now unlikely to be the maker of the product—can correct the defect, short of replacing the product. (Lives there any owner of a 35 mm. camera who has not, at some time, had his camera returned to the factory for "difficult" repairs?)

Finally, the large number of parts in modern products coupled with the larger number of products available produces an inventory organization problem of massive dimensions. (Sears, for example, maintains 500,000 "inventory units" for some 65,000 merchandise items.) [26] Only a large and necessarily bureaucratic organization can administer the large inventories that are characteristic of modern retail establishments. And the size and complexity of this inventory assures numerous delays in identifying, locating, and retrieving the correct part to effect a particular repair. The bicycle episode described earlier is hardly unique.

Product complexity also affects the incidence of complaints arising from innocent and not-so-innocent failures of communication. Since there is more to tell (regarding the characteristics of the product, the prices of components, the terms of the transaction), the probability of an innocent failure in communication is greater. And, unfortunately, the increased amount of information to be communicated enhances the opportunities for deception and fraud.

But product complexity is not the only factor giving rise to more consumer grievances and their less satisfactory resolution. A large part of the problem must be attributed to the vastly changed character of retailing today: Given 1) the mobility that the automobile confers, 2) economies of scale in advertising, financing, and procurement, 3) time economies of scale to consumers in shopping in a single location, 4) the risk-spreading incentive to organize multiestablishment enterprises, it follows that the typical retail outlet of today is likely to have the following characteristics:

1. It is *large* (and hence, impersonal) in terms of personnel, financial resources, and the number of products, brands, and product variants offered;
2. It is *not locally owned,* but is part of a multiestablishment organization, and perhaps, of a multiestablishment, multiindustry organization;

[26] Sources: Sears, Roebuck *Annual Report for 1969,* p. 10, and letter from William P. Zabler, National Service Manager for Sears, dated December 6, 1971.

3. It is *not the maker* of the goods it sells;
4. *Its handling of various functions is performed by specialists*—
in advertising, complaints, credit granting, and so on.

The consequences for the consumer are unfortunate. First, he is less likely to deal with persons he knows either by name or by sight. Thus, the personal factor that in 1776 minimized the number of consumer grievances and facilitated their resolution will usually be missing two centuries later.

Second, when a grievance arises, the consumer complainant is likely to encounter difficulties in placing responsibility for the grievance. Why is this so? The first part of the answer is that the consumer is now dealing with very large retail organizations, subject to all the infirmities to which bureaucracies fall prey—excessive rule-following, the protective avoidance of responsibility, and ambiguities with respect to the placement of responsibility. Since these large organizations contain many "parts" and are often themselves parts of even larger organizations, the opportunities for buck-passing are considerable.

Finally, since the retailer is no longer the manufacturer of the product, problems arise as to the allocation of responsibility between the retailer and the manufacturer. As many car buyers have discovered to their chagrin, automobile dealers and manufacturers tend to have conflicting understandings of their respective responsibilities under new car warranties.

With impersonal buyer-seller relations and an ambiguous placement of responsibility, it is small wonder that more grievances occur, and that the probability of the satisfactory resolution of a grievance is less than two centuries ago.

On the communications front, the use of the mass media for advertising means that there exists no personal relationship between seller and buyer that might inhibit the tendency to dissimulate.

A final, undesirable feature of buyer-seller relations today is that when the consumer seeks correction of a grievance, the contest between the two parties is now vastly unequal. This inequality is explained largely by differences in the nature of the seller's interest in a consumer complaint and the buyer's interest in the same complaint. The seller has a deep, abiding, and highly focused interest in the products he sells and any complaints they generate. By contrast, the complaining consumer has a transient interest in his complaint that could be replaced tomorrow by a different complaint arising from another of the thousands of purchases he makes in a year.

Consider now the capacity of each party to defend his interest. The seller is a specialist in complaints affecting his products. He has accumulated immense experience in handling and defending against complaints. Dealing with many complaints, often of a similar character, he can hire specialized talents at "wholesale" rates reflecting economies of scale and develop standardized procedures for dealing with them. His financial resources are enormous as compared with the buyer's. Finally, reflecting the ascendency of merchants in our society, the law of contract has usually been drawn to protect sellers and hence tends to make the consumer's right to "his day in court" an imaginary, not a realistic right.[27]

By unhappy contrast, the consumer's capacity to further his complaint is limited indeed. First, he is an amateur confronting a professional. Second, the inconvenience and the time costs of achieving redress are often large as compared with the money value of the grievance. Third, if legal action is necessary to achieve redress, it is highly likely that the legal costs will exceed the monetary worth of the complaint. Remember that experienced lawyers charge from $40 to $100 an hour and that even the simplest case will involve interview time with the complainant, time to draft a complaint, time to research the law, time to ascertain and confirm the facts, time to track down and interview witnesses, and finally time to try the case. It follows that there are few cases indeed where the consumer complainant would get off for less than $500 to $1,000 of legal fees. Philip Schrag concludes: "The barriers that the legal system has erected to consumer litigation go a long way toward explaining the relative unconcern of merchants and manufacturers about truthful selling and the quality of their products."[28]

To all of these disabilities there is one major offsetting factor: the interest of most sellers in retaining the consumer complainant, and those he may influence, as possible future customers. Against this must be balanced the cost of correcting the consumer complaint. If the type of complaint is infrequent or the cost of correction "small," then it clearly pays the seller to provide redress politely and willingly. If, however, the cost of correction is "large" or the complaint applies to a large number of consumers, some conscious of the wrong and others unconscious of it, the seller may feel that his interests are best served by correcting the complaint for only the most competent and

[27] For a graphic recital of the difficulties in achieving redress through the law even with the support of a well-staffed, alert supporting organization, see Philip G. Schrag, *Counsel for the Deceived* (New York: Pantheon Books, Inc., 1972).

[28] Philip G. Schrag, "Consumer Rights," *Columbia Forum* (Summer 1970).

most persistent complainants. In so acting, he would hope that, because of consumer ignorance, his organization's standing with others would not be adversely affected. This explanation is consistent with the routine manner in which automobile manufacturers and distributors in instances of auto "recalls" have sometimes sought to notify car purchasers of the need to replace defective parts.

Unsafe Products. Product safety, arising from either failures in production or in design, deserves our special attention. With the generally simpler products of 1776, the common experience and common sense of consumers usually enabled them to detect, and to avoid or correct unsafe products. To the extent that this assumption was true, the cost of design failures was born by producer-sellers.

As products have become increasingly complex, the ability of the consumer to detect unsafe products has decreased until it must be near zero for many classes of products. Unable to identify unsafe or badly designed products, many consumers will purchase them. And unfortunately these consumers will bear the costs of the defective design in the form of bodily or property injury, or uneconomic performance on the part of the product. Until recently the consumer-victim has had no recourse. Legal doctrines, conceived in an era when consumers could be assumed capable of identifying seriously defective products, held that makers and sellers were not liable for harmful effects derived from their products.[29] It turned out that for many sellers, it was less costly to market a potentially unsafe product than to incur possible heavy costs in further testing, redesigning, or postponing the introduction date.

So it is hardly surprising that in recent years many unsafe products have found their way to market. And it is equally unsurprising that the marketing of unsafe products has given a strong impetus to consumerism and to strong demands that the rules be changed so as to reduce the probability of unsafe products being put on sale. The marketing of unsafe products is, of course, a striking contradiction of the concept of consumer sovereignty.

Environmental Effects. Although economists have long been

---

[29] For a discussion of how warranties, disclaimers, the doctrine of privity (non-responsibility for the safety of a product in the absence of a direct relationship between manufacturer and purchaser), and the concept of negligence were used to limit manufacturers' responsibility for the production of a safe product, cf. David L. Rados, "Product Liability: Tougher Ground Rules," *Harvard Business Review*, July–August 1969, pp. 144–152.

aware that the production and consumption activities of one set of people could have adverse (or beneficial) effects on others, the public has not.[30] It was only in the 1960s that environmentalism became a popular "cause." It is a cause embraced by many who are not consumerists. But it is cataloged here because, as anyone who has attended a consumer movement meeting can attest, complaints against sellers who fail to take account of environmental effects in designing and selling products are shared by most who identify themselves as consumerists.

But our concern is with both awareness and the magnitude of environmental effects. There has been an increase in adverse environmental effects between 1776 and the present. Population increases and increased affluence are the primary causes for the increase. The case is disarmingly easy to argue.

As an example, start with the Los Angeles basin in 1910 when cars were few and (we assume) the air was clear. Now add families and cars in the same proportions. Keep adding families and cars long enough (with no technological improvements in the cars) and ultimately you will arrive at some days when the concentration of exhaust fumes causes your eyes to tear. Then you will have experienced an "environmental effect": someone else's consumption has caused your environment to deteriorate. So much for population increases as a cause of environmental effects.

Now modify your mental experiment. Let population remain stable, but let mean income increase and let the population of automobiles and automobile usage increase with income. Again, you will have a searing demonstration. Affluence will have created effluence. Your environment will have been fouled by the consumption activities of others. We cannot be sure whether automobile manufacturers or automobile purchasers/users are more to blame. But we will have discovered an environmental effect that stands as an obstacle to the attainment of consumer sovereignty.

A Summing-up: 1776 versus Bicentennial. Our impressionistic comparison of the status of the consumer in 1776 versus the consumer today has revealed the following major changes, all of which

[30] A. C. Pigou, *The Economics of Welfare*, 4th ed. (New York: St. Martin's Press, Inc., 1960, 1931).

K. W. Kapp, *The Social Costs of Private Enterprise* (Cambridge, Mass.: Harvard University Press, 1950).

Ronald H. Coase, "The Problem of Social Cost," *Journal of Law and Economics* (October 1960).

are conducive to a higher frequency of consumer grievances and a lower likelihood of their successful resolution:

> Complex, multicomponent products have replaced simple products;
> Impersonal relationships between buyer and seller have replaced personal relationships;
> Large, multiestablishment, multiproduct, bureaucratically organized firms in which it is difficult to fix responsibility have replaced small, locally owned businesses in which the placement of responsibility was unambiguous;
> In disputes, a vastly unequal contest between buyer and seller now (with the seller clearly ascendant) has replaced a relatively equal contest back in 1776;
> As a consequence of increased population and affluence, the magnitude of productive and consumption activities has increased greatly relative to the area in which these activities take place, with the result that other peoples' production and consumption have an adverse effect on "our" environment.

For the future, this analysis suggests that consumer grievances constitute a new and increasingly important obstacle to the achievement of consumer sovereignty.

THE UNDERREPRESENTATION OF THE CONSUMER INTEREST

It is the curse of the consumer interest that it commands almost universal approbation and near-zero resources for its furtherance. It is the purpose of this section to understand why this should be so.

We commence our discussion by taking up a task that we have avoided until now: saying what the "consumer interest" *is*. By our definition,

> *The consumer interest* consists of "policies that enhance the attainment of consumer sovereignty *and* enjoy the support of most understanding, fully informed consumers."

We explore the implications of this definition by applying it to three governmental actions/policies that have been widely viewed as "proconsumer." The three: 1) no-fault automobile insurance, 2) maximum interest rate (finance) charges on consumer loans, 3) mandatory installation of seat belt ignition interlocks on automobiles. We examine each in turn to judge whether it *is* in "the consumer interest."

No-Fault Automobile Insurance. Until 1970, the automobile insurance system in the United States was primarily a fault system. Except for several specific coverages,[31] individuals sustaining personal injuries or property damage as a result of an automobile accident had to demonstrate that they were *not at all* "at fault" before they could recover *any* compensation for their losses.[32]

Consumerists and others called for the substitution of a no-fault automobile insurance system for the unsatisfactory fault system. And such a system has been adopted in many states and may perhaps be enacted by the federal government. No-fault legislation, as its name suggests, specifies that compensation for losses in accidents be paid by one's "own" insurance company regardless of fault. Although the principle of compensation without a finding of fault may seem novel when applied to automobile insurance, it is in fact familiar and has enjoyed long usage in life and health insurance. Both pay benefits without inquiring as to whether a death or an accident requiring health care was attributable to negligence on the part of the victim.

The complaints against the fault automobile insurance system are several.[33] 1) It does not achieve its objective of providing protection against the economic losses of *all* victims of automobile accidents, especially the seriously injured. (Of accidents involving $25,000 or more of economic losses, only 30 per cent of the victims achieved any recovery under fault coverage; and of those achieving some recovery, insurance benefits after legal fees covered only 30 per cent of the economic losses sustained.) 2) It is inefficient, with only $.44 of the premium dollar going to the accident victim. (The rest goes for administrative, selling, and legal costs.) 3) It is inequitable with small claims being grossly overpaid and large claims being grossly underpaid. 4) It is slow, the average claim requiring 16 months from accident to payment.

Experience under the state no-fault laws enacted since 1970

---

[31] "Collision" and "medical payments" for example.

[32] This "contributory negligence" doctrine characterized the laws of most states although in recent years some states adopted "comparative negligence" laws as a partial reform measure. Under "comparative negligence" economic losses are partitioned in proportion to each driver's fault between the insurance companies of each party to the accident.

[33] For an eloquent statement of the case for no-fault insurance, see Jeffrey O'Connell, *The Injury Industry and the Remedy of No-Fault Auto Insurance* (Champaign-Urbana, Illinois: University of Illinois Press, 1971).

suggests that many of the shortcomings of the fault system have been eliminated. It suggests also that no-fault has not given birth to major new problems.[34]

To the extent that this discussion is accurate, it seems clear that no-fault fits "the consumer interest": it achieves what consumers want in terms of protection against losses from automobile accidents, more completely and at less cost than the fault system. It is also clear that no-fault automobile insurance had and has widespread support among consumers. Almost all consumer organizations—Consumers Union, Consumers Federation of America, and many local consumer organizations—sought its acceptance. Finally, surveys showed that about two-thirds of the public (consumers) favored it.[35] In terms both of its effects on consumer sovereignty and its support by consumers, no-fault insurance qualifies as being in the consumer interest.

Maximum Interest (Finance) Rates on Consumer Loans. The subject is consumer credit, the objective is access to credit at the lowest possible rate, especially for economically disadvantaged households, and the issue is the means. The means embodied in many state usury laws [36] and traditionally advocated by consumer organizations [37] is

---

[34] A protagonist of many reform ideas, Daniel Patrick Moynihan termed no-fault automobile insurance "the one incontestably successful reform of the 1960s." Cf. Jeffrey O'Connell, *Ending Insult to Injury, No-Fault Insurance for Products and Services* (Urbana: University of Illinois Press, 1975), p. ix. For a journalistic assessment, well larded with supporting data, see "The Early Returns on No-Fault Insurance Shows It's Working," *The New York Times,* October 5, 1975, Section 4, p. 6.

[35] In March, 1973 The Minnesota Poll asked the following question of a representative sample of Minnesota adults:

If you were a member of the Minnesota Legislature this year, would you vote for or against Adopting No-Fault Automobile Insurance?

Responses were distributed as follows:

For	61%
Against	17
No answer	22

Strikingly similar results were attained from a survey conducted in Illinois by the Survey Research Laboratory of the University of Illinois. Cf. Jeffrey O'Connell and Wallace H. Wilson, *Car Insurance and Consumer Desires* (Urbana: University of Illinois Press, 1969).

[36] As of July, 1974, 16 states had usury laws prohibiting consumer loans in excess of 8 per cent whereas another 7 states prohibited rates in excess of 9 per cent.

None of these were applied universally. Most exempted FHA- or VA-insured mortgages, which at that time exceeded the statutory ceiling in two ways: 1) by charging a high rate, and 2) by allowing disguised interest payments in the form of "points" (lump-sum prepayments of interest) or permitted the charging of "fees" at higher-than-cost levels.

Source: Norman N. Bowsher, "Usury Laws: Harmful When Effective," *Monthly Bulletin of Federal Reserve Bank of St. Louis* (August 1974), pp. 16–22.

[37] Consumers Union and Consumer Federation of America supported a maximum

the establishment of maximum rates of interest on consumer loans. In support of this position it is argued that low-income consumers are often the least well informed and, in the absence of ceilings, will be charged unduly high rates. Further, where there is inadequate competition, interest rates will automatically be higher than competitive levels.

But others, including the author, argue that maximum interest rates will achieve the *exact opposite* of the intended result: they will deny credit to the poor. The argument goes as follows. Common sense and common experience suggest that lending to economically vulnerable groups is a high-cost proposition. The bad loan rate for such groups is likely to be higher than for groups whose financial position is more secure. Lenders, quite understandably, will be willing to lend to such groups only if they can cover all their costs, including the costs of bad loans. If the legally allowable interest rate does not enable them to recover all their costs of serving such groups, lenders will not make this type of loan.

But the time for argumentation is past. Happily or unhappily, the several credit "crunches" of the last decade have provided "natural experiments" during which market rates of interest have exceeded the maximums set in various state laws. Numerous statistical studies of these episodes have been conducted, yielding near-unanimous conclusions in support of the following typical summary statement:

> all evidence at the present time (not surprisingly) confirms the theoretical contention that low ceilings rations borrowers and that high ceilings expand credit availability.[38]

What *is* the consumer interest in the matter of interest rate ceilings? In the author's judgment, the statistical evidence is over-

---

interest rate limit in 1970 when the Uniform Consumer Credit Code contained such a proviso.

By 1975, Consumers Union had modified its support of such a limit. Consider the following in the May, 1975, issue of *Consumer Reports* (p. 308): "CU has mixed feelings, however, about nationwide ceilings on maximum rates of interest on consumer loans . . . there is evidence that ceilings intended to assure credit to consumers at reasonable prices often reduce the supply of credit—and limit what is available to relatively good credit risks. On the other hand, an absence of ceilings could result in excessively high prices for credit where there is inadequate competition."

[38] Thomas A. Durkin, "The Economic Effects of Legislation: Consumer Loans Under Very High Rate Ceilings," Paper given at the American Finance Association, San Francisco, December 1974. Also see Bowsher, op. cit., and Arthur J. Rolnick, et al., "Minnesota's Usury Law: An Evaluation," *Ninth District Quarterly*, Federal Reserve Bank of Minneapolis, April 1975, pp. 16–25.

In the author's judgment, however, the Durkin study is definitive.

whelming: interest rate ceilings do *not* facilitate the achievement of consumer sovereignty. What is more, it is the author's judgment that, on further exposure to the accumulating evidence, consumer organizations would, like Consumers Union, shift ultimately from support of interest ceilings to opposition to such ceilings as these organizations became fully informed. If this interpretation is correct, then interest rate ceilings are *not* in the consumer interest.

This example underlines the possibility that consumer organizations may err and that the identification of the consumer interest, especially where tradition and feelings are strong, does not come easily. (On this issue, we were unable to locate any survey evidence regarding the public's attitudes toward interest rate ceilings.)

Safety Belt Ignition Interlock. Most 1974 model automobiles were delivered with a built-in interlock device that prevented the driver from starting the motor until every one in the car was "buckled up." Later that year, Congress passed legislation that did away with the safety belt interlock.

The case for the seat-belt interlock is easily made. Hard statistical evidence shows that fatality and serious injury rates are substantially lower for motorists who use safety belts.[39] But surveys showed, too, that many motorists failed to belt up, especially for in-town driving where safety belts should have their highest payoff.[40] What the interlock was designed to do was to extend the protection afforded by

---

[39] A careful study in two Michigan counties of accidents from which cars had to be towed away, yielded the following relationships between safety belt usage and the probability of severe injury:

Safety Belt Usage	Probability of Severe Injury
No belts used	0.74
Lap belt only	0.60
Both seat and shoulder belt used	0.38

Source: Robert E. Scott and James O' Day, "A Sampling Program For Evaluation of the 1974 Restraint Systems," *HIT Lab Reports* (Highway Safety Research Institute, University of Michigan), April, 1975, p. 9.

Dr. Scott, in conversation with the author, expressed the view that other studies now being processed would give similar results.

Regarding the effect of seat belt usage on fatalities, Westefeld and Phillips assert: "It is estimated that 10,000–15,000 of the 57,000 traffic deaths in 1972 could have been avoided had people worn their safety belts." Albert Westefeld and Benjamin M. Phillips, *Safety Belt Interlock Systems: Usage Survey* (Springfield, Va.: National Technical Information Service, Report DOT HW—801594, 1975), p. ix. But Westefeld and Phillips do not cite the basis for their assertion.

[40] In late 1974, according to observational data collected on urban sites by Westefeld and Phillips, only 16 per cent of occupants of pre-1972 automobiles used both lap and shoulder belts. Ibid., Figure 7, p. 14.

safety belts to the majority of motorists who would not buckle up voluntarily.[41]

And the case against the interlock is made with equal ease. Many found the interlock annoying and inconvenient, especially when they had to "buckle up" to make the trip from their driveway to their garage! Others doubted the statistical evidence supporting safety belt usage or felt that the "averages" did not apply to them. Whatever the basis for people's feelings, there is every reason to believe that Congress was acting with popular approval when it rescinded the interlock requirement in 1975.[42]

What consumer organization support existed for the interlock requirement? The answer seems to be that little, direct support existed. However, consumer organizations had taken a generally supportive view of efforts to make products safer. And this support—along with Ralph Nader's *Unsafe At Any Speed in 1965*—provided the initial impetus for the establishment of the National Highway Traffic Administration in 1967 and the Consumer Safety Product Commission in 1972. As far as can be ascertained, the interlock proposal came from within the government, not directly from consumer organizations. When it was finally introduced, it received lukewarm rather than strong support from consumer groups (to the extent that positions were taken).

Where do we end up with the interlock and the consumer interest? With the reluctant conclusion that many (perhaps) most understanding, fully informed consumers objected to, rather than supported, the interlock requirement. For this reason we conclude that the interlock requirement was *not* in the consumer interest.

Our three illustrative policy/actions underscore the difficulty inherent in determining what policies are in the consumer interest. This difficulty should not blind us to the essential role of consumers and consumer organizations in giving voice to consumer concerns and ultimately thrashing out policies that are in the consumer interest. It was consumer organizations, supported in part by professors, who first gave voice to the consumer information and consumer grievance problems cited earlier in this chapter. It would have been fatuous to expect producer organizations to act in this role.

[41] They succeeded partly, but the effect declined with time. In February-March of 1974 64 per cent of interlock-equipped cars used both their belts; by October, 1974 this per cent had declined to 41 per cent. Ibid., Figure 1, p. 8.

[42] An attitude survey conducted by Westefeld and Phillips showed 36 per cent of owner-drivers to be "favorably" disposed to the safety belt interlock as against 59 per cent who were "unfavorable" to it. Ibid., Figure 15, p. 25.

Consumer Representation, Then and Now. In your mind's eye, pose the issue of consumer representation to the great economic prophets of the eighteenth and nineteenth centuries—Smith, David Ricardo, John Stuart Mill—and imagine their response. It might be as follows:

> Consumer representation, sir, is no issue at all! Each consumer represents himself and "votes" as he spends his income. At his service are multitudes of sellers, each vying with the other to serve him better. It may be argued, even, that our *economic* democracy (here in England) is better developed than our political democracy, where we lag somewhat behind you Americans. . . . What "protects" the consumer you ask? And I answer: his own common sense and "the invisible hand" of competition. If he succeeds ill with one seller, he has only to turn to another.

And, details aside, this answer probably was valid in the workably competitive economy of England in the 1800s, when government functioned mainly as the referee in the economic game. It was a relatively simple game and the referee was probably fair.

In our time, the economic game has become more complex and the task of the referee more difficult. And so consumers have more reason to be concerned with the formulation and administration of the rules. All sorts of rules: to maintain competition, to provide consumer information, to ensure safety, to monitor or set certain prices, to monitor or set that supremely important price—wages, to encourage some activities (by tax or other subsidies), or to discourage some activities (by taxation, regulatory actions, or prohibitions).

Also in our time, the role of government has been extended beyond the referee role. Now the services that governments provide have become quite diverse and very large indeed: highways, education (both higher and lower), research, defense expenditures (counting military personnel, the Department of Defense employs 3.3 million, equal to 3.8 per cent of the civilian/military labor force), postal services (0.7 million, or 0.8 per cent of the labor force), national parks and forests.[43] Together, the employees of federal, state, and local governments total 13.6 million (counting military), or 15.7 per cent of the labor force.[44]

Nor have we yet exhausted the activities of government. Our governments also operate redistribution systems that tax some indi-

[43] *Statistical Abstract of the United States,* 1964, Tables 424, 505, 542.
[44] Ibid.

viduals and make payments to others for sundry purposes: death, retirement, disability benefits through Social Security; medical services benefits through Medicare; pension, death, and retirement benefits to veterans and their dependents; and, of course, collections of monies through the "regular" federal, state, and local tax systems. Consumers would naturally hope that the administration of these governmentally provided services and systems would conform to *their* preferences.

To date, organized consumer groups have concerned themselves almost exclusively with policies or actions affecting the "rules of the game" even though it could be argued that all these functions pose issues falling into the "consumer interest" domain.

With this broad range of government activity potentially affecting the consumer interest, it is relevant to ask to what extent organized representation of the consumer interest exists in our capitols. The answer is hardly at all. In Washington, for example, Consumers Union (at this writing) is represented by three lawyers and the Consumer Federation of America is represented by three professionals. Supplementing these six persons are relatively few lawyers of various public interest law firms. It is also probably accurate to say that a number of legislators, some members of their staffs, and some government officials view *their* roles as ones of identifying and supporting the consumer interest. Nonetheless, compared to this meager representation of the consumer interest, a head count would doubtlessly reveal a veritable "army" representing producer (business or labor) interests. And this picture of the relative underrepresentation of the consumer interest could be reproduced in 50 state capitols and in most cities.

But lurking in the backgrounds, as all politicians are acutely aware, is the enormous political potential of the consumer interest. If even the tiniest fraction of consumers were mobilized on a particular issue, the political effect would be overwhelming.

And so we are left with the political paradox: that the most universal of interests—consumers—is almost unrepresented in our capitols.

Underrepresentation: The Reasons Why. Three factors explain the differential degree of representation of the producer and consumer interest in the capitols where policies are legislated: 1) the extent to which the interest is focused or dispersed, 2) the means of financing, and 3) the concentration or dispersal of benefits from representation.

The Matter of Focus. The producer interest is highly focused, whereas the consumer interest is thinly spread across the informational requirements, the terms, and the grievances arising (in a year) from thousands of transactions and the management of hundreds of possessions, precious few of which contain elements that repeat.

This difference in degree of focus cannot be overemphasized. It contributes to differential effectiveness in two crucial spheres, 1) the ease of representation of an interest and 2) the ease of recruitment of support for that interest. We elaborate on each.

Effective representation of an interest, either producer or consumer, requires an immense investment in knowledge and in contacts. On the knowledge side, the representative must be able to assess the desirability or undesirability of legislative or regulatory proposals or actions. To do this effectively, he must familiarize himself with many background materials: the history of the issue, the arguments and data relied upon by interested parties, and so on. To formulate proposals requires an even deeper knowledge and analysis of the issue.

All this is made easier if the concerns of your interest group remain relatively constant over time. Such is usually the case with the producer interest, but not the consumer interest. Consider the proposal for no-fault automobile insurance cited earlier. Since the representatives of two producer interest groups—insurance companies and trial lawyers (who earned much of their income contesting automobile accident claims)—had been engaged in this representation for some time, they were already familiar with much background information and could concentrate the lesser investment required to master the no-fault issue itself.

This was not true for the consumer representatives,[45] who had to start from the beginning and familiarize themselves with the basic information for the industry (insurance in this example). Only when they had mastered this could they go on to the merits and faults of a particular proposal.

The same concentration facilitates the recruitment of support for the producer interest and impedes recruitment in the consumer interest. In the campaign for no-fault automobile insurance, opponents representing the producer interest [46] often appeared at legislative hearings backed up by solid phalanxes of numerous and articulate trial lawyers or insurance agents. At the same time, representatives of

[45] Except for professional students of the issue who are often associated with university teaching of research organizations. Such people, however, are available to and are employed by both producer and consumer interests.

[46] On this particular issue, one producer interest—the insurance interest—was divided. Very early in the no-fault discussions, one of the major trade associations, the American Insurance Association, changed sides and supported no-fault.

the consumer interest had to plead with their supporting organizations to "get some bodies down here." This is readily understandable. No-fault insurance was likely to have a large impact on the earnings and activities of trial lawyers (and to a lesser extent) insurance agents. On the other hand, the effect on an individual consumer was highly attenuated: perhaps a lower automobile insurance bill and—in what may have seemed a remote possibility—better protection in case of an accident. It is little wonder that the marshaling of trial lawyers and insurance men was easy compared to the enlistment of consumers. The same logic applies to recruitment to membership in producer interest organizations, for example, the American Trial Lawyers Association versus consumer interest groups such as the Minnesota Consumers League.

The Matter of Financing. In terms of financing, the consumer movement is a movement in search of financing whereas producer interests are better financed than they deserve.

Earlier in this chapter we argued that the information-persuasion activities of business (a producer interest) are financed by what amounts to a tax on consumers. The same "tax" finances the representation of this producer interest. Referring once again to the no-fault insurance issue, for most of us, the operation of an automobile requires the purchase of automobile insurance. Most assuredly, the price charged will be high enough to cover the costs of representation in state capitols and in Washington. And this fact gives birth to the irony that the consumer is taxed to finance the representation of an interest of which he is not a part. What is more ironic, the company that taxed him may be supporting a position he would oppose (assuming he was fully informed). It is in this sense that the producer interest is "better financed than it deserves."

We pause to note parenthetically that multiple "producer interests" may exist. Our discussion has spoken of the producer interests of *companies* making and selling goods. Another producer interest is that of employees, unionized or ununionized, who sell their labor services. *Their* interests may in some cases be identical with their employers, for example, attitudes toward a tariff; or different from that of their employers, for example, their views on wages and working conditions. With respect to the producer tax just cited, they are in the position of pure consumers: they may have to pay for the representation of positions to which they are opposed. However, through such assorted devices as "union shops" or "closed shops" combined with checkoffs, labor unions have an effective device for financing the representation of *their* particular producer interest. Whether the cost of financing union activities is ultimately shifted to consumers in the form of higher prices requires a complex analysis we do not undertake here.

For the consumer interest the sole means of financing that has proved itself over time is the selling of product test magazines. This device, first embodied in the *Consumers' Research Bulletin*, has now been reproduced in 31 periodicals published in 29 different countries.[47] In some countries, notably West Germany, Sweden, the Netherlands, Norway, and Great Britain (intermittently), the consumer interest has been financed by government grants. Tried but not yet proven successful are the following means of financing: consumer foundations, inviting individual or organizational contributions; class action litigation, although problems of barratry may stand in the way; the selling of consumer information to the media—television, radio, newspapers, periodicals; the conduct and sale of consumer research.

Our chief conclusion comes easily: the consumer interest still stands in need of additional means of financing.[48]

A second conclusion comes just as easily: the producer interest tends to have professional, specialized representation whereas the consumer interest is underrepresented.[49]

The Distribution of Benefits from Representation. In affecting public policy, both producer interests and consumer interests suffer from the public good problem; that is, persons not contributing to the enactment of a policy/action may derive benefits from it. *All* consumers benefit from no-fault insurance, not just those whose contributions helped the no-fault bill to become law.

The same public good problem afflicts both producer and consumer interests, but the effect is less attenuated for producers than for consumers. Compare the negative effect of no-fault insurance on the incomes and activities of trial lawyers with the positive benefits of no-fault insurance on a particular consumer. Is it surprising that little difficulty is encountered in recruiting lawyers (and their contributions) to the local or national trial lawyers association? Is it sur-

[47] In spring 1975.

[48] Our summary is incomplete. The income tax laws are biased in favor of the producer interest by permitting deduction of expenses incurred in earning income (including expenses of representation), but not expenses incurred in the furtherance of effective consumption.

[49] An exception is the experts from universities and research institutes who will often work for the consumer interest at lower than normal rates of compensation.

prising that it is difficult to recruit consumers (and their contributions) to membership in a local or state consumer association?

THE NONRESPONSIVENESS OF GOVERNMENT BUREAUCRACIES

For the sake of completeness, but with no attempt at careful analysis, we list the nonresponsiveness of government bureaucracies as an additional obstacle to the achievement of consumer sovereignty.

Almost everyone knows, from personal experience, the frustration of dealing with government employees for whom adherence to a set of rules is primary and responding to the supplicant's genuine needs is secondary. For an excellent analysis of the underlying dynamics, the reader is urged to consult Theodore Morgan's article, "The Theory of Error in Centrally Directed Economic Systems." [50] For additional insights into bureaucratic responses and for an imaginative attempt to model bureaucratic behavior formally, see William Niskanen's book, *Bureaucracy and Representative Government*.[51]

A SUMMING-UP

And so, consumerism at once responds to the frustration of consumers and adds to our catalog of obstacles to consumer sovereignty. The analysis of this chapter identifies four new obstacles to the achievement of consumer sovereignty: the consumer information problem, the consumer grievance problem, the underrepresentation of the consumer interest, and the nonresponsiveness of government bureaucracies.

[50] Theodore Morgan, "The Theory of Error in Centrally Directed Economic Systems," *Quarterly Journal of Economics* (August 1964), pp. 395–419.

[51] William A. Niskanen, Jr., *Bureaucracy and Representative Government* (Chicago: Aldine-Atherton Publishing Co., 1971).

INDEX

Names and Sources

INDEX

Subjects

A

Accepted Sequence (of demand creation), 267–268
Activities
  as source of satisfaction, 15, 249–250
  time used, 296–301
Advertising
  category systems in, 114–116
  deceptive advertising, 112–125, 324
    defined, 117–119
  efficiency of, 321–325
  expenditures, 323–324
  implications for profit vs. sales maximization, 302–303
  psychology of, 113–117
  as source of information, 97–99
Affluence
  as cause of informationally imperfect markets, 320–321
  effects on search, 21–22, 28–29
  and non-urgent wants, 266
Air transportation
  as example of:
    consumer redress, 232–234
    price discrimination, 40–43
American Express case, 146–147
Aspirin, 30, 85
Automobile
  purchase as example of
    bargaining, 43–45, 166–168
    consumer payoff, 43–45
    obtaining and evaluating information, 106–110

Automobile (*cont.*)
  repairs as example
    sampling problem, 92–94

B

"Bait and switch," 162
Bandwagon effects, 260
Bargaining
  avoiding, 162–163
  to bargain or not to bargain, 152
  bargainable products, 150
  bluffing, 155, 160–161
  and contracts, 159–160
  defined, 149
  examples
    automobile, 43–46, 166–168, 175–176
    bicycle, 165–166
    house, 169–172
    single-phase bargaining 43–46, 159
  multiple terms, 158
  nature, 152–154
  and price discrimination, 150–151
  single-phase, 159
  tactics, 154–156
    of sellers, 161–175
    and unique goods, 156–157
    the walkout, 156, 174–175
  for used goods, 157–158
  when not to bargain, 157–158
Barriers to entry
  a manifestation of monopoly power, 292

355